Beginning Ruby 3

From Beginner to Pro

Fourth Edition

Carleton DiLeo
Peter Cooper

Apress®

Beginning Ruby 3: From Beginner to Pro

Carleton DiLeo
Boulder, CO, USA

Peter Cooper
Louth, UK

ISBN-13 (pbk): 978-1-4842-6323-5
https://doi.org/10.1007/978-1-4842-6324-2

ISBN-13 (electronic): 978-1-4842- 6324-2

Managing Director, Apress Media LLC: Welmoed Spahr
Acquisitions Editor: Steve Anglin
Development Editor: Matthew Moodie
Coordinating Editor: Mark Powers

Cover designed by eStudioCalamar

Cover image by Jason D on Unsplash (www.unsplash.com)

Distributed to the book trade worldwide by Apress Media, LLC, 1 New York Plaza, New York, NY 10004, U.S.A. Phone 1-800-SPRINGER, fax (201) 348-4505, e-mail orders-ny@springer-sbm.com, or visit www.springeronline.com. Apress Media, LLC is a California LLC and the sole member (owner) is Springer Science + Business Media Finance Inc (SSBM Finance Inc). SSBM Finance Inc is a **Delaware** corporation.

For information on translations, please e-mail booktranslations@springernature.com; for reprint, paperback, or audio rights, please e-mail bookpermissions@springernature.com.

Apress titles may be purchased in bulk for academic, corporate, or promotional use. eBook versions and licenses are also available for most titles. For more information, reference our Print and eBook Bulk Sales web page at http://www.apress.com/bulk-sales.

Any source code or other supplementary material referenced by the author in this book is available to readers on GitHub via the book's product page, located at www.apress.com/9781484263235. For more detailed information, please visit http://www.apress.com/source-code.

Printed on acid-free paper

For Laura, Penny and Imogen
—Peter

For Jennifer and my parents
—Carleton

Table of Contents

About the Authors

Carleton DiLeo is a founder, author, and developer who brings nearly two decades of experience working with technology. His expertise includes building high-traffic websites, big data systems, and video games. This wide base of knowledge provides Carleton with a unique perspective when working with Ruby.

Peter Cooper is an experienced Ruby developer and trainer and editor of *Ruby Weekly* (www.rubyweekly.com/) and *JavaScript Weekly* (https://javascriptweekly.com/).

Since 2004, Peter has developed many commercial websites using Ruby on Rails, the Ruby-based web framework.

In addition to development work, Peter has written professionally about various development techniques and tools since 1998.

He lives in Lincolnshire, England, with his wife, Laura, and children, Penny and Imogen.

About the Technical Reviewer

Ronald Petty, M.B.A., M.S., is founder of Minimum Distance LLC, a management consulting firm based in San Francisco. He spends his time helping technology-based startups do the right thing. He is also an instructor at UC Berkeley Extension.

Foreword

here is a nice mountain in japan.

this one's just a meadow with a horse taking it easy.

oh, nice! a bowl of curry! ⚠ so delicious...

why the lucky stiff

Acknowledgments

I want to thank my parents, Ken and Margaret DiLeo, for supporting me when I started my journey to become a software engineer long ago. Thank you to my close friends Jennifer Reyes, Joseph Guetierrez, and their daughter Madison Guetierrez for being my sounding board and encouraging me to keep going when times were tough. Thank you to Peter Cooper, my coauthor to this book, and to Apress, our publisher.

Finally, thank you to those reading this book. I hope you find the same enjoyment and satisfaction I have found digging into the vast world of software development.

—Carleton DiLeo

It is often said that writing is a lonely task, but it's not until you write a book that you realize the process has to be anything *but* lonely. Without the help and reassurance of the large team of people backing this book, and backing me personally, this book could not have been written.

My first thanks go to Keir Thomas, who approached me with the idea of writing a Ruby book back in 2005. He gave me great freedom over the scope and specification of the book, and was the most essential piece of the puzzle in getting the book approved and everything sorted out in the early stages.

Beth Christmas and Mark Powers of Apress deserve special thanks for their project management and reassurance during the writing of this book across the three editions of this book so far. Without their schedules and assurance that everything was on track, I would have been a nervous wreck.

Jonathan Gennick, Tim Fletcher, Peter Marklund, Alan Bradburne, Ronald Petty, and Peter Szinek deserve much praise for their seemingly unending reading and rereading of this book's chapters throughout the various stages of development. I'd also like to praise Susannah Davidson Pfalzer for her diligent approach to copy editing the first edition of this book by fixing my pronouns, removing my overuse of words like *however* and *therefore*, and generally making it possible to read the book without going insane. As the first edition of this book was my first book for Apress, I depended on

ACKNOWLEDGMENTS

Susannah's deep knowledge of Apress customs a great deal. For the second edition of the book, I thank Damon Larson for performing the same role admirably, and for this third edition, thanks to Kezia Endsley.

Naturally, thanks go to all of the other people I directly worked with on the book, whether they're from Apress or independent—in no particular order, Michelle Lowman, Laura Esterman, Candace English, Nancy Bell, Jason Gilmore, Lori Bring, Nancy Sixsmith, and "why the lucky stiff."

Separately from the book itself, I have to give thanks to many in the Ruby community for working alongside me, producing tools I've used, or just making the Ruby language more appealing in general—in no particular order, "why the lucky stiff" (for an unforgettable foreword), Yukihiro "Matz" Matsumoto, Zach Inglis, Satish Talim, Amy Hoy, Evan Weaver, Geoffrey Grosenbach, Obie Fernandez, Gregg Pollack, Jason Seifer, Damien Tanner, Chris Roos, Martin Sadler, Pat Eyler, Ian Ozsvald, Caius Durling, Jeremy Jarvis, Nic Williams, Shane Vitarana, Josh Catone, Ryan Tomayko, Karel Minarik, Jonathan Conway, Alex MacCaw, Benjamin Curtis, David Heinemeier Hansson, and the late James Golick and Jim Weirich. I am anxious I've missed some names, especially with the exploding population of the Ruby community between the three editions of this book, so if you're missing from this list, I humbly apologize.

Those in my personal life have also supported me a great deal by putting up with my weird work hours and annoying habits, and by asking questions about the book, feeding me, or just being there to talk to. In this regard, I'd like to thank—again in no particular order—Laura Cooper, Clive Cooper, Ann Cooper, David Sculley, Michael Wong, Dave Hunt, Chris Ueland, Ben Neumann, Rob Willie, Kristian Roebuck, Graham Craggs, Lorraine Craggs, and Robert Smith. Laura Cooper deserves a special mention for having had to put up with me nearly 24 hours a day during the writing of this book; she is awesome.

Last, it's necessary to thank *you*, the reader, for choosing to buy this book, for if no one bought it, these acknowledgments and the efforts of many people during the writing would have been wasted. Thank you! If at all possible, both I and all of the fine folks at Apress would be delighted if you'd be able to post a small review of this book on Amazon. com, Amazon.co.uk, or whichever online bookstore is popular in your part of the world. Reading the reviews makes our day!

—Peter Cooper

Introduction

I wanted to minimize my frustration during programming, so I want to minimize my effort in programming. That was my primary goal in designing Ruby. I want to have fun in programming myself.

—Yukihiro Matsumoto (Matz), creator of Ruby

Ruby is a "best of breed" language that has been assembled from the best and most powerful programming features found in its predecessors.

—Jim White

Ruby makes me smile.

—Amy Hoy (slash7.com)

Ruby is a fun toy. It's also a serious programming language. Ruby is the jolly uncle who puts in solid 12-hour days at the construction site during the week but keeps the kids entertained come rain or shine. To hundreds of thousands of programmers, Ruby has become a good friend and a trusted servant, and has revealed a new way of thinking about programming and software development. It's fun and it *works*.

Like the guitar, it's claimed that Ruby is an easy language to learn and a hard one to master. I agree, with some provisions. If you don't know any programming languages already, Ruby will be surprisingly easy to learn. If you already know some languages such as PHP, Python, C#, or Golang, some of the concepts in Ruby will already be familiar to you, but the different perspective Ruby takes could throw you at first. Like the differences between spoken languages, Ruby differs from most other programming languages not only by syntax but by culture, grammar, and customs. In fact, Ruby has more in common with more esoteric languages like LISP and Smalltalk than with better-known languages such as PHP and C#.

While Ruby's roots might be different from other languages, it's heavily used and respected in many industries. Companies that use or support Ruby in one way or another include such prestigious names as Intel, Microsoft, Apple, and Amazon.com. The Ruby on Rails web framework is a system for developing web applications that uses Ruby as its base language, and it powers hundreds of large websites. Ruby is also used as a generic language from the command prompt. Grammarians, biochemists, database administrators, and thousands of other professionals and hobbyists use Ruby to make their work easier. Ruby is a truly international language with almost unlimited application.

This book is designed to cater both to people new to programming and to those with programming experience in other languages. Ruby's culture is different enough from other languages that most of this book will be of use to both groups. Any large sections that can be skipped by already proficient programmers are noted in the text. In any case, I'd suggest that all programmers at least speed-read the sections that might seem obvious to them, as there are some surprising ways in which Ruby is different from what you've done before.

When reading this book, be prepared for a little informality, some quirky examples, and a heavy dose of pragmatism. Ruby is an extremely pragmatic language, less concerned with formalities and more concerned with ease of development and valid results. From time to time, I'll show you how you can do things the "wrong" way in Ruby, merely for illustrative purposes, but mostly you'll be working with code that does things "the Ruby way." When I started to learn Ruby, I learned primarily by example, and with a language as original and idiomatic as Ruby, it's the easiest way to pick up good habits for the future. However, there's always more than one way to do it, so if you think some code in this book could be rewritten in a different way that fits in more with your way of thinking, try it out!

As you start this book, be prepared to think in new ways and to feel motivated to start coding for both fun and profit. Ruby has helped a lot of jaded developers become productive once again, and whether you're a beginner to programming or one of those jaded programmers, it's almost inevitable that you'll see how Ruby can be both fun and productive for you.

Last, if you're coming from other modern scripting languages such as JavaScript, PHP, or Python, you might want to jump to Appendix A before reading Chapter 1. It covers the key differences between Ruby and other scripting languages, which might help you move through the initial chapters of this book more easily.

Good luck, and I hope you enjoy this book. I'll see you in Chapter 1.

PART I

Foundations and Scaffolding

This part of the book is where you build the foundations of your Ruby knowledge. By the end of this part, you'll be able to develop a complete, though basic, Ruby program. You'll learn how to get Ruby working, what object orientation is, how to develop some basic programs, and about the data types and control structures Ruby uses and can operate on. Finally, I'll walk you through creating a small program from start to finish.

CHAPTER 1

Let's Get It Started: Installing Ruby

Ruby is a popular programming language, but not all computers have it installed by default. This chapter takes you through the steps necessary to get Ruby working on your computer.

As an open source language, Ruby has been adapted to run on many different computer platforms and architectures. This means that if you develop a Ruby program on one machine, it's likely you'll be able to run it without any changes on a different machine. You can use Ruby, in one form or another, on all the following operating systems and platforms:

- Microsoft Vista, 7, 8, and 10
- Mac OS X
- Linux (most distributions)
- BSDs (including FreeBSD and OpenBSD)
- Any platform for which a full Java Virtual Machine exists (using JRuby)

Caution   Some specifics of Ruby vary between platforms, but most of the code in this book (particularly in the earlier chapters) runs on all varieties. When we begin to look at more complex code, such as external libraries and interfacing between Ruby and other systems, you should be prepared to make changes in your code or accept that you won't have access to every feature. However, if you're using Windows, Linux, or OS X, almost everything will work as described in this book without changes.

© Carleton DiLeo, Peter Cooper 2021
C. DiLeo and P. Cooper, *Beginning Ruby 3*, https://doi.org/10.1007/978-1-4842-6324-2_1

Before you can start playing with Ruby, you need to get your computer to understand the Ruby language by installing an implementation of Ruby on your system, which I'll cover first. In some cases, Ruby may already be present on your computer, and we will cover these situations also since you may not need to do anything to get started.

Installing Ruby

Typically, when you install Ruby onto your computer, you'll get the *Ruby interpreter*, the program that understands other programs written in the Ruby language, along with a collection of extensions and libraries to make your Ruby more fully featured.

To satisfy the majority of readers without referring to external documentation, I'm providing full instructions for using Ruby on Windows, Mac OS X, and Linux, along with links to Ruby implementations for other platforms. In each case, I provide instructions to check that the installation is successful before sending you on to the programming fun in Chapter 2.

Note   Ruby comes in multiple versions. The code in this book is primarily aimed at versions 3.0 and above, but nearly all of it will work in older versions as well. There are major differences between Ruby versions that can become important when you reach more advanced topics, but at this stage, you can choose whichever is easiest to install on your platform. Or, if Ruby is already installed on your machine, simply use that as is.

Windows

Ruby was initially designed for use under UNIX and UNIX-related operating systems such as Linux, but Windows users have access to an excellent Windows-specific installer that installs Ruby, a horde of extensions, a source code editor, and various documentation. Ruby on Windows is as reliable and useful as it is on other operating systems, and Windows is a reasonable environment for developing Ruby programs.

To get up and running as quickly as possible, follow these steps:

1. Open a web browser and go to `https://rubyinstaller.org/`.

2. Click the big Download button and then choose the latest version to download. There are two sections of downloads: "with devkit" and "without devkit". It's recommended to download the installer under the "with devkit" section. Make sure you select the "x64" download. There are further details about the installer on the sidebar of the download page if you're interested.

3. Run the downloaded file to launch the installer.

4. If Windows gives you a Security Error box, click the Run button to give your approval.

5. A typical installation program appears with some instructions. On the initial screen, click to accept the license and then click Next.

6. Work your way through the installation screens. Unless you have a specific reason not to, let the installation program install Ruby in its default location and its default program group. Check the box for "Add Ruby Executables to Your PATH" if possible, as well as the "Associate .rb and .rbw Files with this Ruby Installation" option.

7. If given the option, install the "MSYS2 development toolchain." It provides a much richer command-line interface than what is provided by Windows. We won't be using it in this book, but I recommend looking into what MSYS2 has to offer.

8. Installation is complete when the installation program gives you a Finish button to exit it.

If Ruby installed correctly, congratulations! To test that your Ruby installation works correctly for Chapter 2, you need to load Interactive Ruby prompt or irb. If you are using Windows 7 or higher, use the search bar to find the irb by searching for "irb". You should see "Interactive Ruby" in the results. Click the "Interactive Ruby" icon to launch the tool. If the program loads successfully, you'll see a screen that looks somewhat like Figure 1-1.

Figure 1-1. *The Interactive Ruby (irb) prompt running on Windows 10*

If irb started properly, Ruby is installed correctly. Congratulations! Lastly, you need to be familiar with running Ruby and its associated utilities from the command prompt and use the search toolbar to search for "Start Command Prompt with Ruby." You should see "Start Command Prompt with Ruby" in your results. Click the icon to start the command prompt.

Throughout this book, commands that can be used at the command prompt will be given. This is because using a command prompt such as this is a standard technique in operating systems such as Linux and OS X. For example, in Chapter 7, we'll look at installing extra features (libraries) for Ruby, and the command prompt will be used for this. Therefore, it's necessary for you to know how to access it and run programs.

If you type irb at this prompt and press Enter, you should see something like the following:

```
irb(main):001:0>
```

If you see the preceding line, everything is set up correctly, and you can type exit and press Enter to be returned to the command prompt.

Now you can move on to Chapter 2 and start to play with the Ruby language itself.

Mac OS X/macOS

Unlike Windows, most modern Apple machines running OS X come with a version of Ruby already installed. OS X Catalina (10.15.4) comes with Ruby 2.6 out of the box. It's not recommended to use this version of Ruby since there are limitations that will make development difficult. Instead, we will use a Homebrew to install ruby. Once you become more advanced, I recommend looking into tools like rbenv (`https://github.com/rbenv/rbenv`) and rvm (`https://rvm.io/`) which help manage multiple versions of Ruby on the same computer.

Installing Ruby on OS X with Homebrew

Since we are not using the system-provided version of Ruby, we will install it using a packaging system called Homebrew (`https://brew.sh/`). Installing Homebrew is easy. Open up a Terminal and type the following command:

```
/bin/bash -c "$(curl -fsSL https://raw.githubusercontent.com/Homebrew/
install/master/install.sh)"
```

Once Homebrew has installed, you can run **brew install ruby** to install the latest version of Ruby. You can then test that Ruby installed correctly using the command **ruby -v**. If this command does not work, restart the terminal and try again.

Note   If you are running OS X Catalina or higher, you may need to link your terminal to the Ruby installation. This can be done by running the following command:

```
echo 'export PATH="/usr/local/opt/ruby/bin:$PATH"'
>> ~/.bash_profile
```

If the Homebrew install command doesn't work, visit the Homebrew site `https://brew.sh/` for details on installing Homebrew.

Linux

As an open source programming language, Ruby is already installed with many Linux distributions. It's not universal, though, but you can check if Ruby is installed by following the instructions in the next section. If this fails, there are further instructions to help you install it.

Checking If Ruby Is Installed on Linux

Try to run the Ruby interpreter from the command prompt (or terminal window), as follows:

```
ruby -v
```

If Ruby is installed, the current Ruby version will be printed on the screen. This book requires 2.7.1 as a bare minimum (with 3.0+ being preferred), so if the version is earlier than 2.7.1, you'll need to continue onward in this chapter and install a more recent version of Ruby. However, if Ruby appears to be installed and up to date, try to run the irb interactive Ruby interpreter, as follows:

```
irb
```

Once you've run irb, you should get the following output:

```
irb(main):001:0>
```

If running irb results in a similar output, you can move on to Chapter 2. (You might wish to type exit and press Enter to get back to the command line!) Otherwise, read on to install a fresh version of Ruby.

Installing Ruby with a Package Manager

The installation procedure for Ruby on Linux varies between different Linux distributions. Some distributions, such as Debian, Arch Linux, and Red Hat, provide "package managers" to make installation of programs easy. Others require that you install directly from source or install a package manager beforehand.

If you're comfortable with using emerge, rpm, or apt-get, you can install Ruby quickly with the following methods:

- *Yum (on Red Hat, CentOS, and Fedora)*: Install as follows: sudo yum install -y ruby

- *Pacman (on Arch Linux)*: Install as follows: sudo pacman -S ruby

- *Debian*: Use apt-get, as such: sudo apt-get install ruby-full

- *Ubuntu-based distributions:* Use snap, as such: sudo snap install ruby --classic

If one of these methods works for you, try to run Ruby and irb as shown in the preceding section, and progress to Chapter 2 if you're ready. Alternatively, you can search your distribution's package repository for Ruby, as the name of the Ruby package in your distribution might be nonstandard or changing over time. However, if all else fails, you can install Ruby directly from its source code in the next section.

Installing Ruby from Source Code

Installing Ruby from its source code is a great option if you don't mind getting your hands dirty. The process is similar on all forms of UNIX (not just Linux—this will work on OS X too). Here are the basic steps:

1. Make sure that your Linux distribution can build applications from source by searching for the "make" and "gcc" tools (on OS X, Xcode allows you to install these). From the terminal, you can use `which gcc` and `which make` to see if the development tools are installed. If not, you need to install these development tools (on Ubuntu, try `apt-get install build-essential`; on Red Hat or CentOS, try `sudo yum groupinstall "Development Tools"`).

2. Open a web browser and go to `www.ruby-lang.org/`.

3. Click the Downloads link at the top of the page.

4. On the download page, scroll down to Compiling Ruby – Source Code and download the archive file containing the latest version. This downloads a `tar.gz` file containing the source code for the latest stable version of Ruby.

5. Uncompress the `tar.gz` file. If you're at a command prompt or terminal window, go to the same directory as the `ruby-3.x.x.tar.gz` file and run `tar xzvf ruby-3.x.x.tar.gz` (where `ruby-3.x.x.tar.gz` is the name of the file you just downloaded).

7. Go into the Ruby folder that was created during decompression. If you're not using a command prompt at this stage, open a terminal window and go to the directory.

8. Run `./configure` to generate the makefile and `config.h` files. If you receive numerous errors, particularly about no C compiler being available, you have not installed the development tools properly on your operating system and should search for further help online on how to achieve this.

9. Run `make` to compile Ruby from source. This might take a while.

10.   Run `make install` to install Ruby to its correct location on the system. You need to do this as a superuser (such as root), so you might need to run it as `sudo make install` and type in your password if you are not logged in as a superuser already.

11.   If there are errors by this stage, read the README file that accompanies the source code files for pointers. Otherwise, try to see what version of Ruby is now installed with `ruby -v`.

If the expected version of Ruby appears at this point, you're ready to move to Chapter 2 and begin programming. If you get an error complaining that Ruby can't be found or the wrong version of Ruby is installed, the place where Ruby was installed might not be in your path (the place your operating system looks for files to run). To fix this, scroll up and find out exactly where Ruby was installed (often in `/usr/local/bin` or `/usr/bin`) and add the relevant directory to your path. The process to do this varies by distribution and shell type, so refer to your Linux documentation on changing your path.

Once you can check which version of Ruby is running and you can run irb and get a Ruby interpreter prompt, your Ruby installation is complete (for now!) and you can move on to Chapter 2.

Other Platforms

If you're not using Windows, OS X, or Linux, it is possible you may be able to use a variant or port of Ruby. Up until version 2.0, the official Ruby interpreter supported a variety of other platforms (including BeOS, MS-DOS, and even the Atari ST), but it is now primarily focused on mainstream operating systems, so in this edition, we will not be providing any pointers, as they are now out of date.

In many cases, the versions of Ruby for some operating systems might be out of date or unsupported. If this is the case and you're confident about being able to compile your own version of Ruby directly from the Ruby source code, the source code is available to download from `www.ruby-lang.org/`.

To test that Ruby is installed sufficiently to continue with this book, you want to check which version of Ruby is installed by asking Ruby for its version, as follows:

```
ruby -v
```

You also need access to Ruby's interactive prompt, irb. You access this simply by running irb (if it's in your path) as follows:

```
irb
```

If Ruby and irb do not work without complaint, you need to seek assistance for your specific platform. Appendix B provides a list of useful resources. If irb does load, you can type exit and press Enter to close it again.

Summary

In this chapter, we've focused on making sure Ruby is properly installed and that you can run the irb tool, which you'll be using over the next several chapters.

Although Ruby is an easy language to learn and develop with, it's easy to become overwhelmed with the administration of Ruby itself, its installation, and its upgrades. As Ruby is a language constantly in development, it's possible that points covered in this chapter will go out of date and other ways to install Ruby will come along.

An important part of being a proficient Ruby developer is being able to use the resources the Ruby community makes available, and being able to find the latest sources of help over time. The Ruby community, including your humble author, can provide help in most cases, and a variety of resources to try are covered in Chapter 5 and Appendix B.

CHAPTER 2

Programming == Joy: A Whistle-Stop Tour of Ruby and Object Orientation

Depending on who you ask, programming is both a science and an art. Telling computers what to do with computer programs requires being able to think analytically, like a scientist, and conceptually, like an artist. Being an artist is essential for coming up with big ideas and being flexible enough to take unique approaches. Being a scientist is essential to understanding how and why certain methodologies need to be taken into account, and to approach testing and debugging from a logical perspective, rather than an emotional one.

Luckily, you don't need to be an artist or a scientist already. As with training the body, programming exercises and thinking about how to solve problems train the mind to make you a better programmer. Anyone can learn to program. The biggest impediments are a lack of motivation and commitment or an unnecessary level of complexity early on. Ruby is one of the easiest programming languages to learn, so that leaves motivation and commitment. You've probably bought this book with a view to creating a certain program, web app, or to solve a certain task, hence your motivation, leaving only commitment. To help cover the commitment angle, we're going to try to keep things smooth and uncomplicated.

By the time you reach the end of this chapter, I hope you can get a taste of the fun that lies ahead with the knowledge of a powerful yet deceptively simple programming language, and you will begin to feel excited about building your own things!

© Carleton DiLeo, Peter Cooper 2021
C. DiLeo and P. Cooper, *Beginning Ruby 3*, https://doi.org/10.1007/978-1-4842-6324-2_2

Note   This chapter does not follow an instructional format as subsequent chapters do. Instead, I'll be moving quickly from concept to concept to give you a *feel* for Ruby as a language before we circle around to the details later.

Baby Steps

In Chapter 1, you focused on installing Ruby so that your computer can understand the language. At the end of the chapter, you loaded a program called irb.

irb: Interactive Ruby

irb stands for "Interactive Ruby." "Interactive" means that as soon as you type something and press Enter, your computer will *immediately* attempt to process it. Sometimes this sort of environment is called an *immediate* or *interactive* environment.

Note   If you cannot remember how to load irb, refer to the section of Chapter 1 dedicated to your computer's operating system.

Start irb and make sure a prompt appears, like so:

```
irb(main):001:0>
```

This prompt is not as complex as it looks. All it means is that you're in the irb program, you're typing your first line (001), and you're at a *depth* of 0. You don't need to place any importance on the depth element at this time.

Type this after the preceding prompt and press Enter:

```
1 + 1
```

The result should come back quickly: 2. The entire process looks like this:

```
irb(main):001:0> 1 + 1
=> 2
irb(main):002:0>
```

Ruby is now ready to accept another command or expression from you.

As a new Ruby programmer, you'll spend a lot of time in irb testing concepts and building up insights into Ruby. It provides the perfect environment for tweaking and testing the language.

irb's interactive environment gives you the benefit of immediate feedback—an essential tool when learning. Rather than writing a program in a text editor, saving it, getting the computer to run it, and then looking through the errors to see where you went wrong, you can just type in small snippets of code, press Enter, and immediately see what happens.

If you want to experiment further, try other arithmetic such as 100 * 5, 57 + 99, 10 – 50, or 100 / 10 (if the last one seems alien to you, in Ruby, the forward slash character, /, is the operator for division).

Ruby Is "English for Computers"

At the lowest level, computer processors are made out of transistors that respond to and act on electronic signals, but thinking about performing operations at this level is time-consuming and complicated, so we tend to use higher-level "languages" to communicate our intentions, much as we do with natural languages like English.

Computers can understand languages, though in a rather different fashion than how most people do. Being logical devices that cannot understand subtlety or ambiguity, languages such as English and French aren't appealing to computers. Computers require languages with logical structures and a well-defined *syntax* so that there's a logical clarity in what you're telling the computer to do.

Clarity is required because almost everything you relay to the computer while programming is an *instruction* (or *command*). Instructions are the basic building blocks of all programs, and for the computer to perform (or *execute*) them properly, the programmer's intentions must be clear and precise. Many hundreds of these instructions are tied together into *programs* that perform certain tasks, which means there's little room for error.

You also need to consider that other programmers might need to maintain computer programs you've written. This won't be the case if you're just programming for fun, but it's important that your programs are easy to understand, so you can understand them when you come back to them later on.

Why Ruby Makes a Great Programming Language

Although English would make a bad programming language, due to its ambiguity and complexity, Ruby can feel surprisingly English-*like* at times. Ruby is just one of hundreds of programming languages, but it's special because it *feels* a lot like a natural language to many programmers while having the clarity required by computers. Consider this example code:

```
10.times do print "Hello, world!" end
```

Read through this code aloud (it helps, really!). It doesn't flow quite as well as English, but the meaning should be immediately clear. It asks the computer to "10 times" "print" "Hello, world!" to the screen. It works. If you've got irb running, type in the preceding code and press Enter to see the results:

```
Hello, world!Hello, world!Hello, world!Hello, world!Hello, world!Hello,
world!Hello, world!Hello, world!Hello, world!Hello, world! => 10
```

If you read the code aloud, the resulting output ("Hello, world!" printed ten times) should not be a surprise. The => 10 on the end might seem more confusing, however, but we'll be covering the meaning of that later.

Note   Experienced programmers might wonder why there's no semicolon at the end of the previous code example. Unlike many other languages, such as C#, PHP, C, and C++, a semicolon is not needed at the end of lines in Ruby (although it won't hurt if you do use one). This can take a little while to get used to at first, but for new programmers it makes Ruby even easier to learn.

Here's a much more complex example that might occur in a real-world web app:

```
user = User.find_by_email('me@privacy.net')
user.country = 'Belgium'
```

Note   Don't copy and paste this code. It won't work outside the context of a particular application.

This code is nowhere near as obvious as the "Hello, world!" example, but you should still be able to take a good guess at what it does. First, it tells the computer you want to work with a concept called User. Next, it tries to find a user with a specified email address. Last, it changes the user's country data to Belgium. Don't worry about how the data is stored for users at this point; that comes later.

This is a reasonably advanced and abstract example, but demonstrates a single concept from a potentially complex application where you can deal with different concepts such as "users." By the end of this chapter, you'll see how you can create your own real-life concepts in Ruby and operate on them in a similar way to this example. Your code can be almost as easy to read as English too.

Trails for the Mind

Learning can be a fun activity in its own right, but merely reading about something won't make you an expert at it. I've read a few cookbooks, but this doesn't seem to improve my cooking when I attempt it from time to time. The missing ingredient is experimentation and testing, as without these, your efforts are academic, at best.

With this in mind, it's essential to get into the mood of experimenting and testing from day one of using Ruby. Throughout the book, I'll ask you to try out different blocks of code and to play with them to see if you get the results you want. You'll occasionally surprise yourself and sometimes chase your code into dead ends; this is all part of the fun. Whatever happens, all good programmers learn from experimentation, and you can only master a language and programming concepts by experimenting as you go along.

This book will lead you through a forest of code and concepts, but without testing and proving the code is correct to yourself, you can quickly become lost. Use irb and the other tools I'll cover frequently, and experiment with the code as much as possible so that the knowledge will stick.

Type in the following code at your irb prompt and press Enter:

```
print "test"
```

The result is simply

```
test => nil
```

Logically, print "test" results in test being printed to the screen. However, the =>
nil suffix is the result of your code as an *expression* (more about these in Chapter 3). This
appears because all lines of code in Ruby are made up of expressions that *return* values.
However, print displays data to the screen rather than return any value as an expression,
so you get nil. More about this in Chapter 3. It is perfectly okay to be semi-confused
about this at this stage.

Let's try something else:

```
print "2+3 is equal to " + 2 + 3
```

This command seems logical on the surface. If 2 + 3 is equal to 5 and you're adding
that to the end of "2+3 is equal to ", you should get "2+3 is equal to 5", right?
Unfortunately, you get this error instead:

```
Traceback (most recent call last):
        5: from bin/irb:23:in `<main>'
        4: from bin/irb:23:in `load'
        3: from exe/irb:11:in `<top (required)>'TypeError (no implicit
            conversion of Integer into String)
        2: from (irb):2
        1: from (irb):2:in `+'
        TypeError (no implicit conversion of Integer into String)
```

Ruby complains when you make an error, and here it's complaining that you can't
convert a number into a string (where a "string" is a collection of text, such as this very
sentence). Numbers and strings can't be mixed in this way. Deciphering the reason
isn't important yet, but experiments such as this along the way will help you learn and
remember more about Ruby than reading this book alone. When an error like this
occurs, you can use the error message as a clue to the solution, whether you find it in this
book, on the Internet, or by asking another developer.

As a quick side activity, copy and paste the "no implicit conversion of
Integer into String" error into Google and see what comes up. If you are like most
programmers, you will do this a lot over your programming career. Not every article you
find will be useful, but sometimes you can get out of tricky situations by seeing what
other people suggest online.

An interim solution to the preceding problem would be to do this:

```
print "2+3 is equal to "
print 2 + 3
```

Or this:

```
print "2+3 is equal to " + (2 + 3).to_s
```

Try them both.

Let's try one more example. What about 10 divided by 3?

```
irb(main):002:0> 10 / 3
=> 3
```

Computers are *supposed* to be precise, but anyone with basic arithmetic skills will know that 10 divided by 3 is 3.33 recurring, rather than 3!

The reason for the curious result is that, by default, Ruby assumes a number such as 10 or 3 to be an *integer*—a whole number. Arithmetic with integers in Ruby gives integer results, so it's necessary to provide Ruby with a *floating point* number (a number with decimal places) to get a floating point answer such as 3.33. Here's an example of how to do that:

```
Irb(main):001:0> 10.0 / 3
=> 3.333333333333
```

Outcomes such as these make testing and experimentation not only a good learning tool but essential tactics when developing larger programs.

That's enough of the errors for now. Let's make something useful!

Turning Ideas into Ruby Code

Part of the artistry of programming is in being able to turn your ideas into computer programs. Once you become proficient with a programming language, you can turn your ideas directly into code. However, before you can do this, you need to see how Ruby understands real-world concepts, and how you can relay your ideas into a form that Ruby appreciates.

How Ruby Understands Concepts with Objects and Classes

Ruby is an *object-oriented* programming language. In the simplest sense, this means that your Ruby programs can define and operate on concepts in a fashion that mimics how we might deal with concepts in the real world. Your program can contain concepts such as "people," "boxes," "tickets," "maps," or any other concept you want to work with. Object-oriented languages make it easy to implement these concepts in a way that you can create *objects* based on them. As an object-oriented language, Ruby can then act on and understand the relationships between these concepts in any way you can define.

For example, you might want to create an application that can manage the booking of tickets for sports events. The concepts involved include "events," "people," "tickets," "venues," and so forth. Ruby lets you put these concepts directly into your programs, create *object instances* of them (instances of an "event" might be the Super Bowl or the final of the World Cup), and perform operations on and define relationships between them. With all these concepts in your program, you can quickly relate "events" to "venues" and "tickets" to "people," meaning that your code forms a logical system from the outset.

If you haven't programmed much before, the idea of taking real-life concepts and using them directly in a computer program might seem like an obvious way to make software development easier. However, object orientation is a reasonably new idea in software development (the concept was developed in the 1960s, but it only became popular in mainstream programming in the 1990s). With non-object-oriented languages, the programmer has to take a more manual approach for handling concepts and the relationships between them, and while this adds more control, it also introduces extra complexity.

The Making of a Person

Let's jump directly into some source code demonstrating a simple concept, a person:

```
class Person
  attr_accessor :name, :age, :gender
end
```

Ruby seemed a lot like English before, but it doesn't seem much like English when defining concepts. Let's go through it step by step:

```
class Person
```

This line is where you start to define the concept of a "person." When we define concepts in Ruby (or in most other object-oriented languages, for that matter), we call them *classes*. A *class* is the definition of a single type of object. Class names in Ruby always start with a capital letter, so your programs will end up with classes with names like User, Person, Place, Topic, Message, and so forth:

```
attr_accessor :name, :age, :gender
```

The preceding line provides three *attributes* for the Person class. An individual person has a name, an age, and a gender, and this line creates those attributes. attr stands for "attribute," and accessor roughly means "make these attributes accessible to be set and changed at will." This means that when you're working with a Person object in your code, you can change that person's name, age, and gender (or, more accurately, the object's name, age, and gender *attributes*):

```
end
```

The end line should be of obvious utility. It matches up with the class definition on the first line and tells Ruby that you're no longer defining the Person class.

To recap, a class defines a concept (such as a Person), and an object is a single thing based *on* class (such as a "Chris" or a "Mrs. Smith").

So let's experiment with our Person class. Go to your irb prompt and type in the Person class found earlier. Your efforts should look like this:

```
irb(main):001:0> class Person
irb(main):002:?>   attr_accessor :name, :age, :gender
irb(main):003:?> end
=> nil
irb(main):004:0>
```

You'll notice that irb recognizes when you were "inside" a class definition because it automatically indents your code.

Once you've finished your class definition and Ruby has processed it, `nil` is returned, because defining a class results in no return value, and `nil` is Ruby's way of representing "nothing." As there were no errors, your `Person` class now exists within Ruby, so let's do something with it:

```
person_instance = Person.new
person_instance.inspect
=> #<Person:0x007fbb0c625f88>
```

What the first line does is create a "new" instance of the `Person` class, so you're creating a "new person" and assigning it to `person_instance`—a placeholder representing the new person, known as a *variable*. The second line is Ruby's response to creating a new person and isn't important at this stage. The `0x007fbb0c625f88` bit will be different from computer to computer and only represents an internal reference that Ruby has assigned to the new person. You don't have to take it into account at all.

Let's immediately do something with `person_instance`:

```
person_instance.name = "Christine"
```

In this basic example, you refer to `person_instance`'s name attribute and give it a value of `"Christine"`. You've just given your person a name. The `Person` class has two other attributes: age and gender. Let's set those:

```
person_instance.age = 52
person_instance.gender = "female"
```

Simple. You've given `person_instance` a basic identity. What about printing the person's name back to the screen?

```
puts person_instance.name
```

`Christine` appears when you press Enter. Try the same with the age and the gender.

Note   In previous examples, you've used `print` to put things on the screen. In the preceding example, you used `puts`. The difference between `print` and `puts` is that `puts` automatically moves the output cursor to the next line (i.e., it adds a newline character to start a new line), whereas `print` continues printing text onto the same line as the previous time. Generally, you'll want to use `puts`, but I used `print` to make the earlier examples more intuitive when reading them out loud.

Basic Variables

In the previous section, you created a person and assigned that person to a *variable* (computer terminology for a "placeholder") called person_instance.

Variables are an important part of programming, and they're easy to understand, especially if you have the barest of knowledge of algebra. Consider this:

```
x = 10
```

This code assigns the value 10 to the variable x. Since x now equals 10, you can do things like this:

```
x * 2
```

```
20
```

> **Note**   Some new programmers can be confused by the definition of = as an assignor of value, rather than an indicator of *equality*. When we say x = 10, we do not mean that x and 10 are equal, but that x should now be considered to *refer* to the value 10.

Variables in Ruby can refer to any value-related concept that Ruby understands, such as numbers, text, and other data structures I'll cover throughout this book. In the previous section, person_instance was a variable that referred to an object instance of the Person class, much like x is a variable containing the number 10. More simply, consider person_instance as a name that refers to a particular, unique Person object.

When you want to store something and use it over multiple lines within a program, you'll use variables as temporary storage places for the data you're working with.

From People to Pets

Previously, you created a simple class (Person), created an object of that class, assigned it as the person_instance variable, and gave it an identity (we called it Christine) that you queried. If these concepts seem simple to you, well done—you understand the bare basics of object orientation! If not, reread the previous section and make sure you follow along on your computer, but also read this section, as I'm going to go into a little more depth.

You started out with a `Person` class, but now you need something a bit more complex, so let's create some "pets" to live inside Ruby. You'll create some cats, dogs, and snakes. The first step is to define the classes. You could do something like this:

```
class Cat
  attr_accessor :name, :age, :gender, :color
end

class Dog
  attr_accessor :name, :age, :gender, :color
end

class Snake
  attr_accessor :name, :age, :gender, :color
end
```

It's just like creating the `Person` class, but multiplied for the three different animals. You could continue by creating animals with code such as `lassie = Dog.new` or `sammy = Snake.new` and setting the attributes for the pets with code such as `lassie.age = 12` or `sammy.color = "Green"`. Type in the preceding code and give it a try if you like.

However, creating the classes in this way would miss out on one of the more interesting features of object-oriented programming: *inheritance.*

Inheritance allows different classes to relate to one another and group concepts by their similarities. In this case, cats, dogs, and snakes are all pets. Inheritance allows you to create a "parent" Pet class, and then let your `Cat`, `Dog`, and `Snake` classes *inherit* ("is-a") the features that all pets have.

Almost everything in real life exists in a similar structure to your classes. Cats can be pets, which are, in turn, animals; which are, in turn, living things; which are, in turn, objects that exist in the universe. A hierarchy of classes exists everywhere, and object-oriented languages let you define those relationships in code.

Note   Chapter 6 features a helpful diagram showing the concept of inheritance between different forms of life such as mammals, plants, and so forth.

Structuring Your Pets Logically

Now that we've come up with some ideas to improve our code, let's retype it from scratch. To totally cleanse out and reset what you're working on, you can restart irb. irb doesn't remember information between the different times you use it. So restart irb (to exit irb, type exit and press Enter) and rewrite the class definitions like so:

```ruby
class Pet
    attr_accessor :name, :age, :gender, :color
end

class Cat < Pet
end

class Dog < Pet
end

class Snake < Pet
end
```

Note   In the code listings in this chapter, any code that's within classes is indented, as with the `attr_accessor` line in the preceding `Pet` class. This is only a matter of style, and it makes the code easier to read. When you type it into irb, it's not necessary to replicate the effect, as it will do some indentation for you. You can simply type what you see. Once you start using a text editor to write longer programs, you'll want to indent your code to make it easier to read too, but it's not important yet.

First, you create the Pet class and define the name, age, gender, and color attributes available to Pet objects. Next, you define the Cat, Dog, and Snake classes that inherit from the Pet class (the < operator, in this case, denotes which class is inherited from). This means that cat, dog, and snake objects will all have the name, age, gender, and color attributes, but because the functionality of these attributes is inherited from the Pet class, the functionality doesn't have to be created specifically in each class. This makes the code easier to maintain and update if you wanted to store more information about the pets or if you wanted to add another type of animal.

What about attributes that aren't relevant to every animal? What if you wanted to store the length of snakes, but didn't want to store the length of dogs or cats? Luckily, inheritance gives you lots of benefits with no downside. You can still add class-specific code wherever you want. Reenter the Snake class like so:

```
class Snake < Pet
  attr_accessor :length
end
```

The Snake class now has a length attribute. However, this is added to the attributes Snake has inherited from Pet, so Snake has name, age, gender, color, and length attributes, whereas Cat and Dog only have the first four attributes. You can test this like so (some output lines have been removed for clarity):

```
irb(main):001:0> snake = Snake.new
irb(main):002:0> snake.name = "Sammy"
irb(main):003:0> snake.length = 500
irb(main):004:0> lassie = Dog.new
irb(main):005:0> lassie.name = "Lassie"
irb(main):006:0> lassie.age = 20
irb(main):007:0> lassie.length = 10
```

```
NoMethodError (undefined method 'length=' for #<Dog:0x32fddc @age=20,
@name="Lassie">)
```

Here you created a dog and a snake. You gave the snake a length of 500, before trying to give the dog a length of 10 (the units aren't important). Trying to give the dog a length results in an error of undefined method 'length=', because you only gave the Snake class the length attribute.

Try playing with the other attributes and creating other pets. Try using attributes that don't exist and see what the error messages are.

Note   You might be wondering why we're using such artificial examples as cats, dogs, and snakes here. They have been chosen to provide a simple to understand and easily mentally visualized model of how classes work. In your eventual apps, you'll work with things like different types of users, events, products, photos, and so forth, and they will work in a somewhat similar way. Feel free to create your own classes using concepts relevant to your planned programs and follow along using those instead, substituting the names of the classes where appropriate.

Controlling Your Pets

So far, you've been creating classes and objects with various changeable attributes. Attributes are data related to individual objects. A snake can have a length, a dog can have a name, and a cat can be of a certain color. What about the *instructions* I spoke of earlier? How do you give your objects instructions to perform? You define *methods* for each class.

Methods are important in Ruby. They enable you to tell objects to *perform actions*. For example, you might want to add a bark method to your Dog class, which, if called on a Dog object, prints Woof! to the screen. You could write it like so:

```ruby
class Dog < Pet
  def bark
    puts "Woof!"
  end
end
```

After entering this code, any dogs you create can now bark. Let's try it out:

```ruby
irb(main):0> a_dog = Dog.new
irb(main):0> a_dog.bark
```

Woof!

Eureka! You'll notice that the way you make the dog bark is simply by referring to the dog (a_dog, in this case) and including a period (.) followed by the bark method's name, whereby your dog "barks." Let's dissect exactly what happened.

First, you added a bark method to your Dog class. The way you did this was by *defining* the method. To define a method, you use the word def followed by the name of the method you wish to define. This is what the def bark line means. It means "I'm defining the bark method within this class until I say end." The following line then simply puts the word "Woof!" on the screen, and the last line of the method ends the definition of that method. The last end ends the class definition (this is why indentation is useful, so you can see which end lines up with which definition). The Dog class then contains a new method called bark, as you used earlier.

Think about how you would create methods for the other Pet classes or for the Pet class itself. Are there any methods that are generic to all pets? If so, they'd go in the Pet class. Are there methods specific to cats? They'd go in the Cat class.

27

Everything Is an Object

In this chapter, we've looked at how Ruby can understand concepts in the form of classes and objects. We created virtual cats and dogs, gave them names, and triggered their methods (e.g., the bark method). These basic concepts form the core of object-oriented programming, and you'll use them constantly throughout this book. Dogs and cats are merely an example of the flexibility object orientation offers, but the concepts we've used so far could apply to most concepts, whether we're giving a "ticket" a command to change its price or a "user" a command to change his or her password. Begin to think of the programs you want to develop in terms of their general concepts and how you can turn them into classes you can manipulate with Ruby.

Among even object-oriented programming languages, Ruby is reasonably unique in that almost *everything* in the language is an object, even the concepts relating to the language itself. Consider the following line of code:

```
puts 1 + 10
```

If you typed this into irb and pressed Enter, you'd see the number 11 in response. You've asked Ruby to print the result of 1 + 10 to the screen. It seems simple enough, but believe it or not, this simple line uses *two objects*. 1 is an object, as is 10. They're objects of class Integer, and this built-in class has methods already defined to perform operations on numbers, such as addition and subtraction.

We've considered how concepts can be related to different classes. Our pets make a good example. However, even defining the concepts that programmers use to write computer programs as classes and objects makes sense. When you write a simple sum such as 2 + 2, you expect the computer to add two numbers together to make 4. In its object-oriented way, Ruby considers the two numbers (2 and 2) to be number objects. 2 + 2 is then merely shorthand for asking the first number object to add the second number object to itself. In fact, the + sign is actually an addition *method*! (It's true; 2.+(2) will work just fine!)

You can prove that everything in Ruby is an object by asking the things of which class they're a member. In the pet example earlier, you could have made a_dog tell you what class it's a member of with the following code:

```
puts a_dog.class
```

Dog

`class` isn't a method you created yourself, such as the `bark` method, but one that Ruby supplies by default to all objects. This means that you can ask any object which class it's a member of by using its `class` method. So `a_dog.class` equals `Dog`.

What about if you ask a number what its class is? Try it out:

```
puts 2.class
```

```
Integer
```

The number 2 is an object of the `Integer` class. This means that all Ruby has to do is implement the logic and code for adding numbers together in the `Integer` class, much like you created the `bark` method for your `Dog` class, and then Ruby will know how to add any two numbers together! Better than that, though, is that you can then add your own methods to the `Integer` class and process numbers in any way you see fit.

Kernel Methods

`Kernel` is a special class (actually, a *module*—but don't worry about that until Chapter 6!) whose methods are made available in every class and scope throughout Ruby (if this sounds complicated, consider the `Kernel` methods to be those available in every situation without fail). You've used a key method provided by `Kernel` already.

Consider the `puts` method. You've been using the `puts` method to print data to the screen, like so:

```
puts "Hello, world!"
```

However, unlike the methods on your own classes, `puts` isn't prefixed by the name of a class or object on which to complete the method. It would seem logical that the full command should be something like `Screen.puts` or `Display.puts`, as `puts` places text on the screen. However, in reality, `puts` is a method made available from the `Kernel` module—a special type of class packed full of standard, commonly used methods, making your code easier to read and write.

Note   The `Kernel` module in Ruby has no relationship to kernels in operating systems or the Linux kernel. As with a kernel and its operating system, the `Kernel` module is part of Ruby's "core," but there is no connection beyond that. The word "kernel" is used merely in a traditional sense.

When you type puts "Hello, world!", Ruby can tell that there's no class or object involved, so it looks through its default, predefined classes and modules for a method called puts, finds it in the Kernel module, and does its thing. When you see lines of code where there's no obvious class or object involved, take time to consider where the method call is going.

To guarantee that you're using the Kernel puts method, you can refer to it explicitly, although this is rarely done with puts:

```
Kernel.puts "Hello, world!"
```

Passing Data to Methods

Asking a dog to bark or asking an object its class is simple with Ruby. You simply refer to a class or object and follow it with a period (.) and the name of the method, such as a_dog.bark, 2.class, or Dog.new. However, there are situations where you don't want to issue a simple command, but you want to associate some data with it too.

Let's create a very simple class that represents a dog:

```
class Dog
  def bark
    puts "Woof!"
  end
end
```

Now we can simply make a dog bark by calling the relevant method:

```
my_dog = Dog.new
my_dog.bark
```

```
Woof!
```

That's simple, but what about if we have an action where some user input would be useful? We can write methods to accept data when they are called, for example:

```
class Dog
  def bark(i)
    i.times do
      puts "Woof!"
    end
  end
end
```

This time we can make the dog bark a certain number of times by passing a value to the bark method:

```
my_dog = Dog.new
my_dog.bark(3)
```

```
Woof!
Woof!
Woof!
```

When we specify the *argument* of 3 in my_dog.bark(3), it is passed to the bark method and is placed into the defined parameter i. We can then use i as a source value for running the puts command three times (or, more accurately, i times) using a times block.

There are a couple of other things to be aware of at this early stage. First, you can specify many different parameters that can be accepted by a method, for example:

```
class Dog
  def say(a, b, c)
    puts a
    puts b
    puts c
  end
end
```

Now we can pass three arguments:

```
my_dog = Dog.new
my_dog.say("Dogs", "can't", "talk!")
```

```
Dogs
can't
talk!
```

You should also be aware that parentheses around the arguments on the end of the method call are optional when there's only a single argument and the method call is not joined to any others. For example, you've previously seen code like this:

```
puts "Hello"
```

But you could just as easily write

```
puts("Hello")
```

You will continue to see many examples of calling methods and passing arguments to them throughout this book. Keep your eyes peeled for the various ways this occurs, with and without arguments and with and without parentheses.

Using the Methods of the String Class

You've played with dogs and numbers, but lines of text (*strings*) can be interesting to play with too:

```
puts "This is a test".length
```

14

You've asked the string `"This is a test"`, which is an object of the `String` class (confirm this with `"This is a test".class`), to print its length onto the screen using the `length` method. The `length` method is available on all strings, so you can replace `"This is a test"` with any text you want and you'll get a valid answer.

Asking a string for its length isn't the only thing you can do. Consider this:

```
puts "This is a test".upcase
```

THIS IS A TEST

The `String` class has many methods, which I'll cover in the next chapter, but experiment with some of the following: `capitalize`, `downcase`, `chop`, `next`, `reverse`, `sum`, and `swapcase`. Table 2-1 demonstrates some of the methods available to strings.

Table 2-1. *The Results of Using Different*
Methods on the String "Test" or "test"

Expression	Output
"Test" + "Test"	TestTest
"test".capitalize	Test
"Test".downcase	test
"Test".chop	Tes
"Test".next	Tesu
"Test".reverse	tseT
"Test".sum	416
"Test".swapcase	tEST
"Test".upcase	TEST
"Test".upcase.reverse	TSET
"Test".upcase.reverse. next	TSEU

Some of the examples in Table 2-1 are obvious, such as changing the case of the text or reversing it, but the last two examples are of particular interest. Rather than processing one method against the text, you process two or three in succession. The reason you can do this is that methods will return the original object after it's been adjusted by the method, so you have a fresh String object upon which to process another method. "Test".upcase results in the string TEST being returned, upon which the reverse method is called, resulting in TSET, upon which the next method is called, which "increments" the last character, resulting in TSEU.

In the next chapter, we'll be looking at strings more deeply, but the concept of chaining methods together to get quick results is an important one in Ruby. You can read the preceding examples aloud and they make sense. Not many other programming languages can give you that level of instant familiarity!

Using Ruby in a Non-object-Oriented Style

So far in this chapter, we've looked at several reasonably complex concepts. With some programming languages, object orientation is almost an afterthought, and beginners' books for these languages don't cover object orientation until readers understand the basics of the language (particularly with Perl and PHP, other popular web development languages). However, this doesn't work for Ruby because Ruby is a *pure* object-oriented language, and you can gain significant advantages over users of other languages by understanding these concepts right away.

Ruby has its roots in other languages, though. Ruby has been heavily influenced by languages such as Perl and C, both usually considered procedural non-object-oriented languages (although Perl has some object-oriented features). As such, even though almost everything in Ruby is an object, you can use Ruby in a similar way as a non-object-oriented language if you like, even if it's less than ideal. Essentially, you'd be "ignoring" Ruby's object-oriented features, even though they'd still be in operation under the hood.

A common demonstration program for a language such as Perl or C involves creating a *subroutine* (essentially a sort of method that has no associated object or class) and calling it, much like you called the bark method on your Dog objects. Here's a similar program, written in Ruby:

```
def dog_barking
  puts "Woof!"
end

dog_barking
```

This looks a lot different from your previous experiments. Rather than appearing to define a method within a class, it looks as if you're defining it on its own, totally independently. The method is a general one and doesn't appear to be tied to any particular class or object. In a language such as Perl or C, this method would be called a *procedure*, *function*, or *subfunction*, as *method* is a word generally used to refer to an action that can take place on an object. In Ruby, this method is still being defined on a class (the Object class), but we can ignore that within this context.

After the method is defined—it's still called a method, even though other languages would consider it to be a subroutine or function—it becomes available to use immediately without using a class or object name, like how puts is available without referring directly to the `Kernel` module. You call the method simply by using its name on its own, as on the last line of the preceding example. Typing the preceding code into irb results in the `dog_barking` method being called, giving the following result:

```
Woof!
```

In Ruby, almost everything's an object, and that includes the magical space where classless methods end up! Understanding exactly where isn't important at this stage, but it's always useful to bear Ruby's object-oriented ways in mind even when you're trying not to use object-oriented techniques!

Note   If you want to experiment, you'll find `dog_barking` at `Object.dog_barking`.

Summary

In this chapter, you learned about several important concepts not only for programming in Ruby but for programming in general. If these concepts seem logical to you already, you're well on the way to being a solid Ruby developer. Let's recap the main concepts before moving on:

- *Class*: A class is a definition of a concept in an object-oriented language such as Ruby. We created classes called `Pet`, `Dog`, `Cat`, `Snake`, and `Person`. Classes can inherit features from other classes, but still have unique features of their own.

- *Object*: An object is a single instance of a class (or, as can be the case, an instance of a class itself). An object of class `Person` is a single person. An object of class `Dog` is a single dog. Think of objects as real-life objects. A class is the classification, whereas an object is the actual object or "thing" itself.

- *Object orientation*: Object orientation is the approach of using classes and objects to model real-world concepts in a programming language, such as Ruby.

- *Variable*: In Ruby, a variable is a placeholder for a single object, which may be a number, string, list (of other objects), or instance of a class that you defined, such as, in this chapter, a `Pet`.

- *Method*: A method represents a set of code (containing multiple commands and statements) within a class and/or an object. For example, our `Dog` class objects had a `bark` method that printed "Woof!" to the screen. Methods can also be directly linked to classes, as with `fred = Person.new`, where `new` is a method that creates a new object based on the `Person` class. Methods can also accept data—known as arguments or parameters—included in parentheses after the method name, as with `puts("Test")`.

- *Arguments/parameters*: These are the data passed to methods in parentheses (or, as in some cases, following the method name without parentheses, as in `puts  "Test"`). Technically, you pass arguments *to* methods, and methods *receive* parameters, but for pragmatic purposes, the terms are interchangeable.

- *Kernel*: Some methods don't require a class or module name to be usable, such as `puts`. These are usually built-in, common methods that don't have an obvious connection to any classes or modules. Many of these methods are included in Ruby's `Kernel` module, a module that provides functions that work from anywhere within Ruby code without being explicitly referred to (a global "grab bag" of useful methods, if you will).

- *Experimentation*: One of the most fulfilling things about programming is that you can turn your dreams into reality. The amount of skill you need varies with your dreams, but generally if you want to develop a certain type of application or service, you can give it a try. Most software comes from necessity or a dream, so keeping your eyes and ears open for things you might want to develop is important. It's even more important when you first get practical knowledge of a new language, as you are while reading this book. If an idea crosses your mind, break it down into the smallest components that you can represent as Ruby classes and see if you can put together the building blocks with the Ruby you've learned so far. Your programming skills can only improve with practice.

In the next few chapters, we're going to look at the topics briefly passed over in this chapter in more detail.

## CHAPTER 3

Ruby's Building Blocks: Data, Expressions, and Flow Control

Computer programs spend nearly all their time manipulating data or waiting for data to arrive from elsewhere. We type in words, phrases, and numbers; listen to music; and watch videos, while the computer performs calculations, makes decisions, and relays information to us. To write computer programs, it's essential to understand the basics of data and its manipulation.

This chapter looks at some of the basic forms of data that Ruby supports, along with how to work with and manipulate them. The topics covered in this chapter will provide the majority of the foundation of knowledge on which your future Ruby programs will be developed.

Numbers and Expressions

At the lowest level, computers are entirely number-based, with everything represented by streams of numbers. A language such as Ruby tries to insulate you from the internal workings of the computer, and numbers in Ruby are used for mostly the same things that you use numbers for in real life, such as counting, logical comparisons, arithmetic, and so on. Let's look at how you can use numbers in these ways in Ruby and how to *do* something with them.

© Carleton DiLeo, Peter Cooper 2021
C. DiLeo and P. Cooper, *Beginning Ruby 3*, https://doi.org/10.1007/978-1-4842-6324-2_3

Basic Expressions

When programming, an *expression* is a combination of data (such as numbers or strings of text), operators (such as + or -), and variables that, when understood by the computer, result in an answer of some form. For example, these are all expressions:

```
5
1 + 2
"a" + "b" + "c"
100 - 5 * (2 - 1)
x + y
```

The top four expressions all work right away with irb (try them out now!) and get the answers you'd expect from such basic operations (1 + 2 results in 3, "a" + "b" + "c" results in abc, and so on). The final expression would fail, but try it out anyway and consider the error returned and how you could resolve the situation. (Tip: Set the x and y variables to something!)

Brackets (parentheses) work the same way as with regular arithmetic. Anything inside brackets is calculated first (or, more technically, given higher *precedence*).

Note   You can work through all the topics in this chapter using irb, the interactive Ruby interpreter. If you get stuck, simply leave irb by typing exit or pressing Ctrl+D at any time, and start irb again as demonstrated in Chapter 1. If this fails, press Ctrl+C and then the Enter key and *then* type exit.

Expressions are used regularly throughout all computer programs and not just with numbers. However, an understanding of how expressions and operations work with numbers immediately translates into a basic knowledge of how they work with text, lists, and other items too.

Variables

In Chapter 2, we ran through a multitude of concepts, including variables. Variables are placeholders or references to objects, including numbers, text, or any types of objects you've chosen to create, for example:

x = 10

```
puts x
```

```
10
```

Here you *assign* the numeric value of 10 to a variable called x. Be aware that you always need to *initialize* variables (i.e., assign a value to them) before using them; otherwise, you will end up with an error.

Note   Ruby 3 adds a new way to assign values to variables. This new feature is called "right assignment." This feature uses a hash rocket operator, =>, instead of an equal operator. We write the value first, then a hash rocket, and finally the variable name:

"Jane Doe" => name   puts name

This new syntax introduces more natural flow to variable assignment, but it's not considered a replacement. Use this syntax where it makes sense and improves code readability.

You can name variables however you like, with only a few limitations. Variable names must be a single unit (no spaces!); must start with either a letter or an underscore; must contain only letters, numbers, or underscores; and are case-sensitive. Table 3-1 demonstrates variable names that are valid and invalid.

Table 3-1. *Valid and Invalid Variable Names*

Variable Name	Valid or Invalid?
x	Valid
y2	Valid
_x	Valid
7x	Invalid (starts with a digit)
this_is_a_test	Valid
this is a test	Invalid (not a single word)
this'is@a'test!	Invalid (contains invalid characters: ', @, and !)
this-is-a-test	Invalid (looks like subtraction)

Variables are important because they allow you to write and use programs that perform operations on varying data. For example, consider a small program that has the sole job of subtracting two numbers:

```
x = 100
y = 10
puts x - y
```

90

If the code was written simply as `puts 100 - 10`, you'd get the same result, but it's not as flexible. Using variables, you can get the values for x and y from the user, a file, or some other source. The only logic is the subtraction.

As variables are placeholders for values and data, they can also be assigned the results of an expression (such as `x = 2 - 1`) and be used in expressions themselves (such as `x - y + 2`). Here's a more complex example:

```
x = 50
y = x * 100
x += y
puts x
```

5050

Step through the example line by line. First, you set x to equal 50. You then set y to the value of `x * 100` (50 * 100 or 5000). Next, you add y to x before printing the result, 5050, to the screen. It makes sense, but the third line isn't obvious at first. Adding y to x looks more logical if you say `x = x + y` rather than `x += y`. This is another Ruby shortcut. Because the act of a variable performing an operation upon itself is so common in programming, you can shorten `x = x + y` to `x += y`. The same works for other operations too, such as multiplication and division, with `x *= y` and `x /= y` being valid too. A common way to increase a variable's value by 1 is `x += 1`, which is shorthand for `x = x + 1`.

Comparison Operators and Expressions

A program without logic is merely a calculator. Computers don't just perform single operations on data. They also use logic to determine different courses of action. A basic form of logic is to use *comparison operators* within expressions to make decisions.

Consider a system that demands the user be over a certain age:

```
age = 10
puts "You're too young to use this system" if age < 18
```

If you try this code, you'll see "You're too young to use this system" because the code prints the text to the screen only when the value of age is under 18 (note the "less than" symbol). Let's make something more complex:

```
age = 24
puts "You're a teenager" if age > 12 && age < 20
```

This code results in no response because someone aged 24 is not a teenager. However, if age were to be between 13 and 19 inclusive, the message would appear. This is a case where two small expressions (age > 12 and age < 20) are joined together with &&, meaning "and." Reading expressions such as this aloud is the best way to understand them: "Print the text if age is larger than 12 *and* age is smaller than 20."

To get the opposite effect, you can use the word unless:

```
age = 24
puts "You're NOT a teenager" unless age > 12 && age < 20
```

This time you'd get the message that you're not a teenager with your age of 24. This is because unless means the opposite of if. You display the message *unless* the age is in the teenage range.

Note   Another cute technique offered by Ruby is the between? method that returns true or false if the object is between or equal to two supplied values. For example, when dealing with integers, at least, age.between?(13, 19) is equivalent to age >= 13 && age <= 19.

You can also test for equality:

```
age = 24
puts "You're 24!" if age == 24
```

Notice that the "equals" concept is represented in two different ways, due to the two different meanings. On the first line, you're saying that age is to equal 24, meaning you want age to refer to the number 24. However, on the second line, you're asking if age "is equal to" 24. In the first case, you're *demanding*, and in the second case, you're *asking*. This difference results in different operators. Therefore, the equality operator is == and the *assignment* operator is just =. A list of comparison operators for numbers is shown in Table 3-2.

Table 3-2. *A Full List of Number Comparison Operators in Ruby*

Comparison	Meaning
x > y	Greater than
x < y	Less than
x == y	Equal to
x >= y	Greater than *or* equal to
x <= y	Less than *or* equal to
x <=> y	Comparison; returns 0 if x and y are equal, 1 if x is higher, and -1 if x is lower
x != y	Not equal to

As you saw earlier, it's possible to group multiple expressions into a single expression, as with the following:

```
puts "You're a teenager" if age > 12 && age < 20
```

&& is used to enforce that *both* age > 12 and age < 20 are true. However, you can also check whether one *or* the other is true by using ||, as so:

```
puts "You're either very young or very old" if age > 80 || age < 10
```

Note   The | symbol used in || is the *pipe symbol*, not the letter *l* nor the number 1.

Grouping together multiple comparisons is also possible with a clever use of parentheses:

```ruby
gender ="male"
age = 6
puts "A very young or old man" if gender == "male" && (age < 18 || age > 85)
```

This example checks if gender is equal to "male" *and* if age is under 18 or over 85. If we did not use the parentheses, the line would be printed even if the gender were "female" and the age were over 85, because the Ruby interpreter would consider the comparisons on an individual basis, rather than making the initial && depend on satisfaction of the age < 18 || age > 85 comparison.

Looping Through Numbers with Blocks and Iterators

Nearly all programs require certain operations to be repeated over and over again to accomplish a result. It would be extremely inefficient (and inflexible!) to write a program to count through numbers like this:

```ruby
x = 1
puts x
x += 1
puts x
x += 1
puts x
...
...
```

What you want to do in these situations is implement a *loop*—a mechanism that makes the program use the same code over and over. Here's a basic way to implement a loop:

```ruby
5.times do puts "Test" end
```

```
Test
Test
Test
Test
Test
```

First, you take the number 5. Next, you call the `times` method, common to all numbers in Ruby. Rather than pass data to this method, you pass it more code: the code between do and end. The `times` method then uses the code five times in succession, producing the preceding five lines of output.

Another way to write this is with curly brackets instead of do and end. Although do and end are encouraged for multiple-line code blocks, curly brackets make the code easier to read on a single line. Therefore, this code works in exactly the same way:

```
5.times { puts "Test" }
```

You'll be using this style for single lines of code from here on, but will be using do and end for longer blocks of code. This is a good habit to pick up, as it's the style nearly all professional Ruby developers follow (although there are always exceptions to the rule).

In Ruby, one mechanism to create a loop is called an *iterator*. An iterator is something that progresses through a list of items one by one. In this case, it loops, or *iterates*, through five steps, resulting in five lines of `Test`. Other iterators are available for numbers, such as the following:

```
1.upto(5) { ...code to loop here... }
10.downto(5) { ...code to loop here... }
0.step(50, 5) { ...code to loop here... }
```

The first example counts from 1 up to 5. The second example counts from 10 down to 5. The last example counts up from 0 to 50 in steps of 5, because you're using the `step` method on the number 0.

What isn't obvious is how to get hold of the number being iterated upon at each step of the way so that you can do something with it in the looped code. What if you wanted to print out the current iteration number? How could you develop a counting program with these iterators? Thankfully, all of the iterators just explained automatically *pass* the state of the iteration to the looped code as a parameter, which you can then retrieve into a variable and use, like so:

```
1.upto(5) { |number| puts number }
```

```
1
2
3
4
5
```

The easiest way to understand this is that the code between { and } (or, potentially, do and end, remember?) is the code being looped upon. At the start of that code, the number from the "1 up to 5" count is sent down a "chute" into a variable called number. You can visualize the chute with the bars surrounding number. This is how parameters are passed into blocks of code that don't have specific names (unlike methods on classes and objects, which have names). In the preceding line of code, you ask Ruby to count from 1 to 5. It starts with 1, which is passed into the code block and displayed with puts. This is repeated for the numbers 2 through 5, resulting in the output shown.

Note that Ruby (and irb) doesn't care whether you spread your code over multiple lines or not (usually—there are exceptions!). For example, this code works in exactly the same way as the previous example:

```
1.upto(5) do |number|
 puts number
end
```

The key point to realize here is that some methods will execute code blocks and pass along data that you can then capture into variables. In the previous example, the upto method available on integers passes the value of each iteration into the code block, and we "captured" it into the variable number.

Floating Point Numbers

In Chapter 2, you ran a test where you divided 10 by 3, like so:

```
puts 10 / 3
```

```
3
```

The result is 3, although the actual answer should be 3.33 recurring. The reason for this is that, by default, Ruby considers any numbers without a floating point (also known as a decimal point) to be an integer—a whole number. When you say 10 / 3, you're asking Ruby to divide two *integers*, and Ruby gives you an integer as a result. Let's refine the code slightly:

```
puts 10.0 / 3.0
```

```
3.33333333333
```

Now you get the desired result. Ruby is now working with number objects of the Float class, and returns a Float, giving you the level of precision you'd expect.

There might be situations where you don't have control over the incoming numbers, but you still want to have them treated as floats. Consider a situation where a user enters two numbers to be divided, and the numbers require a precise answer:

```
x = 10
y = 3
puts x / y
```

```
3
```

Both input numbers are integers, so the result is an integer, as before. Luckily, integers have a special method that converts them to floats on the fly. You'd simply rewrite the code like this:

```
x = 10
y = 3
puts x.to_f / y.to_f
```

```
3.333333333335
```

In this situation, when you reach the division, both x and y are converted to their floating point number equivalents using the Integer class's to_f method. Similarly, floating point numbers can be converted back in the other direction, to integers, using to_i:

```
puts 5.7.to_i
```

```
5
```

We'll look at this technique used in other ways in the section "Converting Objects to Other Classes" later in this chapter.

Constants

Earlier you looked at separating data and logic with variables, concluding that there's rarely a need for data to be a direct part of a computer program. This is true in most cases, but consider some values that never change—the value of pi, for example. These unchanging values are called *constants* and can also be represented in Ruby by a variable name beginning with a capital letter:

```
Pi = 3.141592
```

If you enter the preceding line into irb and then try to change the value of `Pi`, it will let you do it, but you'll get a warning:

```
Pi = 3.141592
Pi = 500
```

```
(irb): warning: already initialized constant Pi
```

Ruby gives you full control over the value of constants, but the warning gives out a clear message. In the future, Ruby might enforce tighter control over constants, so respect this style of usage and try not to reassign constants mid-program.

The eagle-eyed reader might recall that in Chapter 2 you referred to classes by names such as `Dog` and `Cat`, beginning with capital letters. This is because once a class is defined, it's a constant part of the program and therefore acts as a constant too.

Text and Strings

If numbers are the most basic type of data that a computer can process, text is our next rung up the data ladder. Text is used everywhere, especially when communicating with users (directly in email, over the Web, or otherwise). In this section, you'll find out how to manipulate text to your heart's content.

String Literals

We've used strings already in some of our earlier code examples, like so:

```
puts "Hello, world!"
```

A string is a collection of textual characters (including digits, letters, whitespace, and symbols) of any length. All strings in Ruby are objects of the String class, as you can discover by calling a string's class method and printing the result:

```
puts "Hello, world!".class
```

```
String
```

When a string is embedded directly into code, using quotation marks as earlier, the construction is called a *string literal*. This differs from a string whose data comes from a remote source, such as a user typing in text, a file, or the Internet. Any text that's pre-embedded within a program is a string literal.

Like numbers, strings can be included in operations, added to, and compared against. You can also assign strings to variables:

```
x = "Test"
y = "String"
puts "Success!" if x + y == "TestString"
```

```
Success!
```

There are several other ways of including a string literal within a program. For example, you might want to include multiple lines of text. Using quotation marks is only viable for a single line, but if you want to span multiple lines, try this:

```
x = %q{This is a test
of the multi
line capabilities}
```

In this example, the quotation marks have been replaced with %q{ and }. You don't have to use curly brackets, though. You can use < and >, (and), or simply two other delimiters of your choice, such as ! and !. This code works in exactly the same way:

```
x = %q!This is a test
of the multi
line capabilities!
```

However, the important thing to remember is that if you use exclamation marks as your delimiter, then any exclamation marks in the text you're quoting will cause this technique to go awry. If delimiter characters are present in your string, your string literal will end early and Ruby will consider your remaining text erroneous. Choose your delimiters wisely!

Another way to build up a long string literal is by using a *here document or heredoc*, a concept found in many other programming languages. It works in a similar way to the previous example, except that the delimiter can be many characters long. Here's an example:

```
x = <<END_MY_STRING_PLEASE
This is the string
And a second line
END_MY_STRING_PLEASE
```

In this case, `<<` marks the start of the string literal and is followed by a delimiter of your choice (`END_MY_STRING_PLEASE` in this case). The string literal then starts from the next new line and finishes when the delimiter is repeated again on a line on its own. Using this method means that you're unlikely to run into any problems with choosing a bad delimiter, as long as you're creative! Do note that you can't include spaces in your delimiter; it has to be a single group of displayed characters.

String Expressions

Using the + symbol *concatenates* (joins together) the two strings `"Test"` and `"String"` to produce `"TestString"`, meaning that the following comparison is `true`, which results in `"Success!"` being written to the screen:

```
puts "Success!" if "Test" + "String" == "TestString"
```

Likewise, you can *multiply* strings. For example, let's say you want to replicate a string five times, like so:

```
puts "abc" * 5
```

```
abcabcabcabcabc
```

You can also perform "greater than" and "less than" comparisons:

```
puts "x" > "y"
```

```
false
```

```
puts "y" > "x"
```

```
 true
```

Note   "x" > "y" and "y" > "x" are expressions that, by using a comparison operator, result in true or false outcomes.

In this situation, Ruby compares the numbers that represent the characters in the string. As mentioned previously, characters are stored as numbers inside your computer's memory. Every letter and symbol has a value, called an *ASCII value*. These values aren't particularly important, but they do mean you can do comparisons between letters, and even longer strings, in this way. If you're interested to learn what value a particular character has, find out like so:

```
puts "x".ord
```

```
120
```

```
puts "A".ord
```

```
65
```

The String class's ord method returns an integer matching the position of that character in the *ASCII table*, an international standard for representing characters as values.

You can achieve the inverse by using the String class's chr method, for example:

```
puts 120.chr
```

```
x
```

Note   Explaining more about the ASCII character set here is beyond the scope of this book, but there are many resources on the Web if you wish to learn more. One excellent resource is `https://en.wikipedia.org/wiki/ASCII`.

Interpolation

In previous examples, you've printed the results of your code to the screen with the `puts` method. However, your results have had little explanation. If a random user came along and used your code, it wouldn't be obvious what's going on, as they won't be interested in reading your source code. Therefore, it's essential to provide user-friendly output from your programs. You'll go back to using numbers for this example:

```
x = 10
y = 20
puts "#{x} + #{y} = #{x + y}"
```

```
10 + 20 = 30
```

It's kindergarten-level math, but the result highlights an interesting capability. You can embed expressions (and even logic) directly into strings. This process is called *interpolation.*

In this situation, interpolation refers to the process of inserting the result of an expression into a string literal. The way to interpolate within a string is to place the expression within #{ and } symbols. An even more basic example demonstrates

```
puts "100 * 5 = #{100 * 5}"
```

```
100 * 5 = 500
```

The #{100 * 5} section interpolates the result of 100 * 5 (500) into the string at that position, resulting in the output shown. Examine this code:

```
puts "#{x} + #{y} = #{x + y}"
```

You first interpolate the value of x, then the value of y, and then the value of x added to y. You surround each section with the relevant mathematical symbols, and hey presto, you get a complete mathematical equation:

```
10 + 20 = 30
```

You can interpolate other strings too:

```
x = "cat"
puts "The #{x} in the hat"
```

```
The cat in the hat
```

Or if you want to get clever:

```
puts "It's a #{"bad " * 5}world"
```

```
It's a bad bad bad bad bad world
```

In this instance, you interpolate a repetition of a string, "bad ", five times. It's certainly a lot quicker than typing it!

Interpolation also works within strings used in assignments:

```
my_string = "It's a #{"bad " * 5}world"
puts my_string
```

```
It's a bad bad bad bad bad world
```

It's worth noting that you could achieve the same results as the preceding by placing the expressions outside the strings, without using interpolation, for example:

```
x = 10
y = 20
puts x.to_s + " + " + y.to_s + " = " + (x + y).to_s
puts "#{x} + #{y} = #{x + y}"
```

The two `puts` lines result in the same output. The first uses string concatenation (+) to join several different strings together. The numbers in x and y are converted to strings with their `to_s` method. However, the second `puts` line uses interpolation, which doesn't require the numbers to be converted to strings explicitly.

String Methods

We've looked at using strings in expressions, but you can do a lot more with strings than add them together or multiply them. As you experimented in Chapter 2, you can use a number of different methods on a string. Table 3-3 provides a recap of the string methods you looked at in Chapter 2.

Table 3-3. *The Results of Using Different Methods on the String "Test"*

Expression	Output
`"Test" + "Test"`	TestTest
`"test".capitalize`	Test
`"Test".downcase`	test
`"Test".chop`	Tes
`"Test".next`	Tesu
`"Test".reverse`	tseT
`"Test".sum`	416
`"Test".swapcase`	tEST
`"Test".upcase`	TEST
`"Test".upcase.reverse`	TSET
`"Test".upcase.reverse.next`	TSEU

In each example in Table 3-3, you're using a method that the string offers, whether it's concatenation, conversion to uppercase, reversal, or merely incrementing the last letter. You can *chain* methods together, as in the final example of the table. First, you create the "Test" string literal; then you convert it to uppercase, returning TEST; then you reverse *that*, returning TSET; and then you increment the last letter of *that*, returning TSEU.

Another method you used in Chapter 2 was length, like so:

```
puts "This is a test".length
```

14

These methods are useful, but they don't let you do anything particularly impressive with your strings. Let's move on to playing directly with the text itself.

Regular Expressions and String Manipulation

When working with strings at an advanced level, it becomes necessary to learn about *regular expressions*. A regular expression is, essentially, a search query, and not to be confused with the expressions we've discussed already in this chapter. If you type ruby into your favorite search engine, you'd expect information about Ruby to appear. Likewise, if your regular expression is ruby and you run that query against, say, a long string, you'd expect any matches to be returned. A regular expression, therefore, is a string that describes a pattern for matching elements in other strings.

Note   This section provides only a brief introduction to regular expressions. Regular expressions are a major branch of computer science, and many books and websites are dedicated to their use. Ruby supports the majority of standard regular expression syntax, so non-Ruby-specific knowledge about regular expressions obtained from elsewhere can still prove useful in Ruby.

Substitutions

One thing you'll often want to do is substitute something within a string for something else. Take this example:

```
puts "foobar".sub('bar', 'foo')
```

---

foofoo

In this example, you use a method on the string called sub, which substitutes the first instance of the first parameter 'bar' with the second parameter 'foo', resulting in foofoo. sub only does one substitution at a time, on the first instance of the text to match, whereas gsub does multiple substitutions at once, as this example demonstrates:

```
puts "this is a test".gsub('i', '')
```

```
ths s a test
```

Here you've substituted all occurrences of the letter 'i' with an empty string. What about more complex patterns? Simply matching the letter 'i' is not a true example of a regular expression. For example, let's say you want to replace the first two characters of a string with 'Hello':

```
x = "This is a test"
puts x.sub(/^../, 'Hello')
```

```
Hellois is a test
```

In this case, you make a single substitution with sub. The first parameter given to sub isn't a string but a regular expression—forward slashes are used to start and end a regular expression. Within the regular expression is ^... The ^ is an *anchor*, meaning the regular expression will match from the beginning of any lines within the string. The two periods each represent "any character." In all, /^../ means "any two characters immediately after the start of a line." Therefore, Th of "This is a test" gets replaced with Hello.

Likewise, if you want to change the last two letters, you can use a different anchor:

```
x = "This is a test"
puts x.sub(/..$/, 'Hello')
```

```
This is a teHello
```

This time the regular expression matches the two characters that are anchored to the end of any lines within the string.

> **Note**   If you want to anchor to the absolute start or end of a string, you can use
> \A and \z, respectively, whereas ^ and $ anchor to the starts and ends of lines
> within a string.

Iteration with a Regular Expression

Previously, you used iterators to move through sets of numbers, counting from 1 to 10, for example. What if you want to iterate through a string and have access to each section of it separately? scan is the iterator method you require:

```
"xyz".scan(/./) { |letter| puts letter }
```

```
x
y
z
```

scan lives up to its name. It scans through the string looking for anything that matches the regular expression passed to it. In this case, you've supplied a regular expression that looks for a single character at a time. That's why you get x, y, and z separately in the output. Each letter is fed to the block, assigned to letter, and printed to the screen. Try this more elaborate example:

```
"This is a test".scan(/../) { |x| puts x }
```

```
Th
is
i
s
a
te
st
```

This time you're scanning for two characters at a time. Easy! Scanning for all characters results in some weird output, though, with all the spaces mixed in. Let's adjust our regular expression to match only letters and digits, like so:

```
"This is a test".scan(/\w\w/) { |x| puts x }
```

```
Th
is
is
te
st
```

Within regular expressions, there are special characters that are denoted with a backslash, and they have special meanings. \w means "any alphanumeric character or an underscore." There are many others, as illustrated in Table 3-4.

Table 3-4. Basic Special Characters and Symbols Within Regular Expressions

Character	Meaning
^	Anchor for the beginning of a line
$	Anchor for the end of a line
\A	Anchor for the start of a string
\z	Anchor for the end of a string
.	Any character
\w	Any letter, digit, or underscore
\W	Anything that \w doesn't match
\d	Any digit
\D	Anything that \d doesn't match (non-digits)
\s	Whitespace (spaces, tabs, newlines, and so on)
\S	Non-whitespace (any visible character)

Using the knowledge from Table 3-4, you can easily extract numbers from a string:

```
"The car costs $1000 and the cat costs $10".scan(/\d+/) do |x|
  puts x
end
```

```
1000
10
```

You've just gotten Ruby to extract meaning from some arbitrary English text! The scan method was used as before, but you've given it a regular expression that uses \d to match any digit, and the + that follows \d makes \d match as many digits in a row as possible. This means it matches both 1000 and 10, rather than just each individual digit at a time. To prove it, try this:

```
"The car costs $1000 and the cat costs $10".scan(/\d/) do |x|
  puts x
end
```

```
1
0
0
0
1
0
```

So, + after a character in a regular expression means *match one or more* of that type of character. There are other types of modifiers, and these are shown in Table 3-5.

Table 3-5. *Regular Expression Character and Sub-expression Modifiers*

Modifier	Description
*	Match zero or more occurrences of the preceding character, and match as many as possible.
+	Match one or more occurrences of the preceding character, and match as many as possible.
*?	Match zero or more occurrences of the preceding character, and match as *few* as possible.
+?	Match one or more occurrences of the preceding character, and match as *few* as possible.
?	Match either one or none of the preceding character.
{x}	Match x occurrences of the preceding character.
{x,y}	Match at least x occurrences and at most y occurrences.

The last important aspect of regular expressions you need to understand at this stage is *character classes*. These allow you to match against a specific set of characters. For example, you can scan through all the vowels in a string:

```
"This is a test".scan(/[aeiou]/) { |x| puts x }
```

```
i
i
a
e
```

[aeiou] means "match any of a, e, i, o, or u." You can also specify ranges of characters inside the square brackets, like so:

```
"This is a test".scan(/[a-m]/) { |x| puts x }
```

```
h
i
i
a
e
```

This scan matches all lowercase letters between a and m.

Regular expressions can be complex and confusing, and entire books larger than this one have been dedicated to them. Most coders only need to understand the basics, as the more advanced techniques will become apparent with time—but they're a powerful tool when you experiment with and master them.

You'll be using and expanding on all the techniques covered in this section in code examples throughout the rest of the book.

Matching

Making substitutions and extracting certain text from strings is useful, but sometimes you merely want to check whether a certain string matches against the pattern of your choice. You might want to establish quickly if a string contains any vowels:

```
puts "String has vowels" if "This is a test" =~ /[aeiou]/
```

In this example, =~ is another form of operator: a *matching* operator. If the string has a match with the regular expression following the operator, then the expression returns the *position* of the first match (2 in this case—which logically is non-false, so the if condition is satisfied). You can, of course, do the opposite:

```
puts "String contains no digits" unless "This is a test" =~ /[0-9]/
```

This time you're saying that *unless* the range of digits from 0 to 9 matches against the test string, tell the user that there are no digits in the string.

It's also possible to use a method called match, provided by the String class. Whereas =~ returns the position of the first match or nil depending on whether the regular expression matches the string, match provides a lot more power. Here's a basic example:

```
puts "String has vowels" if "This is a test".match(/[aeiou]/)
```

In regular expressions, if you surround a section of the expression with parentheses—(and)—the data matched by that section of the regular expression is made available separately from the rest. match lets you access this data:

```
x = "This is a test".match(/(\w+) (\w+)/)
puts x[0]
puts x[1]
```

```
puts x[2]
```

```
This is
This
is
```

`match` returns a `MatchData` object that can be accessed like an array. The first element (`x[0]`) contains the data matched by the entire regular expression. However, each successive element contains that which was matched by each match group of the regular expression. In this example, the first (`\w+`) matched `This` and the second (`\w+`) matched `is`.

Note   Matching can get far more complex than this, but I'll be covering more advanced uses in the next chapter when you put together your first complete Ruby program.

Arrays and Lists

So far in this chapter, you've created single instances of number and string objects and manipulated them. After a while, it becomes necessary to create collections of these objects and to work with them as a list. In Ruby, you can represent ordered collections of objects using *arrays*.

Basic Arrays

Here's a basic array:

```
x = [1, 2, 3, 4]
```

This array has four *elements*. Each element is an integer, and is separated by commas from its neighboring elements. Square brackets are used to denote an *array literal*.

Elements can be accessed by their index (their position within the array). To access a particular element, an array (or a variable containing an array) is followed by the index contained within square brackets. This is called an *element reference*, for example:

```
x = [1, 2, 3, 4]
puts x[2]
```

```
3
```

As with most programming languages, the indexing for Ruby's arrays starts from 0, so the first element of the array is element 0, and the second element of the array is element 1, and so on. In our example, this means x[2] is addressing what we'd call the third element of the array, which in this case is an object representing the number 3. To change an element, you can simply assign it a new value or manipulate it as you've manipulated numbers and strings earlier in this chapter:

```
x[2] += 1
puts x[2]
```

```
4
```

Or

```
x[2] = "Fish" * 3
puts x[2]
```

```
FishFishFish
```

Arrays don't need to be set up with predefined entries or have elements allocated manually. You can create an empty array like so:

```
x = []
```

The array is empty, and trying to address, say, x[5] results in nil being returned. You can add things to the end of the array by *pushing* data into it, like so:

```
x = []
x << "Word"
```

After this, the array contains a single element: a string saying "Word". With arrays, << is the operator for pushing an item onto the end of an array. You can also use the push method, which is equivalent:

```
x.push("Word")
```

You can also remove entries from an array one by one. Arrays can act as a stack, "last in, first out," where items are pushed onto the end of the array and also *popped* from the end (*popping* is the process of retrieving and removing items from the end of the array):

```
x = []
x << "Word"
x << "Play"
x << "Fun"
puts x.pop
puts x.pop
puts x.length
```

```
Fun
Play
1
```

You push "Word", "Play", and "Fun" into the array held in x and then display the first "popped" element on the screen. Elements are popped from the end of the array, so "Fun" comes out first. Next comes "Play". For good measure, you then print out the length of the array at that point, using the aptly named length method (size works too, and gives exactly the same result), which is 1 because only "Word" is still present in the array.

Another useful feature is that if an array is full of strings, you can join all the elements together into one big string by calling the join method on the array:

```
x = ["Word", "Play", "Fun"]
puts x.join
```

```
WordPlayFun
```

The join method can take an optional parameter that's placed between each element in the resulting string:

```
x = ["Word", "Play", "Fun"]
puts x.join(', ')
```

```
Word, Play, Fun
```

This time you join the array elements together, but between each set of elements you place a comma and a space. This results in cleaner output.

Splitting Strings into Arrays

In the section relating to strings, you used scan to iterate through the contents of the string looking for characters that matched patterns you expressed as regular expressions. With scan, you used a block of code that accepted each set of characters and displayed them on the screen. However, if you use scan *without* a block of code, it returns an array of all the matching parts of the string, like so:

```
puts "This is a test".scan(/\w/).join(',')
```

```
T,h,i,s,i,s,a,t,e,s,t
```

First, you define a string literal, then you scan over it for alphanumeric characters (using /\w/), and finally you join the elements of the returned array together with commas.

What if you don't want to scan for particular characters, but instead want to *split* a string into multiple pieces? You can use the split method and tell it to split a string into an array of strings on the periods, like so:

```
puts "Short sentence. Another. No more.".split(/\./).inspect
```

```
["Short sentence", " Another", " No more"]
```

There are a couple of important points here. First, if you'd used . in the regular expression rather than \., you'd be splitting on every character rather than on full stops, because . represents "any character" in a regular expression. Therefore, you have to *escape* it by prefixing it with a backslash (*escaping* is the process of specifically denoting a character to make its meaning clear). Second, rather than joining and printing out the sentences, you're using the inspect method to get a tidier result.

The inspect method is common to almost all built-in classes in Ruby, and it gives you a textual representation of the object. For example, the preceding output shows the result array in the same way that you might create an array yourself. inspect is incredibly useful when experimenting and debugging!

`split` is also happy splitting on newlines, or multiple characters at once, to get a cleaner result:

```
puts "Words with lots of spaces".split(/\s+/).inspect
```

```
["Words", "with", "lots", "of", "spaces"]
```

With Ruby and some regular expressions, you're never far from solving any text processing problem!

It is also important to cover p, an alternative to using `inspect`. The previous example could also be written in this way:

```
p "Words with lots of spaces".split(/\s+/)
```

```
["Words", "with", "lots", "of", "spaces"]
```

p is an extremely useful alternative to using `puts` when playing with expressions in irb. It automatically shows you the structure of the object(s) returned by the expression following it. We will use p extensively throughout the rest of this chapter. You will almost never need to use it in a production application, but for debugging and learning, it's excellent—not to mention quick to type!

Array Iteration

Iterating through arrays is simple and uses the each method. The each method goes through each element of the array and passes it as a parameter to the code block you supply, for example:

```
[1, "test", 2, 3, 4].each { |element| puts element.to_s + "X" }
```

```
1X
testX
2X
3X
4X
```

Although each iterates through elements of an array, you can also convert an array on the fly using the collect method:

```
[1, 2, 3, 4].collect { |element| element * 2 }
```

```
[2, 4, 6, 8]
```

collect iterates through an array element by element and assigns to that element the result of any expression within the code block. In this example, you multiply the value of the element by 2.

Note   map is functionally equivalent to collect. You may see both being used in this book and in other code you encounter.

Programmers who have come from less dynamic and possibly non-object-oriented languages might see these techniques as being quite modern. It's possible to do things "the old-fashioned way" with Ruby if required:

```
a = [1, "test", 2, 3, 4]
i = 0

while (i < a.length)
 puts a[i].to_s + "X"
 i += 1
end
```

This works in a similar way to the each example from earlier, but loops through the array in a way more familiar to traditional programmers (from languages such as C, BASIC, or JavaScript). However, it should be immediately apparent to anyone why iterators, code blocks, and methods such as each and collect are preferable with Ruby, as they make the code significantly easier to read and understand.

Other Array Methods

Arrays have a lot of interesting methods, some of which I'll cover in this section.

Array Addition and Concatenation

If you have two arrays, you can quickly combine their results into one:

```
x = [1, 2, 3]
y = ["a", "b", "c"]
z = x + y
p z
```

```
[1, 2, 3, "a", "b", "c"]
```

Note   We're using p here instead of puts z.inspect. Go back to the "Splitting Strings into Arrays" section if you missed the explanation of this key point.

Array Subtraction and Difference

You can also compare two arrays by subtracting one against the other. This technique removes any elements from the main array that are in both arrays:

```
x = [1, 2, 3, 4, 5]
y = [1, 2, 3]
z = x - y
p z
```

```
[4, 5]
```

Checking for an Empty Array

If you're about to iterate over an array, you might want to check if it has any items yet. You could do this by checking if array.size or array.length is larger than 0, but a more popular shorthand is to use empty?:

```
x = []
puts "x is empty" if x.empty?
```

```
x is empty
```

Checking an Array for a Certain Item

The include? method returns true if the supplied parameter is in the array, and false otherwise:

```
x = [1, 2, 3]
p x.include?("x")
p x.include?(3)
```

```
false
true
```

Accessing the First and Last Elements of the Array

Accessing the first and last elements of an array is easy with the first and last methods:

```
x = [1, 2, 3]
puts x.first
puts x.last
```

```
1
3
```

If you pass a numeric parameter to first or last, you'll get that number of items from the start or the end of the array:

```
x = [1, 2, 3]
puts x.first(2).join("-")
```

```
1-2
```

Reversing the Order of the Array's Elements

Like a string, an array can be reversed:

```
x = [1, 2, 3]
p x.reverse
```

```
[3, 2, 1]
```

Hashes

Arrays are collections of objects, and so are hashes. However, hashes have a different storage format and way to define each object within the collection. Rather than having an assigned position in a list, objects within a hash are given a *key* that points to them. It's more like a *dictionary* than a list, as there's no guaranteed order, but just simple links between keys and values. Note we are not using the preferred hash syntax. This will change when you learn about symbols. Here's a basic hash with two entries:

```
dictionary = { cat: "feline animal", dog: "canine animal" }
```
The variable storing the hash is dictionary, and it contains two entries, as you can inspect:
```
puts dictionary.size
```

```
2
```

One entry has a key of cat and a value of feline animal, while the other has a key of dog and a value of canine animal. The key in this example is a symbol which is covered later in this chapter. For now, don't worry about the details of symbols. Just know symbols are like strings with different properties. Like arrays, you use square brackets to reference the element you wish to retrieve, for example:

```
puts dictionary[:cat]
```

```
feline animal
```

As you can see, a hash can be viewed as an array that has names for elements instead of position numbers. You can even change values in the same way as an array:

```
dictionary[:cat] = "fluffy animal"
puts dictionary[:cat]
```

```
fluffy animal
```

> **Note**   It won't be immediately useful to you, but it's worth noting that both keys and values can be objects of any type. Therefore, it's possible to use an array (or even another hash) as a key. This might come in useful when you're dealing with more complex data structures in the future.

Basic Hash Methods

As with arrays, hashes have many useful methods that you'll look at in this section.

Iterating Through Hash Elements

With arrays, you can use the each method to iterate through each element of the array. You can do the same with hashes:

```
x = { "a" => 1, "b" => 2 }
x.each { |key, value| puts "#{key} equals #{value}" }
```

```
a equals 1
b equals 2
```

> **Note**   Since Ruby 1.9, the order in which the elements were inserted into the hash will be remembered, and each will return them in that order.

The each iterator method for a hash passes two parameters into the code block: first, a key, and second, the value associated with that key. In this example, you assign them to variables called key and value and use string interpolation to display their contents on the screen.

Retrieving Keys

Sometimes you might not be interested in the values in a hash, but want to get a feel for what the hash contains. A great way to do this is to look at the keys. Ruby gives you an easy way to see the keys in any hash immediately, using the keys method:

```
x = { a: 1, b: 2, c: 3 }
p x.keys
```

```
[:a, :b, :c]
```

keys returns an array of all the keys in the hash, and if you're ever in the mood, values will return an array of all the values in the hash too. Generally, however, you'll look up values based on a key.

Deleting Hash Elements

Deleting hash elements is easy with the delete method. All you do is pass in a key as a parameter, and the element is removed:

```
x = { a: 1, b: 2 }
x.delete(:a)
p x
```

```
{:b=>2}
```

Deleting Hash Elements Conditionally

Let's say you want to delete any hash elements whose value is below a certain figure. Here's an example of how to do this:

```
x = { a: 100, b: 20 }
x.delete_if { |key, value| value < 25 }
p x
```

```
{:a=>100}
```

Hashes Within Hashes

It's possible to have hashes (or, indeed, any sort of object) within hashes, and even arrays within hashes, within hashes! Because everything is an object and hashes and arrays can contain any other objects, you could create giant tree structures with hashes and arrays. Here's a demonstration:

```ruby
people = {
  fred: {
    name: "Fred Elliott",
    age: 63,
    gender: "male",
    favorite_painters: ["Monet", "Constable", "Da Vinci"]
  },
  janet: {
    name: "Janet S Porter",
    age: 55,
    gender: "female"
  }
}

puts people[:fred][:age]
puts people[:janet][:gender]
puts people[:janet]
```

```
63
female
{:name=>"Janet S Porter", :age=>55, :gender=>"female"}
```

Although the structure of the hash looks a little confusing at first, it becomes reasonably fred and janet sections are simple hashes of their own, but they're wrapped up into another giant hash assigned to people. In the code that queries the giant hash, you simply chain the lookups on top of each other, as with puts people[:fred][:age]. First, it gets people[:fred], which returns Fred's hash, and then you request [:age] from that, yielding the result of 63.

Even the array embedded within Fred's hash is easy to access:

```
puts people[:fred][:favorite_painters].length
puts people[:fred][:favorite_painters].join(", ")
```

```
3
Monet, Constable, Da Vinci
```

These techniques are used more and explained in greater depth in the following chapters.

Flow Control

In this chapter, you've used comparisons, together with `if` and `unless`, to perform different operations based on the circumstances. `if` and `unless` work well on single lines of code, but when combined with large sections of code, they become even more powerful. In this section, you'll be looking at how Ruby lets you control the *flow* of your programs with these and other constructs.

if and unless

The first use of `if` within this chapter used this demonstration:

```
age = 10
puts "You're too young to use this system" if age < 18
```

If the value of age is under 18, the string is printed to the screen. The following code is equivalent:

```
age = 10
if age < 18
  puts "You're too young to use this system"
end
```

It looks similar, but the code to be executed if the expression is `true` is contained between the `if` expression and `end`, instead of the `if` expression being added onto the end of a single line of code. This construction makes it possible to put any number of lines of code in between the `if` statement and the end line:

```
age = 10
if age < 18
  puts "You're too young to use this system"
  puts "So we're going to exit your program now"
  exit
end
```

Note   If you copy and paste the previous code directly into irb, the `exit` call on the fifth line will result in irb closing, so don't be surprised by this. You will also see this in the next example.

It's worth noting that `unless` can work in exactly the same way because `unless` is just the opposite of `if`:

```
age = 10
unless age >= 18
  puts "You're too young to use this system"
  puts "So we're going to exit your program now"
  exit
end
```

It's possible to nest logic too, as in this example:

```
age = 19
if age < 21
 puts "You can't drink in most of the United States"
 if age >= 18
   puts "But you can in the United Kingdom!"
 end
end
```

`if` and `unless` also supply the `else` condition, used to delimit lines of code that you want to be executed if the main expression is `false`:

```
age = 10
if age < 18
  puts "You're too young to use this system"
```

```
else
  puts "You can use this system"
end
```

?, the Ternary Operator

The ternary operator makes it possible for an expression to contain a mini if/else statement. It's a construction that's entirely optional to use, and some developers are oblivious to its existence. However, because it can be useful to produce more compact code, it's worth learning early. Let's dive in with an example:

```
age = 10
type = age < 18 ? "child" : "adult"
puts "You are a " + type
```

The second line contains the ternary operator. It starts by assigning the result of an expression to the variable type. The expression is age < 18 ? "child" : "adult". The structure is as follows:

```
<condition> ? <result if condition is true> : <result if condition is false>
```

In our example, age < 18 returns true, so the first result, "child", is returned and assigned to type. However, if age < 18 were to be false, "adult" would be returned.

Consider an alternative:

```
age = 10
type = 'child' if age < 18
type = 'adult' unless age < 18
puts "You are a " + type
```

The double comparison makes it harder to read. Another alternative is to use the multiline if/else option:

```
age = 10
if age < 18
 type = 'child'
else
 type = 'adult'
end
puts "You are a " + type
```

The ternary operator shows its immediate benefit in its conciseness, and as it can be used to build expressions on a single line, you can use it easily in calls to methods or within other expressions where if statements would be invalid. Consider this even simpler version of the first example from this section:

```
age = 10
puts "You are a " + (age < 18 ? "child" : "adult")
```

elsif and case

Sometimes it's desirable to make several comparisons with the same variable at the same time. You could do this with the if statement, as covered previously:

```
fruit = "orange"
color = "orange" if fruit == "orange"
color = "green" if fruit == "apple"
color = "yellow" if fruit == "banana"
```

If you want to use else to assign something different if fruit is not equal to orange, apple, or banana, it will quickly get messy, as you'd need to create an if block to check for the presence of any of these words and then perform the same comparisons as earlier. An alternative is to use elsif, meaning "else if":

```
fruit = "orange"
if fruit == "orange"
  color = "orange"
elsif fruit == "apple"
  color = "green"
elsif fruit == "banana"
  color = "yellow"
else
  color = "unknown"
end
```

elsif blocks act somewhat like else blocks, except that you can specify a whole new comparison expression to be performed, and if none of those match, you can specify a regular else block to be executed.

A variant of this technique is to use a `case` block. Our preceding example, with a `case` block, becomes as follows:

```
fruit = "orange"
case fruit
when "orange"
  color = "orange"
when "apple"
  color = "green"
when "banana"
  color = "yellow"
else
  color = "unknown"
end
```

This code is similar to the `if` block, except that the syntax is a lot cleaner. A `case` block works by processing an expression first and then by finding a contained when block that matches the result of that expression. If no matching when block is found, then the `else` block within the `case` block is executed instead.

`case` has another trick up its sleeve. As all Ruby expressions return a result, you can make the previous example even shorter:

```
fruit = "orange"
color = case fruit
when "orange"
  "orange"
when "apple"
  "green"
when "banana"
  "yellow"
else
  "unknown"
end
```

In this example, you use a `case` block, but you assign the result of whichever inner block is executed directly to `color`.

Note   If you are familiar with the `switch/case` syntax in C (or a C-related language), you might think `case/when` is Ruby's equivalent. It's very similar, but only one "case" can be matched in Ruby, as execution does not continue through the list of options once a match has been made.

---

case pattern matching

Using the case statement and pattern matching provides an easy way to deconstruct complex objects and use their data. It's possible to use pattern matching with case statements. Instead of using case/when, we use case/in with the pattern following the "in" statement:

```
response = { error: 'Bad Gateway', code: 502 }
case response
in { data: data, code: code }
  puts "Success #{data}, Code: #{code}"
in { error: error, code: code }
  puts "Error: #{error}, Code: #{code}"
end
```

```
Error: Bad Gateway, Code: 502
```

In the example, we have a response object which contains an error message and a code. We pass the response to the case statement. Ruby checks each pattern of the case statement until it finds a pattern that matches. Since the response matches the second pattern structure, Ruby binds the matched parts in the hash to the variable error and code. Next, it runs the statement after the pattern which prints the error and the code to the screen. If no patterns match, Ruby throws a NoMatchingPattern error rather than return nil like in a case/when statement.

As you can see, pattern matching is very useful. The best part is pattern matching doesn't only work with hashes. You can use it with arrays, ranges, and objects. Check out the Ruby docs for an in-depth guide to pattern matching: `https://docs.ruby-lang.org/en/master/syntax/pattern_matching_rdoc.html`.

while and until

In previous sections, you've performed loops using iterator methods, like so:

```
1.upto(5) { |number| puts number }
```

```
1
2
3
4
5
```

However, it's possible to loop code in other ways. while and until allow you to loop code based on the result of a comparison made on each loop:

```
x = 1
while x < 100
  puts x
  x = x * 2
end
```

```
1
2
4
8
16
32
64
```

In this example, you have a while block that denotes a section of code that is to be repeated over and over while the expression x < 100 is satisfied. Therefore, x is doubled loop after loop and printed to the screen. Once x is 100 or over, the loop ends.

until provides the opposite functionality, looping *until* a certain condition is met:

```
x = 1
until x > 99
  puts x
  x = x * 2
end
```

It's also possible to use `while` and `until` in a single line setting, as with `if` and `unless`:

```
i = 1
i = i * 2 until i > 1000
puts i
```

```
1024
```

The value of i is doubled over and over until the result is over 1000, at which point the loop ends (1024 being 2 to the power of 10).

Code Blocks

Code blocks have been used in several code examples in this chapter, for example:

```
x = [1, 2, 3]
x.each { |y| puts y }
```

```
1
2
3
```

The each method accepts a single following code block. The code block is defined within the { and } symbols or, alternatively, do and end delimiters:

```
x = [1, 2, 3]
x.each do |y|
 puts y
end
```

The code between { and } or do and end is a code block—essentially an anonymous, nameless method or function. This code is passed to the each method, which then runs the code block for each element of the array.

It's possible to use numbered parameters instead of an explicit variable when defining a block:

```
x = [1, 2, 3]
x.each do
  puts _1
end
```

The new example is the same functionality but uses the number parameter _1, which is automatically defined and assigned to the value passed to the block. Numbered parameters are useful for situations where providing a parameter name doesn't add any additional meaning to the code.

You can write methods of your own to handle code blocks, for example:

```
def each_vowel(&code_block)
  %w{a e i o u}.each { |vowel| code_block.call(vowel) }
end

each_vowel { |vowel| puts vowel }
```

```
a
e
i
o
u
```

each_vowel is a method that accepts a code block, as designated by the ampersand (&) before the variable name code_block in the method definition. It then iterates over each vowel in the literal array %w{a e i o u} and uses the call method on code_block to execute the code block once for each vowel, passing in the vowel variable as a parameter each time.

Note   Code blocks passed in this way result in objects that have many methods of their own, such as call. Remember, almost everything in Ruby is an object! (Many elements of syntax are not objects, nor are code blocks in their literal form.)

An alternate technique is to use the yield method, which automatically detects any passed code block and passes control to it:

```
def each_vowel
 %w{a e i o u}.each { |vowel| yield vowel }
end
each_vowel { |vowel| puts vowel }
```

This example is functionally equivalent to the last, although it's less obvious what it does because you see no code block being accepted in the function definition. Which technique you choose to use is up to you.

Note   Only one code block can be passed at any one time. It's not possible to accept two or more code blocks as parameters to a method. However, code blocks may accept none, one, or more parameters themselves.

It's also possible to store code blocks within variables, using a `Proc`:

```
print_parameter_to_screen = Proc.new { |x| puts x }
print_parameter_to_screen.call(100)
```

```
100
```

As with accepting a code block into a method, you use the `Proc` object's `call` method to execute it, as well as to pass any parameters in.

Note   *lambda* is another way to define code blocks. There are a couple of differences between a proc and lambda. Lambdas check if the number of parameters matches the signature. If a lambda defines two parameters and your code provides one, you get an error. Another difference is a lambda returns just like a Ruby method, while a proc returns from the current context. Don't worry too much if this doesn't make sense right now. Lambdas and procs are an advanced topic you can revisit when you are more comfortable with Ruby.

Other Useful Building Blocks

So far in this chapter, we've covered the primary built-in data classes of numbers, strings, arrays, and hashes. These few types of objects can get you a long way and will be used in all your programs. You'll be looking at objects in more depth in Chapter 6, but before you get that far, there are a few other important points you need to look at first.

Dates and Times

A concept that's useful to represent within many computer programs is time, in the form of dates and times. Ruby provides a class called Time to handle these concepts.

Internally, Time stores times as a number of microseconds since the UNIX time epoch: January 1, 1970 00:00:00 Greenwich Mean Time (GMT)/Coordinated Universal Time (UTC). This makes it easy to compare times using the standard comparison operators, such as < and >.

Let's look at how to use the Time class:

```
puts Time.now
```

```
2020-08-01 00:00:00 +0100
```

Time.now creates an instance of class Time that's set to the current time. However, because you're trying to print it to the screen, it's converted into the preceding string.

You can manipulate time objects by adding and subtracting numbers of seconds to them, for example:

```
puts Time.now
puts Time.now - 10
puts Time.now + 86400
```

```
2020-07-01 00:00:00 +0100
2020-06-30 23:59:50 +0100
2020-07-02 00:00:00 +0100
```

In the first example, you print the current time, and then the current time minus 10 seconds, and then the current time with 86,400 seconds (exactly one day) added on. Because times can be manipulated so easily in Ruby using normal mathematical operators, but because people prefer to work with minutes, hours, and days rather than seconds all of the time, some developers extend the Integer class with some helper methods to make time manipulation even easier:

```ruby
class Integer
  def seconds
    self
  end
  def minutes
    self * 60
  end
  def hours
    self * 60 * 60
  end
  def days
    self * 60 * 60 * 24
  end
end

puts Time.now
puts Time.now + 10.minutes
puts Time.now + 16.hours
puts Time.now - 7.days
```

```
2020-07-01 00:00:00 +0100
2020-07-01 00:10:00 +0100
2020-07-01 16:00:00 +0100
2020-06-24 00:00:00 +0100
```

Don't worry if this code seems confusing and unfamiliar, as we'll be covering this type of technique more in the following chapters. Do note, however, the style used in the final puts statements. It's easy to manipulate dates with these helpers!

The Time class also allows you to create Time objects based on arbitrary dates:

```
year = 2020
month = 1
day = 16
hour = 12
min = 57
sec = 10
msec = 42
Time.local(year, month, day, hour, min, sec, msec)
```

The preceding code creates a Time object based on the current (local) time zone. All arguments from month onward are optional and take default values of 1 or 0. You can specify months numerically (between 1 and 12) or as three-letter abbreviations of their English names:

```
Time.gm(year, month, day, hour, min, sec, msec)
```

The preceding code creates a Time object based on GMT/UTC. Argument requirements are the same as for Time.local:

```
Time.utc(year, month, day, hour, min, sec, msec)
```

The preceding code is identical to Time.gm, although some might prefer this method's name.

You can also convert Time objects to an integer representing the number of seconds since the UNIX time epoch:

```
Time.gm(2020, 02).to_i
```

```
1580515200
```

Likewise, you can convert epoch times back into Time objects. This technique can be useful if you want to store times and dates in a file or a format where only a single integer is needed, rather than an entire Time object:

```
epoch_time = Time.gm(2020, 2).to_i
t = Time.at(epoch_time)
puts t.year, t.month, t.day
```

2020

5

1

As well as demonstrating the conversions of times between `Time` objects and epoch times, this code shows that `Time` objects also have methods that can be used to retrieve certain sections of a date/time. A list of these methods is shown in Table 3-6.

Table 3-6. *Time Object Methods Used to Access Date/Time Attributes*

Method	What the Method Returns
hour	A number representing the hour in 24-hour format (e.g., 21 for 9 p.m.)
min	The number of minutes past the hour
sec	The number of seconds past the minute
usec	The number of microseconds past the second (there are 1,000,000 microseconds per second)
day	The number of the day in the month
mday	Synonym for the day method, considered to be "month" day
wday	The number of the day in terms of the week (Sunday is 0, Saturday is 6)
yday	The number of the day in terms of the year
month	The number of the month of the date (e.g., 11 for November)
year	The year associated with the date
zone	Returns the name of the time zone associated with the time
utc?	Returns true or `false` depending on if the time/date is in the UTC/GMT time zone or not
gmt?	Synonym for the `utc?` method for those who prefer to use the term GMT

Note that these methods are for retrieving attributes from a date or time and cannot be used to set them. If you want to change elements of a date or time, you'll either need to add or subtract seconds or construct a new `Time` object using `Time.gm` or `Time.local`.

Note   In Chapter 16, you'll look at a Ruby gem called *Chronic* that lets you specify dates and times in a natural, English language form and have them converted to valid `Time` objects.

Ranges

Sometimes it's useful to be able to store the concept of a list, instead of its actual contents. For example, if you want to represent all the letters between *A* and *Z*, you could begin to create an array, like so:

```
x = ['A', 'B', 'C', 'D', 'E' .. and so on.. ]
```

It would be nice, though, merely to store the concept of "everything between *A* and *Z*." With a *range*, you can do that. A range is represented in this way:

```
('A'..'Z')
```

The range class offers a simple way to convert a range into an array with `to_a`. This one-line example demonstrates

```
('A'..'Z').to_a.each { |letter| print letter }
```

It converts the range `'A'` to `'Z'` into an array with 26 elements, each one containing a letter of the alphabet. It then iterates over each element using `each`, which you first used in the previous section on arrays, and passes the value into `letter`, which is then printed to the screen.

Note   Remember that as you've used `print`, rather than `puts`, the letters are printed one after another on the same line, whereas `puts` starts a new line every time it's used.

Even though working with arrays is perhaps more obvious, the range class *does* have an each method of its own, so while there is no array involved, the preceding example *could* be rewritten as follows:

```
('A'..'Z').each { |letter| print letter }
```

The range class comes with other methods baked in too. It might also be useful to test if something is included in the set of objects specified by the range. For example, with your ('A'..'Z') range, you can check to see if R is within the range, using the include? method, like so:

```
('A'..'Z').include?('R')
```

```
=> true
```

Being a lowercase letter, however, r is not included:

```
('A'..'Z').include?('r')
```

```
=> false
```

You can also use ranges as array indices to select multiple elements at the same time:

```
a = [2, 4, 6, 8, 10, 12]
p a[1..3]
```

```
[4, 6, 8]
```

Similarly, you can use them to set multiple elements at the same time (and following on from the current contents of a):

```
a[1..3] = ["a", "b", "c"]
p a
```

```
[2, "a", "b", "c", 10, 12]
```

You can use ranges with objects belonging to many different classes, including the ones you create yourself.

Symbols

Symbols are abstract references represented, typically, by a short string prefixed with a colon. Examples include :blue, :good, and :name. Sadly, there is no succinct, easy-to-learn trick to symbols, so you'll need to read this whole section—maybe even more than once—to get it to stick. It certainly took me a while to pick them up when I started with Ruby, but they are used so heavily by Rubyists that it's worth the effort!

Let's jump straight into an illustrative example:

```
current_situation = :good
puts "Everything is fine" if current_situation == :good
puts "PANIC!" if current_situation == :bad
```

```
Everything is fine
```

In this example, :good and :bad are symbols. Symbols don't contain values or objects, like variables do. Instead, they're used as a consistent name within code. For example, in the preceding code, you could easily replace the symbols with strings, like so:

```
current_situation = "good"
puts "Everything is fine" if current_situation == "good"
puts "PANIC!" if current_situation == "bad"
```

This gives the same result, but isn't as efficient. In this example, every mention of "good" and "bad" creates a new object stored separately in memory, whereas symbols are single reference values that are only initialized once. In the first code example, only :good and :bad exist, whereas in the second example, you end up with the full strings of "good", "good", and "bad" taking up memory.

Symbols also result in cleaner code in many situations. Often you'll use symbols to give method parameters a name. Having varying data as strings and fixed information as symbols results in easier-to-read code.

You might want to consider symbols to be literal constants that have no value, but whose name is the most important factor. If you assign the :good symbol to a variable and compare that variable with :good in the future, you'll get a match. This makes symbols useful in situations where you don't necessarily want to store an actual value, but a concept or an option.

Symbols are particularly useful when creating hashes and you want to have a distinction between keys and values, for example:

```
s = { key: "value" }
```

This technique can also be useful when there's a specification or consistency in which key names to use:

```ruby
person1 = { name: "Fred", age: 20, gender: :male }
person2 = { name: "Laura", age: 23, gender: :female }
```

Many methods provided by Ruby classes use this style to pass information into that method (and often for return values). You'll see examples of this construction throughout this book.

Think of symbols as less flexible, straitjacketed strings that are used as identifiers. If it still doesn't make complete sense to you, keep an eye out for where we use symbols later on in the book and refer back to this section.

Converting Objects to Other Classes

Numbers, strings, symbols, and other types of data are just objects belonging to various classes. Numbers belong to `Integer` and/or `Float` classes. Strings are objects of the `String` class, symbols are objects of the `Symbol` class, and so on.

In most cases, you can convert objects between the different classes, so a number can become a string and a string can become a number. Consider the following:

```ruby
puts "12" + "10"
puts 12 + 10
```

```
1210
22
```

The first line joins two strings, which happen to contain representations of numbers, together, resulting in 1210. The second line adds two numbers together, resulting in 22.

However, converting these objects to representations in different classes is possible:

```ruby
puts "12".to_i + "10".to_i
puts 12.to_s + 10.to_s
```

```
22
1210
```

The tables have been turned with the to_ methods. The String class provides the to_i and to_f methods to convert a string to an object of class Integer or Float, respectively. The String class also offers to_sym, which converts a string into a symbol. Symbols provide the inverse, with a to_s method to convert them into strings.

Likewise, the number classes support to_s to convert themselves into textual representations, as well as to_i and to_f to convert to and between integers and floats.

Summary

In this chapter, you've looked at the key building blocks of all computer programs—data, expressions, and logic—and discovered how to implement them with Ruby. The topics in this chapter provide a critical foundation for every other chapter in this book, as almost every future line of your Ruby code will contain an expression, an iterator, or some sort of logic.

Note   It's important to remember that due to the depth of Ruby, I haven't tried to cover every single combination of classes and methods here. There's more than one way to do anything in Ruby, and we've looked at the easiest routes first before moving on to more advanced techniques later in the book.

You have not yet exhausted the different types of data within Ruby. Objects and classes, as covered in Chapter 2, are actually types of data too, although they might appear not to be. In Chapter 6, you'll directly manipulate objects and classes in a similar way to how you've manipulated the numbers and strings in this chapter, and the bigger picture will become clear.

Before moving on to Chapter 4, where you'll develop a full but basic Ruby program, let's reflect on what we've covered so far:

- *Variable*: A placeholder that can hold (or refer to) an object—from numbers, to text, to arrays, to objects of your own creation. (Variables were covered in Chapter 2, but this chapter extended your knowledge of them.)

- *Operator*: Something that's used in an expression to manipulate objects such as + (plus), - (minus), * (multiply), and / (divide). You can also use operators to do comparisons, such as with <, >, and &&.

- *Integer*: A whole number, such as 5 or 923737.

- *Float*: A number with a decimal portion, such as 1.0 or 3.141592.

- *Character*: A single letter, digit, unit of space, or typographic symbol (punctuation and the like).

- *String*: A collection of characters such as Hello, world! or Ruby is cool. In Ruby, we represent strings by enclosing them in quotation marks, such as "Hello" or 'Hello'.

- *Constant*: A variable with a fixed value. Constant variable names begin with a capital letter.

- *Iterator*: A special method such as each, upto, or times that steps through a list element by element. This process is called iteration, and each, upto, and times are *iterator methods*.

- *Interpolation*: The mixing of expressions into strings.

- *Array*: A collection of objects or values with a defined, regular order.

- *Hash*: A collection of objects or values associated with keys. A key can be used to find its respective value inside a hash, but items inside a hash have no specific order. It's a lookup table, much like the index of a book or a dictionary.

- *Regular expression*: A way to describe patterns in text that can be matched and compared against. If you want to play with these and their operation, visit http://rubular.com/ for a handy tool.

- *Flow control*: The process of managing which sections of code to execute based on certain conditions and states.

- *Code block*: A section of code, often used as an argument to an iterator method, that has no discrete name and that is not a method itself, but that can be called and handled by a method that receives it as an argument. Code blocks can also be stored in variables as objects of the Proc class (or as *lambdas*).

- *Range*: The representation for an entire range of values between a start point and an endpoint.

- *Symbol*: A unique reference defined by a string prefixed with a colon (e.g., `:blue` or `:name`). Symbols don't contain values as variables do, but can be used to maintain a consistent reference within code. They can be considered as identifiers or constants that stand alone in what they abstractly represent.

Now it's time to put together some of these basic elements and develop a fully working program, which you'll do in Chapter 4.

Developing Your First Ruby Application

Up to this point, we've focused on covering the basics of the Ruby language and how it works at the ground level. In this chapter, we'll move into the world of real software development and develop a complete, though very basic, Ruby application with a basic set of features. Once we've developed and tested the basic application, we'll look at different ways to extend it to become more useful. On our way, we'll cover some new facets of development that haven't been mentioned so far.

First, let's look at the basics of source code organization before moving on to actual programming.

Working with Source Code Files

So far in this book, we've focused on using the irb immediate Ruby prompt to learn about the language. However, for developing anything you wish to reuse over and over, it's essential to store the source code in a file (or often multiple files) that can be kept on your hard drive, sent over the Internet, kept on a drive, and so forth.

The mechanism by which you create and manipulate source code files on your system varies by operating system and personal preference. On Windows, you might be familiar with the included Notepad software for creating and editing text files. At a Linux prompt, you might be using vi, Emacs, pico, or nano. Mac users have TextEdit or Xcode at their disposal. Whatever you use, you need to be able to create new files and save them as plain text so that Ruby can use them properly. In the next few sections, you're going to look at some available tools that tie in well with Ruby development.

© Carleton DiLeo, Peter Cooper 2021
C. DiLeo and P. Cooper, *Beginning Ruby 3*, https://doi.org/10.1007/978-1-4842-6324-2_4

Creating a Test File

The first step to developing a Ruby application is to get familiar with your text editor. If you're already familiar with text editors and how they relate to writing and saving source code, skip down to the section titled "A Simple Source Code File."

Visual Studio Code

In 2015, Microsoft released a free, cross-platform code editor called Visual Studio Code—not to be confused with their professional Visual Studio suite (Figure 4-1). At https://code.visualstudio.com/, you can download Visual Studio Code for Windows, Mac OS X, and Linux, and quickly install and use it as an editor for your future Ruby code.

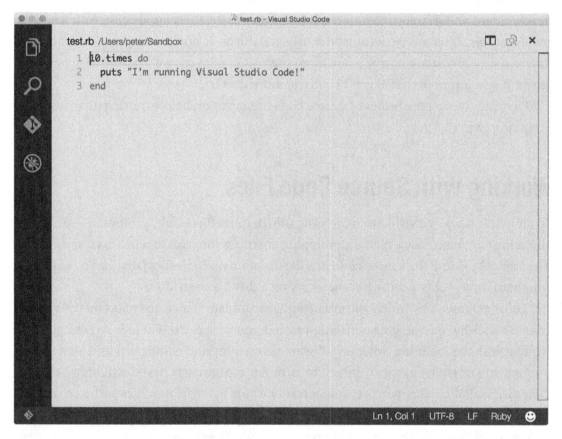

Figure 4-1. *Using Visual Studio Code*

After installing and running Visual Studio Code (as seen in Figure 4-1), you can simply type or paste Ruby code and use the File ➤ Save menu option to save your text to a location on your drive. It would probably be good to create a folder called ruby within your home or user folder and save your initial Ruby source code there (using a filename such as myapp.rb), as this is what the instructions assume in the next section.

If you would prefer a full IDE (integrated development environment) experience that goes beyond what even Visual Studio Code offers, you could use RubyMine by JetBrains, although it is a commercial product. You can find it at www.jetbrains.com/ruby/.

Alternatives to Linux

Visual Studio Code is available for Linux, but desktop Linux distributions typically come with at least one text editor already which you may prefer to use. If you're working entirely from the shell or terminal, you might be familiar with vim, Emacs, pico, or nano, and all of these are suitable for editing Ruby source code. Some editors (such as vi and Emacs) have extensions available that are specifically designed to make working with Ruby easier. If you're using Linux with a graphical interface, you might have Kate (KDE Advanced Text Editor) and/or gedit (GNOME Editor) available. All the preceding are great text and source code editors. Choose one and learn how to use it, if you don't choose to use Visual Studio Code or another IDE.

At this stage, it would be a good idea to create a folder in your home directory called "ruby", or something similar, so that you can save your Ruby code there and have it in an easily remembered place.

A Simple Source Code File

Once you've got an environment where you can edit and save text files, enter the following code:

```
x = 2
print "This program is running okay if 2 + 2 = #{x + x}"
```

Note   If this code looks like nonsense to you, you've skipped too many chapters. Head back to Chapter 3! This chapter requires full knowledge of everything covered in Chapter 3.

Save the code with a filename of `example1.rb` in a folder or directory of your choice. It's advisable that you create a folder called `ruby` located somewhere that's easy to find. On Windows, this might be directly off of your C drive, and on OS X or Linux, this could be a folder located in your home directory.

Note   `.rb` is the de facto standard file extension for Ruby files, much like `.php` is standard for PHP, `.txt` is common for text files, and `.jpg` is standard for JPEG images.

Now you're ready to run the code.

Running Your Source Code

Once you've created the basic Ruby source code file, `example1.rb`, you need to get Ruby to execute it. As always, the process by which to do this varies by operating system. Read the particular following section that matches your operating system. If your operating system isn't listed, the OS X and Linux instructions are most likely to match those for your platform.

Whenever this book asks you to "run" your program, this is what you'll be doing each time.

Note   Even though you're going to be developing an application in this chapter, there are still times when you'll want to use irb to follow along with the tests or basic theory work throughout the chapter. Use your judgment to jump between these two methods of development. irb is extremely useful for testing small concepts and short blocks of code without the overhead of jumping back and forth between a text editor and the Ruby interpreter.

Windows

Running Ruby from the command line provides the most flexibility and the most predictable behavior. To do this, load the command prompt using the item in the Start menu within the Ruby menu. This will ensure that the `ruby` command will work directly from the prompt. Once the command prompt is loaded, you'll need to navigate to the folder containing `example1.rb` using the `cd` command and then type `ruby example1.rb`.

Mac OS X/macOS

The simplest method to run Ruby applications on OS X is from Terminal, much in the same way as irb is run. Terminal was explained in Chapter 1. If you followed the preceding instructions, continue like so:

1. Launch Terminal (found in `Applications/Utilities`, or use Spotlight to launch it).

2. Use `cd` to navigate to the folder where you placed `example1.rb`, like so: `cd ~/ruby`. This tells Terminal to take you to the `ruby` folder located in your home user folder.

3. Type `ruby example1.rb` and press Enter to execute the `example1.rb` Ruby script.

4. If you get an error such as ruby: `No such file or directory -- example1.rb (LoadError)`, you aren't in the same folder as the `example1.rb` source file, and you need to establish where you have saved it.

If you get a satisfactory response from `example1.rb`, you're ready to move on to the "Our Application: A Text Analyzer" section.

Alternatively, if you're using Visual Studio Code or Sublime Text, there are other ways you can run your code directly from the editor. However, it may not always be an option, so it's essential to at least be familiar with how to run Ruby scripts from the terminal too.

Linux and Other UNIX-Based Systems

In Linux or other UNIX-based systems, you run your Ruby applications from the shell (i.e., within a terminal window) in the same way that you ran irb. The process to run irb was explained in Chapter 1, so if you've forgotten how to get that far, you need to recap before continuing, like so:

1. Launch your terminal emulator (such as xterm or, on Ubuntu, simply "Terminal") so you get a Linux shell/command prompt.

2. Navigate to the directory where you placed `example1.rb` using the `cd` command (e.g., `cd ~/ruby` takes you to the ruby directory located directly under your home directory, usually /home/<your username>/).

3. Type `ruby example1.rb` and press Enter to make Ruby execute the `example1.rb` script.

If you get a satisfactory response from `example1.rb`, you're ready to move on.

TEXT EDITORS VS. SOURCE CODE EDITORS

Source code is basically the same as plain text, and although you can write your code in a general text editor, some developers prefer to use a specialist source code editor (typically known as an IDE).

RubyMine is an example of IDEs specifically created for Ruby developers. It allows you to edit text, as with any other text editor, but both offer extended features such as source code syntax coloring and the ability to run code directly from the editor. Sublime Text and Visual Studio Code look like regular text editors, but also offer some IDE-like functionality, including source code syntax coloring.

Some developers find source code syntax coloring an invaluable feature, as it makes their code easier to read. Variable names, expressions, string literals, and other elements of your source code are all given different colors, which makes it easy to pick them out.

Whether you choose an IDE or a basic text editor depends on your own preference, but it's worth trying both. Many developers prefer the freedom of a regular text editor and then running their Ruby programs from the command line, whereas others prefer to work entirely within a single environment. This book will not assume, however, that you are using an IDE, so you may have a separate learning curve for picking up the IDE's functions as well as Ruby's in general.

Our Application: A Text Analyzer

The application you're going to develop in this chapter will be a text analyzer. Your Ruby code will read in text supplied in a separate file, analyze it for various patterns and statistics, and print out the results for the user. It's not a 3D graphical adventure nor a fancy website, but text processing programs are the bread and butter of systems administration and most application development. They can be vital for parsing log files and user-submitted text on websites and manipulating other textual data.

Ruby is well suited for text and document analysis with its regular expression features, along with the ease of use of `scan` and `split`, and you'll be using these heavily in your application.

Note   With this application, you'll be focusing on implementing the features quickly and pragmatically, rather than developing an elaborate object-oriented structure, any documentation, or a testing methodology. The sole aim of this project is to build a simple script that performs a number of operations in sequence. I'll be covering object orientation and its usage in larger programs in depth in Chapter 6, and documentation and testing are covered in Chapter 8.

Required Basic Features

Your text analyzer will provide the following basic statistics:

- Character count
- Character count (excluding spaces)
- Line count
- Word count
- Sentence count
- Paragraph count
- Average number of words per sentence
- Average number of sentences per paragraph

In the last two cases, the statistics are easily calculated from each other. That is, once you have the total number of words and the total number of sentences, it becomes a matter of a simple division to work out the average number of words per sentence.

Building the Basic Application

When starting to develop a new program, it's useful to think of the key steps involved. In the past, it was common to draw *flow charts* to show how the operation of a computer program would flow, but it's easy to experiment, change things about, and remain agile with modern tools such as Ruby. Let's outline the basic steps as follows:

1. Load a file containing the text or document you want to analyze.

2. As you load the file line by line, keep a count of how many lines there were (one of your statistics taken care of).

3. Put the text into a string and measure its length to get your character count.

4. Temporarily remove all whitespace and measure the length of the resulting string to get the character count excluding spaces.

5. Split out all the whitespace to find out how many words there are.

6. Split on full stops to find out how many sentences there are.

7. Split on double newlines to find out how many paragraphs there are.

8. Perform calculations to work out the averages.

Create a new, blank Ruby source file and save it as `analyzer.rb` in your Ruby folder. As you work through the next few sections, you'll be able to fill it out.

Obtaining Some Dummy Text

Before you start to code, the first step is to get some test data that your analyzer can process. The first chapter of Oliver Twist is an ideal piece of text to use, as it's copyright-free and easy to obtain. It's also of a reasonable length. You can find the text at `https://raw.github.com/Apress/beginnning-ruby-4e/master/oliver.txt` for you to copy into a local text file. Save the file in the same folder you saved example1.rb, and call it text.txt. Your application will read from text.txt by default (although you'll make it more dynamic and able to accept other sources of data later on).

Tip   If the preceding web page is unavailable at the time of reading, use your favorite search engine to search for "twist workhouse rendered profound thingummy" (without the quotation marks) and you're guaranteed to find it. Alternatively, use any large block of text you can obtain.

If you're using the *Oliver Twist* text and want your results to match up roughly with those given as examples throughout this chapter, make sure you only copy and paste the text including and between these sections:

```
Among other public buildings in a certain town, which for many
reasons it will be prudent to refrain from mentioning
```

and

```
Oliver cried lustily. If he could have known that he was an
orphan, left to the tender mercies of church-wardens and
overseers, perhaps he would have cried the louder.
```

Loading Text Files and Counting Lines

Now it's time to get coding! The first step is to load the file. Ruby provides a comprehensive set of file manipulation methods via the File class. Whereas other languages can make you jump through hoops to work with files, Ruby keeps the interface simple. Here's some code that opens up your text.txt file:

```
File.open("text.txt").each { |line| puts line }
```

Type this into analyzer.rb and run the code. If text.txt is in the current directory, the result is that you'll see the entire text file flying up the screen.

You're asking the File class to open up text.txt, and then, much like with an array, you can call the each method on the file directly, resulting in each line being passed to the inner code block one by one, where puts sends the line as output to the screen. (In Chapter 9, you'll look at how file access and manipulation work in more detail, along with more robust techniques than are used in this chapter!)

Edit the code to look like this instead:

```ruby
line_count = 0
File.open("text.txt").each { |line| line_count += 1 }
puts line_count
```

You initialize `line_count` to store the line count and then open the file and iterate over each line while incrementing `line_count` by 1 each time. When you're done, you print the total to the screen (approximately 119 if you're using the *Oliver Twist* chapter). You have your first statistic!

You've counted the lines, but still don't have access to the contents of the file to count the words, paragraphs, sentences, and so forth. This is easy to fix. Let's change the code a little and add a variable, `text`, to collect the lines together as one as we go:

```ruby
text = ""
line_count = 0
File.open("text.txt").each do |line|
  line_count += 1
  text += line
end

puts "#{line_count} lines"
```

Note   Remember that using { and } to surround blocks is the standard style for single-line blocks, but using do and end is *preferred* for multiline blocks.

Compared to your previous attempt, this code introduces the `text` variable and adds each line onto the end of it in turn. When the iteration over the file has finished—that is, when you run out of lines—`text` contains the entire file in a single string ready for you to use.

That's a simple-looking way to get the file into a single string and count the lines, but `File` also has other methods that can be used to read files more quickly. For example, you can rewrite the preceding code like this:

```ruby
lines = File.readlines("text.txt")
line_count = lines.size
text = lines.join

puts "#{line_count} lines"
```

Much simpler! File implements a readlines method that reads an entire file into an array, line by line. You can use this both to count the lines and join them all into a single string.

Counting Characters

The second easiest statistic to work out is the number of characters in the file. As you've collected the entire file into the text variable, and text is a string, you can use the length method that all strings supply to get the exact size of the file, and therefore the number of characters.

To the end of the previous code in analyzer.rb, add the following:

```
total_characters = text.length
puts "#{total_characters} characters"
```

If you ran analyzer.rb now with the *Oliver Twist* text, you'd get output like this:

```
119 lines
6289 characters
```

Note   Don't worry about your results being *identical* to those shown in this chapter. As long as they're roughly in the same ballpark, you're on the right track.

The second statistic you wanted to get relating to characters was a character total excluding whitespace. If you can remember back to Chapter 3, strings have a gsub method that performs a global substitution (like a search and replace) upon the string, for example:

```
"this is a test".gsub(/t/, 'X')
```

```
Xhis is a XesX
```

You can use gsub to eradicate the spaces from your text string in the same way and then use the length method to get the length of the newly "de-spacified" text. Add the following code to analyzer.rb:

```
total_characters_nospaces = text.gsub(/\s+/, '').length
puts "#{total_characters_nospaces} characters excluding spaces"
```

If you run `analyzer.rb` in its current state against the *Oliver Twist* text, the results should be similar to the following:

```
119 lines
6289 characters
5142 characters (excluding spaces)
```

Counting Words

A common feature offered by word processing software is a "word counter." All it does is count the number of complete words in your document or a selected area of text. This information is useful to work out how many pages the document will take up when printed. Many assignments also have requirements for a certain number of words, so knowing the number of words in a piece of text is certainly useful.

You can approach this feature in a couple of ways:

1. Count the number of groups of contiguous letters using `scan` to create an array of those groups and then use the length of the array.

2. Split the text on whitespace and count the resulting fragments using `split` and `size`.

Let's look at each method in turn to see what's best. Recall from Chapter 3 that `scan` works by iterating over a string of text and finding certain patterns over and over, for example:

```
puts "this is a test".scan(/\w/).join
thisisatest
```

In this example, `scan` looked through the string for anything matching \w, a special term representing all alphanumeric characters (and underscores), and placed them into an array that you've joined together into a string and printed to the screen.

You can do the same with groups of alphanumeric characters. In Chapter 3, you learned that to match multiple characters with a regular expression, you could follow the character with +. So let's try again:

```
puts "this is a test".scan(/\w+/).join('-')
```

```
this-is-a-test
```

This time, `scan` has looked for all *groups* of alphanumeric characters and placed them into the array that you've then joined together into a string using - as the separation character.

To get the number of words in the string, you can use the `length` or `size` array methods to count the number of elements rather than join them together:

```
puts "this is a test".scan(/\w+/).length
```

```
4
```

Excellent! So what about the `split` approach?

The `split` approach demonstrates a core tenet of Ruby (as well as some other languages, particularly Perl): *there's always more than one way to do it!* Analyzing different methods to solve the same problem is a crucial part of becoming a good programmer, as different methods can vary in their efficacy.

Let's split the string by spaces and get the length of the resulting array, like so:

```
puts "this is a test".split.length
```

```
4
```

As it happens, by *default*, `split` will split by whitespace (single or multiple characters of spaces, tabs, newlines, and so on), and that makes this code shorter and easier to read than the `scan` alternative.

So what's the difference between these two methods? Simply, one is looking for words and returning them to you for you to count, and the other is splitting the string by that which separates words—whitespace—and telling you how many parts the string was broken into. Interestingly, these two approaches can yield different results:

```
text = "First-class decisions require clear-headed thinking."
puts "Scan method: #{text.scan(/\w+/).length}"
puts "Split method: #{text.split.length}"
```

```
Scan method: 7
Split method: 5
```

Interesting! The `scan` method is looking through for all blocks of alphanumeric characters, and, sure enough, there are seven in the sentence. However, if you split by spaces, there are five words. The reason is the hyphenated words. Hyphens aren't "alphanumeric," so `scan` is seeing "first" and "class" as separate words.

Returning to `analyzer.rb`, let's apply what we've learned here. Add the following:

```
word_count = text.split.length
puts "#{word_count} words"
```

Running the complete `analyzer.rb` gets these results:

```
1119 lines
6289 characters
5142 characters (excluding spaces)
1111 words
```

Counting Sentences and Paragraphs

Once you understand the logic of counting words, counting the sentences and paragraphs becomes easy. Rather than splitting on whitespace, sentences and paragraphs have different splitting criteria.

Sentences end with full stops, question marks, and exclamation marks. They can also be separated with dashes and other punctuation, but we won't worry about these rare cases here. The split is simple. Instead of asking Ruby to split the text on one type of character, you simply ask it to split on any of three types of characters, like so:

```
sentence_count = text.split(/\.|\?|!/).length
```

The regular expression looks odd here, but the full stop, question mark, and exclamation mark are clearly visible. Let's look at the regular expression directly:

```
/\.|\?|!/
```

The forward slashes at the start and the end are the usual delimiters for a regular expression, so those can be ignored. The first section is `\.`, and this represents a full stop. The reason why you can't just use `.` without the backslash in front is because `.` represents "any character" in a regular expression (as covered in Chapter 3), so it needs to be *escaped* with the backslash to identify itself as a literal full stop. This also explains why the question mark is escaped with a backslash, as a question mark in a regular expression usually means "zero or one instances of the previous character"—also covered in Chapter 3. The ! is not escaped, as it has no other meaning in terms of regular expressions.

The pipes (| characters) separate the three main characters, which means they're treated separately so that split can match one or another of them. This is what allows the split to split on periods, question marks, *and* exclamation marks all at the same time. You can test it like so:

```ruby
puts "Test code! It works. Does it? Yes.".split(/\.|\?|!/).length
```

```
4
```

Paragraphs can also be split apart with regular expressions. Whereas paragraphs in a printed book, such as this one, tend not to have any spacing between them, paragraphs that are typed on a computer typically do, so you can split by a double newline (as represented by the special combination \n\n—simply, two newlines in succession) to get the paragraphs separated, for example:

```ruby
text = %q{
This is a test of
paragraph one.

This is a test of
paragraph two.

This is a test of
paragraph three.
}

puts text.split(/\n\n/).length
```

```
3
```

Let's add both these concepts to analyzer.rb:

```ruby
paragraph_count = text.split(/\n\n/).length
puts "#{paragraph_count} paragraphs"
```

```ruby
sentence_count = text.split(/\.|\?|!/).length
puts "#{sentence_count} sentences"
```

Calculating Averages

The final statistics required for your basic application are the average number of words per sentence and the average number of sentences per paragraph. You already have the paragraph, sentence, and word counts available in the variables word_count, paragraph_count, and sentence_count, so only basic arithmetic is required, like so:

```ruby
puts "#{sentence_count / paragraph_count} sentences per paragraph
(average)"
puts "#{word_count / sentence_count} words per sentence (average)"
```

The calculations are so simple that they can be interpolated directly into the output commands rather than pre-calculated. When run now, we'd see this:

```
119 lines
6289 characters
5142 characters excluding spaces
1111 words
20 paragraphs
45 sentences
2 sentences per paragraph (average)
24 words per sentence (average)
```

Note The astute reader will notice that we're dividing an integer by an integer in the preceding code—thus resulting in integer division—without first converting the numbers to floating point numbers to gain accurate division (recall from Chapter 2 that 10 / 3 == 3, but 10.0 / 3 == 3.3333333333333). In this case, integer division is fine, as it makes little sense to say that there are, say, 2.8 sentences per paragraph on average—it's nicer just to see "3."

The Source Code So Far

You've been updating the source code as you've gone along, and in each case, you've put the logic next to the `puts` statement that shows the result to the user. However, for the final version of your basic application, it would be tidier to separate the logic from the presentation a little and put the calculations in a separate block of code before everything is printed to the screen.

There are no logic changes, but the finished source for `analyzer.rb` looks a little cleaner this way:

```ruby
lines = File.readlines("text.txt")
line_count = lines.size
text = lines.join
word_count = text.split.length
character_count = text.length
character_count_nospaces = text.gsub(/\s+/, '').length
paragraph_count = text.split(/\n\n/).length
sentence_count = text.split(/\.|\?|!/).length

puts "#{line_count} lines"
puts "#{character_count} characters"
puts "#{character_count_nospaces} characters excluding spaces"
puts "#{word_count} words"
puts "#{paragraph_count} paragraphs"
puts "#{sentence_count} sentences"
puts "#{sentence_count / paragraph_count} sentences per paragraph
(average)"
puts "#{word_count / sentence_count} words per sentence (average)"
```

When run, the result will be somewhat like the following:

```
1119 lines
6289 characters
5142 characters excluding spaces
1111 words
20 paragraphs
45 sentences
2 sentences per paragraph (average)
24 words per sentence (average)
```

If you've made it this far and everything's making sense, congratulations are due. Let's look at how to extend our application a little further with some more interesting statistics.

Adding Extra Features

Your analyzer has a few basic functions, but it's not particularly interesting. Line, paragraph, and word counts are useful statistics, but with the power of Ruby, you can extract significantly more interesting data from the text. The only limit is your imagination, but in this section, you'll look at a couple other features you can implement, and how to do so.

Percentage of "Useful" Words

Most written material, including this very book, contains a large number of words that, although providing context and structure, are not directly useful or interesting. In the last sentence, the words *that, and, are,* and *or* are not of particular interest, even if the sentence would make less sense to a human without them.

These words are typically called *stop words* and are often ignored by computer systems whose job is to analyze and search through text, because they aren't words most people are likely to be searching for (e.g., as opposed to nouns). Google is a perfect example of this, as it doesn't want to have to store information that takes up space and that's generally irrelevant to searches.

Note   For more information about stop words, including links to complete lists, visit `https://en.wikipedia.org/wiki/Stop_words`.

It can be argued that more "interesting" text should have a lower percentage of stop words and a higher percentage of useful or interesting words. You can easily extend your application to work out the percentage of non-stop words in the supplied text.

The first step is to build up a list of stop words. There are hundreds of possible stop words, but you'll start with just a handful. Let's create an array to hold them:

```
stopwords = %w{the a by on for of are with just but and to the my I has
some in}
```

This code results in an array of stop words being assigned to the stopwords variable.

Tip In Chapter 3, you saw arrays being defined like so: x = ['a', 'b', 'c']. However, like many languages, Ruby has a shortcut that builds arrays quickly with string-separated text. This segment can be shortened to the equivalent x = %w{a b c}, as demonstrated in the preceding stop word code.

For demonstration purposes, let's write a small, separate program to test the concept:

```
text = %q{Los Angeles has some of the nicest weather in the country.}
stopwords = %w{the a by on for of are with just but and to the my in I has some}
```

```
words = text.scan(/\w+/)
keywords = words.select { |word| !stopwords.include?(word) }

puts keywords.join(' ')
```

When you run this code, you get the following result:

```
Los Angeles nicest weather country
```

Cool, right? First, you put some text into the program and then the list of stop words. Next, you get all the words from text into an array called words. Then you get to the magic:

```
keywords = words.select { |word| !stopwords.include?(word) }
```

This line first takes your array of words, words, and calls the select method with a block of code to process for each word (like the iterators you played with in Chapter 3). The select method is available to all arrays and hashes that return the elements of that array or hash that match the expression in the code block.

In this case, the code in the code block takes each word via the variable word and asks the stopwords array whether it includes any elements equal to word. This is what stopwords.include?(word) does.

The exclamation mark (!) before the expression negates the expression (an exclamation mark negates any Ruby expression). The reason for this is you *don't* want to select words that *are* in the stopwords array. You want to select words that *aren't*.

In closing, then, you select all elements of words that are *not* included in the stopwords array and assign them to keywords. Don't read on until that makes sense, as this type of single-line construction is common in Ruby programming.

After that, working out the percentage of non-stop words to all words uses some basic arithmetic:

```
((keywords.length.to_f / words.length.to_f) * 100).to_i
```

The reason for the .to_f's is so that the lengths are treated as floating decimal point numbers, and the percentage is worked out more accurately. When you work it up to the real percentage (out of 100), you can convert back to an integer once again.

Here's a look at how we can bring these concepts together with our other program fragments so far:

```ruby
stopwords = %w{the a by on for of are with just but and to the my I has
some in}
lines = File.readlines("text.txt")
line_count = lines.size
text = lines.join

# Count the words, characters, paragraphs and sentences
word_count = text.split.length
character_count = text.length
character_count_nospaces = text.gsub(/\s+/, '').length
paragraph_count = text.split(/\n\n/).length
sentence_count = text.split(/\.|\?|!/).length

# Make a list of words in the text that aren't stop words,
# count them, and work out the percentage of non-stop words
# against all words
all_words = text.scan(/\w+/)
good_words = all_words.reject{ |word| stopwords.include?(word) }
good_percentage = ((good_words.length.to_f / all_words.length.to_f) * 100).
to_i

# Give the analysis back to the user
puts "#{line_count} lines"
puts "#{character_count} characters"
```

```
puts "#{character_count_nospaces} characters (excluding spaces)"
puts "#{word_count} words"
puts "#{sentence_count} sentences"
puts "#{paragraph_count} paragraphs"
puts "#{sentence_count / paragraph_count} sentences per paragraph
(average)"
puts "#{word_count / sentence_count} words per sentence (average)"
puts "#{good_percentage}% of words are non-fluff words"
```

With these results:

```
119 lines
6289 characters
5142 characters (excluding spaces)
1111 words
45 sentences
20 paragraphs
2 sentences per paragraph (average)
24 words per sentence (average)
76% of words are non-fluff words
```

Summarizing by Finding "Interesting" Sentences

Word processors such as Microsoft Word generally have summarization features that can take a long piece of text and seemingly pick out the best sentences to produce an "at-a-glance" summary. The mechanisms for producing summaries have become more complex over the years, but one of the simplest ways to develop a summarizer of your own is to scan for sentences with certain characteristics.

One technique is to look for sentences that are of about average length and that look like they contain nouns. Tiny sentences are unlikely to contain anything useful, and long sentences are likely to be simply too long for a summary. Finding nouns reliably would require systems that are far beyond the scope of this book, so you could "cheat" by looking for words that indicate the presence of useful nouns in the same sentence, such as "is" and "are" (e.g., "Noun is," "Nouns are," "There are x nouns").

Let's assume that you want to throw away two-thirds of the sentences—a third that are the shortest sentences and a third that are the longest sentences—leaving you with an ideal third of the original sentences that are ideally sized for your task.

For ease of development, let's create a new program from scratch and transfer your logic over to the main application later. Create a new program called `summarize.rb` and use this code:

```ruby
text = %q{
Ruby is a great programming language. It is object oriented
and has many groovy features. Some people don't like it, but that's
not our problem! It's easy to learn. It's great. To learn more about Ruby,
visit the official Ruby website today.
}

sentences = text.gsub(/\s+/, ' ').strip.split(/\.|\?|!/)
sentences_sorted = sentences.sort_by { |sentence| sentence.length }
one_third = sentences_sorted.length / 3
ideal_sentences = sentences_sorted.slice(one_third, one_third + 1)
ideal_sentences = ideal_sentences.select { |sentence| sentence =~ /is|are/
}
puts ideal_sentences.join(". ")
```

And for good measure, run it to see what happens:

```
Ruby is a great programming language. It is object oriented and has many
groovy features
```

Seems like a success! Let's walk through the program.

First, you define the variable text to hold the long string of multiple sentences, much like in `analyzer.rb`. Next, you split text into an array of sentences like so:

```ruby
sentences = text.gsub(/\s+/, ' ').strip.split(/\.|\?|!/)
```

This is slightly different from the method used in `analyzer.rb`. There is an extra gsub in the chain, as well as `strip`. The gsub gets rid of all large areas of whitespace and replaces them with a single space (\s+ meaning "one or more whitespace characters"). This is simply for cosmetic reasons. The `strip` removes all extra whitespace from the start and end of the string. The `split` is then the same as that used in the analyzer.

Next, you sort the sentences by their lengths, as you want to ignore the shortest third and the longest third:

```
sentences_sorted = sentences.sort_by { |sentence| sentence.length }
```

Arrays and hashes have the `sort_by` method, which can rearrange them into almost any order you want. `sort_by` takes a code block as its argument, where the code block is an expression that defines what to sort by. In this case, you're sorting the `sentences` array. You pass each sentence in as the `sentence` variable and choose to sort them by their `length`, using the `length` method on the sentence. After this line, `sentences_sorted` contains an array with the sentences in length order.

Next, you need to get the middle third of the length-sorted sentences in `sentences_sorted`, as these are the ones you've deemed to be probably the most interesting. To do this, you can divide the length of the array by 3 to get the number of elements in a third and then grab that number of elements from one third into the array (note that you grab one extra element to compensate for rounding caused by integer division). This is done like so:

```
one_third = sentences_sorted.length / 3
ideal_sentences = sentences_sorted.slice(one_third, one_third + 1)
```

The first line takes the length of the array and divides it by 3 to get the quantity that is equal to "a third of the array." The second line uses the `slice` method to "cut out" a section of the array to assign to `ideal_sentences`. In this case, assume that the `sentences_sorted` is six elements long. 6 divided by 3 is 2, so a third of the array is two elements long. The `slice` method then cuts *from* element 2 for 2 (plus 1) elements, so you effectively carve out elements 2, 3, and 4 (remember that array elements start counting from 0). This means you get the "inner third" of the ideal-length sentences you wanted.

The penultimate line checks to see if the sentence includes the word *is* or *are* and only accepts each sentence if so:

```
ideal_sentences = ideal_sentences.select { |sentence| sentence =~ /is|are/ }
```

It uses the `select` method, as the stop-word removal code in the previous section did. The expression in the code block uses a regular expression that matches against sentence and only returns `true` if *is* or *are* is present within `sentence`. This means `ideal_sentences` now only contains sentences that are in the middle third lengthwise *and* contain either *is* or *are*.

The final line simply joins the ideal_sentences together with a full stop and space between them to make them readable:

```
puts ideal_sentences.join(". ")
```

Analyzing Files Other Than text.txt

So far, your application has the filename text.txt hard-coded into it. This is acceptable, but it would be a lot nicer if you could specify, when you run the program, what file you want the analyzer to process.

Note   This technique is only practical to demonstrate if you're running analyzer.rb from a command prompt or shell or if your IDE supports passing in command-line arguments.

Typically, if you're starting a program from the command line, you can append parameters onto the end of the command, and the program will process them. You can do the same with your Ruby application.

Ruby automatically places any parameters that are appended to the command line when you launch your Ruby program into a special array called ARGV. To test it out, create a new script called argv.rb and use this code:

```
puts ARGV.join('-')
```

From the command prompt, run the script like so:

```
ruby argv.rb
```

The result will be blank, but then try to run it like so:

```
ruby argv.rb test 123
```

```
test-123
```

This time the parameters are taken from ARGV, joined together with a hyphen, and displayed on the screen. You can use this to replace the reference to text.txt in analyzer.rb by replacing "text.txt" with ARGV[0] or ARGV.first (which both mean exactly the same thing—the first element of the ARGV array). The line that reads the file becomes the following:

```
lines = File.readlines(ARGV[0])
```

To process text.txt now, you'd run it like so:

```
ruby analyzer.rb text.txt
```

You'll learn more about deploying programs and making them friendly to other users, along with ARGV, in Chapter 10.

Note   If you ran the preceding code but specified a file that did not exist, the program would still run but File.readlines would throw an error. We look at ways to tackle this issue later.

The Completed Program

You've already got the source for the completed basic program, but it's time to add all the new, extended features from the previous few sections to analyzer.rb to create the final version of your text analyzer.

Note   Remember that source code for this book is available in the Source Code area at www.apress.com, so it isn't strictly necessary to type in code directly from the book.

Here we go:

```
# analyzer.rb -- Text Analyzer

stopwords = %w{the a by on for of are with just but and to the my I has
some in}
lines = File.readlines(ARGV[0])
line_count = lines.size
text = lines.join

# Count the words, characters, paragraphs and sentences
word_count = text.split.length
```

```ruby
character_count = text.length
character_count_nospaces = text.gsub(/\s+/, '').length
paragraph_count = text.split(/\n\n/).length
sentence_count = text.split(/\.|\?|!/).length

# Make a list of words in the text that aren't stop words,
# count them, and work out the percentage of non-stop words
# against all words
all_words = text.scan(/\w+/)
good_words = all_words.reject{ |word| stopwords.include?(word) }
good_percentage = ((good_words.length.to_f / all_words.length.to_f) * 100).
to_i

# Summarize the text by cherry picking some choice
sentences = text.gsub(/\s+/, ' ').strip.split(/\.|\?|!/)
sentences_sorted = sentences.sort_by { |sentence| sentence.length }
one_third = sentences_sorted.length / 3
ideal_sentences = sentences_sorted.slice(one_third, one_third + 1)
ideal_sentences = ideal_sentences.select { |sentence| sentence =~ /is|are/
}

# Give the analysis back to the user
puts "#{line_count} lines"
puts "#{character_count} characters"
puts "#{character_count_nospaces} characters (excluding spaces)"
puts "#{word_count} words"
puts "#{sentence_count} sentences"
puts "#{paragraph_count} paragraphs"
puts "#{sentence_count / paragraph_count} sentences per paragraph
(average)"
puts "#{word_count / sentence_count} words per sentence (average)"
puts "#{good_percentage}% of words are non-fluff words"
puts "Summary:\n\n" + ideal_sentences.join(". ")
puts "-- End of analysis"
```

Note   Have you noticed that the good_words line no longer uses `select` but `reject`? It's a quick exercise to you to work out how these methods differ and why it has been used here instead of the original code.

Running the completed `analyzer.rb` with the *Oliver Twist* text now results in an output like the following:

```
119 lines
6289 characters
5142 characters (excluding spaces)
1111 words
45 sentences
20 paragraphs
2 sentences per paragraph (average)
24 words per sentence (average)
76% of words are non-fluff words
Summary:
' The surgeon leaned over the body, and raised the left hand. Think what it
is to be a mother, there's a dear young lamb do. 'The old story,' he said,
shaking his head: 'no wedding-ring, I see. What an excellent example of
the power of dress, young Oliver Twist was. ' Apparently this consolatory
perspective of a mother's prospects failed in producing its due effect. '
The surgeon had been sitting with his face turned towards the fire: giving
the palms of his hands a warm and a rub alternately. ' 'You needn't mind
sending up to me, if the child cries, nurse,' said the surgeon, putting on
his gloves with great deliberation. She had walked some distance, for her
shoes were worn to pieces; but where she came from, or where she was going
to, nobody knows. ' He put on his hat, and, pausing by the bed-side on his
way to the door, added, 'She was a good-looking girl, too; where did she
come from
-- End of analysis
```

Try `analyzer.rb` with some other text of your choice (a web page, perhaps), and see if you can make improvements to its features. This application is rife for improvement with the concepts you'll learn over the next several chapters, so keep it in mind if you're looking for some code to play with.

CODE COMMENTS

You might notice text in source code prefixed with # symbols. These are *comments* and are generally used in programs for the benefit of the original developer(s), along with anyone else who might need to read the source code. They're particularly useful for making notes to remind you of why you took a particular course of action that you're likely to forget in the future.

You can place comments in any Ruby source code file on their own lines or even at the end of a line of code. Here are some valid examples of commenting in Ruby:

```
puts "2+2 = #{2+2}" # Adds 2+2 to make 4
# A comment on a line by itself
```

As long as a comment is on a line by itself or is the last thing on a line, it's fine. Comment liberally, and your code will be easier to understand, especially if you come back to it a long time later.

Summary

In this chapter, you developed a complete, basic application that realized a set of requirements and desired features. You then extended it with some nonessential but useful elaborations. Ruby makes developing quick applications a snap.

The application you've developed in this chapter has demonstrated that if you have a lot of text to process or a number of calculations to do, and you're dreading doing the work manually, Ruby can take the strain.

To keep things simple, we didn't use any methods or flow control in our application. It simply went through a process step by step to give a set of results. This is the simplest form of a useful program. More complex programs will undoubtedly involve flow control and methods, and we'll be covering those in more depth in the following chapters.

Chapter 4 marks the end of the practical programming exercises in the first part of this book. Next, in Chapter 5, you'll take a look at the history of Ruby, Ruby's community of developers, and the historical reasons behind certain features in Ruby. You'll also learn how to get help from and become part of the Ruby community. Code makes up only half the journey to becoming a great programmer!

CHAPTER 5

The Ruby Ecosystem

As with other programming languages, Ruby has its own culture and "ecosystem." Ruby's ecosystem is made up of thousands of developers, maintainers, documenters, bloggers, companies, and those who help sponsor or fund the development of the language.

Some programmers who are new to a language assume that learning about a language's history and community is pointless, but the most successful developers quickly learn about the ecosystem and get involved in it. The motivations behind a language's development can provide significant clues about the best approaches to take when solving problems, and understanding the vocabulary of other developers greatly helps when it comes to looking for help and advice.

This chapter takes a break from the code-focused tutorials to bring you up to speed with how the Ruby world works, the motivations behind the language, and the best ways to find help and get involved with the community. If you're new to software development, this chapter will also explain some of the terms and phrases used by developers relating to software development.

You'll also take a quick look at Ruby's history, Ruby's creator, the idiomatic processes and terminology that Ruby developers use, and the technologies that have taken Ruby from being relatively unknown to being a first-class programming language of significance.

© Carleton DiLeo, Peter Cooper 2021
C. DiLeo and P. Cooper, *Beginning Ruby 3*, https://doi.org/10.1007/978-1-4842-6324-2_5

Ruby's History

Ruby is relatively young in the world of programming languages, having been first developed in 1993, making it roughly the same age as both Perl and Python. Among the most popular programming languages still in use today, Fortran, for example, was developed in 1953, and C was developed in the early 1970s. Ruby's relative modernity is an asset rather than a downfall, however. From day one, it was designed with object-oriented programming in mind, and its syntax has remained consistent over time. Older languages have frequently been forced to complicate their syntax and change radically to address modern concepts such as object orientation, networking, and graphical environments.

Unlike languages that are formed out of pure necessity or research, Ruby's birth came from a sense of frustration with existing languages. Despite the presence of so many established programming languages, a plucky Japanese computer scientist felt development was becoming ever more complex and tiresome, and decided some fun had to be injected into the world of programming languages.

The Land of the Rising Sun

Ruby began life in Japan as the creation of Yukihiro Matsumoto, known more commonly as Matz. Unlike that of most language developers, Matz's motivation for Ruby was fun and a principle of "least surprise" in order to improve overall developer productivity. He couldn't find a language that resonated with his mindset, so he took his own outlook about how programming should work and created Ruby (named after the gemstone in homage to the "Perl" programming language).

A longtime object-oriented programming fan, Matz felt object orientation was the best model to adopt. However, unlike other languages, such as Perl, object orientation with Ruby wouldn't be an afterthought, but act as the core foundation for the language. Everything (within reason) would be an object, and methods would fill the roles of the procedures and functions developers had come to expect in older procedural languages. As Matz himself said in a 2001 interview, "I wanted a language that was more powerful than Perl, and more object-oriented than Python. That's why I decided to design my own language."

In December 1995, Matz released the first public alpha version of Ruby, and soon thereafter a community began to form in Japan. However, although Ruby quickly became relatively popular in Japan, it struggled to gain a foothold elsewhere.

Note   In software development, the terms *alpha*, *beta*, and *gamma*, among others, are used to denote the development stage of a piece of software. An initial release that's not for general use is often called an alpha. A release that implements most of the required features, but might not be entirely tested or stable, is often called a beta, although this term is becoming muddied by the plethora of websites and games now more permanently using the term "beta" on otherwise fully released products and services.

In 1996, the development of Ruby was opened up significantly, and a small team of core developers and other contributors began to form alongside the more general community of Ruby developers. Ruby 1.0 was released on December 25, 1996. These core developers help Matz develop Ruby and submit their patches (adjustments to the code) and ideas to him. Matz continues to act as a "benevolent dictator" who ultimately controls the direction of the language, despite the ever-widening influence of other developers.

Note   Although developing software privately is still common, many projects are now worked upon in a public manner, allowing them to be extended and worked upon by any competent programmer. In many cases, this makes it possible for other developers to *fork* the project (taking the existing code and splitting it into their own version).

Ruby's Influences

In developing Ruby, Matz was heavily influenced by the programming languages he was familiar with. Larry Wall, the developer of the popular Perl language, was a hero of Matz, and Perl's principle of *there is more than one way to do it* (TMTOWTDI) is present in Ruby.

Some languages, such as Python, prefer to provide more rigid structures and present a clean method for developers to have a small number of options to perform a certain task. Ruby allows its developers to solve problems in any one of many ways. This allows the language great flexibility, and combined with the object-oriented nature of the language, Ruby is highly customizable.

In terms of its object-oriented nature, Ruby has also been heavily influenced by Smalltalk, a prolific object-oriented language developed in the 1970s. As in Smalltalk, almost everything in Ruby is an object, and Ruby also gives programmers the ability to change many details of the language's operation within their own programs on the fly. This feature is called *reflection*.

To a lesser extent, Python, Lisp, Eiffel, Ada, and C++ have also influenced Ruby. These influences demonstrate that Ruby isn't a language that's afraid to take on the best ideas from other languages. This is one of many reasons why Ruby is such a powerful and dynamic language. The implementation of many of these features has also made the migration from other languages to Ruby significantly easier. Learning Ruby means, to a great extent, learning the best features of other programming languages for free. (Refer to Appendix A for a comparison between Ruby and other languages.)

Go West

As a language initially developed for Matz's own use in Japan, the initial documentation was entirely in Japanese, locking most non-Japanese users out. Although Ruby has always used English for its keywords (such as `print`, `puts`, `if`, and so on) like most programming languages, it wasn't until 1997 that the initial documentation actually written in English began to be produced.

Matz first began to officially promote the Ruby language in English in late 1998 with the creation of the `ruby-talk` mailing list, still one of the best places to discuss the Ruby language, as well as a useful resource with more than 300,000 messages archived at the list's website (`http://blade.nagaokaut.ac.jp/ruby/ruby-talk/index.shtml`).

Note   You can subscribe to `ruby-talk` yourself by visiting `www.ruby-lang.org/en/community/mailing-lists/` and using the signup form.

An official English language website soon followed in late 1999 with the creation of `ruby-lang.org` (`www.ruby-lang.org/`), which is still Ruby's official English language website (see Figures 5-1 and 5-2 for a comparison of the official site between then and now).

What's New

- The new stable version 1.4.6 is released (00/08/16)

- The book from Addison Wesley by Dave & Andy is going to be out around mid October. Stay tuned. (00/08/16)

- `Brave GNU World' introduces Ruby. (00/08/14)

  Brave GNU World issue 18 contains the article about Ruby. Brave GNU World is the international column magazine: English, Japanese, German, French, Espanish.

- Perl/Ruby Conference will be held in Kyoto (00/08/03)

  Perl/Ruby Conference in Japan will be held from Nov. 29 to Dev. 1 at Kyoto International Conference Hall. This conference is sponsored by O'Reilly Japan and Japan Linux Association.

- The Page of the Day (00/08/02)

  Thirty-seven Reasons I Love Ruby
  I love this page.

- Nightly snapshot is available. This is tar'ed and gzip'ed file of the latest CVS. It may contain unfixed problems. (as usual ;-) (00/06/30)

- InformIT published an article The Ruby Programming Language. Matz wrote this. (00/06/13)

- Ruby Bug Tracking System is available. (00/04/10)

- IBM developerWork picked up Ruby in Ruby: An open source gem from Japan. (00/02/10)

- new better FAQ is available.

- The first book about Ruby is published: ISBN4-7561-3254-5. (99/10/26)

  But it is written in Japanese! Sorry.

Figure 5-1. *The official English language Ruby homepage in 2000*

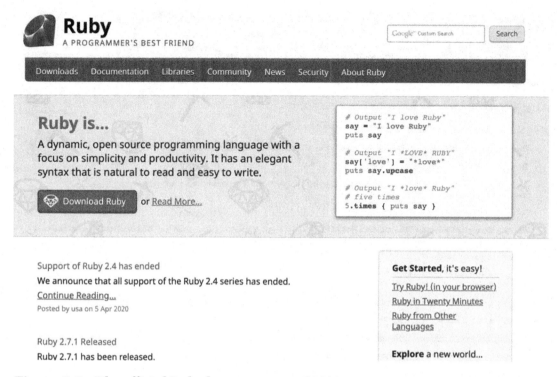

Figure 5-2. *The official Ruby homepage as of 2020*

Ruby failed to catch on with all but a few ardent developers until 2000 and 2001 (with the main Ruby Usenet newsgroup `comp.lang.ruby` being created in May 2000), and even then the English-speaking Ruby community was tiny. Matz didn't consider this to be important though, and was even surprised that other people found his language useful, having only created it to fit his own way of thinking.

However, the exposure of Ruby to the larger audience of software developers continued to be low. IBM published an article with a brief overview of Ruby and an interview with Matz in 2000, and the much-revered *Dr. Dobb's Journal* published an article by Dave Thomas and Andy Hunt with a similar introduction in January 2001.

Despite Ruby's obvious power, it appeared as if Python and PHP were going to win the race to become "the next Perl" as general scripting and web languages, respectively, up until 2004. But then everything changed when a young Dane released Ruby on Rails, a Ruby-powered web application framework that quickly changed the perception of Ruby in the worldwide development community. Before we look at Rails, however, we need to see how else Ruby has flourished in the last several years.

Alternative Ruby Implementations

Until around 2007, the official Ruby implementation as developed by Matz and the Ruby core team (known as MRI—Matz's Ruby Interpreter) was the only *reliable* way to run Ruby scripts. Since then, some alternative Ruby implementations have become viable for certain uses.

This book does not focus on any implementations other than the official ones for learning the language, but as the alternative implementations may have relevance for you in the future, here are a few of the most popular ones:

- *JRuby* (`www.jruby.org/`): A Ruby implementation that runs on the Java Virtual Machine (JVM). Even in 2009, it was on par with Ruby 1.9 in terms of performance, and since then has proven to be faster than MRI in many situations. As a Java-based implementation, JRuby gives Ruby developers access to the whole Java ecosystem, including Java libraries, distribution tools, and application servers. Conversely, developers on the JVM platform get access to Ruby's benefits.

- *IronRuby* (`http://ironruby.net/`): An implementation of Ruby for Microsoft's.NET platform. The head developer was John Lam, who worked for Microsoft. As of 2012, the project appeared to no longer be regularly updated.

In practical terms, as of mid-2016, JRuby is an alternative to MRI for day-to-day and production use, although it has its pros and cons. JRuby's support for all things Java makes it an attractive option in settings where a Java ecosystem is well established. For anyone new to Ruby, however, I would strongly recommend sticking with MRI.

Ruby on Rails

In the last several years, it has become impossible to publish any book or article about Ruby without at least mentioning *Ruby on Rails* (or *Rails*, for short). Rails is a web application framework that has propelled the popularity of Ruby outside of Japan from a humble core of avid developers to hundreds of thousands of developers all now interested in using the language. This section examines Rails, explains why it's important, and discusses how its presence has changed the whole dynamic of the Ruby ecosystem.

Note   An application framework is a set of conventions, structures, and systems that provide an underlying structure to make application development easier. Ruby on Rails is such a framework for web application development.

I'll be covering Ruby on Rails development briefly (the framework advances too quickly for a full tutorial in a long-lasting book like this one) in Chapter 13, but let's first look at the motivation behind the framework and how it has changed the entire Ruby landscape.

Why Rails Came into Existence

37signals (`www.37signals.com/`), a successful web software company recently renamed Basecamp, was founded in 1999 initially as a web design agency that promoted the use of clean, fast, and functional designs over the gee-whiz Flash-based websites that were popular at the time. With only two cofounders running the entire company, they quickly realized they needed some tools to help them run their business efficiently. They tried some off-the-shelf software but found nothing that matched their needs and found most solutions to be bloated and complex. They felt their attitude toward web design should also be applied to applications, and in mid-2003 decided to develop their own project management tool.

As designers rather than coders, 37signals turned to the services of David Heinemeier Hansson, a student in Copenhagen, Denmark, to develop their project management application. Rather than use the then-common tools such as Perl or PHP, Hansson was convinced that 37signals could develop the application far more quickly and completely by using Ruby. Previously a PHP coder, Hansson was beginning to feel the pain of using PHP for large web application development, and felt a new direction should be sought.

As development on the nascent application (called Basecamp) progressed, the team members showed it to others in the industry and quickly realized from the responses they heard that they should release the application to the public rather than keep it for their own use.

With a successful public release of Basecamp in February 2004—only about four months after beginning the project—the development methodology adopted by 37signals and Hansson was proven, and 37signals began a rapid transition into an application development company, with Hansson eventually becoming a partner at the company.

Ruby proved to be the silver bullet that powered the rapid development of Basecamp. Hansson used Ruby's object orientation and reflection features to build a framework that made developing database-driven web applications easier than ever before. This framework became known as Ruby on Rails, and was first released to the public in July 2004. 37signals continued to develop new products quickly using the power of the new framework.

Like Ruby itself, the Ruby on Rails framework didn't immediately experience an explosion of popularity, but found a small number of ardent fans who began to realize its power and, in many cases, wished to replicate 37signals' success.

How the Web (2.0) Was Won

Ruby on Rails wasn't a wallflower for long. 2005 was an epic year for Ruby on Rails, and Ruby's popularity exploded alongside it. The initial fans of Ruby on Rails had begun blogging feverishly about the technology and were winning over converts with an unintentional, but surprisingly potent, grassroots viral marketing campaign.

In January 2005, Slashdot, the world's most popular technology community website at the time, published its first post mentioning Ruby on Rails, and since then has run scores of stories on the technology, each encouraging existing PHP, Perl, and Python developers to give Ruby and Ruby on Rails a try.

In March 2005, Hansson announced the development of the first commercial Rails book, which came out in beta PDF form in May of that year. In September 2005, the print version of the book went on sale and immediately topped the Amazon.com chart for programming books.

In the space of a year, Rails books were under development and being released by a multitude of publishers; tens of thousands of blog posts had been made about the technology; hundreds of thousands of screencasts (video tutorials demonstrating how to use Rails) had been watched online; and David Heinemeier Hansson had won numerous awards, including Google and O'Reilly's "Best Hacker of the Year 2005." Tens of thousands of developers were suddenly flocking to Ruby on Rails and, as a consequence, to Ruby.

The Ruby ecosystem was thrust into the limelight, especially on the back of the then-popular Web 2.0 concept, a coined term that referred to a supposed second generation in Internet-based services, and was often used to refer to the growing culture of blogs, social networking, wikis, and other user content–driven websites. As Ruby and Rails made these sites easy to develop, many developers used these tools to their advantage to get ahead in the Web 2.0 field and beyond.

The Open Source Culture

When Ruby was initially developed, Matz didn't have a specific development culture in mind. He developed the language to be for his own use and to fit his own mindset. For the first couple years, he kept the language mostly to himself. Most of today's culture relating to *how* to develop software with Ruby has evolved in the last several years and is partly shared with other programming languages.

A common element of the Ruby development culture that's crucial to understand is the *open source* movement.

Tip   Feel free to skip this section and move on to "Where and How to Get Help" if you're already familiar with the concepts surrounding open source.

What Is Open Source?

If you've used Linux or downloaded certain types of software, you might be familiar with the term *open source*. Simply, open source means that the source code to an application or library is made available publicly for other people to look at and use. There might be restrictions on what people can do with the code (generally via a license), but it's publicly viewable. Much like Linux, Ruby, along with nearly all its libraries, is released under an open source license—in contrast to, say, Microsoft Windows, whose source code isn't readily available (although Microsoft is continuing to make more moves toward open source in recent years).

The terms of Ruby's license don't require that any applications you produce with Ruby also need to be made open source. You can develop proprietary "closed source" applications with Ruby and never let anyone else see the code. Choosing whether to release your code as open source or not can be a tough decision.

There are often shades of gray in the open source vs. closed source decision. When 37signals developed the first Ruby on Rails–powered application, Basecamp, they didn't release the source openly, but they did extract the Ruby on Rails framework and release that as open source. The result is that their company has received a lot of publicity, and 37signals has hired some great coders who worked on Ruby on Rails for free, benefiting everybody. Software products such as the popular Apache httpd and nginx web servers and the PostgreSQL database system are also available under varying open source licenses and are routinely improved by unpaid coders.

The open source community is one of sharing knowledge freely and collaborating to improve the systems and services that most of us use. Although proprietary software will always have its place, open source is rapidly becoming the de facto way to develop programming languages, libraries, and other non-application types of software.

Understanding open source is an important key to understanding the Ruby community. Although many developers don't necessarily open source the code to their applications, they'll often release the tools and code tricks to the community so that they can benefit from the peer review and popularity that results.

Releasing your code as open source isn't necessarily a bad business decision. It could actually improve the quality of your code and tools, and make you much better known in the industry.

Where and How to Get Help

This book will help you learn all the essentials about Ruby and more besides, but it's often useful to get more timely or domain-specific assistance while coding. In this section, you'll look at a few ways that you can get assistance from the large community of Ruby developers. (There's also a more succinct and complete list of resources in Appendix B that you might prefer for future reference.)

Mailing Lists

For decades, mailing lists have been popular havens for discussion about programming languages. Favored by the more technical members of any programming language's culture, they're a good place to ask questions about the internals or future of the language, along with esoteric queries that only a true language uber-geek could answer. They are not, however, suited for basic queries.

Ruby has three official mailing lists for English speakers to which you can subscribe, as follows:

- `ruby-talk`: Deals with general topics and questions about Ruby

- `ruby-core`: Discussion of core Ruby issues, specifically about the development of the language

- `ruby-doc`: Discussion of the documentation standards and tools for Ruby (rarely used)

Further information about these lists is available at `www.ruby-lang.org/en/community/mailing-lists/`.

Lists are also available in Japanese, French, and Portuguese, and these are similarly listed on the first page in the preceding paragraph. The Japanese mailing lists, being composed of some of the most experienced Ruby developers, are often read by English speakers using translation software. Information about this is also available at the aforementioned web page. Ruby's mailing lists appear to be getting quieter year by year, but do still work.

Chat

On the Internet, there are several ways you can discuss topics with other users in real time. For example, Slack and Discord provide real-time chat via a desktop, mobile, or web app:

> *Ruby on Rails Slack channel (`www.rubyonrails.link/`)*:
> A community of Ruby on Rails developers from all over the world.

> *Ruby Discord Server (`https://discord.gg/bHB8Jkx`)*: A Discord
> server where developers discuss and seek help on various
> Ruby topics.

Documentation

There's a significant amount of documentation available on the Web (as well as within Ruby itself) for Ruby developers. The site `www.ruby-doc.org/` provides a web-based rendering of the documentation that comes with Ruby 1.8 through to 3.0 and allows you to look up references for all of the internal classes and the standard library.

The API documentation for the current stable release of Ruby is available at `www.ruby-doc.org/core/`. Produced automatically from the Ruby source code with Ruby's built-in documentation tool, *rdoc*, the structure of the documentation isn't immediately obvious. Usually you can choose between viewing documentation for certain files that make up Ruby, documentation for each different base class, or documentation for certain methods. You don't get a logical order to follow, and there are no deep tutorials. This sort of documentation is for reference purposes only.

Most Ruby libraries and applications use a similar scheme for their documentation, and the links to this are made available on their official sites. For example, Ruby on Rails' API documentation is available at `https://api.rubyonrails.org/`.

Forums

Forums make up some of the most popular websites on the Internet. Unlike newsgroups or mailing lists, which tend to be the domain of more technical people, forums provide extremely easy access to a non-real-time discussion on the Web. Forums are a particularly good place to ask more basic questions and to get general advice.

Several Ruby forums are available to try:

- *Ruby-Forum.com* (`www.ruby-forum.com/`): Ruby-Forum.com provides a forum style view onto some of the popular Ruby mailing lists. This means it isn't a true forum in the strictest sense, but people used to forums will appreciate the structure.

- *Go Rails Forum* (`https://gorails.com/forum`): Go Rails Forum is an active forum focused on Ruby on Rails.

Joining the Community

One of the reasons for programming communities is for people to get help from others who are experienced with the language, but also to share knowledge and to develop useful tools and documentation together. Solely "taking" from the community is natural at the start of a developer's experience with a new language, but it's essential to give something back once you've developed some knowledge of your own. Ruby developers are proud that their community is one of the friendliest and easiest to get involved with, and there are a number of ways to make a mark.

Give Help to Others

In the previous section, we looked at the ways that you can get help from other Ruby developers, but once you've gained a certain amount of Ruby knowledge, you'll be able to start helping people yourself. You can participate on the IRC chatrooms, forums, and mailing lists and begin to answer some of the questions for those with lesser knowledge than yourself.

Helping others isn't always the selfless, time-consuming act it might seem at first. Often, questions are asked that relate to your knowledge but require you to work out something new or identify a new solution to a problem you've already solved. My personal experience with helping people in the IRC chatrooms has been that my mind has been constantly stretched. Although sometimes I might have the best answer, other times I might give an inaccurate or confusing answer that's then corrected by someone else, helping me to gain new insights.

Don't be afraid to dive in and try to help others. If you feel your answer is right, even if it's not, it's likely that several people will try to help, and the Ruby community is generally forgiving of such errors. In the Ruby community, effort is often prized above prowess.

Contribute Code

Once you begin to develop your own Ruby applications, you might find features missing in the applications or libraries you wish to use, and you'll either develop your own or work on upgrading those that already exist. If a project is open source, you should be able to supply your changes and upgrades back to the project, meaning that you improve the quality of the software for the entire community. Other than benefiting others, this also means your code is likely to be extended and improved itself, and you'll be able to reap even more benefit than if you kept your code to yourself.

All open source Ruby libraries and applications have someone who is in charge of maintaining them, and if no guidance is provided on the project's website, simply contact the maintainer and see whether you can contribute your code.

Alternatively, if you don't feel confident enough to supply code, but see large gaps in the documentation for a project—perhaps even in Ruby itself—maintainers are often ecstatic if you'll supply documentation. You can learn more about how to document Ruby programs in Chapter 7. Many coders aren't good at documentation or don't have the time to complete it, so if you have a skill for it, contributing documentation to a project could make you very popular indeed!

News Sites and Sources

There are a variety of sites and podcasts through which you can get up-to-date Ruby news and articles. The following are some of the most popular:

- *RubyFlow* (`www.rubyflow.com/`): This is a Ruby community link blog where all of the items are supplied by other Ruby developers. You'll find a lot of interesting Ruby-related announcements and links to tutorials scattered across the Web. Of course, if you write anything helpful of your own, you can post it to RubyFlow and get the attention of the Ruby community.

- *Ruby Weekly* (`https://rubyweekly.com/`): A weekly email newsletter dedicated to sharing the latest from the entire Ruby world.

- *Ruby on Reddit* (`https://reddit.com/r/ruby`): The Ruby section of the popular social bookmarking and discussion site aggregates most of the best Ruby blogs into a single page.

By visiting these sites, you'll quickly learn about hundreds of other Ruby resources, tricks, and sources of documentation. If you comment on these sites and begin to update a blog yourself with your experiences of Ruby, you'll quickly become established in the Ruby community.

Summary

In this chapter, we've taken a break from coding to focus on the culture, community, and ecosystem surrounding the Ruby language. Understanding the larger world around the Ruby language is extremely useful, as it's from this community that most developers will get assistance, advice, code, and even paying work.

Being able to get help and give help in return benefits the community, helps the cause of Ruby to progress, and ultimately helps with your own programming skills.

The Ruby community is important and friendly to new Ruby developers, making it ideal to get involved as soon as possible when you begin to learn Ruby. Make sure you use the resources the community provides to the fullest as you learn Ruby and begin to develop applications. A single book cannot turn anyone into a Ruby expert, but a collection of valuable resources and participation in the community can.

Refer to Appendix B for a larger collection of URLs and links to other Ruby resources that are available online.

PART II

The Core of Ruby

This part of the book walks you through the remaining essential elements of Ruby and goes into more detail about some previously seen aspects of the language. By the end of Part 2, you'll be able to develop Ruby applications complete with complex class and object arrangements of your own; you'll know how to test, document, and deploy your applications; and you'll use databases and external data sources to feed your applications.

## CHAPTER 6

Classes, Objects, and Modules

In Chapter 2, we dived straight into the principles of object orientation, the method of representing concepts in Ruby by using *classes* and *objects*. Since then, we've looked at Ruby's standard classes, such as `String` and `Array`, worked with them, and then branched off to look at Ruby's logic and other core features.

In this chapter, the focus is back onto object orientation, but rather than looking at the concepts from afar, we'll be getting into the details. We'll look at why classes and objects behave the way they do, why object orientation is a viable development tool, how you can implement classes to match your own requirements, and how to *override* and *extend* the classes Ruby provides by default. Finally, you'll implement a basic dungeon text adventure to demonstrate how several real-world concepts can combine into an easily maintainable set of interconnected classes.

Why Use Object Orientation?

Object orientation is not the only development approach with which to develop software. The *procedural* style of programming predates it, and continues to be used in languages such as C. Whereas object orientation dictates that you define concepts and processes as classes from which you can create objects, programming procedurally means you focus on the steps required to complete a task instead, without paying particular attention to how the data is managed.

© Carleton DiLeo, Peter Cooper 2021
C. DiLeo and P. Cooper, *Beginning Ruby 3*, https://doi.org/10.1007/978-1-4842-6324-2_6

Imagine two developers within a single software development company who are vying to be respected as the most knowledgeable programmer in the company. Capitalizing on the rivalry, their boss issues both of them the same tasks and uses the best code in each case. There's only one difference between the two programmers. One follows the principles of object-oriented development, and the other is a procedural programmer coding without using classes and objects.

For a forthcoming project, the boss demands some code that can work out the perimeter and area of various shapes. She says the shapes required are squares and triangles.

The procedural programmer rushes away and quickly comes up with four obvious routines:

```ruby
def perimeter_of_square(side_length)
  side_length * 4
end

def area_of_square(side_length)
  side_length * side_length
end

def perimeter_of_triangle(side1, side2, side3)
  side1 + side2 + side3
end

def area_of_triangle(base_width, height)
  base_width * height / 2
end
```

Note   Remember, it's not necessary to use `return` to return values from methods in Ruby. The last expression within the method is used as the return value by default. If it feels right for the situation or seems clearer to you, however, you can certainly use `return` with impunity!

Finishing first, the procedural programmer is sure his code will be chosen.

The object-oriented programmer takes longer. He recognizes that the specifications might change in the future and that it would be useful to define a Shape class and then create classes that would inherit from Shape. This would mean that if extra features needed to be added to shapes in general, the code would be ready. He submits his initial solution:

```ruby
class Shape
end

class Square < Shape
  def initialize(side_length)
    @side_length = side_length
  end

  def area
    @side_length * @side_length
  end

  def perimeter
    @side_length * 4
  end
end

class Triangle < Shape
  def initialize(base_width, height, side1, side2, side3)
    @base_width = base_width
    @height = height
    @side1 = side1
    @side2 = side2
    @side3 = side3
  end

  def area
    @base_width * @height / 2
  end

  def perimeter
    @side1 + @side2 + @side3
  end
end
```

> **Note**   This code might seem complex and alien at this time, but we'll be covering the techniques used here later in this chapter. For now, simply recognize the structure of laying down classes and methods, as covered in Chapter 2.

The procedural programmer scoffs at the object-oriented solution. "Why all the pointless assignments of data? That object-oriented code is 90 percent structure and 10 percent logic!"

The boss is impressed by the shortness of the procedural code, but decides to try out both versions for herself. She quickly spots a big difference:

```
puts area_of_triangle(6,6)
puts perimeter_of_square(5)
```

```
18
20
```

```
my_square = Square.new(5)
my_triangle = Triangle.new(6, 6, 7.81, 7.81, 7.81)
puts my_square.area
puts my_square.perimeter
puts my_triangle.area
puts my_triangle.perimeter
```

```
25
20
18
23.43
```

The boss notices that with the object-oriented code, she can create as many shapes as she wants in a logical way, whereas the procedural code expects her to have a mental note of the shapes she wants to work with. She isn't without her concerns, though.

"More lines of code means more time required," she says. "Is it worth taking the object-oriented route if it means more lines of code, more time, and more hassles?"

The object-oriented developer has heard this complaint before and immediately springs into action. "Try dealing with a large number of random shapes," he says.

The boss isn't entirely up to date with modern development trends, but when she discovers that many new types of shapes can be produced easily by copying and pasting the existing classes with some minor tweaks, she begins to be won over. She also realizes that if a shape could be stored as an object referenced by a single variable and that if each shape class accepted the same methods, the type of shape presented wouldn't matter (this quality is often referred to as *polymorphism*). She could call the `perimeter` or `area` method on *any* shape without worry. The procedural code, on the other hand, is just a jumble of different routines, and the developer would be forced to keep track of the different types of shapes to know which procedures to run. The Shape class also provides a way to give general functionality to all the different types of shapes if it's necessary in the future. The boss knows which code to choose!

"Object-oriented code requires a little more setup, but when it comes to scaling that code to fit real-life requirements, there's no contest," she says.

Note   It's worth noting that in the latter triangle example, the data provided is erroneous (how can a side be 7.81 units long, yet the base be 6 units long?). The beauty of object-oriented programming, however, is that since the triangle is a single object, it would be easy to add a "validation" routine to check the parameters used to define the object and reject or recalculate those that are incorrect. With the procedural code, the developer should perform any "checks" manually every time he wants to work with a triangle built from fresh data!

The basic advantage with object-oriented programming is that even if there's more structure involved in setting up your code, it's easy for a non-expert to understand how classes and objects relate, and it's easier to maintain and update the code to deal with real-life situations.

Object Orientation Basics

Let's recap the basic knowledge of classes and objects that you acquired over the past few chapters.

A *class* is a blueprint for objects. You have only one class called Shape, but with it, you can create multiple *instances* of shapes (Shape *objects*), all of which have the methods and attributes defined by the Shape class.

An *object* is an *instance* of a class. If Shape is the class, then x = Shape.new creates a new Shape instance and makes x reference that object. You would then say x is a Shape object, or an object of class Shape.

Local, Global, Object, and Class Variables

In Chapter 2, you created some classes and added methods to them. To recap, here's a simple demonstration of a class with two methods and how to use it. First, here's the class itself:

```
class Square
  def initialize(side_length)
    @side_length = side_length
  end

  def area
    @side_length * @side_length
  end
end
```

Next, let's create some square objects and use their area methods:

```
a = Square.new(10)
b = Square.new(5)
puts a.area
puts b.area
```

```
100
25
```

The first method—and when I say "first," I mean the first method in our example; the actual order of methods in code is irrelevant—in the Square class is initialize. initialize is a special method that's called when a new object based on that class is created. When you call Square.new(10), the Square class creates a new object instance of itself and then calls initialize on that object.

In this case, `initialize` accepts a single argument into `side_length` as passed by `Square.new(10)` and assigns the number 10 (now referenced by `side_length`) to a variable called `@side_length`. The @ symbol before the variable name is important in this case. But why? To understand why some variables are prefixed with certain symbols requires understanding that there are multiple types of variables, such as local, global, object, and class variables.

Local Variables

In previous examples, you've created variables simply, like so:

```
x = 10
puts x
```

```
10
```

In Ruby, this sort of basic variable is called a *local variable*. It can be used only in the same place it is defined. If you jump to using an object's methods or a separate method of your own, the variable x doesn't come with you. It's considered to be local in *scope*. That is, it's only present within the local area of code. Here's an example that demonstrates this:

```
def basic_method
  puts x
end

x = 10
basic_method
```

This example defines x to equal 10 and then jumps to a local method called `basic_method`. If you ran this code through irb, you would get an error like this:

```
NameError (undefined local variable or method `x' for main:Object)
```

What's happening is that when you jump to `basic_method`, you're no longer in the same *scope* as the variable x that you created. Because x is a local variable, it exists only where it was defined. To avoid this problem, it's important to remember to use only local variables where they're being directly used.

Here's an example where you have two local variables with the same name but in different scopes:

```
def basic_method
  x = 50
  puts x
end

x = 10
basic_method
puts x
```

```
50
10
```

This demonstrates that local variables live entirely in their original scope. You set x to 10 in the main code and set x to 50 inside the method, but x is still 10 when you return to the original scope. The x variable inside `basic_method` is not the same x variable that's outside of the method. They're separate variables, distinct within their own scopes.

Global Variables

In opposition to local variables, Ruby can also use *global variables*. As their name suggests, global variables are available from everywhere within an application, including inside classes or objects.

Global variables can be useful, but aren't commonly used in Ruby. They don't mesh well with the ideals of object-oriented programming, as once you start using global variables across an application, your code is likely to become dependent on them. Because the ability to separate blocks of logic from one another is a useful aspect of object-oriented programming, global variables are not favored.

You define global variables by putting a dollar sign ($) in front of the variable name, like so:

```
def basic_method
  puts $x
end

$x = 10
```

```
basic_method
```

```
10
```

$x is defined as a global variable, and you can use it anywhere in your application.

Note   The $ and @ characters that denote global variables and object variables (as demonstrated in the next section) are technically called *sigils*. Many developers are, however, unaware of this. This book is not beyond giving you knowledge that can make you more popular at cocktail parties!

Instance or Object Variables

Where local variables are specific to the local scope and global variables have global scope, *instance variables* (also known as *object variables*) are so named because they have scope within, and are associated with, the current object. A demonstration of this concept was shown at the start of this section with the Square class:

```
class Square
  def initialize(side_length)
    @side_length = side_length
  end

  def area
    @side_length * @side_length
  end
end
```

Instance variables are prefixed with an @ symbol. In the Square class, you assign the side_length provided to the class to @side_length. @side_length, as an instance variable, is then accessible from any other method inside that object. That's how the area method can then use @side_length to calculate the area of the square represented by the object:

```
a = Square.new(10)
b = Square.new(5)
```

```
puts a.area
puts b.area
```

```
100
25
```

The results are different, even though the code to work out the area in both cases is `@side_length * @side_length`. This is because `@side_length` is an instance variable associated only with the current object or instance.

Tip   If you didn't fully understand the `Shape/Square/Triangle` example at the start of this chapter, now would be a good time to look back at it, as it used several object variables to develop its functionality.

Class Variables

The last major type of variable is the *class variable*. The scope of a class variable is within the class itself, as opposed to within specific objects of that class. Class variables start with two @ symbols (@@) as opposed to the single @ symbol of instance variables.

Class variables can be useful for storing information relevant to all objects of a certain class. For example, you could store the number of objects created so far in a certain class using a class variable like so:

```
class Square
  def initialize
    if defined?(@@number_of_squares)
      @@number_of_squares += 1
    else
      @@number_of_squares = 1
    end
  end

  def self.count
    @@number_of_squares
  end
end
```

```
a = Square.new
b = Square.new
puts Square.count
```

2

Because @@number_of_squares is a class variable, it's already defined each time you create a new object (except for the first time, but that's why you check to see if it's defined and, if not, give it an initial value of 1).

Note   In recent years, class variables have begun to fall out of favor among professional Ruby developers. Fashions come and go in the Ruby world but ultimately enable developers to work together more smoothly. Since all classes are themselves objects within Ruby, it has become more popular to simply use object variables within the context of class methods in order to keep things simple.

Class Methods vs. Instance Methods

In your Square class, you defined two methods: initialize and area. Both are instance methods, as they relate to, and operate directly on, an instance of an object. Here's the code again:

```
class Square
  def initialize(side_length)
    @side_length = side_length
  end

  def area
    @side_length * @side_length
  end
end
```

Once you've created a square with s = Square.new(10), you can use s.area to get back the area of the square represented by s. The area method is made available in all objects of class Square, so it's considered to be an *instance method*.

However, methods are not just useful to have available on object instances. It can be useful to have methods that work directly on the class itself. In the previous section, you used a class variable to keep a count of how many square objects had been created, and it would be useful to access the @@number_of_squares class variable in some way other than through Square objects.

Here's a simple demonstration of a class method:

```
class Square
  def self.test_method
    puts "Hello from the Square class!"
  end

  def test_method
    puts "Hello from an instance of class Square!"
  end
end

Square.test_method
Square.new.test_method
```

```
Hello from the Square class!
Hello from an instance of class Square!
```

This class has two methods. The first is a class method, and the second is an instance method, although both have the same name of test_method. The difference is that the class method is denoted with self., where self represents the current class, so def self.test_method defines the method as being specific to the class. However, with no prefix, methods are automatically instance methods.

Class methods give you the mechanism to implement the "object counter" hinted at earlier:

```
class Square
  def initialize
    if defined?(@@number_of_squares)
      @@number_of_squares += 1
    else
      @@number_of_squares = 1
```

```
    end
  end

  def self.count
    @@number_of_squares
  end
end
```

Let's give it a try:

```
a = Square.new
puts Square.count
b = Square.new
puts Square.count
c = Square.new
puts Square.count
```

```
1
2
3
```

Notice you don't refer to a, b, or c at all to get the count. You use the Square.count class method directly. Consider it as if you're asking the class to do something that's relevant to the class as a whole, rather than asking the objects.

Inheritance

An interesting object-oriented programming concept is *inheritance*, which allows you to generate a taxonomy of classes and objects. If you consider all living things as a class called LivingThing (see Figure 6-1), under that class you could have (and let's keep this simple, biologists!) Plant and Animal classes. Under Animal, you'd have Mammal, Fish, Amphibian, and so forth. Digging into Mammal, you could work through Primate and Human. A Human is a living thing, a Human is an Animal, a Human is a Mammal, and so forth, but each level down is more specific and targeted than that above it. This is class inheritance in action! The same system applied to the Shape example where Triangle and Square inherited directly from Shape.

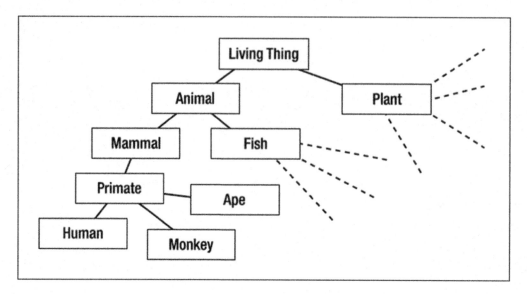

Figure 6-1. *An example of a hierarchy of "living things"*

The benefit of inheritance is that classes lower down the hierarchy get the features of those higher up, but can also add specific features of their own. The basic "all living things" class is so generic that the only functionality you could give to it is a basic "living or dead" method. However, at the animal level, you could add methods such as eat, excrete, or breathe. At the human level, you'd inherit all this functionality but be able to add human methods and qualities such as sing, dance, and love.

Ruby's inheritance features are similarly simple. Any class can inherit the features and functionality of another class, but a class can inherit only from a *single* other class. Some other languages support *multiple inheritance*, a feature that allows classes to inherit features from multiple classes, but Ruby doesn't support this. Multiple inheritance can cause some confusing situations—for instance, classes could inherit from one another in an endless loop—and the efficacy of multiple inheritance is debatable.

Let's look at how inheritance works in code form:

```
class ParentClass
  def method1
    puts "Hello from method1 in the parent class"
  end

  def method2
    puts "Hello from method2 in the parent class"
```

```
    end
end

class ChildClass < ParentClass
  def method2
    puts "Hello from method2 in the child class"
  end
end

my_object = ChildClass.new
my_object.method1
```

```
Hello from method1 in the parent class
```

```
my_object.method2
```

```
Hello from method2 in the child class
```

First, you create the ParentClass with two methods, method1 and method2. Then you create ChildClass and make it inherit from ParentClass using the ChildClass < ParentClass notation. Last, you create an object instance of ChildClass and call its method1 and method2 methods.

The first result demonstrates inheritance perfectly. ChildClass has no method1 of its own, but because it has inherited from ParentClass, and ParentClass has a method1, it uses it.

However, in the second case, ChildClass already has a method2 method, so the method2 method supplied by the parent class is ignored. In many cases, this is ideal behavior, as it allows your more specific classes to override behavior provided by more general classes. However, in some situations you might want a child method to call an inherited method and do something with the result.

Consider some basic classes that represent different types of people:

```
class Person
  def initialize(name)
    @name = name
  end
```

```ruby
  def name
    @name
  end
end

class Doctor < Person
  def name
    "Dr. " + super
  end
end
```

In this case, you have a `Person` class that implements the basic functionality of storing and returning a person's name. The `Doctor` class inherits from `Person` and overrides the `name` method. Within the `name` method for doctors, it returns a string starting with `Dr.`, appended with the name as usual. This occurs by using `super`, which looks up the inheritance chain and calls the method of the same name on the next highest class. In this example, you only have two tiers, so using `super` within the `name` method in `Doctor` then uses the `name` method in `Person`.

The benefit of using inheritance in this way is that you can implement generic functionality in generic classes and then implement only the specific functionality that more specific child classes require. This saves a lot of repetition and means that if you make changes to the parent classes, child classes will inherit these changes too. A good example of this might be if you changed `Person` to take two arguments, `firstname` and `lastname`. The `Doctor` class wouldn't need to be changed at all to support this change. With one child class, this doesn't seem too important, but when you have hundreds of different classes in an application, it pays to cut down on repetition!

Note   In the Ruby world, the concept of cutting down on repetition is commonly called *DRY*, meaning Don't Repeat Yourself. If you can code something once and reuse it from multiple places, that's usually the best way to practice "DRY."

Overriding Existing Methods

Because it's a dynamic language, one clever thing you can do with Ruby is override existing classes and methods. For example, consider Ruby's String class. As covered in Chapter 3, if you create a string, you end up with an object of class String, for example:

```
x = "This is a test"
puts x.class
```

```
String
```

You can call a number of different methods upon the String object stored in x:

```
puts x.length
puts x.upcase
```

```
14
THIS IS A TEST
```

Let's stir things up a bit by overriding the length method of the String class:

```
class String
  def length
    20
  end
end
```

Many newcomers to Ruby, even experienced developers, initially fail to believe this will work, but the results are exactly as the code dictates:

```
puts "This is a test".length
puts "a".length
puts "A really long line of text".length
```

```
20
20
20
```

Some libraries and extensions (add-ons) to Ruby override the methods supplied by the core classes to extend the functionality of Ruby in general. However, this demonstration shows why it's always necessary to tread with caution and be aware of what's going on in your application. If you were relying on being able to measure the length of strings, and the length method gets overridden, you're going to have a hard time!

You should also note that you can override your own methods. In fact, you've probably been doing it a lot already by following these examples in irb:

```ruby
class Dog
  def talk
    puts "Woof!"
  end
end

my_dog = Dog.new
my_dog.talk
```

```
Woof!
```

```ruby
class Dog
  def talk
    puts "Howl!"
  end
end

my_dog.talk
```

```
Howl!
```

In this example, you created a basic class with a simple method, then reopened that class, and redefined a method on the fly. The results of the redefinition were made effective immediately, and my_dog began to howl as a result.

This ability to reopen classes and add and redefine methods is relatively unique among object-oriented languages. Although it allows you to perform a number of interesting tricks (some of which you'll see in action later), it can also cause the same sections of code to act in different ways depending on whether certain classes upon which you depend were changed in the application, as demonstrated by your redefinition of String's length method previously.

Note   You might have noticed this class-reopening technique in action in some of our earlier examples where you created methods in one example, only to add new methods in a later example. If running under irb or within the same program, reopening a class lets you add new methods or change old ones without losing anything.

Reflection and Discovering an Object's Methods

Reflection is the process by which a computer program can inspect, analyze, and modify itself while it's running and being used. Ruby takes reflection to an extreme and allows you to change the functionality of great swathes of the language itself while running your own code.

It's possible to query almost any object within Ruby for the methods that are defined within it. This is another part of reflection:

```
a = "This is a test"
puts a.methods.join(' ')
```

```
unicode_normalize unicode_normalize! ascii_only? to_r unpack encode
encode! unpack1 % include? * + count partition +@ -@ <=> << to_c == ===
sum =~ next [] casecmp casecmp? insert []= match match? bytesize empty?
eql? succ! next! upto index rindex replace clear chr getbyte setbyte
scrub! scrub undump byteslice freeze inspect capitalize upcase dump
downcase! swapcase downcase hex capitalize! upcase! lines length size
codepoints succ split swapcase! bytes oct prepend grapheme_clusters concat
start_with? reverse reverse! to_str to_sym crypt ord strip end_with? to_s
to_i to_f center intern gsub ljust chars delete_suffix sub rstrip scan
chomp rjust lstrip chop! delete_prefix chop sub! gsub! delete_prefix!
chomp! strip! lstrip! rstrip! squeeze delete_suffix! tr tr_s delete each_
line tr! tr_s! delete! squeeze! slice each_byte each_char each_codepoint
each_grapheme_cluster b slice! rpartition encoding force_encoding valid_
encoding? hash unicode_normalized? clamp between? <= >= > < dup itself
yield_self then taint tainted? untaint untrust untrusted? trust frozen?
methods singleton_methods protected_methods private_methods public_methods
instance_variables instance_variable_get instance_variable_set instance_
```

```
variable_defined? remove_instance_variable instance_of? kind_of? is_a?
tap display class singleton_class clone public_send method public_method
singleton_method define_singleton_method extend to_enum enum_for !~ nil?
respond_to? object_id send __send__ ! != __id__ equal? instance_eval
instance_exec
```

The methods method on any object (unless it has been overridden, of course!) returns an array of methods made available by that object. Due to Ruby's heavily object-oriented structure, that's usually a significantly larger number of methods than those you have specifically defined yourself!

Note   The preceding method list may vary depending on your environment and the specific Ruby interpreter you're using. As long as your list is *similar*, you're doing fine.

The results reveal some other reflective methods too. For example, protected_methods, private_methods, and public_methods all reveal methods encapsulated in different ways (more on this in the next section).

Another interesting method is instance_variables. It returns the names of any object variables associated with an instance (as opposed to class variables):

```
class Person
  attr_accessor :name, :age
end

p = Person.new
p.name = "Fred"
p.age = 20
puts p.instance_variables
```

```
@age
@name
```

Note   If you received an error while running the last example, try restarting *irb* and running it again. Since we used the class Person in previous examples, *irb* may still have the class definition loaded in memory.

At this stage, you might not see the value in these reflective methods, but as you progress toward becoming more proficient with Ruby and object orientation, they'll become more important. This book doesn't go deeply into metaprogramming and advanced reflective techniques since they are beyond the scope of a beginner's book.

Encapsulation

Encapsulation describes the way in which data and methods can be bundled together into objects that operate as a single unit. Encapsulation keeps functionality hidden inside your classes and allows you to control how the outside world manipulates your object's data (thus maintaining the overall "single unit" of data and code bound together). You can extend and change your classes without worrying that other elements of your application will break.

Here's an example class that represents a person:

```ruby
class Person
  def initialize(name)
    set_name(name)
  end

  def name
    @first_name + ' ' + @last_name
  end

  def set_name(name)
    first_name, last_name = name.split(/\s+/)
    set_first_name(first_name)
    set_last_name(last_name)
  end

  def set_first_name(name)
    @first_name = name
  end

  def set_last_name(name)
    @last_name = name
  end
end
```

In previous examples, you would have written this with a single `attr_accessor` `:name` and simply assigned the name to an object variable. Our example is only to highlight the concept of encapsulation. You should use `attr_accessor` to accomplish the same functionality in your real code.

In this case, the first name and last name are stored separately within each `Person` object, in object variables called `@first_name` and `@last_name`. When a `Person` object is created, the name is split into two halves and each is assigned to the correct object variable by `set_first_name` and `set_last_name`, respectively. One possible reason for such a construction could be that although you want to work with complete names in your application, the database design might demand you have first names and last names in separate columns. Therefore, you need to hide this difference by handling it in the class code, as in the preceding code.

Note   A side benefit of this approach is that you can perform checks on the data before assigning it to the object variables. For example, in the `set_first_name` and `set_last_name` methods, you could check that the names contain enough characters to be considered valid names. If not, you can then raise an error.

The code appears to work fine:

```
p = Person.new("Fred Bloggs")
puts p.name
```

```
Fred Bloggs
```

However, you still seem to have some problems:

```
p = Person.new("Fred Bloggs")
p.set_last_name("Smith")
puts p.name
```

```
Fred Smith
```

Uh-oh! You wanted to abstract the first name/last name requirement and only allow full names to be set or retrieved. However, the `set_first_name` and `set_last_name` are still public and you can use them directly from any code where you have `Person` objects. Luckily, encapsulation lets you solve the problem:

```ruby
class Person
  def initialize(name)
    set_name(name)
  end

  def name
    @first_name + ' ' + @last_name
  end

private

  def set_name(name)
    first_name, last_name = name.split(/\s+/)
    set_first_name(first_name)
    set_last_name(last_name)
  end

  def set_first_name(name)
    @first_name = name
  end

  def set_last_name(name)
    @last_name = name
  end
end
```

The only difference in the Person class from the first example is the keyword private has been added. private tells Ruby that any methods declared in this class from there on should be kept private. This means that only code within the object's methods can access those private methods, whereas code outside of the class cannot. For example, this code no longer works:

```ruby
p = Person.new("Fred Bloggs")
p.set_last_name("Smith")
```

```
NoMethodError (undefined method `set_last_name' for
#<Person:0x00007faedfb31538 @age="Fred Bloggs">)
```

The opposite of the private keyword is public. You could put private before one method, but then revert to public methods again afterward using public, like so:

```ruby
class Person
  def anyone_can_access_this
    ...
  end

  private
  def this_is_private
    ...
  end

  public
  def another_public_method
    ...
  end
end
```

You can also use `private` as a command by passing in symbols representing the methods you want to keep private, like so:

```ruby
class Person
  def anyone_can_access_this; ...; end

  def this_is_private; ...; end

  def this_is_also_private; ...; end

  def another_public_method; ...; end

  private :this_is_private, :this_is_also_private
end
```

Note   Ruby supports ending lines of code with semicolons (;) and allows you to put multiple lines of code onto a single line (e.g., x = 10; x += 1; putsx). In this case, it's been done to save on lines of code in the example, although it's not considered good style in production-quality Ruby code.

The command tells Ruby that `this_is_private` and `this_is_also_private` are to be made into `private` methods. Whether you choose to use `private` as a directive before methods or as a command specifying the method names directly is up to you, and is another of many technically unimportant stylistic decisions you'll make as a Ruby programmer. However, it's important to note that in the preceding example, the `private` declaration has to come after the methods are defined.

Ruby supports a third form of encapsulation (other than `public` and `private`) called `protected` that makes a method private, but within the scope of a class rather than within a single object. For example, you were unable to directly call a private method outside the scope of that object and its methods. However, you can call a `protected` method from the scope of the methods of any object that's a member of the same class:

```ruby
class Person
  def initialize(age)
    @age = age
  end

  def age
    @age
  end

  def age_difference_with(other_person)
    (self.age - other_person.age).abs
  end

  protected :age
end

fred = Person.new(34)
chris = Person.new(25)
puts chris.age_difference_with(fred)
puts chris.age
```

```
9
MethodError (protected method `age' called for #<Person:0x00007faedfaebad8
@age=25>)
```

The preceding example uses a `protected` method so that the `age` method cannot be used directly, except within any method belonging to an object of the `Person` class. However, if `age` were made `private`, the preceding example would fail because `other_person.age` would be invalid. That's because `private` makes methods accessible only by methods of a specific object.

Note that when you use `age` directly, on the last line, Ruby throws an exception.

Polymorphism

Polymorphism is the concept of writing code that can work with objects of multiple types and classes at once. For example, the + method works for adding numbers, joining strings, and adding arrays together. What + does depends entirely on *what* type of things you're adding together.

Here's a Ruby interpretation of a common demonstration of polymorphism:

```ruby
class Animal
  attr_accessor :name

  def initialize(name)
    @name = name
  end
end

class Cat < Animal
  def talk
    "Meaow!"
  end
end

class Dog < Animal
  def talk
    "Woof!"
  end
end

animals = [Cat.new("Flossie"), Dog.new("Clive"), Cat.new("Max")]
animals.each do |animal|
```

```
  puts animal.talk
end
```

```
Meaow!
Woof!
Meaow!
```

In this example, you define three classes: an Animal class and Dog and Cat classes that inherit from Animal. In the code at the bottom, you create an array of various animal objects: two Cat objects and a Dog object (whose names are all processed by the generic initialize method from the Animal class).

Next, you iterate over each of the animals, and on each loop, you place the animal object into the local variable, animal. Last, you run puts animal.talk for each animal in turn. As the talk method is defined on both the Cat and Dog class, but with different output, you get the correct output of two "Meaow!"s and two "Woof!"s.

This demonstration shows how you can loop over and work on objects of different classes, but get the expected results in each case if each class implements the same methods.

If you were to create new classes under the Cat or Dog classes with inheritance (e.g., class Labrador < Dog), then Labrador.new.talk would still return "Woof!" thanks to inheritance.

Some of Ruby's built-in standard classes (such as Array, Hash, String, and so on) have polymorphic methods of their own. For example, you can call the to_s method on many built-in classes to return the contents of the object as a string:

```
puts 1000.to_s
puts [1,2,3].to_s
puts ({ name: 'Fred', age:10 }).to_s
```

```
1000
[1,2,3]
{:name => 'Fred', :age => 10}
```

The output isn't particularly useful in this case, but being able to rely on most objects to return a string with to_s can come in useful in many situations, such as when putting representations of objects into strings.

Nested Classes

In Ruby, it's possible to define classes *within* other classes. These are called *nested* classes. Nested classes are useful when a class depends on other classes, but those classes aren't necessarily useful anywhere else. They can also be useful when you want to separate classes into groups of classes rather than keep them all distinct. Here's an example:

```ruby
class Drawing
  class Line
  end

  class Circle
  end
end
```

Nested classes are defined in the same way as usual. However, they're used differently.

From within Drawing, you can access the Line and Circle classes directly, but from outside the Drawing class, you can only access Line and Circle as Drawing::Line and Drawing::Circle, for example:

```ruby
class Drawing
  def self.give_me_a_circle
    Circle.new
  end

  class Line
  end

  class Circle
    def what_am_i
      "This is a circle"
    end
  end
end

a = Drawing.give_me_a_circle
puts a.what_am_i
```

```
b = Drawing::Circle.new
puts b.what_am_i
c = Circle.new
puts c.what_am_i
```

```
This is a circle
NameError (uninitialized constant Circle)
This is a circle
```

a = Drawing.give_me_a_circle calls the give_me_a_circle class method, which returns a new instance of Drawing::Circle. Next, a = Drawing::Circle.new gets a new instance of Drawing::Circle directly, which also works. The third attempt, a = Circle. new, does not work, however, because Circle doesn't exist. That's because as a nested class under Drawing, it's known as Drawing::Circle instead.

You're going to use nested classes in a project at the end of this chapter, where you'll see how they work in the scope of an entire program.

The Scope of Constants

In Chapter 3, you looked at constants: special variables whose value(s) are unchanging and permanent throughout an application, such as Pi = 3.141592. Here's an example:

```
def circumference_of_circle(radius)
  2 * Pi * radius
end

Pi = 3.141592
puts circumference_of_circle(10)
```

```
62.83184
```

In this sense, a constant appears to work like a global variable, but it's not. Constants are defined within the scope of the current class and are made available to all child classes, unless they're overridden, for example:

```
Pi = 3.141592
```

```
class OtherPlanet
  Pi = 4.5
  def self.circumference_of_circle(radius)
    radius * 2 * Pi
  end
end

puts OtherPlanet.circumference_of_circle(10)
```

```
90.0
```

```
puts OtherPlanet::Pi
```

```
4.5
```

```
puts Pi
```

```
3.141592
```

This example demonstrates that constants have scope within the context of classes. The OtherPlanet class has its own definition of Pi. However, if you hadn't redefined it there, the original Pi would have been available to OtherPlanet, as the OtherPlanet class is defined within the global scope.

The second section of the preceding example also demonstrates that you can interrogate constants within other classes directly. OtherPlanet::Pi refers directly to the Pi constant within OtherPlanet.

Modules, Namespaces, and Mix-Ins

Modules provide a structure to collect Ruby classes, methods, and constants into a single, separately named and defined unit. This is useful so you can avoid clashes with existing classes, methods, and constants, and also so that you can add (mix-in) the functionality of modules into your classes. First, we'll look at how to use modules to create *namespaces* to avoid name-related clashes.

Namespaces

One common feature used in Ruby is the ability to include code situated in other files into the current program (this is covered in depth in the next chapter). When including other files, you can quickly run into conflicts, particularly if files or libraries you're including then include multiple files of their own. You cannot guarantee that no file that's included (or one that's included in a long chain of `includes`) will clash with code you've already written or processed.

Take this example:

```ruby
def random
  rand(1000000)
end

puts random
```

The `random` method returns a random number between 0 and 999,999. This method could be in a remote file where it's easily forgotten, which would cause problems if you had another file you included using `require` that implemented a method like so:

```ruby
def random
  (rand(26) + 65).chr
end
```

This `random` method returns a random capital letter.

Note   `(rand(26) + 65).chr` generates a random number between 0 and 25 and adds 65 to it, giving a number in the range of 65 to 90. The `chr` method then converts a number into a character using the ASCII standard where 65 is A, through to 90, which is Z. You can learn more about the ASCII character set at `https://en.wikipedia.org/wiki/ASCII`, or refer to Chapter 3, where this topic was covered in more detail.

Now you have two methods called `random`. If the first `random` method is in a file called `number_stuff.rb` and the second `random` method is in a file called `letter_stuff.rb`, you're going to hit problems:

```ruby
require './number_stuff'
```

```
require './letter_stuff'
```

```
puts random
```

Which version of the random method is called?

Note   require is a Ruby statement used to load in code contained within another file. This is covered in detail in the next chapter.

As the last file loaded, it turns out to be the latter version of random, and a random letter should appear onscreen. Unfortunately, however, it means your other random method has been "lost."

This situation is known as a *name conflict*, and it can happen in even more gruesome situations than the simplistic example shown in the preceding code. For example, class names can clash similarly, and you could end up with two classes mixed into one by accident. If a class called Song is defined in one external file and then defined in a second external file, the class Song available in your program will be a dirty mix of the two. Sometimes this might be the intended behavior, but in other cases, this can cause significant problems.

Modules help to solve these conflicts by providing *namespaces* that can contain any number of classes, methods, and constants and allow you to address them directly, for example:

```
module NumberStuff
  def self.random
    rand(1000000)
  end
end
```

```
module LetterStuff
  def self.random
    (rand(26) + 65).chr
  end
end
```

```
puts NumberStuff.random
```

```
puts LetterStuff.random
```

```
184783
X
```

Note   Due to the randomness introduced by using `rand`, the results will vary every time you run the program!

In this demonstration, it's clear which version of `random` you're trying to use in the two last lines. The `modules` defined in the preceding code look a little like classes, except they're defined with the word `module` instead of `class`. However, in reality you cannot create instances of a module, as they're not actually classes, nor can they inherit from anything. Modules simply provide ways to organize methods, classes, and constants into separate namespaces.

A more complex example could involve demonstrating two classes with the same name, but in different modules:

```
module ToolBox
  class Ruler
    attr_accessor :length
  end
end

module Country
  class Ruler
  attr_accessor :name
  end
end

a = ToolBox::Ruler.new
a.length = 50
b = Country::Ruler.new
b.name = "Genghis Khan from Moskau"
```

Rather than having the `Ruler` classes fighting it out for supremacy, or ending up with a mutant `Ruler` class with both `name` and `length` attributes (how many measuring rulers have names?), the `Ruler` classes are kept separately in the `ToolBox` and `Country` namespaces.

You'll be looking at why namespaces are even more useful than this later, but first you have to look at the second reason why modules are so useful.

Mix-Ins

Earlier you studied inheritance: the feature of object orientation that allows classes (and their instance objects) to inherit methods from other classes. You discovered that Ruby doesn't support *multiple inheritance*, the ability to inherit from multiple classes at the same time. Instead, Ruby's inheritance functionality only lets you create simple trees of classes, avoiding the confusion inherent with multiple inheritance systems.

However, in some cases it can be useful to share functionality between disparate classes. In this sense, modules act like a sort of bundle of methods, classes, and constants that can be *included* into other classes, extending that class with the methods the module offers, for example:

```ruby
module UsefulFeatures
  def class_name
    self.class.to_s
  end
end

class Person
  include UsefulFeatures
end

x = Person.new
puts x.class_name
```

```
Person
```

In this code, UsefulFeatures looks almost like a class and, well, it almost is. However, modules are organizational tools rather than classes themselves. The class_ name method exists within the module and is then *included* in the Person class. Here's another example:

```ruby
module AnotherModule
  def do_stuff
    puts "This is a test"
```

```
  end
end

include AnotherModule
do_stuff
```

```
This is a test
```

As you can see, you can include module methods in the current scope, even if you're not directly within a class. Somewhat like a class, though, you can use the methods directly:

```
AnotherModule.do_stuff
```

Therefore, `include` takes a module and includes its contents into the current scope.

Ruby comes with several modules by standard that you can use. For example, the `Kernel` module contains all the "standard" commands you use in Ruby (such as `load`, `require`, `exit`, `puts`, and `eval`) without getting involved with objects or classes. None of those methods are taking place directly in the scope of an object (as with the methods in your own programs), but they're special methods that get included in all classes (including the `main` scope), by default, through the `Kernel` module.

However, of more interest to us are the modules Ruby provides that you can include in your own classes to gain more functionality immediately. Two such modules are `Enumerable` and `Comparable`.

Enumerable

In previous chapters, you've performed the process of *iteration*, like so:

```
[1,2,3,4,5].each { |number| puts number }
```

In this case, you create a temporary array containing the numbers 1 through 5 and use the *each* iterator to pass each value into the code block, assigning each value to `number` that you then print to the screen with `puts`.

The each iterator gives you a lot of power, as it allows you to go through all the elements of an array or a hash and use the data you retrieve to work out, for example, the mean of an array of numbers, or the length of the longest string in an array, like so:

```
my_array = %w{this is a test of the longest word check}
```

```
longest_word = ''
my_array.each do |word|
  longest_word = word if longest_word.length < word.length
end
puts longest_word
```

```
longest
```

In this case, you loop through my_array, and if the currently stored longest word is shorter than the length of word, you assign it to longest_word. When the loop finishes, the longest word is in longest_word.

The same code could be tweaked to find the largest (or smallest) number in a set of numbers:

```
my_array = %w{10 56 92 3 49 588 18}
highest_number = 0
my_array.each do |number|
  number = number.to_i
  highest_number = number if number > highest_number
end
puts highest_number
```

```
588
```

However, the Array class (for one) has pre-included the methods provided by the Enumerable module, a module that supplies about 20 useful counting and iteration-related methods, including collect, detect, find, find_all, include?, max, min, select, sort, and to_a. All of these use Array's each method to do their jobs, and if your class can implement an *each* method, you can include Enumerable, and get all those methods for free in your own class!

First, some examples of the methods provided by Enumerable:

```
[1,2,3,4].collect { |i| i.to_s + "x" }
```

```
=> ["1x", "2x", "3x", "4x"]
```

```
[1,2,3,4].detect { |i| i.between?(2,3) }
```

```
=> 2
```

```
[1,2,3,4].select { |i| i.between?(2,3) }
```

```
=> [2,3]
```

```
[4,1,3,2].sort
```

```
=> [1,2,3,4]
```

```
[1,2,3,4].max
```

```
=> 4
```

```
[1,2,3,4].min
```

```
=> 1
```

You can make your own class, implement an *each* method, and get these methods for "free":

```
class AllVowels
  VOWELS = %w{a e i o u}

  def each
    VOWELS.each { |v| yield v }
  end
end
```

This is a class that, in reality, doesn't need to provide multiple objects, as it only provides an enumeration of vowels. However, to keep the demonstration simple, it is ideal. Here's how it works:

```
x = AllVowels.new
x.each { |v| puts v }
```

```
a
e
i
o
u
```

Your `AllVowels` class contains an array constant containing the vowels, and the instance-level each method iterates through the array constant `VOWELS` and yields to the code block supplied to each, passing in each vowel, using `yield v`. Let's get Enumerable involved:

```
class AllVowels
  include Enumerable

  VOWELS = %w{a e i o u}

  def each
    VOWELS.each { |v| yield v }
  end
end
```

Note   `yield` and its relationship to code blocks were covered near the end of Chapter 3; refer to that if you need a refresher.

Now let's try to use those methods provided by `Enumerable` again. First, let's get an `AllVowels` object:

```
x = AllVowels.new
```

Now you can call the methods on x:

```
x.collect { |i| i + "x" }
```

```
=> ["ax", "ex", "ix", "ox", "ux"]
```

```
x.detect { |i| i > "j" }
```

```
=> "o"
```

```
x.select { |i| i > "j" }
```

```
=> ["o", "u"]
```

```
x.sort
```

```
=> ["a", "e", "i", "o", "u"]
```

```
x.max
```

```
=> "u"
```

```
x.min
```

```
=> "a"
```

Comparable

The Comparable module provides methods that give other classes comparison operators such as < (less than), <= (less than or equal to), == (equal to), >= (greater than or equal to), and > (greater than), as well as the between? method that returns true if the value is between (inclusively) the two parameters supplied (e.g., 4.between?(3,10) == true).

To provide these methods, the Comparable module uses the <=> comparison operator on the class that includes it. <=> returns -1 if the supplied parameter is higher than the object's value, 0 if they are equal, or 1 if the object's value is higher than the parameter, for example:

```
1 <=> 2
```

```
-1
```

```
1 <=> 1
```

```
0
```

```
2 <=> 1
```

```
1
```

With this simple method, the Comparable module can provide the other basic comparison operators and between?. Create your own class to try it out:

```
class Song
  include Comparable

  attr_accessor :length

  def <=>(other)
    @length <=> other.length
  end

  def initialize(song_name, length)
    @song_name = song_name
    @length = length
  end
end

a = Song.new('Rock around the clock', 143)
b = Song.new('Bohemian Rhapsody', 544)
c = Song.new('Minute Waltz', 60)
```

Here are the results of including the Comparable module:

```
a < b
```

```
=> true
```

```
b >= c
```

```
=> true
```

```
c > a
```

```
=> false
```

```
a.between?(c,b)
```

```
=> true
```

You can compare the songs as if you're comparing numbers. Technically, you are. By implementing the <=> method on the Song class, individual song objects can be compared directly, and you use their lengths to do so. You could have implemented <=> to compare by the length of the song title, or any other attribute, if you wished.

Modules give you the same ability to implement similar generic sets of functionality that you can then apply to arbitrary classes. For example, you could create a module that implements longest and shortest methods that could be included into Array, Hash, or other classes and returns the longest or shortest string in a list.

Using Mix-Ins with Namespaces and Classes

In a previous example, I demonstrated how you can use modules to define namespaces using the following code:

```
module ToolBox
  class Ruler
  attr_accessor :length
  end
end

module Country
  class Ruler
    attr_accessor :name
  end
end

a = ToolBox::Ruler.new
```

```
a.length = 50
b = Country::Ruler.new
b.name = "Genghis Khan of Moskau"
```

In this case, the `Ruler` classes were accessed by directly addressing them via their respective modules (as `ToolBox::Ruler` and `Country::Ruler`).

However, what if you wanted to assume temporarily that `Ruler` (with no module name prefixed) was `Country::Ruler` and that if you wanted to access any other `Ruler` class, you'd refer to it directly? `include` makes it possible.

In the previous sections, you've used `include` to include the methods of a module in the current class and scope, but it also includes the classes present within a module (if any) and makes them locally accessible too. Say, after the prior code, you did this:

```
include Country
c = Ruler.new
c.name = "King Henry VIII"
```

Success! The `Country` module's contents (in this case, just the `Ruler` class) are brought into the current scope, and you can use `Ruler` as if it's a local class. If you want to use the `Ruler` class located under `ToolBox`, you can still refer to it directly as `ToolBox::Ruler`.

STATIC TYPING

As you are aware by this point in the book, Ruby is a dynamically typed language. This means a variable's type is determined at runtime. For example, if you assign the value 3 to a variable named `count`, Ruby interprets that line and sets `count` to the type Integer:

```
count = 3
puts count.class
=> Integer
```

Dynamic typing provides flexibility, which in turn makes Ruby great for rapid development and creating expressive code. These benefits come at a cost. Managing large projects written in Ruby can be a significant undertaking. Statically typed languages like C# negate these issues by performing several checks at compile time to catch issues that would appear only at runtime for Ruby.

Since Ruby 3, it's possible to use static typing via an opt-in system called RBS. There are many benefits when using RBS:

- *Uncover more bugs*: Since RBS provides a way to define precisely what type a class, method, or property requires, we can perform checks similar to statically typed languages before runtime. This will uncover issues like undefined methods and type mismatches. Problems like this are common as a codebase matures and receives numerous refactors. Catching these issues before runtime will save you many headaches.

- *Nil safety*: RBS makes it possible to specify whether or not a method can accept a nil value.

- *Guided duck typing*: In Ruby, if it sounds like a duck and acts like a duck, it must be a duck. This concept is fundamental in duck typing. RBS removes the guessing and provides interface types to ensure an object is a duck. Interface types specify the exact method signatures an object needs to implement to pass to a method.

- *IDE integration*: RBS provides IDEs with a better understanding of our source code. This means better integration with your favorite IDE. While all of this sounds great, it requires some work on the developer's part to implement.

To use RBS, create a separate .rbs file with the same name as the .rb file you want to enable static typing. Having a separate file means we don't need to use static typing on all of our classes. We can slowly adopt RBS on a per-class basis.

Look at this example:

```
# sig/employee.rbs
class Employee
  attr_reader name: String
  attr_reader security_level: Integer
  attr_reader email_addresses: Array[String]

  def initialize: (name: String, security_level:Integer) -> void

  def access_granted?: (level:Integer) -> bool
end
```

Here we define an rbs file for the class Employee. You will notice this looks similar to a standard Ruby class except for some additional syntax. At the end of the **attr_reader** definition, there is a type declaration. This type declaration states the property can only accept values of the specified type. In the example, **name** accepts String values, while **security_level** accepts Integer values. It's also possible to specify more complex types. The property **email_addresses** only allows arrays of type String.

Next, notice the method signatures. With RBS, we can specify the parameter types as well as the type of the return value. The initialize method doesn't return anything value, so its return type is void, meaning nothing. The access_granted? method returns a bool or Boolean value.

We have only skimmed the surface of RBS. Visit the GitHub page for more info: `https://github.com/ruby/rbs`.

Building a Dungeon Text Adventure with Objects

So far in this chapter, you've looked at object-oriented concepts in depth, mostly in a technical sense. At this point, it would be useful to extend that knowledge by applying it in a real-world scenario.

In this section, you're going to implement a mini text adventure/virtual dungeon. Text adventures were popular in the 1980s, but have fallen out of favor with modern gamers seeking graphical thrills. They're perfect playgrounds for experimenting with classes and objects, though, as replicating the real world in a virtual form requires a complete understanding of mapping real-world concepts into classes.

Dungeon Concepts

Before you can develop your classes, you have to figure out what you're trying to model. Your dungeon isn't going to be complex at all, but you'll design it to cope with at least the following concepts:

- *Dungeon*: You need a general class that encapsulates the entire concept of the dungeon game.

- *Player*: The player provides the link between the dungeon and you. All experience of the dungeon comes through the player. The player can move between rooms in the dungeon.

- *Rooms*: The rooms of the dungeon are the locations that the player can navigate between. These will be linked together in multiple ways (e.g., doors to the north, west, east, and south) and have descriptions.

A complete adventure would also have concepts representing items, enemies, other characters, waypoints, spells, and triggers for various puzzles and outcomes. You could easily extend what you'll develop into a more complete game later on if you want.

Creating the Initial Classes

Our first concept to develop is that of the dungeon and the game itself. Within this framework come the other concepts, such as the player and rooms.

Using nested classes, you can lay down the initial code like so:

```
class Dungeon
  attr_accessor :player

  def initialize(player)
    @player = player
    @rooms = {}
  end
end

class Player
  attr_accessor :name, :location

  def initialize(player_name)
    @name = player_name
  end
end

class Room
  attr_accessor :reference, :name, :description, :connections

  def initialize (reference, name, description, connections)
    @reference = reference
    @name = name
    @description = description
    @connections = connections
  end
end
```

185

This code lays down the framework for your dungeon.

Your dungeon currently has instance variables to store the player (since the player may change the state of the dungeon in some way) and the list of rooms (`@rooms = {}` creates an empty `Hash`; it's equivalent to `@rooms = Hash.new`).

The `Player` class lets the `player` object keep track of his or her name and current location. The `Room` class lets room objects store their name, description (e.g., "Torture Chamber" and "This is a dark, foreboding room."), and connections to other rooms, as well as a reference (to be used by other rooms for their connections).

When you create a dungeon with `Dungeon.new`, it expects to receive the name of the player, whereupon it creates that player and assigns it to the dungeon's object variable `@player`. This is because the player and the dungeon need to be linked, so storing the `player` object within the dungeon object makes sense. You can easily access the `player` because the player variable has been made into an accessor with `attr_accessor`, for example:

```
me = Player.new("Fred Bloggs")
my_dungeon = Dungeon.new(me)
puts my_dungeon.player.name
```

```
Fred Bloggs
```

You can access the player functionality directly by going *through* the dungeon object. As `@player` contains the `player` object, and as `@player` has been made publicly accessible with `attr_accessor :player`, you get complete access.

Structs: Quick and Easy Data Classes

One thing should stand out about the main code listing so far. It's repetitive. The `Room` and `Player` classes are merely acting as basic placeholders for data rather than as true classes with logic and functionality. There's an easier way to create this sort of special data-holding class in Ruby with a single line of a class called a *struct*.

A struct is a special class whose only job is to have attributes and to hold data. Here's a demonstration:

```
Person = Struct.new(:name, :gender, :age)
fred = Person.new("Fred", "male", 50)
```

```ruby
chris = Person.new("Chris", "male", 25)
puts fred.age + chris.age
```

75

Simply, the Struct class builds classes to store data. On the first line, you create a new class called Person that has built-in name, gender, and age attributes. On the second line, you create a new object instance of Person and set the attributes on the fly. The first line is equivalent to this longhand method:

```ruby
class Person
  attr_accessor :name, :gender, :age

  def initialize(name, gender, age)
    @name = name
    @gender = gender
    @age = age
  end
end
```

Note   In actuality, this code is not *exactly* equivalent to the struct code (though pragmatically it's close enough), because parameters are optional when initializing a Struct class, whereas the preceding Person class code requires the three parameters (name, gender, and age) be present.

This code creates a Person class the "long way." If all you want to do is store some data, then the struct technique is quicker to type and easier to read, although if you ultimately want to add more functionality to the class, creating a class the long way is worth the effort. However, the good thing is that you can start out with a struct and recode it into a full class when you're ready. This is what you're going to do with your dungeon. Let's rewrite it from scratch:

```ruby
class Dungeon
  attr_accessor :player

  def initialize(player)
    @player = player
```

```
      @rooms = {}
   end
end

Player = Struct.new(:name, :location)
Room = Struct.new(:reference, :name, :description, :connections)
```

It's certainly shorter, and because parameters are optional when creating instances of Struct classes, you can still use Player.new(player_name), and the location attribute is merely set to nil. If you ever need to add methods to Player or Room, you can rewrite them as classes and add the attributes back with attr_accessor.

ATTR_ACCESSOR

Throughout the code in this chapter, as well as in Chapter 2, you have used attr_accessor within classes to provide attributes for your objects. Recall that attr_accessor allows you to do this:

```
class Person
  attr_accessor :name, :age
end

x = Person.new
x.name = "Fred"
x.age = 10
puts x.name, x.age
```

However, in reality attr_accessor isn't doing anything magical. It's simply writing some code *for* you. This code is equivalent to the single attr_accessor :name, :age line in the preceding Person class:

```
class Person
  def name
    @name
  end

  def name=(name)
    @name = name
  end
```

```ruby
  def age
    @age
  end

  def age=(age)
    @age = age
  end
end
```

This code defines the name and age methods that return the current object variables for those attributes, so that x.name and x.age (as in the prior code) work. It also defines two "setter" methods that assign the values to the @name and @age object variables.

If you pay attention to the names of the setter methods, you'll see they're the same as the methods that return values but suffixed with an equals sign (=). This means they're the methods that are run for code such as x.name = "Fred" and x.age = 10. In Ruby, assignments are just calls to regular methods! Indeed, x.name = "Fred" is merely shorthand for x.name=("Fred").

Creating Rooms

Your dungeon now has the basic classes in place, but there's still no way to create rooms, so let's add a method to the Dungeon class:

```ruby
class Dungeon
  def add_room(reference, name, description, connections)
    @rooms[reference] = Room.new(reference, name, description, connections)
  end
end
```

You want to add rooms to the dungeon, so adding a method to dungeon objects makes the most sense. Now you can create rooms like so (if my_dungeon is still defined, of course):

```ruby
my_dungeon.add_room(:largecave, "Large Cave", "a large cavernous cave", {
west: :smallcave })


my_dungeon.add_room(:smallcave, "Small Cave", "a small, claustrophobic
cave", { east: :largecave })
```

add_room accepts the reference, name, description, and connections arguments and creates a new Room object with them before adding that object to the @rooms hash.

The reference, name, and descriptions arguments should seem obvious, but the connections argument is designed to accept a hash that represents the connections that a particular room has with other rooms. For example, { west: :smallcave } ties two symbols (:west and :smallcave) together. Your dungeon logic uses this link to connect the rooms. A connections hash of { west: :smallcave, south: :another_room } would create two connections (one to the west heading to "small cave" and one to the south heading to "another room").

Making the Dungeon Work

You have all the rooms loaded for your basic dungeon (and can add more whenever you like with the add_room method), but you have no way of navigating the dungeon itself.

The first step is to create a method within Dungeon that starts everything off by placing the user into the dungeon and giving you the description of the initial location:

```ruby
class Dungeon
  def start(location)
    @player.location = location
    show_current_description
  end

  def show_current_description
    puts find_room_in_dungeon(@player.location).full_description
  end

  def find_room_in_dungeon(reference)
    @rooms[reference]
  end
end

class Room
  def full_description
    @name + "\n\nYou are in " + @description
  end
end
```

You define a start method within the dungeon that sets the player's location attribute. It then calls the dungeon's show_current_description method, which finds the room based on the player's location, and then prints the full description of that location to the screen. full_description does the work of taking the location's name and description and turning it into a full, useful description. find_room_in_dungeon, on the other hand, returns the room whose reference matches that of the current location.

However, the problem with the preceding code is that Room is a struct, rather than a full class, so it becomes necessary to turn it into a full class once again (as hinted at earlier). This change requires a few key changes, so to keep things simple, here's the complete code so far, along with the change of Room to a regular class and some additional methods to aid navigation of the dungeon:

```ruby
class Dungeon
  attr_accessor :player

  def initialize(player)
    @player = player
    @rooms = {}
  end

  def add_room(reference, name, description, connections)
    @rooms[reference] = Room.new(reference, name, description, connections)
  end

  def start(location)
    @player.location = location
    show_current_description
  end

  def show_current_description
    puts find_room_in_dungeon(@player.location).full_description
  end

  def find_room_in_dungeon(reference)
    @rooms[reference]
  end

  def find_room_in_direction(direction)
    find_room_in_dungeon(@player.location).connections[direction]
```

```ruby
  end

  def go(direction)
    puts "You go " + direction.to_s
    @player.location = find_room_in_direction(direction)
    show_current_description
  end
end

class Player
  attr_accessor :name, :location
  def initialize(name)
    @name = name
  end
end

class Room
  attr_accessor :reference, :name, :description, :connections
  def initialize(reference, name, description, connections)
    @reference = reference
    @name = name
    @description = description
    @connections = connections
  end

  def full_description
    @name + "\n\nYou are in " + @description
  end
end

player = Player.new("Fred Bloggs")
my_dungeon = Dungeon.new(player)

# Add rooms to the dungeon
my_dungeon.add_room(:largecave,
                    "Large Cave",
                    "a large cavernous cave",
                    { west: :smallcave })
```

```
my_dungeon.add_room(:smallcave,
                    "Small Cave",
                    "a small, claustrophobic cave",
                    { east: :largecave })

# Start the dungeon by placing the player in the large cave
my_dungeon.start(:largecave)
```

```
Large Cave
You are in a large cavernous cave
```

It's a long piece of source code, but most of it should make sense by now. You've changed Room and Player into true classes once more and implemented the basics of the dungeon.

Two particularly interesting methods have been added to the Dungeon class:

```
def find_room_in_direction(direction)
  find_room_in_dungeon(@player.location).connections[direction]
end

def go(direction)
  puts "You go " + direction.to_s
  @player.location = find_room_in_direction(direction)
  show_current_description
end
```

The go method is what makes navigating the dungeon possible. It takes a single argument—the direction to travel in—and uses that to change the player's location to the room that's in that direction. It does this by calling find_room_in_direction, a method that takes the reference related to the relevant direction's connection on the current room, and returns the reference of the destination room. Remember that you define a room like so:

```
my_dungeon.add_room(:largecave,
                    "Large Cave",
                    "a large cavernous cave",
                    { west: :smallcave })
```

If :largecave is the current room, then find_room_in_direction(:west) will use the connections on that room to return :smallcave, and this is then assigned to @player. location to define that as the new current location.

To test the navigation of the dungeon, you can simply type the go commands if you're using irb, or if you're working with a source file in an editor, you'll need to add the go commands to the end of your source code and re-run it. Here's what happens:

```
my_dungeon.show_current_description
```

```
Large Cave
You are in a large cavernous cave
```

```
my_dungeon.go(:west)
```

```
You go west
Small Cave
You are in a small, claustrophobic cave
```

```
my_dungeon.go(:east)
```

```
You go east
Large Cave

You are in a large cavernous cave
```

The code has no error checking (try going to a nonexistent room with my_dungeon. go(:south)) and lacks items, an inventory, and other basic text-adventure features, but you now have an operational group of objects that represents a dungeon, and that can be navigated in a basic fashion.

This code is rife for extension and manipulation. With another class and several more methods, you could easily add support for items within the game that you can place at different locations, pick up, and then drop at other locations.

If you want an exercise, you can try turning the preceding dungeon code into a truly interactive program by creating a loop that uses the gets method to retrieve instructions from the player and then to "go" wherever the player determines. You can use chomp to strip off the newline characters from the incoming text and to_sym to convert strings into symbols for the go method. This might seem like a tough task at this stage, but if you pull it off, I guarantee you'll have learned a lot and you'll be confident about going on to the next chapter.

In Chapter 9, you'll look at how to interact with files and read data from the keyboard. At that point, you could extend the dungeon game to be properly interactive and accept input from the user, validate that it represents a valid direction, and then call the go method if so. With these additions and the addition of several more rooms, you're most of the way to a viable text adventure!

Summary

In this chapter, we covered the essentials of object orientation and the features Ruby provides to make object-oriented code a reality. You looked at the concepts that apply to object orientation in most languages, such as inheritance, encapsulation, class methods, instance methods, and the types of variables that you can use. Lastly, you developed a basic set of classes to produce a simple dungeon.

Let's reflect on some of the concepts we covered in this chapter:

- *Classes*: A class is a collection of methods and data that are used as a blueprint to create multiple objects relating to that class.

- *Objects*: An object is a single instance of a class. An object of class Person is a single person. An object of class Dog is a single dog. If you think of objects as real-life objects, a class is the classification, whereas an object is the actual object or "thing" itself.

- *Local variable*: A variable that can only be accessed and used from the current scope.

- *Instance/object variable*: A variable that can be accessed and used from the scope of a single object. An object's methods can all access that object's object variables.

- *Global variable*: A variable that can be accessed and used from anywhere within the current program.

- *Class variable*: A variable that can be accessed and used within the scope of a class and all of its child objects.

- *Encapsulation*: The concept of objects containing both data and methods that operate on that data, as well as allowing those methods to have differing degrees of visibility outside of their class or associated object.

- *Polymorphism*: The concept of methods being able to deal with different classes of data and offering a more generic implementation (as with the `area` and `perimeter` methods offered by your `Square` and `Triangle` classes).

- *Module*: An organizational element that collects together any number of classes, methods, and constants into a single namespace.

- *Namespace*: A named element of organization that keeps classes, methods, and constants from clashing.

- *Mix-in*: A module that can mix its methods in to a class to extend that class's functionality.

- *Enumerable*: A mix-in module, provided as standard with Ruby, that implements iterators and list-related methods for other classes, such as `collect`, `map`, `min`, and `max`. Ruby uses this module by default with the `Array` and `Hash` classes.

- *Comparable*: A mix-in module, provided as standard with Ruby, that implements comparison operators (such as `<`, `>`, and `==`) on classes that implement the generic comparison operator `<=>`.

Throughout the next several chapters, I'll assume you have knowledge of how classes and objects work and how the different scopes of variables (including local, global, instance, and class variables) work.

CHAPTER 7

Projects and Libraries

In previous chapters, we've looked at and worked with Ruby from a low-level perspective by working directly with classes, objects, and functions. Each line of code we've used in the small projects so far has been written specifically for that project from scratch. In this chapter, we'll look at how to build larger projects with Ruby and how to reuse code written previously. Finally, we'll look at how to use code already written and prepared by other developers within your own applications so that you don't need to reinvent the wheel every time you create a new program.

This chapter is about the bigger picture: dealing with projects and libraries.

Projects and Using Code from Other Files

As you become more familiar with Ruby and find more uses for it, it's likely that you'll want to move from writing single small programs (with fewer than 100 or so lines) to more complex applications and systems made up of multiple parts. Larger applications and systems therefore often become known as *projects* and are managed in a different way than simple one-file scripts.

The most common way to separate functionality in Ruby is to put different classes in different files. This gives you the ability to write classes that could be used in multiple projects simply by copying the file into your other project.

Basic File Inclusion

Consider this code:

```
puts "This is a test".vowels.join('-')
```

© Carleton DiLeo, Peter Cooper 2021
C. DiLeo and P. Cooper, *Beginning Ruby 3*, https://doi.org/10.1007/978-1-4842-6324-2_7

If you try to execute this code, you'll get an error complaining that the `vowels` method is not available for the "This is a test" object of class `String`. This is true because Ruby doesn't provide that method. Let's write an extension to the `String` class to provide it:

```ruby
class String
  def vowels
    self.scan(/[aeiou]/i)
  end
end
```

If this definition were included in the same file as the prior `puts` code—say, `my_test.rb`—the result would be as follows:

```
i-i-a-e
```

In this case, you've extended `String` with a `vowels` method that uses `scan` to return an array of all the vowels (the `i` option on the end makes the regular expression case-insensitive).

However, you might want to write a number of methods to add to `String` that you'd like to use in multiple programs. Rather than copy and paste the code each time, you can copy it to a separate file and use the `require` command to load the external file into the current program. For example, put this code in a file called `string_extensions.rb`:

```ruby
class String
  def vowels
    self.scan(/[aeiou]/i)
  end
end
```

And put this code in a file called `vowel_test.rb`:

```ruby
require './string_extensions'
puts "This is a test".vowels.join('-')
```

If you run `vowel_test.rb`, the expected result would appear onscreen. The first line, `require './string_extensions'`, simply loads in the `string_extensions.rb` file from the current directory (as signified by the `./`) and processes it as if the code were local. This means that, in this case, the `vowels` method is available, all with a single line.

Ruby does not include the current directory in the path of directories to search for Ruby files by default, so you can either specify the current directory specifically by using ./, as earlier, or by using require_relative. So this example is operationally identical to the previous one:

```
require_relative 'string_extensions'
puts "This is a test".vowels.join('-')
```

As well as require and require_relative, you can use load to load external source code files into your program. For example, this code would seem to function identically to the preceding code:

```
load 'string_extensions.rb'
puts "This is a test".vowels.join('-')
```

Note   load requires a full filename, including the .rb suffix, whereas require assumes the .rb suffix.

The output is the same in this case, but let's try a different example to see the difference. Put this in a .rb:

```
puts "Hello from a.rb"
```

And put this in a file called b.rb:

```
require_relative 'a'
puts "Hello from b.rb"
require_relative 'a'
puts "Hello again from b.rb"
```

Run with ruby b.rb to get the result:

```
Hello from a.rb
Hello rom  b.rb
Hello again from b.rb
```

In this example, the a.rb file is included only once. It's included on line 1, and "Hello from a.rb" gets printed to the screen, but then when it's included again on line 3 of b.rb, nothing occurs. In contrast, consider this code:

```
load 'a.rb'
puts "Hello from b.rb"
load 'a.rb'
puts "Hello again from b.rb"
```

```
Hello from a.rb
Hello from b.rb
Hello from a.rb
Hello again from b.rb
```

With load, the code is loaded and reprocessed anew each time you use the load method. require and require_relative, on the other hand, process external files only once.

Note   Ruby programmers nearly always use require or require_relative rather than load. The effects of load are useful only if the code in the external file has changed or if it contains active code that will be executed immediately.

Inclusions from Other Directories

load and require have different approaches to finding files to load. load and require_relative can bring in local files, but require does not. require 'a' looks for a.rb in a multitude of other directories on your storage drive. By default, these other directories are the various directories where Ruby stores its own files and libraries, although you can override this when necessary.

Ruby stores the list of directories to search for included files in a special variable called $: (or, if you prefer, $LOAD_PATH). You can see what $: contains by default using irb:

```
$:.each { |d| puts d }
/Library/Ruby/Site/3.0.0
/Library/Ruby/Site/3.0.0/x86_64-darwin19
/Library/Ruby/Site/3.0.0/universal-darwin19.
```

Note   This result is what appears on my machine, but the list of directories will probably differ significantly on your machine, particularly if you're using Windows, where the path layout will be entirely different, with the drive letter at the start and backslashes instead of forward slashes.

If you want to add directories to this, it's simple:

```
$:.push '/your/directory/here'
require 'yourfile'
```

`$:` is an array, so you can push extra items to it or use `unshift` to add an element to the start of the list (if you want your directory to be searched before the default Ruby ones—useful if you want to override Ruby's standard libraries).

Logic and Including Code

`require` and `load` both act like normal code in Ruby programs. You can put them at any point in your Ruby code, and they'll behave as if they were processed at that point, for example:

```
$debug_mode = 0
require_relative $debug_mode == 0 ? "normal-classes" : "debug-classes"
```

It's an obscure example, but it checks if the global variable `$debug_mode` is set to 0. If it is, it requires `normal-classes.rb` and, if not, `debug-classes.rb`. This gives you the power to include a different source file dependent on the value of a variable, ideal for situations where your application has "regular" and "debug" modes. You could even write an application that works perfectly, but then use a different `require` to include a whole different set of files that have new or experimental functionality.

A commonly used shortcut uses arrays to quickly load a collection of libraries at once, for example:

```
%w{file1 file2 file3 file4 file5}.each { |file| require file }
```

This loads five different external files or libraries with just two lines of code. However, some coders are not keen on this style, as it can make the code harder to read, even if it's more efficient.

Nested Inclusions

Code from files that are included in others with `require` and `load` has the same freedom as if the code were pasted directly into the original file. This means files that you include can call `load`, `require`, or `require_relative` themselves. For example, assume `a.rb` contains the following:

```
require_relative 'b'
```

and `b.rb` contains the following:

```
require_relative 'c'
```

and `c.rb` contains the following:

```
def example
  puts "Hello!"
end
```

and `d.rb` contains the following:

```
require_relative 'a'
example
```

When `d.rb` is then run,

```
Hello!
```

---

d.rb includes `a.rb` with `require`, `a.rb` includes `b.rb`, and `b.rb` includes `c.rb`, meaning the example method is available to `d.rb`.

This functionality makes it easy to put together large projects with interdependent parts, as the structure can be as deep as you like.

Libraries

In computer programming, a *library* is a collection of routines that can be called by separate programs but that exist independently of those programs. For example, you could create a library to load and process a data file and then use the routines in that library from any number of other programs.

Earlier in this chapter, we looked at using the `require` command to load external files into your Ruby programs, and back in Chapter 6, we looked at how modules can be used to separate elements of functionality into separate namespaces. You can use both of these concepts, jointly, to make libraries in Ruby.

At the start of this chapter, you developed an extremely simple library called `string_extensions.rb`, like so:

```ruby
class String
  def vowels
    self.scan(/[aeiou]/i)
  end
end
```

And you used this library with the following code:

```ruby
require 'string_extensions'
puts "This is a test".vowels.join('-')
```

```
i-i-a-e
```

Nearly all libraries are more complex than this simple example, but nonetheless, *this* is a basic demonstration of how a library works.

Next, we're going to look at the libraries that come standard with Ruby and look at a way to download and use libraries that other developers have made available on the Internet.

The Standard Libraries

Ruby comes with many standard libraries. They provide Ruby with a wide selection of functionality "out of the box," from webserving and networking tools through to encryption, benchmarking, and testing routines.

Note   Collectively the "standard libraries" are often called "the Standard Library." When you see this term (it's used particularly often in Chapter 16), it's important to remember it most likely refers to the collection rather than one library in particular—a "library of libraries," if you will.

In this section, we're going to look at how you can use just two random standard libraries (net/http and OpenStruct), so that you're prepared for using and working with other libraries in later chapters, where you'll be using many other standard libraries in a similar way. The choice of these two libraries is reasonably arbitrary, although both are commonly used by Rubyists whereas some of the standard libraries get little use at all.

A list of all the standard libraries, including documentation, is available at www.ruby-doc.org/stdlib/, although a sizable number of them are covered in more detail in Chapter 16 of this book.

Note   Some users might discover that the number of standard libraries might have been trimmed down, particularly if using a preinstalled version of Ruby. However, if you installed Ruby from source, all the demonstrations in this section should work.

---

net/http

HTTP stands for HyperText Transfer Protocol, and it's the main protocol that makes the World Wide Web work, as it provides the mechanism by which web pages, files, and other media can be sent between web servers and clients.

Ruby provides basic support for HTTP via the net/http library. For example, it's trivial to write a Ruby script that can download and print out the contents of a particular web page:

```ruby
require 'net/http'
uri = URI('https://ruby-doc.org')
http_request = Net::HTTP.new(uri.host, uri.port)
http_request.use_ssl = true
response = http_request.get('/')
puts response.body.force_encoding("ISO-8859-1")
```

If you run this code, after a few seconds, many pages of HTML code should fly past on your screen. The first line loads the net/http library into the current program, and the second line creates a URI (another standard library, and one that's loaded automatically by net/http) to decipher a URL into its constituent parts for the net/http library to use to make its request. The third line creates an instance of the Net::HTTP class (where Net is a module defining the Net namespace and HTTP is a subclass). The fourth line tells the Net::HTTP class to use ssl. On the fifth line, we call the get method which performs a HTTP GET request to https://ruby-doc.org/ and store the response in a variable. On the last line, we display the contents of the web page by calling the body method on the response variable. Since we are requesting a page that uses SSL, we need to tell Ruby to force the string encoding to ISO-8859-1. Hence, the additional method call force_encoding after calling body. Don't worry too much if you don't understand what encoding is and why we are using it. Just note that not all text is stored the same way on a computer. Sometimes we need to convert between different formats.

You may also see the net/http library being used like this:

```
require 'net/http'
url = URI.parse('https://ruby-doc.org/')
response = Net::HTTP.start(url.host, url.port, use_ssl: true) do |http|
  http.get(url.path)
end
content = response.body
```

In this example, a HTTP connection is "started," and within the scope of that connection, a GET request is made with the get method (if this doesn't make sense, don't worry; it's part of how the HTTP protocol works). Finally, you retrieve the content from response.body, a string containing the contents of the web page at https://ruby-doc.org/.

Note   The net/http library is only a basic library, and it requires its input to be sanitized in advance, as in the preceding examples. The URI library is ideally suited to this task.

In Chapter 14, we'll look at net/http and some of its sister libraries, such as net/pop and net/smtp, in more detail.

OpenStruct

In Chapter 6, you worked with a special type of data structure called Struct. Struct allowed you to create small data-handling classes on the fly, like so:

```
Person = Struct.new(:name, :age)
me = Person.new("Fred Bloggs", 25)
me.age += 1
```

Struct gives you the luxury of being able to create simple classes without having to define a class in the long-handed way.

The OpenStruct class provided by the ostruct library makes it even easier. It allows you to create data objects without specifying the attributes and allows you to create attributes on the fly:

```
require 'ostruct'
person = OpenStruct.new
person.name = "Fred Bloggs"
person.age = 25
```

person is a variable pointing to an object of class OpenStruct, and OpenStruct allows you to call attributes whatever you like, on the fly. It's similar to how a hash works, but using the object notation.

As the name implies, OpenStruct is more flexible than Struct, but this comes at the cost of harder-to-read code. There's no way to determine exactly, at a glance, which attributes have been used. However, with traditional structs, you can see the attribute names at the same place the struct is created.

RubyGems

RubyGems is a packaging system for Ruby programs and libraries. It enables developers to package their Ruby libraries in a form that's easy for users to maintain and install. RubyGems makes it easy to manage different versions of the same libraries on your machine and gives you the ability to install them with a single line at the command prompt.

Each individually packaged Ruby library (or application) is known simply as a gem or RubyGem. Gems have names, version numbers, and descriptions. You can manage your computer's local installations of gems using the gem command, available from the command line. RubyGems comes standard with Ruby nowadays, but it was not included with distributions of Ruby 1.8. You no longer need to be concerned with how it is installed as it's available "out of the box"!

Finding Gems

It's useful to get a list of the gems that are installed on your machine, as well as get a list of the gems available for download and installation. To do this, you use gem's list command. If you run the following command from your command line:

```
gem list
```

you'll get a result similar to this:

```
***   LOCAL    GEMS   ***

bigdecimal (2.0.0)
json (2.3.0)
minitest (5.14.0)
```

It's not much, but it's a start. This list shows that you have three different gems installed, along with their version numbers. Your list of gems may be significantly longer than this, but as long as it looks like a list and not an error message, you're good to go.

You can query the remote gem server (currently hosted by rubygems.org, but you can add other sources later) like so:

```
gem list --remote
abstract (1.0.0)
ackbar (0.1.1, 0.1.0)
action_profiler (1.0.0)
```

[..1,000s of lines about other gems removed for brevity..]

Within a minute or so, many thousands of gems and descriptions should go flying past.

Wading through such a list is impractical for most purposes, but generally you'll be aware of which gem you want to install before you get to this stage. People on the Internet will recommend gems, or you'll be asked to install a particular gem by this book or another tutorial.

However, if you wish to "browse," the best way to do so is to visit https://rubygems.org/, the home for the RubyGems repository. The site features search tools and more information about each gem in the repository.

Installing a Gem

Once you've found the name of a gem you wish to install, you can install it with a single command at the command line (where chronic would be replaced with the name of the gem you wish to install, although feedtools is a fine gem to test with):

```
gem install chronic
```

If all goes well, you'll get output like this:

```
Fetching: chronic-0.10.2.gem (100%)
Successfully installed chronic-0.10.2
Parsing documentation for chronic-0.10.2
Installing ri documentation for chronic-0.10.2
Done installing documentation for chronic after 1 seconds
1 gem installed
```

First, RubyGems looks to see if the gem exists in the current directory (you can keep your own store of gems locally, if you like), and if not, it heads off to rubygems.org to download the gem and install it from afar. Last, it builds the documentation for the library using rdoc (covered in Chapter 8), and installation is complete. This process is the same for nearly all gems.

> **Note**   In many cases, installing one gem requires other gems to be installed too. That is, the gem you're trying to install might have other gems it needs to operate, also known as "dependencies."

If you run gem list again at this point, your local list of gems will include the newly installed gem (in this case, chronic).

If you are aware that you need to install a specific version of a gem (such as version 0.10.2 of Chronic, as earlier), you can specify this like so:

```
gem install -v 0.10.2 chronic
```

Using Gems

As the RubyGems system isn't an integrated part of Ruby, it's necessary to tell your programs that you want to use and load gems.

We will use gem install chronic, as demonstrated earlier, to install the gem.

Once the gem is installed, run irb or create a new Ruby source file, and use the chronic gem like so:

```
require 'chronic'
puts Chronic.parse('may 10th')
```

```
2020-05-10 12:00:00 +0100
```

In this example, we load the Chronic library with require. The **'chronic'** refers to the main Ruby file and then we can use the Chronic class to do various things—in this case, time manipulation.

Upgrading and Uninstalling Gems

One of the main features of RubyGems is that gems can be updated easily. You can update all of your currently installed gems with a single line:

```
gem update
```

This makes RubyGems go to the remote gem repository, look for new versions of all the gems you currently have installed, and if there are new versions, install them. If you want to upgrade only a specific gem, suffix the preceding command line with the name of the gem in question.

Uninstalling gems is the simplest task of all. Use the `uninstall` command (where `feedtools` is replaced by the name of the gem you wish to uninstall):

```
gem uninstall feedtools
```

Note   Again, remember to use `sudo` when the situation demands it, as covered in previous sections.

If there are multiple versions of the same gem on the machine, RubyGems will ask you which version you want to uninstall first (or you can tell it to uninstall all versions at once), as in this example:

```
$ gem uninstall rubyforge
```

```
Select RubyGem to uninstall:
1. rubyforge-0.3.0
2. rubyforge-0.3.1
3. All versions
```

Creating Your Own Gems

Naturally, it's possible to create gems from your own libraries and applications. This entire process is covered in Chapter 10, along with the other ways you can deploy your applications to users.

Bundler

Bundler (`https://bundler.io/`) is a tool that was developed to help you manage the dependencies of a project (essentially, the libraries upon which your project depends) in a more structured way. It comes by default on some Ruby installs, but you can always ensure it's installed with `gem install bundler`.

Consider, for example, that you create a project that depends on several libraries or gems. To run this application locally, you'd need to make sure that you have the right versions of each gem installed on your system. But if you have numerous projects with wide varieties of dependencies, you'll start to find it hard to track which gems you have installed and what versions they are.

Bundler lets you create a file (called Gemfile) within a project's directory that specifies what libraries the project depends on. Here's an example of a very simple Gemfile:

```
source 'https://rubygems.org'
gem 'nokogiri'
gem 'rack', '~>1.5'
```

This specifies where the gems are to be downloaded from by default and then which two gems the current project depends upon. Nokogiri is specified without a version number, but in Rack's case, a version query is specified at the end of the line which says any version that's 1.5 or above (but not version 2 or above—so 1.5, 1.6, 1.6.13, etc.).

If you run bundle install from the directory where a Gemfile is present, Bundler ensures that the right gems are installed or upgraded to the right versions:

```
Fetching gem metadata from https://rubygems.org/.........
Resolving dependencies...
Using bundler 2.1.4
Using mini_portile2 2.4.0
Using nokogiri 1.10.9
Using rack 1.6.13
Bundle complete! 2 Gemfile dependencies, 4 gems now installed.
Use 'bundle show [gemname]` to see where a bundled gem is installed.
```

The correct gems, as specified in Gemfile, are now installed. You can use these from within your project, or if you want to ensure that the right versions are loaded, you can specify require 'bundler/setup' within your program, like so:

```
require 'bundler/setup'
require 'rack'
# Now Rack 1.5 or above is loaded properly and you can check by typing the
following:
Rack.version
Rack.release
```

One other thing to be aware of is that when you install or upgrade gems, another file is created or updated called Gemfile.lock. This is not a file you are meant to change yourself, but it simply reflects what the precise set of dependencies are, along with their version numbers, so that if you distribute the project anywhere else, the very same set of libraries and versions will be installed properly. Here's an example of the Gemfile.lock produced by the install earlier:

```
GEM
  remote: https://rubygems.org/
  specs:
    mini_portile2 (2.4.0)
    nokogiri (1.10.9)
      mini_portile2 (~> 2.4.0)
    rack (1.6.13)

PLATFORMS
  ruby

DEPENDENCIES
  nokogiri
  rack (~> 1.5)

BUNDLED WITH
   2.1.4
```

Even though our main Gemfile specifies any version of Rack over 1.5 and under 2.0, we specifically have 1.6.13 installed as that's the latest matching version at the time of writing. If I transferred this project to you in the future, however, 1.7 may be the latest matching Rack, and this could break the code. The Gemfile.lock's job, therefore, is to explicitly communicate which versions of which libraries are working with the project right now.

If you want to learn more about Bundler, visit https://bundler.io/.

Summary

In this chapter, we've looked at some of the methods Ruby provides to make it possible to handle large projects, as well as access the vast universe of prewritten code libraries to make development easier.

Ruby provides a wealth of useful libraries within the main distribution, but using tools such as RubyGems allows you to get access to code written by thousands of other Ruby developers, allowing you to implement more-complex programs more quickly than would otherwise be possible.

Let's reflect on the main concepts covered in this chapter:

- *Project*: Any collection of multiple files and subdirectories that form a single instance of a Ruby application or library.

- *Library*: A collection of routines, classes, methods, and/or modules that provides a set of features that many other applications can use.

- *RubyGems*: The packaging system for Ruby libraries and/or applications that makes them easier to install and maintain by developers.

- *Gem*: A single library (or application) packaged using the RubyGems system. Can also be called a "RubyGem."

- `require`: A method that loads and processes the Ruby code from a separate file, including whatever classes, modules, methods, and constants are in that file, into the current scope. `load` is similar, but rather than performing the inclusion operation once, it reprocesses the code every time `load` is called. `require_relative` is like `require` but lets you load files from the current directory too without prefixing their names with `./`.

- *Bundler*: A tool that makes it easier to handle the libraries that a particular application depends on. It can install gems, handle the upgrading of gems, and help lock certain versions of gems to your specific projects.

In many of the chapters from here on, we'll be using the power of libraries and combining multiple libraries to make single applications. One such example is the Ruby on Rails framework we'll be covering in Chapter 13, which is, in essence, a giant library made up of several libraries itself!

## CHAPTER 8

Documentation, Error Handling, Debugging, and Testing

In this chapter, we're going to look at the finer details of developing reliable programs: documentation, error handling, debugging, and testing. These tasks aren't what most people think of as "development," but are as important to the overall process as general coding tasks. Without documenting, debugging, and testing your code, it's unlikely that anyone but you could work on the code with much success, and you run the risk of releasing faulty scripts and applications.

This chapter demonstrates how to produce documentation, handle errors in your programs, test the efficiency of your code, and make sure that your code is (mostly) bug-free, all using tools that come with Ruby.

Documentation

Even if you're the only person to use and work on your Ruby code, it's inevitable that over time you'll forget the nuances of how it was put together and how it works. To guard against code amnesia, you should document your code as you develop it.

In the past, documentation would often be completed by a third party rather than the developer or would be written after the majority of the development had been completed. Although developers have used comments in their code, true documentation of a quality such that other developers and users can understand it without seeing the source code was an afterthought.

Ruby makes it extremely easy to document your code as you create it, using a utility called *RDoc* (standing for "Ruby Documentation").

© Carleton DiLeo, Peter Cooper 2021
C. DiLeo and P. Cooper, *Beginning Ruby 3*, https://doi.org/10.1007/978-1-4842-6324-2_8

Generating Documentation with RDoc

RDoc calls itself a "Document Generator for Ruby Source." It's a tool that reads through your Ruby source code files and creates structured HTML documentation. It comes with the standard Ruby distribution, so it's easy to find and use.

RDoc understands a lot of Ruby syntax and can create documentation for classes, methods, modules, and numerous other Ruby constructs without much prompting.

The way you document your code in a way that RDoc can use is to leave comments prior to the definition of the class, method, or module you want to document, for example:

```ruby
# This class stores information about people.
class Person
  attr_accessor :name, :age, :gender

  # Create the person object and store their name
  def initialize(name)
    @name = name
  end

  # Print this person's name to the screen
  def print_name
    puts "Person called #{@name}"
  end
end
```

This is a simple class that's been documented using comments. It's quite readable already, but RDoc can turn it into a pretty set of HTML documentation in seconds.

To use RDoc, simply run it from the command line using rdoc <name of source file>.rb, like so:

```
rdoc person.rb
```

Note   On Linux and OS X, this should simply work "out of the box" (as long as the directory containing RDoc—usually /usr/bin or /usr/local/bin—is in the path). On Windows, it might be necessary to prefix rdoc with its full location or add it to the PATH environment variable.

This command tells RDoc to process `person.rb` and produce the HTML documentation. By default, it does this by creating a directory called `doc` from the current directory and placing its HTML and CSS files in there. Once RDoc has completed, you can open `index.html`, located within `doc`, and you should see some basic documentation, as in Figure 8-1.

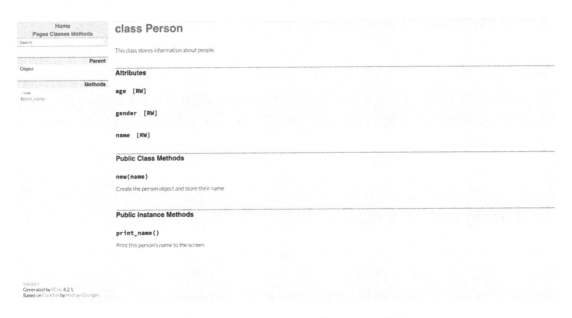

Figure 8-1. *Basic RDoc HTML output as seen from a web browser*

The HTML documentation is shown with three frames across the top containing links to the documented files, classes, and methods, respectively, and a main frame at the bottom containing the documentation being viewed at present. The top three frames let you jump between the various classes and methods with a single click. In a large set of documentation, this quickly becomes useful.

When viewing the documentation for the `Person` class, the documentation shows what methods it contains, the documentation for those methods, and the attributes the class provides for its objects. RDoc works this out entirely from the source code and your comments.

RDoc Techniques

In the prior section, you got RDoc to generate documentation from a few simple comments in your source file. However, RDoc is rarely useful on such a small example, and its real power comes into play when you're working on larger projects and using its advanced functions. This section will cover some of these functions so you can comment the code on your larger projects correctly.

Note   The following sections give only a basic overview of some of RDoc's features. To read the full documentation for RDoc and learn about features that are beyond the scope of this book, visit the official RDoc site at `https://ruby.github.io/rdoc/`.

Producing Documentation for an Entire Project

Previously you used `rdoc` along with a filename to produce documentation for a single file. However, in the case of a large project, you could have many hundreds of files that you want processed. If you run RDoc with no filenames supplied, RDoc will process all the Ruby files found in the current directory and all other directories under that. The full documentation is placed into the `doc` directory, as before, and the entire set of documentation is available from `index.html`.

Basic Formatting

Formatting your documentation for RDoc is easy. RDoc automatically recognizes paragraphs within your comments and can even use spacing to recognize structure. Here's an example of some of the formatting RDoc recognizes:

```
#= This is a 1st level heading
#
#
#* First item in an outer list
#  * First item in an inner list
#  * Second item in an inner list
#* Second item in an outer list
```

```
#   * Only item in this inner list
#
#== This is a second level heading
#
#Visit https://www.apress.com
#
#== Test of text formatting features
#
#Want to see *bold* or _italic_ text? You can even embed
#+text that looks like code+ by surrounding it with plus
#symbols. Indented code will be automatically formatted:
#
# class MyClass
#   def method_name
#     puts "test"
#   end
# end

class MyClass
end
```

If you process this with RDoc, you'll get a result that looks like Figure 8-2. To learn more about RDoc's general formatting features, the best method is to look at existing code that is extensively prepared for RDoc, such as the source code to the Ruby on Rails framework, or refer to the documentation at `https://ruby.github.io/rdoc/RDoc/Markup.html`.

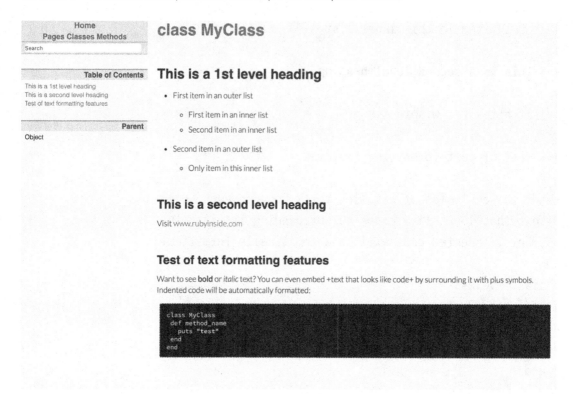

Figure 8-2. *How RDoc renders the formatting feature test file*

Modifiers and Options

RDoc can work without the developer knowing much about it, but to get the most from RDoc, it's necessary to know how several of its features work and how they can be customized. RDoc supports a number of modifiers within comments, along with a plethora of command-line options.

:nodoc: Modifier

By default, RDoc will attempt to use anything it considers relevant to build up its documentation. Sometimes, however, you'd rather RDoc ignore certain modules, classes, or methods, particularly if you haven't documented them yet. To make RDoc ignore something in this way, simply follow the module, class, or method definition with a comment of :nodoc:, like so:

```
# This is a class that does nothing
class MyClass
```

```
  # This method is documented
  def some_method
  end
  def secret_method #:nodoc:
  end
end
```

In this instance, RDoc will ignore `secret_method`.

`:nodoc:` only operates directly on the elements upon which it is placed. If you want `:nodoc:` to apply to the current element and all those beneath it (e.g., all methods within a class), do this:

```
# This is a class that does nothing
class MyClass #:nodoc: all
  # This method is documented (or is it?)
  def some_method
  end

  def secret_method
  end
end
```

Now *none* of `MyClass` is documented by RDoc.

Turning RDoc Processing On and Off

You can stop RDoc from processing comments temporarily using #++ and #--, like so:

```
# This section is documented and read by RDoc.
#--
# This section is hidden from RDoc and could contain developer
# notes, private messages between developers, etc.
#++
# RDoc begins processing again here after the ++.
```

This feature is particularly ideal in sections where you want to leave comments to yourself that aren't for general consumption.

> **Note**   RDoc doesn't process comments that are within methods, so your usual code comments are not used in the documentation produced. RDoc will also not process comments that are separated from other comments with blank lines.

Command-Line Options

Like most command-line applications, including Ruby itself, you can give RDoc a number of options, as follows:

- `--all`: Usually RDoc processes only public methods, but `--all` forces RDoc to document *all* methods within the source files.

- `--fmt <format name>`: Produce documentation in a certain format (which currently includes darkfish, pot, and ri).

- `--help`: Get help with using RDoc's command-line options and find out which output formatters are available.

- `--main <name>`: Set the class, module, or file that appears as the main index page for the documentation to <name> (e.g., `rdoc --main MyClass`).

After any command-line options, `rdoc` is suffixed with the filename(s) of the files you want to have RDoc document. Alternatively, if you specify nothing, RDoc will traverse the current directory and all subdirectories and generate documentation for your entire project.

> **Note**   RDoc supports many more command-line options than these, and they are all covered in RDoc's official documentation. Alternatively, run RDoc with `rdoc --help` at the command line to get a list of its options.

Debugging and Errors

Errors happen. It's unavoidable that programs you develop will contain bugs, and you won't immediately be able to see what the errors are. A misplaced character in a regular expression, or a typo with a mathematical symbol, can make the difference between a reliable program and one that constantly throws errors or generates undesirable output.

Exceptions and Error Handling

An exception is an event that occurs when an error arises within a program. An exception can cause the program to quit immediately with an error message or can be handled by *error-handling* routines within the program to recover from the error in a sensible way.

For example, a program might depend on a network connection (e.g., the Internet), and if the network connection is unavailable, an error will arise when the program attempts to use the network. Rather than brusquely terminating with an obscure error message, the code can handle the exception and print a human-friendly error message to the screen first. Alternatively, the program might have a mechanism by which it can work offline, and you can use the exception raised by trying to access an inaccessible network or server to enter that mode of operation instead.

Raising Exceptions

In Ruby, exceptions are packaged into objects of class `Exception` or one of `Exception`'s many subclasses. Ruby has many predefined exception classes that deal with different types of errors, such as `NoMemoryError`, `StandardError`, `RuntimeError`, `SecurityError`, `ZeroDivisionError`, and `NoMethodError`. You might have already seen some of these in error messages while working in irb.

When an exception is *raised* (exceptions are said to be *raised* when they occur within the execution of a program), Ruby immediately looks back up the tree of routines that called the current one (known as the *stack*) and looks for a routine that can handle that particular exception. If it can't find any error-handling routines, it quits the program with the raw error message, for example:

```
irb(main):001:0> puts 10 / 0
ZeroDivisionError (divided by 0)
        from (irb):1:in `/'
        from (irb):1
```

This error message shows that an exception of type `ZeroDivisionError` has been raised, because you attempted to divide ten by zero.

Ruby can raise exceptions automatically when you perform incorrect functions, and you can raise exceptions from your own code too. You do this with the `raise` method and by using an existing exception class or by creating one of your own that inherits from the `Exception` class.

One of the standard exception classes is `ArgumentError`, which is used when the arguments provided to a method are fatally flawed. You can use this class as an exception if bad data is supplied to a method of your own:

```ruby
class Person
  def initialize(name)
    raise ArgumentError, "No name present" if name.empty?
  end
end
```

If you create a new object from `Person` and supply a blank name, an exception will be raised:

```ruby
fred = Person.new('')
```

```
ArgumentError: No name present
```

Note   You can call `raise` with no arguments at all, and a generic `RuntimeError` exception will be raised. This is not good practice, though, as the exception will have no message or meaning along with it. Always provide a message and a class with `raise`, if possible.

However, you could create your own type of exception if you wanted to, for example:

```ruby
class BadDataException < RuntimeError
end

class Person
  def initialize(name)
    raise BadDataException, "No name present" if name.empty?
  end
end
```

This time you've created a `BadDataException` class inheriting from Ruby's standard `RuntimeError` exception class.

Now, creating a new object with the wrong type of parameter raises a BadDataException:

```
fred = Person.new('')
```

```
BadDataException (No name present)
```

At this point, it might seem meaningless as to why raising different types of exceptions is useful. The reason is so that you can handle different exceptions in different ways with your error-handling code, as you'll do next.

Handling Exceptions

In the previous section, we looked at how exceptions work. When raised, exceptions halt the execution of the program and trace their way back up the stack to find some code that can handle them. If no handler for the exception is found, the program ceases execution and dies with an error message with information about the exception.

However, in most situations, stopping a program because of a single error isn't necessary. The error might only be minor, or there might be an alternative option to try. Therefore, it's possible to *handle* exceptions. In Ruby, the rescue clause is used, along with begin and end, to define blocks of code to handle exceptions, for example:

```
begin
  puts 10 / 0
rescue
  puts "You caused an error!"
end
```

```
You caused an error!
```

In this case, begin and end define a section of code to be run, where if an exception arises, it's handled with the code inside the rescue block. First, you try to work out ten divided by zero, which raises an exception of class ZeroDivisionError. However, being inside a block containing a rescue section means that the exception is handled by the code inside that rescue section. Rather than dying with a ZeroDivisionError, the text "You caused an error!" is instead printed to the screen.

This can become important in programs that rely on external sources of data. Consider this pseudo-code:

```
data = ""
begin
  <..code to retrieve the contents of a Web page..>
  data = <..content of Web page..>
rescue
  puts "The Web page could not be loaded! Using default data instead."
  data = <..load data from local file..>
end
puts data
```

This code demonstrates why handling exceptions is extremely useful. If retrieving the contents of a web page fails (e.g., if you're not connected to the Internet), then the error-handling routine rescues the exception, alerts the user of an error, and then loads some data from a local file instead—certainly better than exiting the program immediately!

In the previous section, we looked at how to create your own exception classes, and the motivation for doing this is that it's possible to rescue different types of exceptions in a different way. For example, you might want to react differently if there's a fatal flaw in the code vs. a simple error such as a lack of network connectivity. There might also be errors you want to ignore and only specific exceptions you wish to handle.

rescue's syntax makes handling different exceptions in different ways easy:

```
begin
  ... code here ...
rescue ZeroDivisionError
  ... code to rescue the zero division exception here ...
rescue YourOwnException
  ... code to rescue a different type of exception here ...
rescue
  ... code that rescues all other types of exception here ...
end
```

This code contains multiple rescue blocks, each of which is caused depending on the type of exception raised. If a ZeroDivisionError is raised within the code between begin and the rescue blocks, the rescue ZeroDivisionError code is executed to handle the exception.

Handling Passed Exceptions

As well as handling different types of exceptions using different code blocks, it's possible to *receive* exceptions and use them. This is achieved with a little extra syntax on the rescue block:

```
begin
  puts 10 / 0
rescue => e
  puts "You caused the error -> #{e.class}"
end
```

```
ZeroDivisionError
```

Rather than merely performing some code when an exception is raised, the exception object itself is assigned to the variable e, whereupon you can use that variable however you wish. This is particularly useful if the exception class contains extra functionality or attributes that you want to access.

Catch and Throw

Although creating your own exceptions and exception handlers is useful for resolving error situations, sometimes you want to be able to break out of a thread of execution (say, a loop) during normal operation in a similar way to an exception, but without actually generating an error. Ruby provides two methods, catch and throw, for this purpose.

catch and throw work in a way a little reminiscent of raise and rescue, but catch and throw work with symbols rather than exceptions. They're designed to be used in situations where no error has occurred, but being able to escape quickly from a nested loop, method call, or similar is necessary.

The following example creates a block using catch. The catch block with the :finish symbol as an argument will immediately terminate (and move on to any code after that block) if throw is called with the :finish symbol:

```
catch(:finish) do
  1000.times do
    x = rand(1000)
    throw :finish if x == 123
  end

  puts "Generated 1000 random numbers without generating 123!"
end
```

Within the `catch` block, you generate 1000 random numbers, and if the random number is ever 123, you immediately escape out of the block using throw :`finish`. However, if you manage to generate 1000 random numbers without generating the number 123, the loop and the block complete, and you see the message.

`catch` and `throw` don't have to be directly in the same scope. `throw` works from methods called from within a `catch` block:

```
def generate_random_number_except_123
  x = rand(1000)
  throw :finish if x > 123 && x < 200
end

catch(:finish) do
  1000.times { generate_random_number_except_123 }
  puts "Generated 1000 random numbers without generating 123!"
end
```

This code operates in an identical way to the first. When `throw` can't find a code block using :`finish` in its current scope, it jumps back up the stack until it can.

The Ruby Debugger

Debugging is the process of fixing the bugs in a piece of code. This process can be as simple as changing a small section of your program, running it, monitoring the output, and then looping through this process again and again until the output is correct and the program behaves as expected.

However, constantly editing and re-running your program gives you no insight into what's actually happening deep within your code. Sometimes you want to know what each variable contains at a certain point within your program's execution, or you might want to force a variable to contain a certain value. You can use `puts` to show what variables contain at certain points in your program, but you can soon make your code messy by interspersing it with debugging tricks.

A debugging tool can *step* through your code line by line (if you wish), set *breakpoints* (places where execution will stop for you to check things out), and debug your code. Code execution pauses giving you control to analyze variables and run methods. It's a little like irb, except you don't need to type out a whole program. You can specify your program's filename, and you'll be acting as if you are within that program.

Ruby provides a debugger, but at the time of writing this book, it's not the primary way developers debug their code. There are two debuggers currently used: Pry and byebug. Since byebug is available by default in Rails, we will be covering it in this book. You will need to install byebug to use it with Ruby. Run the following command to install byebug:

gem install byebug

For example, create a basic Ruby script called `debugtest.rb`:

```
i = 1
j = 0
until i > 1000000
  i *= 2
  j += 1
end
puts "i = #{i}, j = #{j}"
```

If you run this code with `ruby debugtest.rb`, you'll get the following result:

```
i = 1048576, j = 20
```

But say you run it with byebug like this:

```
byebug debugtest.rb
```

You'll see something like this appear:

```
=> 1: i = 1
   2: j = 0
   3: until i > 1000000
```

```
    4:   i *= 2
    5:   j += 1
    6: end
    7: puts "i = #{i}, j = #{j}"
    8:
(byebug)
```

This means the debugger has loaded. Each line of our code is numbered and there is a hash rocket informing you where the debugger paused (the first line, in this case). In our example, the next line Ruby will interpret is line 1.

You may also place a **byebug** statement anywhere in your code to stop execution at that line:

```
require 'byebug'
i = 1
j = 0
byebug
until i > 1000000
  i *= 2
  j += 1
end
puts "i = #{i}, j = #{j}"
```

Using the byebug syntax means we can run the program using the ruby interpreter:

```
ruby debugtest.rb
```

which will output the following:

```
    1: require 'byebug'
    2:
    3: i = 1
    4: j = 0
    5: byebug
=>  6: until i > 1000000
    7:   i *= 2
    8:   j += 1
```

```
 9: end
10: puts "i = #{i}, j = #{j}"
(byebug)
```

Placing the byebug statement in your source code directly provides greater control over where the debugger stops the program execution. This method is used more often by developers.

The function of byebug is similar to irb, and you can type expressions and statements directly onto the prompt here. However, its main strength is that you can use special commands to run debugtest.rb line by line or set breakpoints.

Here are some useful commands to use at the debugger prompt. To use the command, you type either the first letter of the word or the whole word:

- (s)tep: Runs the next line of the program. Steps into method calls. After each step, you can check variables, change values, and so on. This allows you to trace the exact point at which bugs occur. Follow step by the number of lines you wish to execute if it's higher than one, such as step 2 to execute two lines.

- (n)ext: Runs the next line of the program. Same functionality as step, except next steps "over" method calls.

- (c)ontinue: Runs the program without stepping. Execution will continue until the program ends or reaches a breakpoint.

- (b)reak: Sets a breakpoint at the current line number. This means that if you continue execution with **continue**, execution will run until the breakpoint and stop again. This is useful for stopping execution inside of a loop.

- backtrace (bt or w): Displays the current stack trace. This is useful if you want to see which methods were called prior to the current method.

- (q)uit: Exits the debugger.

- restart: Restarts the program as well as byebug.

You can view the contents of a variable by typing the variable name and pressing Enter. Also, you can run any method or instantiate any class available to you in the current context. I recommend testing out different commands and looking at the documentation for byebug which can be found at `https://github.com/deivid-rodriguez/byebug`.

Testing

Testing is a powerful part of modern software development and can help you resolve many development snafus. Without a proper testing system in place, you can never be confident that your app is bug-free. With a good testing system in place, you might only be 99 percent bug-free, but it's a significant improvement.

Previously, we've looked at how to handle explicit errors, but sometimes your programs might perform oddly in certain situations. For example, certain data might cause an algorithm to return an incorrect result, or invalid data might be produced that, although invalid, does not result in an explicit error.

One way to resolve these problems is to debug your code, as you've seen, but debugging solves only one problem at a time. It's possible to debug your code to solve one problem, but create many others! Therefore, debugging alone has become viewed as a poor method of resolving bugs, and testing the overall functionality of code has become important.

In the past, users and developers might have performed testing manually by performing certain actions and seeing what happens. If an error occurs, the bug in question is fixed and testing continues. Indeed, there was a time when it was commonplace solely to use user feedback as a testing mechanism!

However, things have changed quickly with the rapidly growing popularity of test-driven development (also often known as test-first development), a new philosophy that turns software development practices on their head. Ruby developers have been at the forefront of promoting and encouraging this technique.

The Philosophy of Test-Driven Development

Test-driven development is a technique where developers create a set of tests for a system to pass before coding the system itself and then rigidly use these tests to maintain the integrity of the code. In a lighter form, however, it can also refer to the technique of implementing tests for any code, even if you don't necessarily create the tests before the code you're testing.

Note   This section provides only a basic overview of test-driven development. The topic is vast, and many books and resources are available on the topic if you wish to learn more. Wikipedia's entry on the topic at `https://en.wikipedia.org/wiki/Test-driven_development` is a great place to start.

For example, you might add a simple method to `String` that's designed to capitalize text into titles:

```ruby
class String
  def titleize
    self.capitalize
  end
end
```

Your intention is to create a method that can turn "this is a test" into "This Is A Test", that is, a method that makes strings look as if they're titles. `titleize`, therefore, capitalizes the current string with the `capitalize` method. If you're in a rush or not bothering to test your code, disaster will soon strike when the code is released into the wild. `capitalize` capitalizes only the first letter of a string, not the whole string!

```ruby
puts "this is a test".titleize
```

```
"This is a test"
```

That's not the intended behavior! However, with test-driven development, you could have avoided the pain of releasing broken code by first writing some tests to demonstrate the outcome you expect:

```ruby
raise "Fail 1" unless "this is a test".titleize == "This Is A Test"
```

```
raise "Fail 2" unless "another test 1234".titleize == "Another Test 1234"
raise "Fail 3" unless "We're testing titleize".titleize == "We're Testing
Titleize"
```

These three lines of code raise exceptions unless the output of titleize is what you expect it to be.

Note   These tests are also known as *assertions*, as they're *asserting* that a certain condition is true.

If titleize passes these three tests, you can expect the functionality to be okay for other examples.

Note   A set of tests or assertions that test a single component or a certain set of functionalities is known as a *test case*.

Your current code fails on the first test of this test case, so let's write the code to make it work:

```
class String
  def titleize
    self.gsub(/\b\w/) { |letter| letter.upcase }
  end
end
```

This code takes the current string, finds all word boundaries (with \b), passes in the first letter of each word (as obtained with \w), and converts it to uppercase. Job done? Run the three tests again:

```
RuntimeError (Fail 3)
```

Why does test 3 fail?

```
puts "We're testing titleize".titleize
```

```
We'Re Testing Titleize
```

\b isn't smart enough to detect true word boundaries. It merely uses whitespace or "non-word" characters to discriminate words from non-words. Therefore, in "We're," both the *W* and the *R* get capitalized. You need to tweak your code:

```
class String
  def titleize
    self.gsub(/\s\w/) { |letter| letter.upcase }
  end
end
```

If you make sure the character before the letter to capitalize is whitespace, you're guaranteed to now be scanning with a true, new word.

Re-run the tests:

```
RuntimeError: Failed test 1
```

You're back to square one.

One thing you failed to take into account is that looking for whitespace before a word doesn't allow the *first* word of each string to be capitalized, because those strings *start with a letter and not whitespace*. It sounds trivial, but it's a great demonstration of how complex simple functions can become and why testing is so vital to eradicate bugs. However, the ultimate solution is simple:

```
class String
  def titleize
    self.gsub(/(\A|\s)\w/){ |letter| letter.upcase }
  end
end
```

If you run the tests again, you'll notice they pass straight through. Success!

This basic example provides a sharp demonstration of why testing is important. Small changes can lead to significant changes in functionality, but with a set of trusted tests in place, you can focus on solving problems rather than worrying if your existing code has bugs.

Rather than writing code and waiting for bugs to appear, you can proactively determine what your code should do and then act as soon as the results don't match up with the expectations.

Unit Testing

In the previous section, you created some basic tests using `raise`, `unless`, and `==` and compared the results of a method call with the expected results. It's possible to test a lot in this way, but with more than a few tests, it soon becomes messy, as there's no logical place for the tests to go (and you certainly don't want to include tests with your actual, functional code).

Luckily, there are a couple of popular options for Ruby, Minitest, and RSpec. These gems make testing easy and organize test cases into a clean structure. This book will use Minitest, but RSpec is a popular option as well. Before Ruby 2.2, Minitest came bundled with Ruby. Due to issues maintaining Minitest as a part of Ruby's core library, it was removed and placed in a gem. To install Minitest, run the following command:

```
gem install minitest
```

Unit testing is the primary component of test-driven development and means that you're testing each individual unit of functionality within a program or system. Minitest is Ruby's official library for performing unit tests.

One of the benefits of Minitest is that it gives you a standardized framework for writing and performing tests. Rather than writing assertions in an inconsistent number of ways, Minitest gives you a core set of assertions to use.

Let's take the `titleize` method from before to use as a demonstration of Minitest's features and create a new file called `test_titleize.rb`:

```ruby
class String
  def titleize
    self.gsub(/(\A|\s)\w/){ |letter| letter.upcase }
  end
end

require 'minitest/autorun'

class TestTitleize < Minitest::Test
  def test_basic
    assert_equal("This Is A Test", "this is a test".titleize)
    assert_equal("Another Test 1234", "another test 1234".titleize)
    assert_equal("We're Testing", "We're testing".titleize)
  end
end
```

First, you include the `titleize` extension to `String` (typically this would be in its own file that you'd then `require` in, but for this simple example, we'll keep it associated with the test code). Next, you load the Minitest class using `require`. Finally, you create a test case by inheriting from `Minitest::Test`. Within this class, you have a single method (though you can have as many as you like to separate your tests logically) that contains three assertions, similar to the assertions made in the previous section.

If you run this script, you'll see the tests in action:

```
Run options: --seed 45484
# Running:

.

Finished in 0.002585s, 386.8906 runs/s, 1160.6718 assertions/s.
1 runs, 3 assertions, 0 failures, 0 errors, 0 skips
```

This output shows that the tests are started, a single test method is run (`test_basic`, in this case), and that a single test method with three assertions passed successfully.

Say you add an assertion to `test_basic` that's certainly going to fail, like so:

```
assert_equal("Let's make a test fail!", "foo".titleize)
```

and re-run the tests:

```
Run options: --seed 4300

# Running:

F

Failure:
TestTitleize#test_basic [test_titleize.rb:11]:
Expected: "Let's make a test fail!"
  Actual: "Foo"

rails test test_titleize.rb:10

Finished in 0.000813s, 1230.0124 runs/s, 1230.0124 assertions/s.
1 runs, 1 assertions, 1 failures, 0 errors, 0 skips
```

You've added an assertion that was bound to fail, and it has. However, Minitest has given you a full explanation of what happened. Using this information, you can go back and either fix the assertion or fix the code that caused the test to fail. In this case, you forced it to fail, but if your assertions are created normally, a failure such as this would demonstrate a bug in your code.

More Minitest Assertions

In the previous section, you used a single type of assertion, `assert_equal`. `assert_equal` asserts that the first and second arguments are equal (whether they're numbers, strings, arrays, or objects of any other kind). The first argument is assumed to be the *expected* outcome, and the second argument is assumed to be the generated output, as with your prior assertion:

```
assert_equal("This Is A Test", "this is a test".titleize)
```

Note   `assert_equal` can also accept an optional third argument as a message to be displayed if the assertion fails. A message might, in some cases, prove more useful than the default assertion failure message.

You're likely to find several other types of assertions useful as follows:

- `assert(<boolean expression>)`: Passes only if the Boolean expression isn't `false` or `nil` (e.g., `assert 2 == 1` will always fail). `refute` is its direct opposite.

- `assert_equal(expected, actual)`: Passes only if the *expected* and *actual* values are equal (as compared with the `==` operator). `assert_equal('A', 'a'.upcase)` will pass.

- `refute_equal(expected, actual)`: Is the opposite of `assert_equal`. This test will fail if the *expected* and *actual* values are equal. Any negative/"not" assertions can be prefixed with `refute_`, but it's a personal preference as to which you use.

- `assert_raises(exception_type, ..) { <code block> }`: Passes only if the code block following the assertion raises an exception of the type(s) passed as arguments. `assert_raises (ZeroDivisionError) { 2 / 0 }` will pass.

- `assert_instance_of(class_expected, object)`: Passes only if object is of class `class_expected`.

- `flunk`: Is a special type of assertion in that it will *always* fail. It's useful if you haven't quite finished writing your tests and you want to add a strong reminder that your test case isn't complete!

Note   All the preceding assertions, including `flunk`, can take an optional message argument as the last argument, as with `assert_equal`.

You'll use assertions and unit testing more in Chapter 12, where you'll develop a set of tests for a library you'll build.

Benchmarking and Profiling

Once your code is bug-free and working correctly, you may think it's ready for release. Sometimes, however, code can be inefficient and waste system resources. Before Ruby 1.9, the Ruby interpreter was not particularly fast. Ruby 1.9, with its entirely new implementation, is significantly faster than prior versions (2x speed improvements). There were additional improvements with each release of Ruby 2.x, but Ruby 3.0 provides the most significant improvements yet (3x speed improvements). With Ruby 3.0, the Ruby runtime is no longer a performance concern for most applications.

If Ruby is so fast, then why worry about performance? While Ruby is fast, our code may not be. To verify your code is fast enough, create a benchmark. Testing the performance of your code with a benchmark is especially vital if your code runs often.

Simple Benchmarking

Ruby's standard library includes a module called `Benchmark`. `Benchmark` provides several methods that measure the speed it takes to complete the code you provide, for example:

```
require 'benchmark'
puts Benchmark.measure { 10000.times { print "." } }
```

This code measures how long it takes to print 10,000 periods to the screen. Ignoring the periods produced, the output (on my machine; yours might vary) is as follows:

```
0.050000     0.040000     0.090000 (   0.455168)
```

The columns, in order, represent the amount of user CPU time, system CPU time, total CPU, and "real" time taken. In this case, although it took nine-hundredths of a second of CPU time to send 10,000 periods to the screen or terminal, it took almost half a second for them to finish being printed to the screen among all the other things the computer was doing.

Because measure accepts code blocks, you can make it as elaborate as you wish:

```
require 'benchmark'
iterations = 1000000

b = Benchmark.measure do
  for i in 1..iterations
    x = i
  end
end

c = Benchmark.measure do
  iterations.times do |i|
    x = i
  end
end

puts b
puts c
```

In this example, you benchmark two different ways of counting from one to one million. The results might look like this:

```
0.800000   0.010000   0.810000 (  0.949338)
0.890000   0.010000   0.900000 (  1.033589)
```

These results show little difference, except that slightly more user CPU time is used when using the times method rather than using for. You can use this same technique to test different ways of calculating the same answers in your code and optimize your code to use the fastest methods.

Benchmark also includes a way to make completing multiple tests more convenient. You can rewrite the preceding benchmarking scenario like this:

```
require 'benchmark'
iterations = 1000000
```

```
Benchmark.bm do |bm|
  bm.report("for:") do
    for i in 1..iterations
      x = i
    end
  end
  bm.report("times:") do
    iterations.times do |i|
      x = i
    end
  end
end
```

The primary difference with using the bm method is that it allows you to collect a group of benchmark tests together and display the results in a prettier way. Example output for the preceding code is as follows:

```
        User   system   total    real
for:    0.850000        0.000000         0.850000 (   0.967980)
times:  0.970000        0.010000         0.980000 (   1.301703)
```

bm makes the results even easier to read and provides headings for each column.

Another method, bmbm, repeats the benchmark set twice, using the first as a "rehearsal" and the second for the true results, as in some situations CPU caching, memory caching, and other factors can taint the results. Therefore, repeating the test can lead to more accurate figures. Replacing the bm method with bmbm in the preceding example (for the Benchmark method) gives results like these:

```
Rehearsal -------------------------------------
for:  0.780000    0.000001    0.780001 ( 0.958378)
times: 0.100000   0.010000    0.110000 ( 1.342837)
------------------------------ total: 0.890001sec

        User   system    total    real
for:  0.850000    0.000000    0.850000 ( 0.967980)
times: 0.970000   0.010000    0.980000 ( 1.301703)
```

bmbm runs the tests twice and gives both sets of results, where the latter set should be the most accurate.

Profiling

Whereas benchmarking is the process of measuring the total time it takes to achieve something and comparing those results between different versions of code, *profiling* tells you *what code* is taking *what amount of time*. For example, you might have a single line in your code that's causing the program to run slowly, so by profiling your code you can immediately see where you should focus your optimization efforts.

Note   Some people consider profiling to be the holy grail of optimization. Rather than thinking of efficient ways to write your application ahead of time, some developers suggest writing your application, profiling it, and then fixing the slowest areas. This is to prevent premature optimization. After all, you might prematurely optimize something that didn't actually warrant it, but miss out on an area of code that could do with significant optimization.

Ruby comes with a code profiler, but it is increasingly showing its age, and I would recommend instead installing ruby-prof (https://github.com/ruby-prof/ruby-prof). This is available as a gem, so can be simply installed with

```
gem install ruby-prof
```

Note   The installation process on Windows is a little more involved, so look at the ruby-prof GitHub repository at https://github.com/ruby-prof/ruby-prof for further guidance.

Once installed successfully, simply use ruby-prof to run your Ruby code and you'll get a print out of the profiler's findings.

For example, let's say we have the following Ruby program:

```
require 'ruby-prof'
class Calculator
  def self.count_to_large_number
    x = 0
    100000.times { x += 1 }
  end
```

```
  def self.count_to_small_number
    x = 0
    1000.times { x += 1 }
  end
end

Calculator.count_to_large_number
Calculator.count_to_small_number
```

This can then be run using ruby-prof:

```
ruby-prof calculator.rb
```

```
Measure Mode: wall_time
Thread ID: 560
Fiber ID: 540
Total: 0.011410
Sort by: self_time
```

%self	total	self	wait	child	calls	name
96.82	0.011	0.011	0.000	0.000	2	
Integer#times						
1.94	0.011	0.000	0.000	0.011	1	
Kernel#load						
0.28	0.000	0.000	0.000	0.000	5	
<Class::File>#file?						
0.17	0.000	0.000	0.000	0.000	4	Array#each
0.16	0.000	0.000	0.000	0.000	2	
<Class::File>#symlink?						

There's a lot of information given, but it's easy to read. The code itself is simple. Two class methods are defined that both count up to different numbers. Calculator. count_to_large_ number contains a loop that repeats 100,000 times, and Calculator. count_to_ small_number contains a loop that repeats 1000 times.

Note   The reason larger numbers, such as the 1,000,000 loops in the benchmarking tests, weren't used is because profiling adds a severe overhead to the operating speed of a program, unlike benchmarking. Although the program will run slower, this slowdown is consistent, so the accuracy of the profiling results is ensured regardless.

The result contains a number of columns. The first is the percentage of time spent within the method named in the far right column. In the preceding example, the profiler shows that 96.82 percent of the total execution time was spent in the times method in the Integer class. The second column shows the amount of time in seconds rather than as a percentage.

The calls column specifies how many times that method was called. In our case, times was called only twice.

You can use the profiler's results to discover the "sticky" points in your program and help you work around using inefficient methods that suck up CPU time. It's not worth spending time optimizing routines that barely consume any time, so use the profile to find those routines that are using the lion's share of the CPU, and focus on optimizing those.

Tip   ruby-prof can also be used from within code, rather than via the ruby-prof program, in order to profile certain pieces of code rather than an entire script. See ruby-prof's documentation for more information.

Summary

In this chapter, we've looked at the process behind, and the tools Ruby supplies for, documentation, error handling, testing, benchmarking, and profiling.

The quality of the documentation, error handling, and tests associated with a program or section of code demonstrates the professionalism of the developer and the program. Small, quickly developed scripts might not require any of these elements, but if you're developing a system that's designed to be used by other people or that's mission-critical, it's essential to understand the basics of error handling and testing to avoid the embarrassment of your code causing problems and behaving erroneously.

Furthermore, it's important to benchmark and profile your code so that your code has the ability to scale over time. You might expect your code to perform only a certain small set of functions—for example, processing small files—but in the future you might need to process significantly larger amounts of data with the same code and add extra, unanticipated features. The small amount of time taken to benchmark, profile, and optimize your code can pay dividends with reduced execution times later.

Let's reflect on the main concepts covered in this chapter:

- *RDoc*: A tool that comes with Ruby that builds HTML documentation using the structure and comments in your source code.

- *Debugging*: The process of resolving errors in source code, often by stepping through and inspecting the state of a program in situ.

- *Test-driven development/test-first development*: The development process of first writing tests that enforce certain expectations, then writing the code to produce the correct results. *Behavior-driven development* is a popular alternative that merely uses different semantics.

- *Test case*: A group of tests to check the functionality of a section of your program (e.g., a class or module).

- *Assertion*: A single test to see whether a certain condition or result is met, which checks that a certain piece of code is working properly.

- *Unit testing*: The process of testing code by making assertions on its various pieces of functionality to make sure each operates as expected.

- *Optimization*: The process of improving the efficiency of your code by reworking algorithms and finding new ways of solving problems.

- *Benchmarking*: A process involving testing the speed of your code to see how quick it is under certain conditions, or using certain methods and algorithms. You can use the benchmark results to compare different versions of code, or compare coding techniques.

- *Profiling*: A process that shows you which methods and routines are taking up the most execution time (or memory) in your programs.

Most of these concepts are not used directly in the code samples in this book, as they're principally relevant to longer-term projects or code being prepared for release. This doesn't mean they're unimportant concepts, but as in-depth parts of a longer development process, they aren't within the scope of the code examples used in other chapters.

We'll look briefly at testing methodologies again in Chapter 12, where we implement some simple tests while developing a library.

## CHAPTER 9

Files and Databases

In this chapter, we're going to look at how to store, process, and interact with external sources of data from our Ruby programs. In Chapter 4, we briefly looked at how to load files to get data into an application, but this chapter will extend upon that greatly and allow you to create files from scratch from your Ruby programs.

Later in this chapter, we'll look at databases—specialized organizations of data—and how to interact with them, along with some notes on interacting with popular database systems such as SQLite, MySQL, and PostgreSQL. You can use databases for simple tasks such as storing information about a small set of items or as an address book, but databases are also used in the world's busiest data processing environments. By the end of this chapter, you'll be able to use databases the same way as, or at least in a similar way to, those used by professional developers around the world.

Input and Output

Interaction, in computer terms, relates to the input and output of data, or *I/O* for short. Most programming languages have built-in support for I/O, and Ruby's is well designed and easy to use.

I/O streams are the basis for all input and output in Ruby. An *I/O stream* is a conduit or channel for input and output operations between one resource and another. Usually this will be between your Ruby program and the keyboard or between your Ruby program and a file. Along this stream, input and output operations can take place. In some cases, such as when using the keyboard, I/O only works in one direction, as you can't send data *to* a keyboard, and data can only be sent *to*, and not from, a display.

In this section, we're going to look at using the keyboard, using files, and other forms of I/O in Ruby and how they can be used.

© Carleton DiLeo, Peter Cooper 2021
C. DiLeo and P. Cooper, *Beginning Ruby 3*, https://doi.org/10.1007/978-1-4842-6324-2_9

Keyboard Input

The simplest way to get external data into a program is to use the keyboard, for example:

```
a = gets
puts a
```

gets accepts a single line of data from the *standard input*—the keyboard in this case—and assigns it to a. You then print it, using puts, to the standard output—the screen in this case.

STANDARD INPUT AND OUTPUT

The *standard input* is a default stream available in many operating systems that relates to the standard way to accept input from a user or external process. In our case, the standard input is the keyboard, but if, for example, you were to redirect data to a Ruby program from a UNIX-like operating system, such as Linux or Mac OS X, the standard input would be the data being directed to it. For example, let's assume we put the preceding code example into a file called test.rb and then ran it like so:

```
ruby test.rb < somedata.txt
```

The output provided this time would be the first line of somedata.txt, as gets would retrieve a single line from the standard input that, in this case, would be the contents of the file somedata.txt. Essentially, the file is now the input, not the keyboard.

Conversely, *standard output* is usually referring to the screen or display, but if the results of your Ruby script are being redirected to a file or another program, that destination file or program becomes the target for the standard output.

Alternatively, you can read multiple lines in one go by using readlines:

```
lines = readlines
puts lines.length
```

readlines accepts line after line of input until a terminator, most commonly known as EOF (end of file), is found. You can create EOF on most platforms by pressing Ctrl+D. When the terminating line is found, all the lines of input given are put into an array that's assigned to lines. This is particularly ideal for programs that accept piped or redirected input on standard input.

Note that on the second line earlier we then look at the length of the `lines` array. So if the preceding code were in a file called `linecount.rb` and you passed in a text file containing ten lines:

```
ruby linecount.rb < textfile.txt
```

you'd get this result:

```
10
```

In reality, however, this mechanism is rarely used, unless writing shell scripts for use at a UNIX prompt. In most cases, you'll be writing to and from files directly, and you'll require only minimal keyboard input that you can get with `gets`.

File I/O

In Chapter 4, you used the `File` class to open a text file so you could read in the contents for your program to process. The `File` class is used as an abstraction to access and handle file objects that can be accessed from a Ruby program. The `File` class lets you write to both plain text and binary files (there's not really an inherent difference—they're both just sets of data) and offers a collection of methods to make handling files easy.

Opening and Reading Files

The most common file-related procedure is reading a file's data for use within a program. As you saw in Chapter 4, this is easily done:

```
File.open("text.txt").each { |line| puts line }
```

The `File` class's open method is used to open the text file, `text.txt`, and upon that `File` object, the each method returns each line one by one. You can also do it this way:

```
File.new("text.txt", "r").each { |line| puts line }
```

This method clarifies the process involved. By opening a file, you're creating a new `File` object that you can then use. The second parameter, `"r"`, defines that you're opening the file for reading. This is the default mode, but when using `File.new`, it can help to clarify what you want to do with the file (as "new" might imply the creation of a file, which is not usually the case). This becomes important later when you write to files or create new ones from scratch.

For opening and reading files, `File.new` and `File.open` are identical, but `File.open` has one, extra feature. `File.open` can accept a code block, and once the block is finished, the file will be closed automatically. However, `File.new` only returns a `File` object referring to the file. To close the file, you have to use its `close` method. Let's compare the two methods. First, look at `File.open`:

```
File.open("text.txt") do |f|
  puts f.gets
end
```

This code opens `text.txt` and then passes the file handle into the code block as `f`.

`puts f.gets` takes a line of data from the file and prints it to the screen. Now, have a look at the `File.new` approach:

```
f = File.new("text.txt", "r")
puts f.gets
f.close
```

In this example, a file handle/object is assigned to `f` directly. You close the file handle manually with the `close` method at the end.

Both the code block and file handle techniques have their uses. Using a code block is a clean way to open a single file quickly and perform operations in a single location. However, assigning the `File` object with `File.new` (or `File.open`, if you choose) makes the file reference available throughout the entire current scope without needing to contain file manipulation code within a single block.

Note   You might need to specify the location of files directly, as `text.txt` might not appear to be in the current directory. Simply replace `f = File.new("text.txt", "r")` with `f = File.new("c:\ full\ path\here\text.txt", "r")`, including the full path as necessary (this example demonstrates a Windows-style path). Alternatively, use the result of `Dir::pwd` to see what the current working directory is and put `text.txt` there.

You could also choose to assign the file handle to a class or instance variable:

```
class MyFile
  attr_reader :handle

  def initialize(filename)
    @handle = File.new(filename, "r")
  end

  def finished
    @handle.close
  end
end

f = MyFile.new("text.txt")
puts f.handle.gets
f.finished
```

More File Reading Techniques

In the previous section, you used a `File` object's each method to read each line one by one within a code block. However, you can do a lot more than that. Let's assume your `text.txt` file contains this dummy data:

```
Fred Bloggs,Manager,Male,45
Laura Smith,Cook,Female,23
Debbie Watts,Professor,Female,38
```

Next, we'll look at some of the different techniques you can use to read the file, along with their outputs. First, you can read an I/O stream line by line using each:

```
File.open("text.txt").each { |line| puts line }
Fred Bloggs,Manager,Male,45
Laura Smith,Cook,Female,23
Debbie Watts,Professor,Female,38
```

Note   each technically reads from the file delimiter by delimiter, where the standard delimiter is a "newline" character. You can change this delimiter.

You can read an I/O stream with each using a custom delimiter of your choosing:

```
File.open("text.txt").each(',') { |line| puts line }
Fred Bloggs,
Manager,
Male,
45
Laura Smith,
Cook,
Female,
23
Debbie Watts,
Professor,
Female,
38
```

In this case, you passed an optional argument to each that specified a different delimiter from the default "newline" delimiter. Commas delimit the input.

Tip You can override the default delimiter by setting the special variable $/ to any delimiter you choose.

You can read an I/O stream byte by byte with each_byte:

```
File.open("text.txt").each_byte { |byte| puts byte }
70
114
101
100
...many lines skipped for brevity...
51
56
10
```

Note   When reading byte by byte, you get the single byte values of each character rather than the characters themselves, much like when you do something like `puts "test"[0]`. To convert into text characters, you can use the `chr` method.

There's also an alternative called `each_char` that lets you read character by character. In some character sets, characters may be represented by more than one byte, so this can be useful:

```
File.open("text.txt").each_char { |byte| puts byte }
```

```
F
r
e
d
...many lines skipped for brevity...
,
3
8
```

Here's how to read an I/O stream line by line using `gets`:

```
File.open("text.txt") do |f|
  2.times { puts f.gets }
end
```

```
Fred Bloggs,Manager,Male,45
Laura Smith,Cook,Female,23
```

`gets` isn't an iterator like `each` or `each_byte`. Therefore, you have to call it multiple times to get multiple lines. In this example, it was used twice, and pulled out the first two lines of the example file. Like `each`, however, `gets` can accept an optional delimiter:

```
File.open("text.txt") do |f|
  2.times { puts f.gets(',') }
end
```

```
Fred Bloggs,
Manager,
```

There's also a noniterative version of each_byte called getc:

```
File.open("text.txt") do |f|
  2.times { puts f.getc }
end
```

```
F
r
```

You can also read an entire file into an array, split by lines, using `readlines`:

```
puts File.open("text.txt").readlines.join("--")
```

```
Fred Bloggs,Manager,Male,45
--Laura Smith,Cook,Female,23
--Debbie Watts,Professor,Female,38
```

Note   The "newline" characters that are present at the end of each line of the file are not removed, meaning that a newline occurs before each instance of `--`.

Lastly, you can choose to read an arbitrary number of bytes from a file into a single variable using `read`:

```
File.open("text.txt") do |f|
  puts f.read(6)
end
```

```
Fred B
```

Note   You can use all these methods on any file, such as binary files (images, executables, etc.), not just text files. However, on Windows, you might need to open the file in binary mode. This is covered in the section "Writing to Files."

The File class makes some convenient methods available so that you don't need to do things like `File.open("text.txt").read` to be able to read a file into a string. Instead, you can do this:

```
data = File.read("text.txt")
```

This acts as a shorthand for opening the file, using the standard `read` method, and then closing the file again.

You can also do this:

```
array_of_lines = File.readlines("text.txt")
```

Simple!

Generally, you should try to use these shortcut methods wherever possible, as they result in shorter, easier-to-read code, and you don't have to worry about closing the files. Everything is taken care of for you in one step. Of course, if reading a file line by line is necessary (perhaps if you're working with extremely large files), then you can use the techniques demonstrated earlier in this chapter for reading line by line.

Your Position Within a File

When reading a file, it can be useful to know where you are within that file. The `pos` method gives you access to this information:

```
f = File.open("text.txt")
puts f.pos
puts f.gets
puts f.pos
```

```
0
Fred Bloggs,Manager,Male,45
28
```

Before you begin to read any text from the file, the position is shown as 0. Once you've read a line of text, the position is shown as 28. This is because `pos` returns the position of the file pointer (i.e., the current location within the file that you're reading from) in the number of bytes from the start of the file.

However, `pos` can work both ways, as it has a sister method, `pos=`:

```
f = File.open("text.txt")
f.pos = 8
puts f.gets
puts f.pos
```

```
ggs,Manager,Male,45
28
```

In this instance, the file pointer was placed eight bytes into the file before reading anything. This meant that "Fred Blo" was skipped, and only the rest of the line was retrieved.

Writing to Files

The ability to jump easily around files, read lines based on delimiters, and handle data byte by byte makes Ruby ideal for manipulating data, but I haven't yet covered how to write new information to files or how to make changes to existing files.

Generally, you can mirror most of the techniques used to read files when writing to files, for example:

```
File.open("text.txt", "w") do |f|
  f.puts "This is a test"
end
```

This code creates a new file (or overwrites an existing file) called text.txt and puts a single line of text within it. Previously, you've used puts on its own to output data to the screen. However, when used with a File object, puts writes the data to the file instead. Simple!

The "w" passed as the second argument to File.open tells Ruby to open the file for writing only and to create a new file or overwrite what is already in the file. This is in contrast with the "r" mode used earlier when opening a file for reading only.

However, you can use several different file modes, as covered in Table 9-1.

Table 9-1. *File Modes Usable with File.open/File.new*

File Mode	Properties of the I/O Stream
r	Read-only. The file pointer is placed at the start of the file.
r+	Both reading and writing are allowed. The file pointer is placed at the start of the file.
w	Write-only. A new file is created (or an old one overwritten as if new).
w+	Both reading and writing are allowed, but File.new creates a new file from scratch (or overwrites an old one as if new).
a	Write (in append mode). The file pointer is placed at the end of the file and writes will make the file longer.
a+	Both reading and writing are allowed (in append mode). The file pointer is placed at the end of the file and writes will make the file longer.
b	Binary file mode. You can use it in conjunction with any of the other modes listed.

Using the append mode described in Table 9-1, it's trivial to create a program that appends a line of text to a file each time it's run:

```
f = File.new("logfile.txt", "a")
f.puts Time.now
f.close
```

If you run this code multiple times, logfile.txt will contain several dates and times, one after the other. Append mode is particularly ideal for log file situations where new information has to be added at different times.

The read and write modes work in a simple manner. If you want to open a file in a mode where it can be read from and written to at the same time, you can do just that:

```
f = File.open("text.txt", "r+")
puts f.gets
f.puts "This is a test"
puts f.gets
f.close
```

The second line of this code reads the first line of text from the file, meaning the file pointer is waiting at the start of the second line of data. However, the following f.puts statement then puts a new line of text into the file *at* that position. Unfortunately, this action will not push the previously existing second line to the third line of the file. All it does is overwrite the equivalent number of bytes, so you end up with a broken third line! This behavior means you really need to think carefully before writing data into the middle of an existing file, as you may not get the outcome you thought you would!

Whereas puts outputs lines of text, you can perform the writing equivalents of getc and read with putc and write:

```
f = File.open("text.txt", "r+")
f.putc "X"
f.close
```

This example opens text.txt for reading and writing and changes the first character of the first line to X. Similarly:

```
f = File.open("text.txt", "r+")
f.write "123456"
f.close
```

This example overwrites the first six characters of the first line with 123456.

Note   It's worth noticing that putc and write overwrite existing content in the file rather than *inserting* it.

Character Sets and Encodings

Ruby 1.9 and later come with built-in support for automatically handling alternative character encodings when reading files. Character encodings are explained and covered in depth in Chapter 11's "Unicode, Character Encodings, and UTF-8 Support" section.

Whereas strings have just "internal" encodings, I/O objects also have "external" encodings, since I/O objects deal with data coming from, or going to, somewhere else.

In all of the previous file reading examples in this chapter, Ruby used the default encoding to represent data that is read in, even though this may be incorrect. Specifying an external encoding when opening a file requires that you append any supplied file mode with a colon and then specify the encoding's name. For example, if you want to read a file that uses the UTF-8 encoding scheme:

```
File.new("text.txt", "r:utf-8").each { |line| puts line }
```

In this example, we're reading a file (as specified by the "r" mode), but we're also telling the File object to treat the data as if it's in the UTF-8 encoding (whether it actually is or not). This encoding is then applied for all data read from (or written to, if you're in the right mode) the file.

It is possible to determine the external encoding of an I/O object (such as those of the File class) using its external_encoding method:

```
p File.open("text.txt", "r:iso-8859-1").external_encoding
p File.open("text.txt", "r").external_encoding
```

```
#<Encoding:ISO-8859-1>
#<Encoding:UTF-8>
```

Note   If your default encoding is not UTF-8, the second line will return whatever your default encoding actually is, since no external encoding was specified when creating the File object.

Another function of Ruby I/O encoding support is in *transcoding* from one encoding to another. For example, you might be opening a file in the UTF-8 encoding system, but want Ruby to "translate" it to another encoding on the fly as the data is read. This is achieved by adding another colon and encoding the name to the file mode parameter:

```
File.open("text.txt", "r:utf-8:iso-8859-1") do |f|
  p f.external_encoding
  first_line = f.gets
  p first_line.encoding
end
```

```
#<Encoding:UTF-8>
#<Encoding:ISO-8859-1>
```

The transcoding feature will be useful if you want to represent all text within your application in a certain encoding (UTF-8 would be a good choice, as you will see in Chapter 11), but need to read files of varying encodings. In each case, use the relevant external coding, but get Ruby to convert everything into UTF-8!

Renaming and Deleting Files

If you want to change the name of a file, you *could* create a new file with the new name and read into that file all the data from the original file. However, this isn't necessary, and you can simply use File.rename like so:

```
File.rename("file1.txt", "file2.txt")
```

Deleting a file is just as simple. You can delete either one file at a time or many at once:

```
File.delete("file1.txt")
File.delete("file2.txt", "file3.txt", "file4.txt")
File.unlink("file1.txt")
```

Note   File.unlink does exactly the same thing as File.delete.

File Operations

The File class offers you more than just the ability to read and write files. You can also perform a number of checks and operations upon files.

Creating Filenames Platform Independently

Windows and UNIX-related operating systems have different ways of denoting filenames. Windows filenames look like c:\directory\filename.ext, whereas UNIX-style filenames look like /directory/filename.ext. If your Ruby scripts work with filenames and need to operate under both systems, the File class provides the join method.

Under both systems, filenames (and complete paths) are built up from directory names and local filenames. For example, in the preceding examples, the directory is called directory, but on Windows, backslashes are used as opposed to forward slashes.

Note   In modern versions of Ruby on Windows, it's fine to use UNIX-style pathnames using forward slashes as directory separators, rather than having to format filenames in a Windows style with backslashes. However, this section is included for completeness, or for instances where you need to work with libraries that don't respect UNIX-style pathnames on other operating systems.

On Windows, you can use `File.join` to put together a filename using directory names and a final filename:

```
File.join('full', 'path', 'here', 'filename.txt')
full\path\here\filename.txt
```

Note   Depending on how your system is set up, you might even see a forward slash version of the preceding code on Windows, although that is technically a UNIX-style path.

On UNIX-related operating systems, such as Linux, the code is the same:

```
File.join('full', 'path', 'here', 'filename.txt')
```

```
full/path/here/filename.txt
```

The `File.join` method is simple to use, and it allows you to write the same code to run on both systems rather than choosing between backslashes and forward slashes in your code.

The separator itself is stored in a constant called `File::SEPARATOR`, so you can easily turn a filename into an absolute filename (with an absolute path) by appending the directory separator to the start, like so:

```
File.join(File::SEPARATOR , 'full', 'path', 'here', 'filename.txt')
```

```
/full/path/here/filename.txt
```

Similarly, you can use `File.expand_path` to turn basic filenames into complete paths, for example:

```
File.expand_path("text.txt")
```

```
/Users/carleton/text.txt
```

Note   The result of `File.expand_path` will vary according to the operating system the code is run under. As `text.txt` is a relative filename, it converts it to an absolute filename and references the current working directory.

Seeking

In a previous example, you changed the position of the file pointer using `pos=`. However, this only allows you to specify the exact position of the file pointer. If you want to move the pointer forward by a certain offset or move the pointer to a certain position backward from the *end* of the file, you need to use `seek`.

seek has three modes of operation:

- `IO::SEEK_CUR`: Seeks a certain number of bytes ahead of the current position.

- `IO::SEEK_END`: Seeks to a position based on the end of the file. This means that to seek to a certain position from the end of the file, you'll probably need to use a negative value.

- `IO::SEEK_SET`: Seeks to an absolute position in the file. This is identical to `pos=`.

Therefore, to position the file pointer five bytes from the end of the file and change the character to an X, you would use `seek` as follows:

```
f = File.open("text.txt", "r+")
f.seek(-5, IO::SEEK_END)
f.putc "X"
f.close
```

Note   Notice that because you're writing to the file, you use the `r+` file mode to enable writing as well as reading.

Or you could do this to print every fifth character in a file:

```
f = File.open("text.txt", "r")
```

```
while a = f.getc
  puts a.chr
  f.seek(5, IO::SEEK_CUR)
end
```

Finding Out When a File Was Last Modified

To establish when a file was last modified, use `File.mtime`:

```
puts File.mtime("text.txt")
```

```
2020-05-08 13:51:27 -0600
```

The time is returned as a `Time` object, so you can get more information directly:

```
t = File.mtime("text.txt")
puts t.hour
puts t.min
puts t.sec
```

```
00
05
02
```

Note   You can learn more about the `Time` class and its methods in Chapter 3.

Checking Whether a File Exists

It's useful to check whether a file actually exists, particularly if your program relies on that file or if a user supplied the filename. If the file doesn't exist, you can raise a user-friendly error or exception. Invoke the `File.exist?` method to check for the existence of a file:

```
puts "It exists!" if File.exist?("comic-books.txt")
```

File.exist? returns true if the named file exists. You could edit the MyFile class created in a previous example to check for the existence of a file before opening it to avoid a potential exception being thrown, like so:

```
class MyFile
  attr_reader :handle

  def initialize(filename)
    if File.exist?(filename)
      @handle = File.new(filename, "r")
    else
      return false
    end
  end
end
```

Getting the Size of a File

File.size returns the size of a file in bytes. If the file doesn't exist, an exception is thrown, so it would make sense to check its existence with File.exist? first:

```
puts File.size("text.txt")
```

How to Know When You're at the End of a File

In previous examples, either you've used iterators to give you all the lines or bytes in a file, or you've pulled only a few lines from a file here and there. However, it would be useful to have a foolproof way to know when the file pointer is at, or has gone past, the end of the file. The eof? method provides this feature:

```
f = File.new("text.txt", "r")
while !f.eof?
  puts f.gets
end
f.close
```

This example uses an "infinite" loop that will only conclude once f.eof? is true. This specific example is not particularly useful, as f.each could have performed a similar task, but in situations where you might be moving the file pointer around manually, or making large jumps through a file, checking for an "end of file" situation is useful.

Directories

All files are contained within various *directories*, and Ruby has no problem handling these. Whereas the File class handles files, directories are handled with the Dir class.

Navigating Through Directories

To change directory within a Ruby program, use Dir.chdir:

```
Dir.chdir("/usr/bin")
```

This example changes the current directory to /usr/bin.

You can find out what the current directory is with Dir.pwd. For example, here's the result on my installation:

```
puts Dir.pwd
```

```
/Users/carleton
```

```
current = Dir.pwd
Dir.chdir("/usr/bin")
puts Dir.pwd
```

```
/usr/bin
```

```
Dir.chdir(current)
puts Dir.pwd
```

```
/Users/carleton
```

You can get a list of the files and directories within a specific directory using Dir.entries:

```
puts Dir.entries("/usr/bin").join(' ')
```

```
... a2p aclocal aclocal-1.6 addftinfo afmtodit alias amlint ant appleping
appletviewer apply apropos apt ar arch as asa at at_cho_prn atlookup atos
atprint ...items removed for brevity... zless zmore znew zprint
```

`Dir.entries` returns an array with all the entries within the specified directory. `Dir.foreach` provides the same feature, but as an iterator:

```
Dir.foreach("/usr/bin") do |entry|
  puts entry
end
```

An even more concise way of getting directory listings is by using `Dir`'s class array method:

```
Dir["/usr/bin/*"]
```

```
["/usr/bin/a2p", "/usr/bin/aclocal", "/usr/bin/aclocal-1.6",
"/usr/bin/addftinfo", "/usr/bin/afmtodit", "/usr/bin/alias", "/usr/bin/
amlint", "/usr/bin/ant", ...items removed for brevity... ]
```

In this case, each entry is returned as an absolute filename, making it easy to use the `File` class's methods to perform checks on each entry if you wished.

Creating a Directory

You use `Dir.mkdir` to create directories, like so:

```
Dir.mkdir("mynewdir")
```

Once the directory has been created, you can navigate to it with `Dir.chdir`.

You can also specify absolute paths to create directories under other specific directories:

```
Dir.mkdir("/mynewdir")
Dir.mkdir("c:\test")
```

However, you cannot create directories under directories that don't yet exist themselves. If you want to create an entire structure of directories, you must create them one by one from the top down.

Note   On UNIX-related operating systems, `Dir.mkdir` accepts a second optional argument: an integer specifying the permissions for the directory. You can specify this in octal, as with 0666 or 0777, representing modes 666 and 777, respectively.

Deleting a Directory

Deleting a directory is similar to deleting a file:

```
Dir.delete("mynewdir")
```

Note   `Dir.unlink` and `Dir.rmdir` perform exactly the same function and are provided for convenience.

As with `Dir.mkdir`, you can use absolute pathnames.

One thing you need to consider when deleting directories is whether they're empty. If a directory isn't empty, you cannot delete it with a single call to `Dir.delete`. You need to iterate through each of the subdirectories and files and remove them all first. You can do that iteration with `Dir.foreach`, looping recursively through the file tree by pushing new directories and files to remove onto an array.

Alternatively, you can use the `rm_f` method of the `FileUtils` library that comes with Ruby:

```
require 'fileutils'
FileUtils.rm_f(<directory_name>)
```

Caution   If you choose to use `rm_f`, tread carefully, as you might accidentally delete the wrong thing!

Creating Files in the Temporary Directory

Most operating systems have the concept of a "temporary" directory where temporary files can be stored. Temporary files are those that might be created briefly during a program's execution but aren't a permanent store of information.

`Dir.tmpdir` provides the path to the temporary directory on the current system, although the method is not available by default. To make `Dir.tmpdir` available, it's necessary to use `require 'tmpdir'`:

```
require 'tmpdir'
puts Dir.tmpdir
```

```
/tmp
```

> **Note**   On Mac OS X, the result might be somewhat more esoteric. For example, I was given the temporary directory of `/var/folders/80/80DFegkBHLmcQjJ HdZ5SCE+++TI/-Tmp-`. On Windows, I got `C:/Users/username/AppData/ Local/Temp`.

You can use `Dir.tmpdir` with `File.join` to create a platform-independent way of creating a temporary file:

```ruby
require 'tmpdir'
tempfilename = File.join(Dir.tmpdir, "myapp.dat")
tempfile = File.new(tempfilename, "w")
tempfile.puts "This is only temporary"
tempfile.close
File.delete(tempfilename)
```

This code creates a temporary file, writes data to it, and deletes it.

Ruby's standard library also includes a library called `tempfile` that can create temporary files for you:

```ruby
require 'tempfile'
f = Tempfile.new('myapp')
f.puts "Hello"
puts f.path
f.close
```

```
/tmp/myfile1842.0
```

Unlike creating and managing your own temporary files, `tempfile` automatically deletes the files it creates after they have been used. This is an important consideration when choosing between the two techniques.

Basic Databases

Many applications need to store, access, or manipulate data. In some cases, this is by loading files, making changes to them, and outputting data to the screen or back to a file. In many situations, however, a database is required.

A database is a system for organizing data on a computer in a systematic way. A database can be as simple as a text file containing data that can be manipulated by a computer program or as complex as many gigabytes of data spread across hundreds of dedicated database servers. You can use Ruby in these scenarios and for those in between.

First, we're going to look at how to use simple text files as a form of organized data.

Text File Databases

One simple type of database can be stored in a text file in a format commonly known as CSV. CSV stands for comma-separated values and means that for each item of data you're storing, you can have multiple attributes separated with commas. The dummy data in your `text.txt` file in the previous section used CSV data. To recap, `text.txt` initially contained this code:

```
Fred Bloggs,Manager,Male,45
Laura Smith,Cook,Female,23
Debbie Watts,Professor,Female,38
```

Each line represents a different person, and commas separate the attributes relating to each person. The commas allow you to access (and change) each attribute separately.

Ruby's standard library includes a library called `csv` that allows you to use text files containing CSV data as simple databases that are easy to read, create, and manipulate.

Reading and Searching CSV Data

The CSV class provided by the `csv` standard library will manage the manipulation of CSV data for you:

```
require 'csv'
CSV.open('text.txt').each do |person|
  p person
end
```

```
["Fred Bloggs", "Manager", "Male", "45"]
["Laura Smith", "Cook", "Female", "23"]
["Debbie Watts", "Professor", "Female", "38"]
```

You open the `text.txt` file by using `CSV.open`, and each line (i.e., each individual "person" in the file) is passed into the block one by one using `each`. The `inspect` method demonstrates that each entry is now represented in array form. This makes it easier to read the data than when it was in its plain text form.

You can also use CSV alongside the `File` class:

```
require 'csv'
people = CSV.parse(File.read('text.txt'))
puts people[0][0]
puts people[1][0]
puts people[2][0]
```

```
Fred Bloggs
Laura Smith
Debbie Watts
```

This example uses the `File` class to open and read in the contents of a file, and `CSV.parse` immediately uses these to convert the data into an array of arrays. The elements in the main array represent each line in the file, and each element in those elements represents a different attribute (or field) of that line. Therefore, by printing out the first element of each entry, you get the people's names only.

An even more succinct way of loading the data from a CSV-formatted file into an array is with `CSV.read`:

```
require 'csv'
p CSV.read('text.txt')
```

```
[["Fred Bloggs", "Manager", "Male", "45"], ["Laura Smith", "Cook",
"Female", "23"],
["Debbie Watts", "Professor", "Female", "38"]]
```

The find and find_all methods (also known as detect and select, respectively) provided by the Enumerable module to Array make it easy for you to perform searches on the data available in the array. For example, you'd use this code if you wanted to pick out the first person in the data called Laura:

```
require 'csv'
people = CSV.read('text.txt')
laura = people.find { |person| person[0] =~ /Laura/ }
p laura
```

```
["Laura Smith", "Cook", "Female", "23"]
```

Using the find (or detect) method with a code block that looks for the first matching line where the name contains "Laura" gives you back the data you were looking for.

Where find returns the first matching element of an array or hash, find_all (or select) returns all valid matches. Let's say you want to find the people in your database whose ages are between 20 and 40:

```
young_people = people.find_all do |p|
  p[3].to_i.between?(20, 40)
end
p young_people
```

```
[["Laura Smith", "Cook", "Female", "23"], ["Debbie Watts", "Professor",
"Female", "38"]]
```

This operation provides you with the two matching people contained within an array that you can iterate through.

Saving Data Back to the CSV File

Once you can read and query data, the next step is being able to change it, delete it, and rewrite your CSV file with a new version of the data for future use. Luckily, this is as simple as reopening the file with write access and "pushing" the data back to the file. The CSV module handles all of the conversion:

```
require 'csv'
```

```
people = CSV.read('text.txt')
laura = people.find { |person| person[0] =~ /Laura/ }
laura[0] = "Lauren Smith"

CSV.open('text.txt', 'w') do |csv|
  people.each do |person|
    csv << person
  end
end
```

You load in the data, find a person to change, change her name, and then open the CSV file and rewrite the data back to it. Notice, however, that you have to write the data person by person. Once complete, `text.txt` is updated with the name change. This is how to write back CSV data to file.

Storing Objects and Data Structures

Working with CSV is easy, but it doesn't feel very smooth. You're always dealing with arrays, so rather than getting nice names such as `name`, `age`, or `job` for the different attributes, you have to remember in which element and at which position each attribute is located.

You're also forced to store simple arrays for each separate entry. There's no nesting, no way to relate one thing to another, no relationship to object orientation, and the data is "flat." This is sufficient for basic data, but what if you simply want to take data that already exists in structures like arrays and hashes and save that data to disk for later use?

PStore

PStore is a core Ruby library that allows you to use Ruby objects and data structures as you normally would and then store them in a file. Later on, you can reload the objects back into memory from the disk file. This technique is known as *object persistence*, and relies on a technique called *marshalling*, where standard data structures are turned into a form of flat data that can be stored to disk or transmitted over a network for later reconstruction.

Let's create a class to represent the structure of the data you were using in the CSV examples:

```
class Person
  attr_accessor :name, :job, :gender, :age
end
```

You can re-create your data like so:

```
fred = Person.new
fred.name = "Fred Bloggs"
fred.age = 45

laura = Person.new
laura.name = "Laura Smith"
laura.age = 23
```

Note   For brevity, you'll work only with these two objects in this example.

Rather than have your data in arrays, you now have your data available in a fully object-oriented fashion. You could create methods within the `Person` class to help you manipulate your objects and so forth. This style of storing and manipulating data is true to the Ruby way of things and is entirely object-oriented. However, until now, your objects have only lasted until the end of a program, but with PStore it's easy to write them to a file:

```
require 'pstore'
store = PStore.new("storagefile")
store.transaction do
  store[:people] ||= Array.new
  store[:people] << fred
  store[:people] << laura
end
```

In this example, you create a new PStore in a file called `storagefile`. You then start a transaction (data within a PStore file can only be read or updated while inside a "transaction" to prevent data corruption), and within the transaction you make sure the `:people` element of the store contains something or gets assigned to be an array. Next, you push the `fred` and `laura` objects to the `:people` element of the store and then end the transaction.

The reason for the hash syntax is because a PStore is, effectively, a disk-based hash. You can then store whatever objects you like within that hash. In this example, you've created an array *within* store[:people] and pushed your two Person objects to it.

Later on, you can retrieve the data from the PStore database:

```
require 'pstore'
store = PStore.new("storagefile")
people = []
store.transaction do
  people = store[:people]
end

# At this point the Person objects inside people can be treated
# as totally local objects.
people.each do |person|
  puts person.name
end
```

```
Fred Bloggs
Laura Smith
```

> **Note**   It's necessary for the Person class to be defined and ready to use before loading the Person objects from the PStore file, so if you ran the previous example separately from the first, make sure you include the Person class definition again.

With only a simple storage and retrieval process, PStore makes it easy to add storage facilities to existing Ruby programs by allowing you to store existing objects into a PStore database. Object persistence is not ideal for many types of data storage, but if your program is heavily dependent on objects and you want to store those objects to disk for later use, PStore provides a simple method to use.

YAML

YAML (standing for YAML Ain't Markup Language) is a special text-based markup language that was designed as a data serialization format that's readable by humans. You can use it in a similar way to PStore to serialize data structures, but unlike PStore's data, humans can easily read YAML data and even directly edit it with a text editor and a basic knowledge of YAML syntax.

The YAML library comes as part of Ruby's standard library, so it's easy to use. Unlike PStore, though, the YAML library converts data structures to and from YAML and doesn't provide a hash to use, so the technique is a little different. This example writes an array of objects to disk:

```
require 'yaml'

class Person
  attr_accessor :name, :age
end

fred = Person.new
fred.name = "Fred Bloggs"
fred.age = 45

laura = Person.new
laura.name = "Laura Smith"
laura.age = 23
test_data = [ fred, laura ]

puts test_data.to_yaml
```

```
---
- !ruby/object:Person
  age: 45
  name: Fred Bloggs
- !ruby/object:Person
  name: Laura Smith
  age: 23
```

You can use the to_yaml method to convert your Person object array into YAML data, which, as you might agree, is extremely readable! YAML.load performs the operation in the other direction, turning YAML code into working Ruby objects. For example, let's modify the YAML data a little and see if it translates back into working objects:

```
require 'yaml'

class Person
```

```
  attr_accessor :name, :age
end

yaml_string = <<END_OF_DATA
---
- !ruby/object:Person
  age: 45
  name: Jimmy
- !ruby/object:Person
  age: 23
  name: Laura Smith
END_OF_DATA
test_data = YAML.load(yaml_string)
puts test_data[0].name
puts test_data[1].name
```

```
Jimmy
Laura Smith
```

Here YAML.load converts the YAML data back into the test_data array of Person objects successfully.

You can use YAML to convert between most types of Ruby objects (including basic types such as Array and Hash) and YAML. This makes it an ideal intermediary format for storing data (such as configuration files) your applications need to access.

Note   When dealing with serialized objects, you must still have the classes used by those objects defined within the program somewhere; otherwise, they won't be usable.

As plain text, you can safely transmit YAML via email, store it in normal text files, and move it around more easily than the binary data created by libraries such as PStore.

To learn more about YAML formatting, read its Wikipedia entry at https:// en.wikipedia.org/wiki/YAML, or refer to the official YAML website at www.yaml.org/.

Relational Databases and SQL

In the previous section, you created some extremely simplistic "databases" using text files and object persistence. Text files, of course, have their limitations. They're not reliable if many processes are using them at the same time, and they're slow. Loading a CSV file into memory is fine when the dataset is small, but when it grows, the process of working directly with files can soon become sluggish.

When developing more robust systems, you pass database filing and management off to a separate application or system, and applications simply connect to a database system to pass data back and forth. In the previous section, you were working with database files and the data within them quite directly, and that's unacceptable when performance and reliability are necessary.

Relational Database Concepts

One major benefit of using a dedicated database system is getting support for *relational databases*. A relational database is composed of data grouped into one or more *tables* that can be linked together. A table stores information about one type of thing. For example, an address book database might be made up of a people table, an addresses table, and a phonenumbers table. Each table stores information about people, addresses, and phone numbers, respectively.

The people table would likely have a number of attributes (known as *columns*, in database land) such as name, age, and gender. Each row of the table—that is, an individual person—would then have information in each column. Figure 9-1 shows an example.

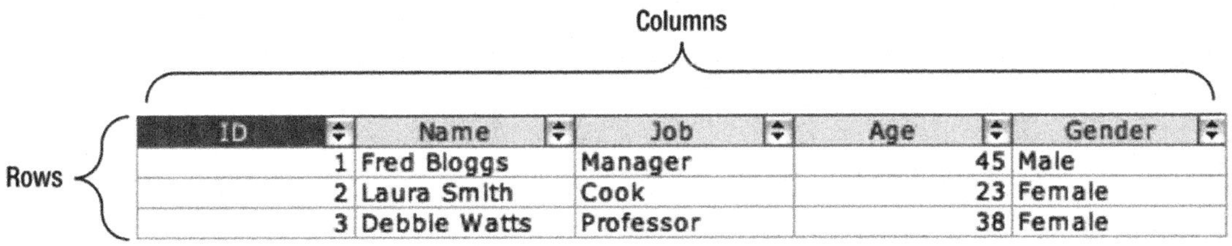

Figure 9-1. *A basic people table containing three rows*

Figure 9-1's example also includes a column called id. In relational databases, it's standard procedure to have an id column on most tables to identify each row uniquely. Although you could look up and retrieve data based on other columns, such as name, numeric IDs are useful when you're creating *relationships* between tables.

Note   In Figure 9-1, the table headings are written in a typical style, as you'd expect in a normal address book or spreadsheet. However, when dealing with relational databases at a lower level, it's common to use all lowercase names for column and table names. This explains why the text and later code examples in this chapter refer to table and column names in lowercase only.

One benefit of relational databases is the way rows in different tables can be related to one another. For example, your people table could have an address_id column that stores the ID of the address associated with this user. If you want to find out the address of a particular person, you can look up his or her address_id and then look up the relevant row of the addresses table.

The reason for this sort of relationship is that many people in your people database might share the same address, and rather than store the address separately for each person, it's more efficient to store a reference instead. This also means that if you update the address in the future, it updates for all the relevant users at the same time.

The relationship functionality also supports the definition of many-to-many relationships. You could create a separate table called related_people that has two columns, first_person_id and second_person_id. This table could store pairs of ID numbers that signify two people are related to each other. To work out to whom a person is related, you can simply look for any rows mentioning his or her ID number, and you'd get back the ID numbers of that person's related people. This sort of relationship is used in most databases and is what makes relational databases so useful.

MySQL, PostgreSQL, and SQLite

Three well-known relational database systems available today that work on both Windows and UNIX operating systems are MySQL, PostgreSQL, and SQLite. Each has significantly different features from the others and therefore has different uses.

Most web developers will be familiar with MySQL, as it comes with most web hosting packages and servers, making it easily the most commonly used database engine on the Internet.

For our purposes in the next few sections of this chapter, we'll be using a system called SQLite. Unlike MySQL, or PostgreSQL, SQLite doesn't run as a "server," so it doesn't require any special resources. Whereas MySQL and PostgreSQL both run as permanent server applications, SQLite is "on-demand" and works entirely on your local machine. Despite this, it's still fast and reliable and is ideal for local database purposes. You can easily carry much of the knowledge you learn with SQLite across to other systems. SQLite is also the default database engine used with Ruby on Rails apps, as you'll discover in Chapter 13.

Nonetheless, toward the end of this chapter, we'll look at how you can connect to databases using these other architectures, so that you can get direct access to any existing databases you might have from your Ruby applications.

Installing SQLite

The first step to getting a database system up and running quickly is to install SQLite3—the latest version of SQLite. Mac OS X comes with SQLite 3 by default, as do some Linux distributions. On Ubuntu or Debian Linux, you can run `apt-get install sqlite3 libsqlite3-dev`.

Once the SQLite3 libraries are installed at the operating system level, you can install the Ruby library that gives Ruby access to SQLite3 databases. It's packaged as a gem called **sqlite3-ruby** and can be installed on all systems with **gem install sqlite3** or **sudo gem install sqlite3** on UNIX-related operating systems if you aren't running as a superuser. (For information about installing Ruby gems, refer to Chapter 7.)

You can check that everything was installed okay with this code:

```
require 'sqlite3'
puts "It's all okay!" if defined?(SQLite3::Database)
```

```
It's all okay!
```

If the installation didn't progress smoothly, links to SQLite resources are available in Appendix B.

A Crash Course in Basic Database Operations and SQL

To manage databases with any of the various database systems at a basic level, knowledge of several SQL commands is required. In this section, we're going to look at how to create tables, add data to them, retrieve data, delete data, and change data.

Throughout this section, think entirely in terms of databases separately from Ruby. A demonstration of how Ruby can use SQL to manipulate a database is covered in detail in the later section "Using SQLite with Ruby."

Note   If you're already familiar with SQL, you can skip the next few sections and jump straight to the section "Using SQLite with Ruby" to see SQL in action alongside Ruby.

What Is SQL?

Structured Query Language (SQL) is a special language, often known as a query language, used to interact with database systems. You can use SQL to create, retrieve, update, and delete data, as well as create and manipulate structures that hold that data. Its basic purpose is to support the interaction between a client and a database system. In this section, I'm going to give you a primer on SQL's syntax and how you can use it from Ruby.

Be aware that this section is only a very basic introduction to SQL, as a full and deep explanation of SQL is beyond the scope of this book.

Note that the way different database systems use and implement SQL can vary wildly, which is why the following sections will only cover that which is reasonably standard and enables you to perform basic data operations.

If you want to play along at home, you can use the command-line `sqlite3` client to create a database and perform SQL queries upon it without getting involved with Ruby at all. Just run `sqlite3 test.db`, where `test.db` is your chosen database filename. You can then type SQL and press Enter to execute it. To leave the client, you can type `.quit` on a separate line and press Enter.

Note   There are also libraries that remove the necessity of writing SQL in order to work with databases. We mention some of these at the end of the chapter. Regardless, at least reading about how SQL works is going to be beneficial to you in the long term.

CREATE TABLE

Before you can add data into a database, it's necessary to create one or many tables to hold it. To create a table, you need to know what you want to store in it, what you want to call it, and what attributes you want to store.

For your people table, you want to have name, job, gender, and age columns, as well as a unique id column for possible relationships with other tables. To create a table, you use a syntax like so:

```
CREATE TABLE table_name (
column_name data_type options,
column_name data_type options,
...,
...
);
```

Note   SQL commands are typically written in capital letters for clarity (and it's somewhat traditional). However, you don't have to do this. Table names and attributes, however, can be case-sensitive with some database systems, so stick to lowercase for those!

Therefore, for your people table, you'd use this syntax:

```
CREATE TABLE people (
id integer primary key,
name varchar(50),
job varchar(50),
gender varchar(6),
age integer);
```

This SQL command creates a people table and gives it five columns. The data types for the name, job, and gender columns are all VARCHARs, meaning they're variable-length character fields. In basic terms, it means they can contain strings. The number in brackets refers to the maximum length of that string, so the name column can hold a maximum of 50 characters.

Note   SQLite is a reasonably pragmatic database, and it ignores most conventions relating to data types in SQL. Almost any form of data will fit into any type of column. SQLite ignores the maximum lengths for these VARCHAR columns. This is one reason why SQLite is great for quick and easy development, but not so great for crucial systems!

The `id` column has the words `primary key` as its options. This means that the `id` column is the primary reference to each row and that the ID must be unique for each row. This means SQLite will automatically assign a unique ID to each row, so you don't need to specify one yourself each time you add a new row.

INSERT INTO

You use the INSERT command to add rows to tables:

```
INSERT INTO people (name, age, gender, job) VALUES ("Chris Scott", 25,
"Male", ↵ "Technician");
```

First, you specify the table you want to add a row to, and then list the columns you wish to fill out, before passing in the values with which to fill the row.

You can omit the list of columns if the data passed after VALUES is in the correct order:

```
INSERT INTO people VALUES ("Chris Scott", 25, "Male", "Technician");
```

Caution   This particular INSERT would cause an error on your `people` table! It's missing the `id` column.

However, it's safer and more convenient if you specify the columns beforehand, as in the first example. The second example clearly demonstrates why this is the case, as it's hard to tell which item of data relates to which column.

Columns that don't have any data specified for them will be filled in automatically with the defaults specified in the CREATE TABLE statement for that table. In the case of the `people` table, the `id` column will automatically receive a unique ID number for each row added.

SELECT

You use the SELECT command to retrieve data from tables. You specify which columns
you want to retrieve (or use * as a wildcard to retrieve them all) and the table you want to
retrieve data from and optionally include a condition upon which to base the retrieval.
For example, you might only want to choose a particular row or rows that match certain
criteria.

This SQL statement retrieves the data from all columns for all rows in the people
table:

```
SELECT * FROM people;
```

This SQL retrieves all the values from just the name column of rows in the people
table (e.g., "Fred Bloggs," "Chris Scott," "Laura Smith"):

```
SELECT name FROM people;
```

This SQL retrieves rows with an id column equal to 2 from the people table (usually,
because id is a column containing unique values, only one row would be returned for
such a query):

```
SELECT * FROM people WHERE id = 2;
```

This SQL retrieves any rows that have a name column equal to "Chris Scott":

```
SELECT * FROM people WHERE name = "Chris Scott";
```

This SQL retrieves all rows of people whose ages are between 20 and 40, inclusive:

```
SELECT * FROM people WHERE age >= 20 AND age <= 40;
```

The conditions used in SQL are somewhat similar to those used in Ruby and other
programming languages, except that logical operators such as AND and OR are written as
plain English. Also, as in Ruby, you can use parentheses to group expressions and build
up more complex requests.

It's also possible to have the results returned in a certain order by appending an
ORDER BY clause such as ORDER column_name to the SQL query. You can further append
ASC to the column name to sort in an ascending fashion, or DESC to sort in a descending
fashion. For example, this SQL returns all rows from the people table ordered by the name
column in descending order (so names starting with Z come before those beginning
with A):

```
SELECT * FROM people ORDER BY name DESC;
```

This SQL returns all rows of those people between the ages of 20 and 40 in order of age, youngest first:

```
SELECT * FROM people WHERE age >= 20 AND age <= 40 ORDER BY age ASC;
```

Another useful addition to a SELECT command is LIMIT. LIMIT allows you to place a limit on the amount of rows returned on a single query:

```
SELECT * FROM people ORDER BY name DESC LIMIT 5;
```

In conjunction with ORDER, you can use LIMIT to find extremes in the data. For example, finding the oldest person is easy:

```
SELECT * FROM people ORDER BY age DESC LIMIT 1;
```

This sorts the rows in descending order by age and returns the first result: the highest. To get the youngest person, you could use ASC instead of DESC on the ordering.

Note   Database engines sort columns automatically by their data type. Strings of text are formatted alphanumerically, whereas integer and other number columns are sorted by their numeric value.

DELETE

The DELETE SQL command deletes rows from tables. You can delete rows based on an SQL condition, for example:

```
DELETE FROM people WHERE name="Chris";
DELETE FROM people WHERE age > 100;
DELETE FROM people WHERE gender = "Male" AND age < 50;
```

As with SELECT, you can place limits on the number of deletions:

```
DELETE FROM people WHERE age > 100 LIMIT 10;
```

In this case, only ten rows with an age over 100 would be deleted.

Think of the DELETE command to be like SELECT, but instead of returning the rows, it erases them. The format is otherwise reasonably similar.

UPDATE

UPDATE provides the ability to update and amend information within the database. As with DELETE, the syntax for UPDATE is similar to that of SELECT. Consider this:

```
SELECT * FROM people WHERE name = "Chris";
UPDATE people SET name = "Christopher" WHERE name = "Chris";
```

UPDATE first accepts the name of a table whose row(s) might be updated, then accepts the column(s) to be changed along with the new data, and finally accepts an optional condition for the change. Some examples follow.

This SQL changes the name column to "Christopher" on all rows where the name column is currently equal to "Chris":

```
UPDATE people SET name = "Christopher" WHERE name = "Chris";
```

This SQL changes the name column to "Christopher" and the age column to 44 where the name column is currently equal to "Chris":

```
UPDATE people SET name = "Christopher", age = 44 WHERE name = "Chris";
```

This SQL changes the name column to "Christopher" where the name column is "Chris" *and* the age column equals 25. Therefore, a row where the name is Chris and the age is 21 will *not* be updated by this example query:

```
UPDATE people SET name = "Christopher" WHERE name = "Chris" AND age = 25;
```

This SQL changes the name column to "Christopher" on every row of the people table. This demonstrates why it pays to be careful when building SQL queries, as short statements can have big ramifications!

```
UPDATE people SET name = "Christopher";
```

Using SQLite with Ruby

Now that you've installed SQLite and we've covered the basics of how SQL works, let's put together a basic demonstration of how it all works in conjunction with Ruby. To do this, you're going to write a program that allows you to manipulate a database based on the people table that we've talked about so far in this chapter.

The first step is to write the basic code that can load or create a database. The sqlite ruby gem makes this simple with the SQLite3::Database.new method, for example:

```
require 'sqlite3'
$db = SQLite3::Database.new("dbfile")
$db.results_as_hash = true
```

From this point, you can use $db in a similar way to the file handles you used earlier in this chapter. For example, $db.close will similarly close the database file, just as you closed regular files.

The $db.results_as_hash = true line forces SQLite to return data in a hash format rather than as an array of attributes (as with CSV). This makes the results easier to access.

Note   The database handle has been assigned to a global variable, $db, so that you can split your program into multiple methods without creating a class. You can therefore access the database handle, $db, from anywhere you wish. This isn't what you'd do in a large program, but for learning to use SQLite3 here, it will suffice.

To cope with the closing situation, you'll create a method specifically for disconnecting the database and ending the program:

```
def disconnect_and_quit
  $db.close
  puts "Bye!"
  exit
end
```

Note   Remember that you must define methods before you use them, so put these separate methods at the top of your source file.

Now let's create a method that will use the CREATE TABLE SQL statement to create the table where you'll store your data:

```
def create_table
  puts "Creating people table"
  $db.execute %q{
    CREATE TABLE people (
    id integer primary key,
    name varchar(50),
    job varchar(50),
    gender varchar(6),
    age integer)
  }
end
```

A database handle will allow you to execute arbitrary SQL with the execute method. All you need to do is pass the SQL as an argument, and SQLite will execute the SQL upon the database.

Next, let's create a method that asks for input from the user to add a new person to the database:

```
def add_person
  puts "Enter name:"
  name = gets.chomp
  puts "Enter job:"
  job = gets.chomp
  puts "Enter gender:"
  gender = gets.chomp
  puts "Enter age:"
  age = gets.chomp
  $db.execute("INSERT INTO people (name, job, gender, age) VALUES (?, ?, ?,
?)", ↵
    name, job, gender, age)
end
```

Note   The chomp method added to gets removes the newline characters that appear at the end of keyboard output retrieved with gets.

The start of the add_person method is mundane. You ask for each of the person's attributes in turn and assign them to variables. However, $db.execute is more intriguing this time. In the previous section, the INSERT SQL was shown with the data in the main statement, but in this method, you're using question marks (?) as placeholders for the data.

Ruby performs an automatic substitution from the other parameters passed to execute into the placeholders. This acts as a way of securing your database. The reason is that if you interpolated the user's input directly into the SQL, the user might type some SQL that could break your query. However, when you use the placeholder method, the sqlite ruby library will clean up the supplied data for you and make sure it's safe to put into the database.

Now you need a way to be able to access the data entered. Time for another method! This code example shows how to retrieve the associated data for a given name and ID:

```ruby
def find_person
  puts "Enter name or ID of person to find:"
  id = gets.chomp

  person = $db.execute("SELECT * FROM people WHERE name = ? OR id = ?", id,
  id.to_i).first

  unless person
    puts "No result found"
    return
  end

  puts %Q{Name: #{person['name']}
Job: #{person['job']}
Gender: #{person['gender']}
Age: #{person['age']}}
end
```

The find_person method asks the user to enter either the name or the ID of the person he or she is looking for. The $db.execute line cleverly checks both the name and id columns at the same time. Therefore, a match on either the id or name will work. If no match is found, the user will be told, and the method will end early. If there's a match, the information for that user will be extracted and printed on the screen.

You can tie it up with a main routine that acts as a menu system for the four methods described earlier. You already have the database connection code in place, so creating a menu is simple:

```
loop do
  puts %q{Please select an option:
    1. Create people table
    2. Add a person
    3. Look for a person
    4. Quit}

  case gets.chomp
  when '1'
    create_table
  when '2'
    add_person
  when '3'
    find_person
  when '4'
    disconnect_and_quit
  end
end
```

If the code is put together properly and then run, a typical first session could go like this:

```
Please select an option:

1. Create people table
2. Add a person
3. Look for a person
4. Quit
1
Creating people table
Please select an option:

1. Create people table
2. Add a person
```

```
3. Look for a person
4. Quit
2
Enter name:
Fred Bloggs
Enter job:
Manager
Enter gender:
Male
Enter age:
48
Please select an option:

1. Create people table
2. Add a person
3. Look for a person
4. Quit
3
Enter name or ID of person to find:
1
Name: Fred Bloggs
Job: Manager
Gender: Male
Age: 48
Please select an option:
1. Create people table
2. Add a person
3. Look for a person
4. Quit
3
Enter name or ID of person to find:
Jane Smith

No result
```

Your quick and basic application provides a way to add data and retrieve data from a remote data source in only a handful of lines!

Note   You should note that we have broken some of the best practices highlighted through this book in the previous program. We used global variables and applied almost no structure to the code at all. The goal here was solely to use SQLite3 quickly, but consider how you could dramatically improve the structure of the program now that it works.

Connecting to Other Database Systems

In the previous section, we looked at SQL and how to use it with the SQLite library, a library that provides a basic database system on the local machine. More commonly, however, you might want to use more elaborate databases or connect to databases located on other machines (and potentially not even run by you).

Sequel (`https://sequel.jeremyevans.net/`) is a "database toolkit" for Ruby that uses a DSL (domain-specific language) to abstract away some of the details of using a database and interfaces with the libraries used to talk to various database systems. If you write your code in a certain way, using Sequel, you can, as long as you do not use any database-specific features, switch that code between, say, MySQL and PostgreSQL and it would continue to work.

Sequel has "adapters" for a wide variety of database systems, the most popular including MySQL, IBM DB, Oracle, PostgreSQL, and SQLite3. It also supports a variety of common database features like prepared statements, stored procedures, and transactions, so if you're already familiar with using databases, it's a library well worth checking out.

Installing Sequel is easy:

```
gem install sequel
```

Once it's installed, you'll want to make sure you have the underlying driver library for your database of choice installed too. For example, for MySQL, you could install the `mysql2` library. For PostgreSQL, install the `pg` library:

```
gem install pg
```

While this isn't going to be a complete tour of Sequel, once you have things installed, you can begin to write code like this:

```ruby
require 'sequel'
require 'pg'

DB = Sequel.connect('postgres://user:password@localhost/dbname')

DB.create_table :people do
  primary_key :id
  String :first_name
  String :last_name
  Integer :age
end

people = DB[:people]
people.insert( :first_name => "Fred", :last_name => "Bloggs", :age => 32 )

puts "There are #{people.count} people in the database"

people.each do |person|
  puts person[:first_name]
end

DB.fetch("SELECT * FROM people") do |row|
  puts row[:first_name]
end
```

In a relatively short program, we've seen how we can create a table, populate that table with data, then query the length of the table, and look up rows within that table in two different ways. As you may notice, this is a lot more straightforward than working with a database driver library directly, as we did with the `sqlite3` library earlier!

Note   In the preceding program, you could `require` in `sqlite3` and then change the first main line of code to DB = `Sequel.sqlite` to create a temporary, in-memory SQLite database. This will let you run the code if you don't have access to a PostgreSQL server.

Refer to `https://sequel.jeremyevans.net/` for more about using Sequel.

ActiveRecord: A Sneak Peek

So far in this chapter, you've worked directly with databases and had to learn a whole new language: SQL. Working with a database with SQL in mind can make things more efficient and reliable than putting data into text files, say, as you did earlier, but ActiveRecord makes it easier still (and even easier than Sequel). ActiveRecord is a product of the Ruby on Rails framework, which we'll look at in Chapter 13, but can be used independently of it. ActiveRecord will be covered in more depth in that chapter, but deserves a brief summary here.

ActiveRecord abstracts away the details of SQL and makes it possible to relate to items within databases in an object-oriented fashion, as you did with PStore.

ActiveRecord gives you objects that correspond to rows and classes that correspond to tables, and you can work with the data using Ruby syntax, like so:

```
person = Person.where(name: "Chris").first
person.age = 50
person.save
```

This code looks through the people table for a row whose name column matches "Chris" and puts an object relating to that row into person. ActiveRecord makes attributes available for all that row's columns, so changing the age column is as easy as assigning to the object's attribute. However, once the object's value has been changed, you issue the save method to save the changes back to the database.

Note   The pluralization from a Person class to a people table is an automatic part of ActiveRecord's functionality.

The previous code could replace SQL such as this:

```
SELECT * FROM people WHERE name = "Chris";
UPDATE people SET age = 50 WHERE name = "Chris";
```

Even SQL gurus familiar with Ruby tend to find Ruby's syntax more natural, particularly in the scope of a Ruby program. There's no need to mix two different languages in one program if both sets of features can be provided in Ruby alone.

ActiveRecord will be covered again in Chapter 13.

Summary

In this chapter, we've looked at how data can flow into and out of your Ruby programs. Initially, we looked at the low-level concept of I/O streams before quickly moving on to the pragmatism of databases. Databases provide a way to work with data in a more abstracted fashion without worrying about the underlying structure of the data on the computer's filesystem. Indeed, databases can be located within memory or on totally different machines, and our code could remain the same.

Let's reflect on the main concepts covered in this chapter:

- *I/O*: Input/output. The concept of receiving input and sending output by various means on a computer, often via I/O streams.

- *I/O stream*: A channel along which data can be sent and/or received.

- *Standard input (stdin)*: A stream that relates to the default way of accepting data into the application, usually the keyboard.

- *Standard output (stdout)*: A stream that relates to the default way of outputting data from the application, usually to the screen.

- *File pointer*: An abstract reference to the current "location" within a file.

- *Database*: An organized collection of data structured in a way that makes it easy to be accessed programmatically.

- *CSV (comma-separated values)*: A way of structuring data with attributes separated with commas. CSV can be stored in plain text files.

- *Marshalling*: The process of converting a live data structure or object into a flat set of data that can be stored on disk, sent across a network, and then used to reconstruct the original data structure or object elsewhere or at some other time.

- *Table*: A collection of data organized into rows, with multiple columns, where each column represents a different attribute of each row. There are usually multiple tables within a database, containing different types of data.

- *SQLite*: An open source, public-domain relational database API and library that works on a single-user basis on a local machine. It supports SQL as its querying language.

- *MySQL*: An open source relational database system available in both community and professional editions. It is maintained by MySQL AB. Web hosting companies commonly offer MySQL database support.

- *PostgreSQL*: A free, open source relational database system licensed under the BSD license, making it possible to repackage and sell within commercial products. PostgreSQL is often considered to be of higher performance and have better conformity to SQL standards than MySQL, although it's less popular at the time of writing.

- *Primary key*: A column (or multiple columns) on a table whose data uniquely identifies each row.

- *SQL (Structured Query Language)*: A language specifically designed to create, amend, retrieve, and otherwise manipulate data in relational database systems.

- *ActiveRecord*: A library that abstracts databases, rows, columns, and SQL into standard Ruby syntax using classes and objects. It's a major part of the Ruby on Rails framework, which is covered in Chapter 13.

With the ability to load, manipulate, and store data, the number of useful Ruby applications you can develop increases significantly. Few applications depend entirely on data typed in every time, and having access to files and databases makes it easy to build powerful systems that can be used over time to manage data.

Next, in Chapter 10, we're going to look at a few ways that you can make your applications and libraries available to the world.

Distributing Ruby Code and Libraries

In this chapter, we're going to look at how to distribute the Ruby code you write to other developers and users.

Developing Ruby applications and libraries is so simple that you'll soon want to release them to the world. As covered in Chapter 5, Ruby has a proud history of community and sharing, and nearly every Ruby developer will release code or completed applications at some point.

This chapter will walk you through the considerations and processes of deploying Ruby applications, libraries, and remotely accessible services using HTTP daemons and CGI scripts.

Distributing Basic Ruby Programs

Ruby is an interpreted language, so to distribute Ruby programs you can simply distribute the source code files you've written. Anyone else who has Ruby installed can then run the files in the same way that you do.

This process of distributing the actual source code for a program is typically how most programs developed using a scripting language, such as Ruby, are shared; but more traditionally, software has been distributed without the source code included. Popular desktop application development languages such as C and C++ are *compiled* languages whose source code is converted directly into *machine code* that runs on a certain platform. This software can be distributed by copying the resulting compiled machine code files, rather than the source, from machine to machine. However, this technique is not possible with Ruby, as there is currently no Ruby compiler available (with the exception of that in JRuby, but this is still a nascent area), so you have to distribute your source code in one sense or another for other people to be able to run your programs.

© Carleton DiLeo, Peter Cooper 2021
C. DiLeo and P. Cooper, *Beginning Ruby 3*, https://doi.org/10.1007/978-1-4842-6324-2_10

Note   Later in this chapter, we'll look at making the functionality of your Ruby programs available across a network. This technique does not require you to make your source code available, although it does require you to maintain a running copy of your program on a machine that's network accessible (such as a web server).

To see how you can distribute Ruby source code, let's take an example Ruby file and call it **test.rb**:

```
puts "Your program works!"
```

If you copy **test.rb** to another computer that has the Ruby interpreter installed on it, you can run the program directly with the Ruby interpreter as you would normally:

```
ruby test.rb
```

```
Your program works!
```

This technique works well if you're passing programs between your own machines or servers or if you're distributing your programs to other developers. As long as the other users and machines have the same Ruby libraries or gems that your program uses, your program should run fine. For example, if you develop something to work with the standard version of Ruby that comes with Mac OS X, your program should work just fine on other Mac OS X machines (assuming they are running the same or a later version of OS X that includes Ruby).

This ability to interpret the code in the same way on varying machines is one benefit of interpreted languages over compiled languages. If the same version of the Ruby interpreter is available on a different platform, it should run the same programs that your Ruby interpreter does. With compiled code (code that is specifically compiled down to machine code for a specific platform), it is not the case that it will run identically on all platforms; in fact, it usually won't!

What if you want to distribute your Ruby program to people who aren't *au fait* with the Ruby interpreter? Depending on the target operating system (i.e., the operating system the user is running), there are several ways to make deploying Ruby applications simpler.

The Shebang Line

On UNIX-related operating systems (Linux, OS X, BSD, etc.), you can engineer your program to run more simply by using a *shebang line*.

Note   In certain situations, such as when using the Apache HTTP server, shebang lines can work in Windows. You can use shebang lines such as #!ruby and #!c:\ ruby\bin\ruby.exe to make Ruby CGI scripts work under Apache on Windows.

For example, say your script were to look like this:

```
#!/usr/bin/ruby

puts "Your program works!"
```

UNIX-related operating systems support putting the name of the interpreter of a file on the first line of the file with a shebang line, where the "shebang" is simply the pound (#) sign and the exclamation mark (!).

Note   The shebang line only needs to be in the file that's initially run. It doesn't need to be in library or support files used by the main program.

In this case, /usr/bin/ruby, the Ruby interpreter, is used to interpret the rest of the file. One problem you might run into, though, is that your Ruby interpreter might be located in /usr/bin/local/ruby or have a different name entirely. However, there's a reasonably portable way to work around this problem. Many UNIX-related operating systems (including most Linuxes and OS X) have a tool called env that stores the location of certain applications and settings. You can use this tool to load Ruby without knowing its exact location, for example:

```
#!/usr/bin/env ruby

puts "Your program works!"
```

You could copy this example to many different Linux or OS X machines, for example, and it would work on the majority (env is not universal).

If this script were called **test.rb** and located in the current working directory, you could simply run it from a command line, like so:

```
./test.rb
```

Note   On most UNIX-like operating systems (including Mac OS X), as well as adding a shebang line, it's necessary to make the Ruby script "executable" by using chmod for the preceding example to work, as in chmod +x test.rb.

Naturally, if you copied the script elsewhere (e.g., /usr/bin), you could access it directly:

```
/usr/bin/test.rb
```

Or if the script's location is in the path, it's even easier:

```
test.rb
```

You could even remove the **.rb** suffix and make it look like a regular executable if you wished.

Associated File Types in Windows

Whereas shebang lines are used on UNIX-like operating systems, Windows users are more familiar with file extensions (such as DOC, EXE, JPG, MP3, or TXT) dictating how a file is processed.

If you use My Computer or Windows Explorer to find a folder containing a Ruby file, the file might or might not already be associated with the Ruby interpreter (depending on which Ruby package you installed). Alternatively, Ruby files might be associated with your text editor. In any case, if you want to be able to double-click Ruby files in Windows and have them run directly as regular Ruby programs, you can do this by changing the default action for files with an extension of RB (or any other arbitrary extension you wish to use).

The easiest way to set an association is to right-click the icon representing a Ruby file and choose the Open With option from the menu (or Open, if it's currently not associated with any program). Associate the program with the ruby.exe Ruby interpreter on your computer and check the Always Use the Selected Program to Open This Kind of File option. This will cause Ruby files to be executed directly by the Ruby interpreter in the future.

Detecting Ruby's Runtime Environment

Deploying Ruby programs can be made easier with the tools covered in the previous section, but you can use a number of techniques directly within Ruby to make Ruby's interactions with its surrounding environment even better.

For example, it's possible to detect information about the machine upon which a Ruby script is running and then change the way the program operates on the fly. You can also retrieve parameters passed to the program via the command line.

Detecting the runtime environment while the program is running can be useful to restrict access to users on specific platforms if your program isn't relevant to other users, or to tailor internal settings in your program so that your program will work better on the user's operating system. It can also be a useful way to get system-specific information (rather than operating system–specific information) that's relevant directly to the machine the program is running on, as it could affect the operation of your program. A common example of this is retrieving the current user's *path*: a string of various directory names on the system that can be searched as default locations for files. There are also environment variables dictating where to store temporary files, and so forth.

Easy OS Detection with RUBY_PLATFORM

Among the myriad special variables Ruby makes accessible, a variable called RUBY_PLATFORM contains the name of the current environment (operating system) you're running under. You can easily query this variable to detect what operating system your program is running under. This can be useful if you want to use a certain filesystem notation or features that are implemented differently under different operating systems.

On my Windows machine, RUBY_PLATFORM contains i386-mswin32, on my OS X machine it contains x86_64-darwin13, and on my Linux machine it contains i686-linux. This gives you the immediate power to segregate features and settings by operating system:

```ruby
if RUBY_PLATFORM =~ /win32/
  puts "We're in Windows!"
elsif RUBY_PLATFORM =~ /linux/
  puts "We're in Linux!"
elsif RUBY_PLATFORM =~ /darwin/
  puts "We're in Mac OS X!"
```

```
elsif RUBY_PLATFORM =~ /freebsd/
  puts "We're in FreeBSD!"
else
  puts "We're running under an unknown operating system."
end
```

Environment Variables

Whenever a program is run on a computer, it's contained with a certain *environment*, whether that's the command line or a GUI. The operating system sets a number of special variables called *environment variables* that contain information about the environment. They vary by operating system, but can be a good way of detecting things that could be useful in your programs.

You can quickly and easily inspect the environment variables (as supplied by your operating system) on your current machine with irb by using the special ENV hash:

```
irb(main):001:0> pp ENV.each {|e| puts e.join(': ') }
```

```
TERM: vt100
SHELL: /bin/bash
USER: carleton
PATH: /bin:/sbin:/usr/bin:/usr/sbin:/usr/local/bin:/opt/local/bin:/usr/
local/sbin
PWD: /Users/carleton
SHLVL: 1
HOME: /Users/carleton
LOGNAME: carleton
SECURITYSESSIONID: 51bbd0
_: /usr/bin/irb
LINES: 32
COLUMNS: 120
```

Specifically, these are the results from my machine, and yours will probably be quite different. For example, when I try the same code on a Windows machine, I get results such as these:

```
ALLUSERSPROFILE: F:\Documents and Settings\All Users
APPDATA: F:\Documents and Settings\carleton\Application Data
CLIENTNAME: Console
HOMEDRIVE: F:
HOMEPATH: \Documents and Settings\carleton
LOGONSERVER: \\PSHUTTLE
NUMBER_OF_PROCESSORS: 2
OS: Windows_NT
Path: F:\ruby\bin;F:\WINDOWS\system32;F:\WINDOWS
PATHEXT: .COM;.EXE;.BAT;.CMD;.VBS;.VBE;.JS;.JSE;.WSF;.WSH;.RB;.RBW
ProgramFiles: F:\Program Files
SystemDrive: F:
SystemRoot: F:\WINDOWS
TEMP: F:\DOCUME~1\Carleton\LOCALS~1\Temp
TMP: F:\DOCUME~1\Carleton\LOCALS~1\Temp
USERDOMAIN: PSHUTTLE
USERNAME: Carleton
USERPROFILE: F:\Documents and Settings\carleton
windir: F:\WINDOWS
```

You can use these environment variables to decide where to store temporary files or to find out what sort of features your operating system offers, in real time, much as you did with RUBY_PLATFORM:

```
tmp_dir = '/tmp'
if ENV['OS'] =~ /Windows_NT/
  puts "This program is running under Windows NT/2000/XP!"
  tmp_dir = ENV['TMP']
elsif ENV['PATH'] =~ /\/usr/
  puts "This program has access to a UNIX-style file system!"
else
  puts "I cannot figure out what environment I'm running in!"
  exit
end

# [.. do something here ..]
```

Note   You can also set environment variables with ENV['variable_name'] = value. However, setting environment variables from within a program only applies to the local process and any child processes.

Although ENV acts like a hash, it's technically a special object, but you can convert it to a true hash using its .to_hash method, as in ENV.to_hash.

Accessing Command-Line Arguments

In Chapter 4, you used a special array called ARGV. ARGV is an array automatically created by the Ruby interpreter that contains the parameters passed to the Ruby program (whether on the command line or by other means). For example, say you created a script called **argvtest.rb**:

```
p ARGV
```

You could run it like so:

```
ruby argvtest.rb these are command line parameters
```

```
["these", "are", "command", "line", "parameters"]
```

The parameters are passed into the program and become present in the ARGV array, where they can be processed as you wish. Use of ARGV is ideal for command-line tools where filenames and options are passed in this way.

Using ARGV also works if you call a script directly. On UNIX operating systems, you could adjust **argvtest.rb** to be like this:

```
#!/usr/bin/env ruby
p ARGV
```

And you could call it in this way:

```
./argvtest.rb these are command line parameters
```

```
["these", "are", "command", "line", "parameters"]
```

You generally use command-line arguments to pass options, settings, and data fragments that might change between executions of a program. For example, a common utility found on most operating systems is copy or cp, which is used to copy files. It's used like so:

```
cp /directory1/from_filename /directory2/destination_filename
```

This would copy a file from one place to another (and rename it along the way) within the filesystem. The two filenames are both command-line arguments, and a Ruby script could receive data in the same way, like so:

```
#!/usr/bin/env ruby
from_filename = ARGV[0]
destination_filename = ARGV[1]
```

Distributing Ruby Libraries As Gems

Over time, it's likely you'll develop your own libraries to solve various problems with Ruby so that you don't need to write the same code over and over in different programs, but can call on the library for support.

Usually you'll want to make these libraries available to use on other machines, on servers upon which you deploy applications, or to other developers. You might even open source your libraries to get community input and a larger developer base.

If you've read Chapter 5, you'll have a good feel for Ruby's commitment to open source and how open source is important to Ruby developers. This section looks at how to release your code and libraries in such a way that other developers can find them useful.

Luckily, deploying libraries is generally less problematic than deploying entire applications, as the target audience is made up of other developers who are usually familiar with installing libraries.

In Chapter 7, we looked at RubyGems, a library installation and management system for Ruby. We looked at how RubyGems makes it easy to install libraries, but RubyGems also makes it easy to create "gems" of your own from your own code.

Creating a Gem

There are easy ways to create gems and slightly less easy ways. I'm going to take a "raw" approach by showing how to create a gem from the ground up. Later, we'll look at a library that will do most of the grunt work for you.

Let's first create a simple library that extends the String class and puts it in a file called **string_extend.rb**:

```ruby
class String
  def vowels
    scan(/[aeiou]/i)
  end
end
```

This code adds a `vowels` method to the `String` `class`, which returns an array of all the vowels in a string:

```ruby
"This is a test".vowels
```

```ruby
["i", "i", "a", "e"]
```

As a local library within the scope of a larger application, it could be loaded with `require` or `require_relative`:

```ruby
require_relative 'string_extend'
```

However, you want to turn it into a gem that you can use anywhere. Building a gem involves three steps. The first is to organize your code and other files into a structure that can be turned into a gem. The second is to create a *specification file* that lists information about the gem. The third is to use the *gem* program to build the gem from the source files and the specification.

Structuring Your Files

Before you can build a gem, it's necessary to collect all the files you want to make up the gem. This is usually done using a standard structure. So far, you have your **string_extend.rb** file, and this is the only file you want within your gem.

First, it's necessary to create a folder to contain all the gem's folders, so you create a folder called `string_extend`. Under this folder, you create several other folders as follows:

- `lib`: This directory will contain the Ruby code related to the library.

- `test or spec`: This directory will contain any unit tests or other testing scripts related to the library.

- `doc`: This is an optional directory that could contain documentation about the library, particularly documentation created with or by RDoc.

- bin: This is another optional directory that can contain system tools and command-line scripts that are related to the library. For example, RubyGems itself installs the gem command-line tool; such a tool would be placed into bin.

At a minimum, you should end up with string_extend/lib and string_extend/test.

In this example, you should place string_extend.rb within the string_extend/lib directory. If you have tests, documentation, or command-line scripts, place them into the respective directories.

Note   The preceding directory names are written in UNIX style, but on Windows would be represented similarly to this: c:\gems\string_extend, c:\gems\string_extend\lib, and so on. Take this into account throughout this entire section.

Creating a Specification File

Once your files are organized, it's time to create a specification file that describes the gem and provides RubyGems with enough information to create the final gem. Create a text file called **string_extend.gemspec** (or a filename that matches your own project name) in the main **string_extend** folder, and fill it out like so:

```ruby
Gem::Specification.new do |s|
  s.name = 'string_extend'
  s.version = '0.0.1'
  s.summary = "StringExtend adds useful features to the String class"
  s.platform = Gem::Platform::RUBY
  s.files = Dir.glob("**/**/**")
  s.test_files = Dir.glob("test/*_test.rb")
  s.authors = ["Your Name"]
  s.email = "your-email-address@email.com"
  s.required_ruby_version = '>= 2.0.0'
end
```

This is a basic specification file. The specification file is effectively a simple Ruby script that passes information through to `Gem::Specification`. The information it provides is mostly simple, but let's look at a few key areas.

First, you define the name of the gem, setting it to `'string_extend'`:

```
s.name = 'string_extend'
```

Next, you define the version number. Typically, version numbers for Ruby projects (and for Ruby itself) contain three parts in order of significance. Early versions of software—before an official release, perhaps—often begin with 0, as in `0.0.1` here:

```
s.version = '0.0.1'
```

The summary line is displayed by `gem list`, and can be useful to people prior to installing the gem. Simply put together a short description of your library/gem here:

```
s.summary = "StringExtend adds useful features to the String class"
```

The files attribute accepts an array of all the files to include within the gem. In this case, you use `Dir.glob` to get an array of all the files under the current directory:

```
s.files = Dir.glob("**/**/**")
```

However, you could explicitly reference every file in an array in the preceding line.

The `test_files` attribute, like the `files` attribute, accepts an array of files, in this case associated with tests. You can leave this line intact even if you have no `test` folder, as `Dir.glob` will just return an empty array, for example:

```
s.test_files = Dir.glob("test/*_test.rb")
or
s.test_files = Dir.glob("spec/*_spec.rb")
```

Last, sometimes libraries rely on features in certain versions of Ruby. You can specify the required version of Ruby with the `require_ruby_version` parameter. If there's no required version, you can simply omit this line:

```
s.required_ruby_version = '>= 2.0.0'
```

Note   A full list of the parameters you can use in a RubyGems specification file is available at `https://guides.rubygems.org/specification-reference/`. Also, you can learn more about versioning by visiting `https://semver.org/`.

Building the Gem

Once the specifications file is complete, building the final `.gem` file is as simple as this:

```
gem build <spec file>
```

Note   `gem build` should be run from the directory that the `spec` file is in.

In your case:

```
gem build string_extend.gemspec
```

This makes gem create the final gem file, called `string_extend-0.0.1.gem`. You may receive some warnings if there is any missing information. Read the warning carefully to determine how to remove it.

Note   In the future, once you change and update your library, simply update the version numbers and rebuild, and you'll have a new gem ready to go that can be installed to upgrade the existing installed gem.

Beyond this point, you could install your own gem with gem `install string_extend`, and then use it from other scripts using `require 'string_extend'`. It's that simple.

Easier Gem Creation

In Chapter 7, we looked at a popular tool within the Ruby world called Bundler. Bundler makes it easy to manage the dependencies of your Ruby programs, but it also has a feature to create all of the boilerplate code that you saw in the past few pages. Knowing how this code operates is important, which is why we covered it, but once you're up to speed, using Bundler to automatically generate the files will save you time.

To create a new gem using Bundler is as simple as

```
bundle gem string_extend
```

Note   Bear in mind if you followed the previous section and created a gem by hand, what we're doing here will conflict with that, so consider moving to a different directory or creating something with a different name.

You will be asked to select a testing framework, if you want to us the MIT license and if you want to include the code of conduct. In the following output, I'm using RSpec, the MIT license and the code of conduct. The result is a directory and a set of files, as well as the initialization of a Git repository:

```
      create  string_extend/Gemfile
      create  string_extend/lib/string_extend.rb
      create  string_extend/lib/string_extend/version.rb
      create  string_extend/string_extend.gemspec
      create  string_extend/Rakefile
      create  string_extend/README.md
      create  string_extend/bin/console
      create  string_extend/bin/setup
      create  string_extend/.gitignore
      create  string_extend/.travis.yml
      create  string_extend/.rspec
      create  string_extend/spec/spec_helper.rb
      create  string_extend/spec/string_extend_spec.rb
      create  string_extend/LICENSE.txt
      create  string_extend/CODE_OF_CONDUCT.md
Initializing git repo in /users/jane/ruby/string_extend
```

Due to Bundler's boilerplate code needing to cope with almost any example of creating a gem out of the box, its gem specification file is slightly more complex than the one we created earlier but follows the same structure:

```
require_relative 'lib/string_extend/version'

Gem::Specification.new do |spec|
  spec.name         = "string_extend"
  spec.version      = StringExtend::VERSION
  spec.authors      = ["Carleton DiLeo"]
  spec.email        = ["example@email.com"]

  spec.summary      = %q{TODO: Write a short summary, because RubyGems
requires one.}
```

```
spec.description    = %q{TODO: Write a longer description or delete this line.}
spec.homepage       = "TODO: Put your gem's website or public repo URL here."
spec.license        = "MIT"
spec.required_ruby_version = Gem::Requirement.new(">= 2.3.0")

spec.metadata["allowed_push_host"] = "TODO: Set to 'http://mygemserver.com'"

spec.metadata["homepage_uri"] = spec.homepage
spec.metadata["source_code_uri"] = "TODO: Put your gem's public repo URL
here."
spec.metadata["changelog_uri"] = "TODO: Put your gem's CHANGELOG.md URL
here."

# Specify which files should be added to the gem when it is released.
# The `git ls-files -z` loads the files in the RubyGem that have been
  added into git.
spec.files          = Dir.chdir(File.expand_path('..', __FILE__)) do
  `git ls-files -z`.split("\x0").reject { |f| f.match(%r{^(test|spec|feat
  ures)/}) }
end
spec.bindir         = "exe"
spec.executables    = spec.files.grep(%r{^exe/}) { |f| File.basename(f) }
spec.require_paths = ["lib"]
end
```

All that's left now is to fill out the blanks and carry on developing your library.

Installing Your Gem

Distributing a gem is easy. You can upload it to a website or transfer it in any way you would normally transfer a file. You can then install the gem with the command **gem install** and refer to the local file.

The best way to distribute gems, however, is in a form where they can be installed over the Internet without specifying a source, for example:

```
gem install gem_name
```

This command installs the gem **gem_name** by looking for it on the Internet and downloading it to the local machine. But how does gem know where to download gems? By default, RubyGems searches a Ruby project repository called RubyGems.org for gems if no source is specified. We'll look at how to make gems available in the default database using RubyGems.org next.

RubyGems.org

RubyGems.org (https://rubygems.org/) is the largest community repository for Ruby projects and libraries. It contains thousands of projects and acts as a centralized location for the hosting of gems. Nearly all the major Ruby libraries are available from or hosted there, including Ruby on Rails.

If you want your gem to be installed easily by users, hosting it on RubyGems.org is key. And, happily, it's entirely free.

To host a project on RubyGems.org, you first need an account, but once you're set up you'll be able to push any valid gem you've created on your local machine up to the RubyGems.org site like so:

```
gem push your_gems_filename-0.0.1.gem
```

Note   You will get an error if you push up a gem that has the same name as a gem that already exists on the RubyGems.org site, so you might want to check if your name conflicts before you even start to build your library, or at least be prepared to rename or namespace it.

If you use the Bundler approach to create a gem, as explained in the previous section, you can use Rake instead:

```
rake release
```

Deploying Ruby Applications As Remote Services

An alternative to giving people your source or packaging it up to be run locally on a user's machine is making a program's functionality available as a remote service over a network. This only works for a small subset of functionality, but providing functionality remotely gives you more control over your code and how it is used.

Ruby's networking and web features will be covered in more depth in Chapters 14 and 15, but in this section, we'll look at how to put together basic services with Ruby that allow users to access a program's functionality over a network.

Note   If you want to build a true web application, refer to Chapter 13. This section is about building small, ad hoc services.

CGI Scripts

A common way to make scripts available online is to upload them to web hosting providers as CGI scripts. Common Gateway Interface (CGI) is a standard that allows web server software (such as Apache or Microsoft IIS) to launch programs and send data back and forth between them and the web client.

Many people associate the term CGI with the Perl language, as Perl has been the most common language with which to write CGI scripts. However, CGI is language agnostic, and you can just as easily write CGI scripts with Ruby (more easily, in fact!).

A Basic CGI Script

The most basic Ruby CGI script looks like this:

```
#!/usr/bin/ruby
puts "Content-type: text/html\n\n"
puts "<html><body>This is a test</body></html>"
```

If you called this script `test.cgi` and uploaded it to a UNIX-based web hosting provider (the most common type) with the right permissions, you could use it as a CGI script. For example, if you have the website `www.example.com/` hosted with a Linux web hosting provider and you upload `test.cgi` to the main directory and give it `execute` permissions, then visiting `www.example.com/test.cgi` should return an HTML page saying, "`This is a test`".

Note   Although `/usr/bin/ruby` is referenced in the previous example, for many users or web hosting providers, Ruby might be located at `/usr/local/bin/ruby`. Make sure to check or try using `/usr/bin/env ruby`.

When `test.cgi` is requested from a web browser, the web server looks for `test.` `cgi` on the website and then executes it using the Ruby interpreter (due to the shebang line—as covered earlier in this chapter). The Ruby script returns a basic HTTP header (specifying the content type as HTML) and then returns a basic HTML document.

Ruby comes with a special library called *cgi* that enables more sophisticated interactions than those with the preceding CGI script. Let's create a basic CGI script that uses cgi:

```ruby
#!/usr/bin/env ruby

require 'cgi'

cgi = CGI.new

puts cgi.header
puts "<html><body>This is a test</body></html>"
```

In this example, you created a `CGI` object and used it to print the header line for you. This is easier than remembering what header to output, and it can be tailored. However, the real benefit of using the cgi library is so that you can do things such as accept data coming from a web browser (or an HTML form) and return more complex data to the user.

Accepting CGI Variables

A benefit of CGI scripts is that they can process information passed to them from a form on an HTML page or merely specified within the URL. For example, if you had a web form with an `<input>` element with a name of "text" that posted to `test.cgi`, you can access the data passed to it like this:

```ruby
#!/usr/bin/env ruby

require 'cgi'
cgi = CGI.new

text = cgi['text']

puts cgi.header
puts "<html><body>#{text.reverse}</body></html>"
```

In this case, the user would see the text he or she entered on the form reversed. You could also test this CGI script by passing the text directly within the URL, such as with www.example.com/test.cgi?text=this+is+a+test.

Here's a more complete example:

```
#!/usr/bin/env ruby

require 'cgi'
cgi = CGI.new

from = cgi['from'].to_i
to = cgi['to'].to_i

number = rand(to-from+1) + from

puts cgi.header
puts "<html><body>#{number}</body></html>"
```

This CGI script responds with a random number that's between the number supplied in the from CGI variable and the to CGI variable. An associated but basic form that could send the correct data would have HTML code like so:

```
<form method="POST" action="http://www.example.com/test.cgi">
For a number between <input type="text" name="from" value="" /> and
<input type="text" name="to" value="" /> <input type="submit"
value="Click here!" /></form>
```

In Chapter 16, the cgi library is covered in more depth, along with information about using HTTP cookies and sessions, so if this mode of deployment is of interest to you, refer there for extended information and longer examples.

In general, however, CGI execution isn't a popular option due to its lack of speed and the need for a Ruby interpreter to be executed on every request. This makes CGI unsuitable for high-use or heavy-load situations.

Tip   Depending on your setup (or hosting environment), you might find that Sinatra offers a nicer way to do what we've looked at in this section. See the Sinatra section in Chapter 13.

Generic HTTP Servers

HTTP is the communications protocol of the World Wide Web. Even though it's commonly used to shuttle web pages from one place to another, it can also be used on an internal network or even to communicate between services on a single machine.

Creating an HTTP server from your Ruby program can provide a way for users (or even other programs) to make requests to your Ruby program, meaning you don't need to distribute the source code, but can instead make your program's functionality available over a network (such as the Internet).

In this section, we're going to look directly at creating a basic HTTP server using WEBrick, part of Ruby's standard library. It's useful to have experience building servers directly so that you can see how things work at a low level, even though, ultimately, you will almost certainly choose to use a web app framework (as covered in Chapter 13) to make life easier. Given this, if you find any code in this section intimidating, skip to the Sinatra-based approach demonstrated in Chapter 13 as it will be a lot more straightforward and hide many of the details covered here.

Note   In this section, we're creating scripts that are HTTP servers themselves and do not rely on established HTTP servers such as Apache.

WEBrick

WEBrick is a Ruby library that makes it easy to build an HTTP server with Ruby. It comes with most installations of Ruby by default (it's part of the standard library), so you can usually create a basic web/HTTP server with only several lines of code:

```
require 'webrick'

server = WEBrick::GenericServer.new( :Port => 1234 )

trap("INT"){ server.shutdown }

server.start do |socket|
   socket.puts Time.now
end
```

This code creates a generic WEBrick server on the local machine on port 1234, shuts the server down if the process is interrupted (often done with Ctrl+C), and for each new connection prints the current date and time. If you run this code, you could try to view the results in your web browser by visiting http://127.0.0.1:1234/ or http://localhost:1234/.

Caution   Because your test program doesn't output valid HTTP, it might fail with some particularly sensitive web browsers. However, if you understand how to use the *telnet* program, you can use telnet 127.0.0.1 1234 to see the result. Otherwise, continue to the next example, where valid HTTP is returned for web browsers to view.

However, a more powerful technique is when you create *servlets* that exist in their own class and have more control over the requests and responses made to them:

```
require 'webrick'

class MyServlet < WEBrick::HTTPServlet::AbstractServlet
  def do_GET(request, response)
    response.status = 200
    response.content_type = "text/plain"
    response.body = "Hello, world!"
  end
end

server = WEBrick::HTTPServer.new( :Port => 1234 )
server.mount "/", MyServlet
trap("INT"){ server.shutdown }
server.start
```

This code is more elaborate, but you now have access to request and response objects that represent both the incoming request and the outgoing response.

For example, you can now find out what URL the user tried to access in his or her browser with such a line:

```
response.body = "You are trying to load #{request.path}"
```

request.path contains the path within the URL (e.g., /abcd from http://127.0.0.1:1234/abcd), meaning you can interpret what the user was trying to request, call a different method, and provide the correct output.

Here's a more elaborate example:

```ruby
require 'webrick'

class MyNormalClass
  def MyNormalClass.add(a, b)
    a.to_i + b.to_i
  end
  def MyNormalClass.subtract(a,b)
    a.to_i - b.to_i
  end
end

class MyServlet < WEBrick::HTTPServlet::AbstractServlet
  def do_GET(request, response)
    if request.query['a'] && request.query['b']
      a = request.query['a']
      b = request.query['b']
      response.status = 200
      response.content_type = 'text/plain'
      result = nil

      case request.path
        when '/add'
          result = MyNormalClass.add(a,b)
        when '/subtract'
          result = MyNormalClass.subtract(a,b)
        else
          result = "No such method"
      end

      response.body = result.to_s + "\n"
    else
      response.status = 400
```

```
      response.body = "You did not provide the correct parameters"
    end
  end
end

server = WEBrick::HTTPServer.new(:Port => 1234)
server.mount '/', MyServlet
trap('INT'){ server.shutdown }
server.start
```

In this example, you have a regular, basic Ruby class called MyNormalClass that implements two basic arithmetic methods. The WEBrick servlet uses the request object to retrieve parameters from the URL, as well as get the Ruby method requested from request.path. If the parameters aren't passed, an HTTP error is returned.

To use the preceding script, you'd use URLs such as these:

```
http://127.0.0.1:1234/add?a=10&b=20
```

30

```
http://127.0.0.1:1234/subtract?a=100&b=10
```

90

```
http://127.0.0.1:1234/subtract
```

You did not provide the correct parameters.

```
http://127.0.0.1:1234/abcd?a=10&b=20
```

No such method.

Summary

In this chapter, we looked at how to deploy Ruby programs and libraries, as well as how to make their functions available to web browsers and other applications over a network. We also interrogated the environment so we can pursue different techniques on a per-operating system basis if we choose.

Let's reflect on the main concepts covered in this chapter:

- *Shebang line*: A special line at the start of a source code file that determines which interpreter is used to process the file. Used primarily on UNIX-based operating systems, shebang lines can also work on Windows when used with the Apache web server.

- RUBY_PLATFORM: A special variable preset by Ruby that contains the name of the current platform (environment).

- *Environment variables*: Special variables set by the operating system or other processes that contain information relevant to the current execution environment and information about the operating system.

- RubyGems.org: A centralized repository and website dedicated to hosting and distributing Ruby projects and libraries.

- *GitHub*: A popular hub and community site for users of the Git source code management system—now popular in the Ruby world. You can find it at `https://github.com/`.

- *CGI*: Common Gateway Interface. A standard that enables web servers to execute scripts and provide an interface between web users and scripts located on that server.

- *WEBrick*: A simple and easy HTTP server library for Ruby that comes with Ruby as standard.

In Chapter 15, we're going to return to looking at network servers, albeit in a different fashion; but first, in Chapter 11, we're going to take a look at some more advanced Ruby topics to flesh out the ideas we've covered so far.

CHAPTER 11

Advanced Ruby Features

In this chapter, we're going to look at some advanced Ruby techniques that have not been covered in prior chapters. This chapter is the last instructional chapter in the second part of the book, and although we'll be covering useful libraries, frameworks, and Ruby-related technologies in Part 3, this chapter rounds off the mandatory knowledge that any proficient Ruby programmer should have. This means that although this chapter will jump between several different topics, each is essential to becoming a professional Ruby developer.

The myriad topics covered in this chapter include how to create Ruby code dynamically on the fly, methods to make your Ruby code safe, how to issue commands to the operating system, how to integrate with Microsoft Windows, and how to create libraries for Ruby using other programming languages. Essentially, this chapter is designed to cover a range of discrete, important topics that you might find you need to use, but that fall outside the immediate scope of other chapters.

Dynamic Code Execution

As a dynamic, interpreted language, Ruby is able to execute code created *dynamically*. The way to do this is with the eval method, for example:

```
eval "puts 2 + 2"
```

```
4
```

Note that while 4 is displayed, 4 is not returned as the result of the whole eval expression. puts always returns nil. To return 4 from eval, you can do this:

© Carleton DiLeo, Peter Cooper 2021
C. DiLeo and P. Cooper, *Beginning Ruby 3*, https://doi.org/10.1007/978-1-4842-6324-2_11

```
puts eval("2 + 2")
```

```
4
```

Here's a more complex example that uses strings and interpolation:

```
my_number = 15
my_code = %{#{my_number} * 2}
puts eval(my_code)
```

```
30
```

The eval method simply executes (or *evaluates*) the code passed to it and returns the result. The first example made eval execute puts 2 + 2, whereas the second used string interpolation to build an expression of 15 * 2, which was then evaluated and printed to the screen using puts.

Bindings

In Ruby, a *binding* is a reference to a context, scope, or state of execution. A binding includes things such as the current value of variables and other details of the execution environment.

It's possible to pass a binding to eval and to have eval execute the supplied code under that binding rather than the current one. In this way, you can keep things that happen with eval separate from the main execution context of your code.

Here's an example:

```
def binding_elsewhere
  x = 20
  return binding
end

remote_binding = binding_elsewhere
```

```
x = 10
eval("puts x")
eval("puts x", remote_binding)
```

10

20

This code demonstrates that `eval` accepts an optional second parameter, a binding, which in this case is returned from the `binding_elsewhere` method. The variable `remote_binding` contains a reference to the execution context within the `binding_elsewhere` method rather than in the main code. Therefore, when you print x, 20 is shown, as x is defined as equal to 20 in `binding_elsewhere`!

Note   You can obtain the binding of the current scope at any point with the `Kernel` module's `binding` method.

Let's build on the previous example:

```
eval("x = 10")
eval("x = 50", remote_binding)
eval("puts x")
eval("puts x", remote_binding)
```

10

50

In this example, two bindings are in play: the default binding and the `remote_binding` (from the `binding_elsewhere` method).

Therefore, even though you set x first to 10, and then to 50, you're not dealing with the *same* x in each case. One x is a local variable in the current context, and the other x is a variable in the context of `binding_elsewhere`.

Other Forms of eval

Although eval executes code within the current context (or the context supplied with a binding), class_eval, module_eval, and instance_eval can evaluate code within the context of classes, modules, and object instances, respectively.

class_eval is ideal for adding methods to a class dynamically:

```
class Person
end

def add_accessor_to_person(accessor_name)
  Person.class_eval %{
    attr_accessor :#{accessor_name}
  }
end

person = Person.new
add_accessor_to_person :name
add_accessor_to_person :gender
person.name = "Carleton DiLeo"
person.gender = "male"
puts "#{person.name} is #{person.gender}"
```

```
Carleton DiLeo is male
```

In this example, you use the add_accessor_to_person method to add accessors dynamically to the Person class. Prior to using the add_accessor_to_person method, neither the name nor gender accessors exist within Person.

Note that the key part of the code, the class_eval method, operates by using string interpolation to create the desired code for Person:

```
Person.class_eval %{
  attr_accessor :#{accessor_name}
}
```

String interpolation makes the eval methods powerful tools for generating different features on the fly. This ability is a power unseen in the majority of programming languages, and is one that's used to great effect in systems such as Ruby on Rails (covered in Chapter 13).

It's possible to take the previous example a lot further and add an `add_accessor` method to every class by putting your `class_eval` cleverness in a new method, defined within the `Class` class (from which all other classes descend):

```ruby
class Class
  def add_accessor(accessor_name)
    self.class_eval %{
      attr_accessor :#{accessor_name}
    }
  end
end

class Person
end

person = Person.new
Person.add_accessor :name
Person.add_accessor :gender
person.name = "Carleton DiLeo"
person.gender = "male"
puts "#{person.name} is #{person.gender}"
```

In this example, you add the `add_accessor` method to the `Class` class, thereby adding it to every other class defined within your program. This makes it possible to add accessors to any class dynamically, by calling `add_accessor`. (If the logic of this approach isn't clear, make sure to try this code yourself, step through each process, and establish what is occurring at each step of execution.)

The technique used in the previous example also lets you define classes like this:

```ruby
class SomethingElse
  add_accessor :whatever
end
```

Because `add_accessor` is being used within a class, the method call will work its way up to the `add_accessor` method defined in class `Class`.

Moving back to simpler techniques, using `instance_eval` is somewhat like using regular `eval`, but within the context of an object (rather than a method). In this example, you use `instance_eval` to execute code within the scope of an object:

```ruby
class MyClass
  def initialize
    @my_variable = 'Hello, world!'
  end
end

obj = MyClass.new
obj.instance_eval { puts @my_variable }
```

Hello, world!

Creating Your Own Version of attr_accessor

So far, you've used the `attr_accessor` method within your classes to generate accessor functions for instance variables quickly. For example, in longhand you might have this code:

```ruby
class Person
  def name
    @name
  end

  def name=(name)
    @name = name
  end
end
```

This allows you to do things such as `puts person.name` and `person.name = 'Fred'`. Alternatively, however, you can use `attr_accessor`:

```ruby
class Person
  attr_accessor :name
end
```

This version of the class is more concise and has exactly the same functionality as the longhand version. Now it's time to ask the question, how does `attr_accessor` work?

It turns out that attr_accessor isn't as magical as it looks, and it's extremely easy to implement your own version using eval. Consider this code:

```
class Class
  def add_accessor(accessor_name)
    self.class_eval %{
      def #{accessor_name}
        @#{accessor_name}
      end

      def #{accessor_name}=(value)
        @#{accessor_name} = value
      end
    }
  end
end
```

At first, this code looks complex, but it's very similar to the add_accessor code you created in the previous section. You use class_eval to define getter and setter methods dynamically for the attribute within the current class.

If accessor_name is equal to name, then the code that class_eval is executing is equivalent to this code:

```
def name
  @name
end

def name=(value)
  @name = value
end
```

Thus, you have duplicated the functionality of attr_accessor.

You can use this technique to create a multitude of different "code generators" and methods that can act as a "macro" language to perform things in Ruby that are otherwise lengthy to type out.

Running Other Programs from Ruby

Often, it's useful to be able to run other programs on the system from your own programs. In this way, you can reduce the amount of features your program needs to implement, as you can pass off work to other programs that are already written. It can also be useful to hook up several of your own programs so that functionality is spread among them. Rather than using the RPC systems covered in the previous chapter, you can simply run other programs from your own with one of a few different methods made available by Ruby.

Getting Results from Other Programs

There are three simple ways to run another program from within Ruby: the `system` method (defined in the `Kernel` module), *backtick* syntax (` `` `), and *delimited input literals* (`%x{}`). Using `system` is ideal when you want to run another program and aren't concerned with its output, whereas you should use backticks when you want the output of the remote program returned.

These lines demonstrate two ways of running the system's directory **list** program:

On OS X or Linux:

```
x = system("ls")
x = `ls`
```

On Windows:

```
x = system("dir")
x = `dir`
```

For the first line, the **list** program output displays in the console and x equals `true`. For the second line, x contains the output of the **list** command. Which method you use depends on what you're trying to achieve. If you don't want the output of the other program to show on the same screen as that of your Ruby script, then use backticks (or a literal, `%x{}`).

Note   `%x{}` is functionally equivalent to using backticks, for example, `%x{ls}` or `%x{dir}`.

Transferring Execution to Another Program

Sometimes it's desirable to jump immediately to another program and cease execution of the current program. This is useful if you have a multistep process and have written an application for each. To end the current program and invoke another, simply use the exec method in place of system, for example:

```
exec "ruby another_script.rb"
puts "This will never be displayed"
```

In this example, execution is transferred to a different program, and the current program ceases immediately—the second line is never executed.

Running Two Programs at the Same Time

Forking is where an instance of a program (a *process*) duplicates itself, resulting in two processes of that program running *concurrently*. You can run other programs from this second process by using exec, and the first (parent) process will continue running the original program.

fork is a method provided by the Kernel module that creates a fork of the current process. It returns the child process's *process ID* in the parent, but nil in the child process—you can use this to determine which process a script is in. The following example forks the current process into two processes and only executes the exec command within the child process (the process generated by the fork):

```
if fork.nil?
  exec "ruby some_other_file.rb"
end
puts "This Ruby script now runs alongside some_other_file.rb"
```

Caution   Don't run the preceding code from irb. If irb forks, you'll end up with two copies of irb running simultaneously, and the result will be unpredictable.

If the other program (being run by exec) is expected to finish at some point and you want to wait for it to finish executing before doing something in the parent program, you can use `Process.wait` to wait for all child processes to finish before continuing. Here's an example:

```ruby
child = fork do
  sleep 3
  puts "Child says 'hi'!"
end

puts "Waiting for the child process..."
Process.wait child
puts "All done!"
```

```
Waiting for the child process...

<3 second delay>

Child says 'hi'!

All done!
```

> **Note**   Forking is not possible with the Windows version of Ruby, as POSIX-style forking is not natively supported on that platform. You will use the `spawn()` method instead. More information at `https://ruby-doc.org/core/Kernel.html#method-i-spawn`.

Interacting with Another Program

The previous methods are fine for simple situations where you just want to get basic results from a remote program and don't need to interact directly with it in any way while it's running. However, sometimes you might want to pass data back and forth between two separate programs.

Ruby's IO module has a popen method that allows you to run another program and have an I/O stream between it and the current program. The I/O stream between programs works like the other types of I/O streams we looked at in Chapter 9, but instead of reading and writing to a file, you're reading and writing to another program. Obviously, this technique only works successfully with programs that accept direct input and produce direct output at a command prompt level (so not GUI applications).

Here's a simple read-only example:

```
ls = IO.popen("ls", "r")
while line = ls.gets
  puts line
end
ls.close
```

In this example, you open an I/O stream with ls (the UNIX command to list the contents of the current directory—try it with dir if you're using Microsoft Windows). You read the lines one by one, as with other forms of I/O streams, and close the stream when you're done.

Similarly, you can also open a program with a read/write I/O stream and handle data in both directions:

```
handle = IO.popen("other_program", "r+")
handle.puts "send input to other program"
handle.close_write
while line = handle.gets
  puts line
end
```

Note   The reason for handle.close_write is to close the I/O stream's writing stream, thereby sending any data waiting to be written out to the remote program. IO also has a flush method that can be used if the write stream needs to remain open.

Threads

Thread is short for *thread of execution*. You use threads to split the execution of a program into multiple parts that can be run concurrently. For example, a program designed to email thousands of people at once might split the task between 20 different threads that all send email at once. Such parallelism is faster than processing one item after another, especially on systems with more than one CPU, because different threads of execution can be run on different processors. It can also be faster because rather than wasting time waiting for a response from a remote machine, you can continue with other operations.

Ruby 1.8 didn't support threads in the traditional sense. Typically, threading capabilities are provided by the operating system and vary from one system to another. However, Ruby 1.8 provided Ruby's threading capabilities directly which meant they lacked some of the power of traditional system-level threads. In Ruby 1.9, Ruby began to use system-based threads, and this is now the default expectation among Rubyists.

While Ruby 1.9 and 2.x's threads are system (native) threads, in order to remain compatible with 1.8 code, a *global interpreter lock* (GIL) has been left in place so that threads do not truly run simultaneously. This means that all of what is covered in this section is relevant to all of 1.8, 1.9, 2.0, and beyond. A Ruby 1.9-and-beyond–only alternative, fibers, is covered in the next primary section of this chapter which now supports non-blocking concurrency.

Basic Ruby Threads in Action

Here's a basic demonstration of Ruby threading in action:

```
threads = []

10.times do
  thread = Thread.new do
    10.times { |i| print i; $stdout.flush; sleep rand(2) }
  end

  threads << thread
end

threads.each { |thread| thread.join }
```

You create an array to hold your Thread objects so that you can easily keep track of them. Then you create ten threads, sending the block of code to be executed in each thread to Thread.new, and add each generated thread to the array.

Note   When you create a thread, it can access any variables that are within scope at that point. However, any local variables that are then created within the thread are entirely local to that thread. This is similar to the behavior of other types of code blocks.

Once you've created the threads, you wait for all of them to complete before the program finishes. You wait by looping through all the thread objects in threads and calling each thread's join method. The join method makes the main program wait until a thread's execution is complete before continuing. In this way, you make sure all the threads are complete before exiting.

The preceding program results in output similar to the following (the variation is due to the randomness of the sleeping):

```
0010120001001010121231212423251232345323433663454436554674454877655788668
97567656797

9789878889899999
```

The example has created ten Ruby threads whose sole job is to count and sleep randomly. This results in the preceding pseudo-random output.

Rather than sleeping, the threads could have been fetching web pages, performing math operations, or sending emails. In fact, Ruby threads are ideal for almost every situation where concurrency within a single Ruby program is desired.

Note   In Chapter 15, you'll be using threads to create a server that creates new threads of execution for each client that connects to it, so that you can develop a simple chat system.

Advanced Thread Operations

As you've seen, creating and running basic threads is fairly simple, but threads also offer a number of advanced features. These are discussed in the following subsections.

Waiting for Threads to Finish Redux

When you waited for your threads to finish by using the join method, you could have specified a timeout value (in seconds) for which to wait. If the thread doesn't finish within that time, join returns nil. Here's an example where each thread is given only one second to execute:

```
threads.each do |thread|
  puts "Thread #{thread.object_id} didn't finish in 1s" unless thread.join(1)
end
```

Getting a List of All Threads

It's possible to get a global list of all threads running within your program using Thread. list. In fact, if you didn't want to keep your own store of threads, you could rewrite the earlier example from the section "Basic Ruby Threads in Action" down to these two lines:

```
10.times { Thread.new { 10.times { |i| print i; $stdout.flush; sleep
rand(2) } } } Thread.list.each { |thread| thread.join unless thread ==
Thread.main }
```

However, keeping your own list of threads is essential if you're likely to have more than one group of threads working within an application and you want to keep them separate from one another when it comes to using join or other features.

The list of threads also includes the *main* thread representing the main program's thread of execution, which is why we explicitly do not join it in the prior code.

Thread Operations from Within Threads Themselves

Threads aren't just tiny, dumb fragments of code. They have the ability to talk with the Ruby thread scheduler and provide updates on their status. For example, a thread can stop itself:

```ruby
Thread.new do
  10.times do |i|
    print i
    $stdout.flush
    Thread.stop
  end
end
```

Every time the thread created in this example prints a number to the screen, it stops itself. It can then only be restarted or resumed by the parent program calling the run method on the thread, like so:

```ruby
Thread.list.each { |thread| thread.run }
```

A thread can also tell the Ruby thread scheduler that it wants to pass execution over to another thread. The technique of voluntarily ceding control to another thread is often known as *cooperative multitasking*, because the thread or process itself is saying that it's okay to pass execution on to another thread or process. Used properly, cooperative multitasking can make threading even more efficient, as you can code in pass requests at ideal locations. Here's an example showing how to cede control from a thread:

```ruby
2.times{Thread.new{10.times{|i|printi;$stdout.flush;Thread.pass}}}Thread.list.each{
|thread| thread.join unless thread == Thread.main }
```

```
00112233445566778899
```

In this example, execution flip-flops between the two threads, causing the pattern shown in the results.

Fibers

Fibers offer an alternative to threads in Ruby 1.9 and beyond. In Ruby 3, Fiber was rewritten, so it no longer blocks on IO operations and supports non-blocking fibers. Fibers are lightweight units of execution that control their own scheduling (often referred to as *cooperative scheduling*). Whereas threads will typically run continually, fibers hand over control once they have performed certain tasks. Unlike regular methods, however, once a fiber hands over control, it continues to exist and can be *resumed* at will.

In short, fibers are pragmatically similar to threads, but fibers aren't scheduled to all run together. You have to manually control the scheduling.

A Fiber in Action

Nothing will demonstrate fibers as succinctly as a demonstration, so let's look at a very simple implementation to generate a sequence of square numbers:

```ruby
sg = Fiber.new do
  s = 0
  loop do
    square = s * s
    Fiber.yield square
    s += 1
  end
end

10.times { puts sg.resume }
```

```
0

1

4

9

16

25

36

49

64

81
```

In this example, we create a fiber using a block, much in the same style as we created threads earlier. The difference, however, is that the fiber will run solely on its own until the `Fiber.yield` method is used to yield control back to whatever last told the fiber to run (which, in this case, is the `sg.resume` method call). Alternatively, if the fiber "ends," the value of the last executed expression is returned.

In this example, it's worth noting that you don't have to use the fiber forever, although since the fiber contains an infinite loop, it would certainly be possible to do so. Even though the fiber contains an infinite loop, however, the fiber is not continually running, so it results in no performance issues.

If you do develop a fiber that has a natural ending point, calling its `resume` method once it has concluded will result in an exception (which, of course, you can catch—refer to Chapter 8's "Handling Exceptions" section) that states you are trying to resume a dead fiber.

Passing Data to a Fiber

It is possible to pass data back into a fiber when you resume its execution as well as receive data from it. For example, let's tweak the square number generator fiber to support receiving back an optional new base from which to provide square numbers:

```
sg = Fiber.new do
  s = 0
  loop do
    square = s * s
    s += 1
    s = Fiber.yield(square) || s
  end
end

puts sg.resume
puts sg.resume
puts sg.resume
puts sg.resume
puts sg.resume 40
puts sg.resume
puts sg.resume
```

```
puts sg.resume 0
puts sg.resume
puts sg.resume
```

```
0

1

4

9

1600

1681

1764

0

1

4
```

In this case, we start out by getting back square numbers one at a time as before. On the fifth attempt, however, we pass back the number 40, which is then assigned to the fiber's s variable and used to generate square numbers. After a couple of iterations, we then reset the counter to 0. The number is received by the fiber as the result of calling Fiber.yield.

It is not possible to send data into the fiber in this way with the *first* resume, however, since the first resume call does not follow on from the fiber yielding or concluding in any way. In that case, any data you passed is passed into the fiber block, much as if it were a method.

Non-blocking Fiber

Ruby 3 introduces the ability to create non-blocking fibers. Creating a non-blocking fiber is simple: specify the parameter blocking: false in the constructor. This option prevents blocking on blocking operations such as I/O, sleep, and so on:

```
non_blocking = Fiber.new(blocking: false) do
  puts "Blocking Fiber? #{Fiber.current.blocking?}"

  # Will not block
  sleep 2
end

3.times { puts non_blocking.resume }
```

```
Blocking Fiber? false

Blocking Fiber? false

Blocking Fiber? false
```

When used correctly, non-blocking fibers will increase performance since multiple operations are performed at once. Since non-blocking fibers are opt-in, Ruby 3 will not break existing code. By default, all I/O operations in fiber are non-blocking with Ruby 3.

Why Fibers?

A motivation to use fibers over threads in some situations is efficiency. Creating hundreds of fibers is a *lot* faster than creating the equivalent threads, since threads are created at the operating system level. There are also significant memory efficiency benefits.

One of the greatest benefits of fibers is in implementing lightweight I/O management routines within other libraries, so even if you don't use fibers directly, you might still end up benefiting from their use elsewhere.

Unicode, Character Encodings, and UTF-8 Support

Unicode is the industry standard way of representing characters from every writing system (character set) in the world. It's the only viable way to be able to manage multiple different alphabets and character sets in a reasonably standard context.

One of Ruby 1.8's most cited flaws was in the way it dealt with character encodings—namely, hardly at all. There were some workarounds, but they were hackish. Ruby 1.8 treated strings as simple collections of bytes rather than true *characters*, which is just fine if you're using a standard English character set, but if you wanted to work with, say, Arabic or Japanese, you have problems!

Ruby 1.9 and beyond, on the other hand, support Unicode, alternative character sets, and encodings out of the box. In this chapter, we'll focus on the direct support in Ruby 1.9 and up.

Note For a full rundown of Unicode and how it works and relates to software development, read `www.joelonsoftware.com/articles/Unicode.html`. The official Unicode site, at `http://unicode.org/`, also has specifications and further details.

Ruby 1.9 and Beyond's Character Encoding Support

Unlike with Ruby 1.8, no hacks or workarounds are necessary to work with multiple character sets and encodings in Ruby 1.9 and above. Ruby 1.9 supports a large number of encodings out of the box (over 100 at the time of writing), and the interface is seamless. You not only get character encoding support for strings within your programs, but for your source code itself too.

Note `Encoding.list` returns an array of `Encoding` objects that represent the different character encodings that your Ruby interpreter supports.

Strings

Strings have encoding support out of the box. To determine the current encoding for a string, you can call its encoding method:

```
"this is a test".encoding
```

```
=> #<Encoding:US-ASCII>
```

By default, a regular ASCII string will be encoded using the US-ASCII, UTF-8, or CP850 encodings, depending on how your system is set up, but if you get a bit more elaborate, then UTF-8 (a character encoding that can be used to represent any Unicode character) will typically be used:

```
"ça va?".encoding
```

```
=> #<Encoding:UTF-8>
```

To convert a string into a different encoding, use its encode method:

```
"ça va?".encode("ISO-8859-1")
```

Not every character encoding will support being able to represent every type of character that exists in your text. For example, the cedilla character (ç) in the preceding example cannot be represented in plain US-ASCII. If we try to do a conversion to US-ASCII, therefore, we get the necessary error:

```
"ça va?".encode("US-ASCII")
```

```
Encoding::UndefinedConversionError: "\xC3\xA7" from UTF-8 to US-ASCII
```

I would personally suggest that, where possible, you try and use the UTF-8 encoding exclusively in any apps that are likely to accept input from people typing in many different languages. UTF-8 is an excellent "global" encoding that can represent any character in the Unicode standard, so using it globally throughout your projects will ensure that everything works as expected.

Tip Make sure to refer to Chapter 9 to see how to open files and read data that is in different character encodings.

Source Code

As well as supporting character encodings out of the box for strings and files, Ruby 1.9 and beyond also allow you to use any of the supported character sets for your actual source code files.

All you need to do is include a comment on the first or second line (in case you're using a shebang line) that contains coding: [format name], for example:

```
# coding: utf-8
```

The primary reason for doing this is so that you can use UTF-8 (or whichever encoding you choose to specify) within literal strings defined with your source files without running into snags with String#length, regular expressions, and the like.

Another fun (but not endorsed by me!) option is to use alternate non-ASCII characters in method names, variable names, and so forth. The danger of this, of course, is that you reduce the usability of your code with developers who might prefer to use other encodings.

Summary

In this chapter, we looked at an array of advanced Ruby topics, from dynamic code execution to writing high-performance functions in the C programming language. This is the last chapter that covers general Ruby-related knowledge that any intermediate Ruby programmer should be familiar with. In Chapter 12, we'll be taking a different approach and will develop an entire Ruby application, much as we did in Chapter 4.

Let's reflect on the main concepts covered in this chapter:

- *Binding*: A representation of a scope (execution) context as an object.

- *Forking*: When an instance of a program duplicates itself into two processes, one as a parent and one as a child, both continuing execution.

- *Threads*: Separate "strands" of execution that run concurrently with each other. Ruby's threads in 1.8 were implemented entirely by the Ruby interpreter, but since Ruby 1.9 use system-based threads, and are a commonly used tool in application development.

- *Fibers*: Lightweight cooperative alternatives to threads. They must yield execution in order to be scheduled.

- *Character encoding*: This describes a system and code that pair characters (whether they're Roman letters, Chinese symbols, Arabic letters, etc.) to a set of numbers that a computer can use to represent those characters.

- *UTF-8 (Unicode Transformation Format-8)*: This is a character encoding that can support any character in the Unicode standard. It supports variable-length characters, and is designed to support ASCII coding natively, while also providing the ability to use up to four bytes to represent characters from other character sets.

Now you can move on to Chapter 12, where you'll develop an entire Ruby application using much of the knowledge obtained in this book so far.

Tying It Together: Developing a Larger Ruby Application

In this chapter, we're going to step back from focusing on individual facets of Ruby and develop an entire program using much of the knowledge you've gained so far. We'll focus on the structural concerns of developing a program and look at how a flexible structure can benefit you and other developers in the long run.

The important thing to remember while working through this chapter is that the program itself is not as important as the concepts used while developing it. We'll be rapidly (and relatively shallowly) covering a number of areas relevant to most development you'll do, such as testing and basic refactoring.

Let's Build a Bot

Before we get to any code, we're going to look at what we're going to build, why we're going to build it, and how we're going to do it.

What Is a Bot?

In this chapter, we're going to build a robot. Not a sci-fi type of robot, such as that in *Lost in Space*, but a computer program that can hold a conversation with us. These types of programs are commonly known as *bots* or *chatterbots*. Bots are present in a lot of different software and tools these days. You can ask them for gift ideas and movie times. In short, it's a little like talking to a customer service agent, except the agent is entirely automated.

© Carleton DiLeo, Peter Cooper 2021
C. DiLeo and P. Cooper, *Beginning Ruby 3*, https://doi.org/10.1007/978-1-4842-6324-2_12

You might be familiar with bots on your own computer. Microsoft Office used to come with the "Clippy" bot turned on by default, and many websites have automated chatbots in an attempt to cut down on support costs and, supposedly, to improve usability.

The history of bots goes back to the 1960s, when a computer scientist at MIT named Joseph Weizenbaum developed a bot called ELIZA. It eventually became so popular that most computer users throughout the 1980s and 1990s were exposed to it in one form or another through the many "talk to your computer"–type programs that became popular.

The conversations you can have with ELIZA-type bots aren't mind blowing, but can prove entertaining, as shown in Figure 12-1. The general mechanism ELIZA bots use is to take whatever you say and twist it around into a statement or question to you. For example, if you were to say "I am bored," ELIZA might respond, "How long have you been bored?" or "Why are you bored?" This form of bouncing back the user's input seems crude when described in this way, but people are often fooled into believing they're talking to something more intelligent simply because of its reflective nature (this is known as the *ELIZA effect*).

```
Eliza: Hi. I'm Eliza. Tell me your problems!
You  : I don't have any problems!
Eliza: We have to find the reason why you don't have any problems!
You  : How can there be a reason for that?
Eliza: Why do you ask?
You  : It was a rhetorical question.
Eliza: Perhaps you would like to talk about a problem?
You  : Okay, let's talk about my book.
Eliza: What does this mean for you, saying " Okay, let's talk about your book "?
You  : Huh?
Eliza: I understand!
You  : I'm glad about that.
Eliza: How long are you glad about that?
You  : Five seconds?
Eliza: I'm not sure wether I understand you!
You  : And you sure can't spell.
Eliza: Come on! Explain your thinkings!
```

Figure 12-1. *A demonstration of a session with an online ELIZA bot*

Our bot won't be exactly like ELIZA—that is, it won't be an ELIZA *clone*—but will share some of the same features and use some similar techniques. We'll also look at how to extend our bot with other features.

Note   If you want to learn about or play with some Internet-hosted versions of ELIZA, visit `https://en.wikipedia.org/wiki/ELIZA`.

Why a Bot?

The good thing about developing a bot is that it can be as simple or as complex as you like. Toward the end of this chapter, we'll be looking at ways you can extend the bot, but the initial construction is quite simple.

You'll be using most of the techniques covered so far in this book to build your bot. You'll be doing a bit of testing and documentation, as well as using classes and complex data structures. You'll also be using files to store information the bot uses, and looking at how to make your bot available to the general public using HTTP servers and CGI scripts. This project also demands you use a lot of string and list-related functions, along with comparison logic. These are all things you're likely to use in a larger development project, and as Ruby is a particularly good language for text processing, this project is perfect for demonstrating Ruby's strengths.

A bot also allows you to have some fun and experiment. Working on a contact information management tool (for example) isn't that much fun, even though such a system would use similar techniques to your bot. You can still implement testing, documentation, classes, and storage systems, but end up with a fun result that can be extended and improved indefinitely.

How?

The primary focus of this chapter is to keep each fragment of functionality in your bot loosely coupled to the others. This is an important decision when developing certain types of applications if you plan to extend them in the future. The plan for this bot is to make it as easy to extend, or change, as possible, allowing you to customize it, add features, and make it your own.

In terms of the general operation of the chatterbot, your bot will exist within a class, allowing you to replicate bots easily by creating new instances. When you create a bot, it will be "blank," except for the logic contained within the class, and you'll pass in a special data file to give it a set of knowledge and a set of responses it can use when conversing with users. User input will be via the keyboard, but the input mechanism will be kept flexible enough so that the bot could easily be used from a website or elsewhere.

Your bot will only have a few public methods to begin with. It needs to be able to load its data file into memory and accept input given by the user and then return its responses. Behind the scenes, the bot will need to parse what the users "say" and be able to build up a coherent reply. Therefore, the first step is to begin processing language and recognizing words.

Creating a Simple Text Processing Library

Several stages are required to accept input such as "I am bored" and turn it into a response such as "Why are you bored?" The first is to perform some *preprocessing*—tasks that make the text easier to parse—such as cleaning up the text, expanding terms such as "I'm" into "I am," "you're" into "you are," and so forth. Next, you'll split up the input into sentences and words, choose the best sentence to respond to, and finally look up responses from your data files that match the input.

Some of these language tasks are generic enough that they could be useful in other applications, so you'll develop a basic library for them. This will make your bot code simpler and give you a library to use in other applications if you need. Logic and methods that are specific to bots can go in the bot's source code, and generic methods that perform operations on text can go into the library.

This section covers the development of a simple library, including testing and documentation.

Building the WordPlay Library

You're going to call your text manipulation and processing library WordPlay, so create a file called wordplay.rb with a basic class:

```
class WordPlay
end
```

Now that you've got the library's main file set up, you'll move on to implementing some of the text manipulation and processing features you know your bot will require, but are reasonably application agnostic. (I covered the construction of classes in depth in Chapter 6.)

Splitting Text into Sentences

Your bot, like most others, is only interested in single-sentence inputs. Therefore, it's important to accept only the first sentence of each line of input. However, rather than specifically tear out the first sentence, you'll split the input into sentences and then choose the first one. The reason for this approach is to have a generic sentence-splitting method, rather than to create a unique solution for each case.

You'll create a sentences method on Ruby's String class to keep the resulting code clean. You could create a class method within the WordPlay class and use it like WordPlay.sentences(our_input), but it wouldn't feel as intuitive and as object-oriented as our_input.sentences, where sentences is a method of the String class:

```ruby
class String
  def sentences
    gsub(/\n|\r/, ' ').split(/\.\s*/)
  end
end
```

Note   The preceding sentences method only splits text into sentences based on a period followed by whitespace. A more accurate technique could involve dealing with other punctuation (e.g., question marks and semicolons).

You can test it easily:

```ruby
p %q{Hello. This is a test of
basic sentence splitting. It
even works over multiple lines.}.sentences
```

```
["Hello", "This is a test of basic sentence splitting", "It even works
over multiple lines"]
```

Splitting Sentences into Words

You also need your library to be able to split sentences into words. As with the sentences method, add a words method to the String class:

```
class String
  def words
    scan(/\w[\w\'\-]*/)
  end
end

p "This is a test of words' capabilities".words
```

```
["This", "is", "a", "test", "of", "words'", "capabilities"]
```

You can test words in conjunction with sentences:

```
p %q{Hello. This is a test of
basic sentence splitting. It
even works over multiple lines}.sentences[1].words[3]
```

```
test
```

This test picks out the second sentence with sentences[1] and then the fourth word with words[3]—remember, arrays are zero-based. (The splitting techniques covered in this section were also explained in Chapter 3.)

Word Matching

You can use the new methods, along with existing array methods, to extract sentences that match certain words, as in this example:

```
hot_words = %w{test ruby great}
my_string = "This is a test. Dull sentence here. Ruby is great. So is
cake."
t = my_string.sentences.find_all do |s|
  s.downcase.words.any? { |word| hot_words.include?(word) }
end
```

```
p t.to_a
```

```
["This is a test", "Ruby is great"]
```

In this example, you define three "hot" words that you want to find within sentences, and you look through the sentences in `my_string` for any that contain either of your hot words. The way you do this is by seeing if, for any of the words in the sentence, it's true that the `hot_words` array also contains that word.

Experienced readers will wonder if regular expressions could be used in this situation. They could, but the focus here is on clean list logic that's easy to extend and adjust. You also get the benefit, if you wish, to use the difference in lengths between the word array, and the word array with hot words removed, to rank sentences in the order of which match the most hot words. This could be useful if you decided to tweak your bot (or any other software using WordPlay) to pick out and process the *most important* sentence, rather than just the first one, for example:

```
class WordPlay
  def self.best_sentence(sentences, desired_words)
    ranked_sentences = sentences.sort_by do |s|
      s.words.length - (s.downcase.words - desired_words).length
    end

    ranked_sentences.last
  end
end

puts WordPlay.best_sentence(my_string.sentences, hot_words)
```

```
Ruby is great
```

This class method accepts an array of sentences and an array of "desired words" as arguments. Next, it sorts the sentences by how many words difference each sentence has from the desired words list. If the difference is high, then there must be many desired words in that sentence. At the end of `best_sentence`, the sentence with the biggest number of matching words is returned.

Switching Subject and Object Pronouns

Switching pronouns is when you swap "you" and "I," "I" and "you," "my" and "your," and "your" and "my." This simple change makes sentences easy to use as a response. Consider what happens if you simply reflect back whatever the user says by switching the pronouns in his or her input. Some examples are shown in Table 12-1.

Table 12-1. *Inputs Coupled with Potential Responses*

Input	Response
My cat is sick.	Your cat is sick.
I hate my car.	You hate your car.
You are an awful bot.	I are an awful bot.

These aren't elaborate conversations, but the first two responses are valid English and are the sort of thing your bot can use. The third response highlights that you also need to pay attention to conjugating "am" to "are" and vice versa when using "I" and "you."

You'll add the basic pronoun-switching feature as a class method on the WordPlay class. As this feature won't be chained with other methods and doesn't need to be particularly concise, you can put it into the WordPlay class rather than continue to add more methods to the String class:

```
def self.switch_pronouns(text)
  text.gsub(/\b(I am|You are|I|You|Your|My)\b/i) do |pronoun|
    case pronoun.downcase
    when "i"
      "you"
    when "you"
      "I"
    when "i am"
      "you are"
    when "you are"
      "i am"
    when "your"
```

```
            "my"
        when "my"
            "your"
      end
    end
end
```

This method accepts any text supplied as a string and performs a substitution on each instance of "I am," "you are," "I," "you," "your," or "my." Next, a `case` construction is used to substitute each pronoun with its opposing pronoun. (You first used the `case/when` syntax in Chapter 3, where you can also find a deeper explanation of how it works.)

The reason for performing a substitution in this way is so that you only change each pronoun once. If you'd used four `gsubs` to change all "I's" to "you's," "you's" to "I's," and so on, changes made by the previous `gsub` would be overwritten by the next. Therefore, it's important to use one `gsub` that scans through the input pronoun by pronoun rather than making several blanket substitutions in succession.

If you use *irb* and require in the WordPlay library, you can quickly check the results:

```
WordPlay.switch_pronouns("Your cat is fighting with my cat")
```

```
my cat is fighting with your cat
```

```
WordPlay.switch_pronouns("You are my robot")
```

```
i am your robot
```

It's easy to find an exception to these results, though:

```
WordPlay.switch_pronouns("I gave you life")
```

```
you gave I life
```

When the "you" or "I" is the *object* of the sentence, rather than the *subject*, "you" becomes "me" and "me" becomes "you," whereas "I" becomes "you" and "you" becomes "I" on the *subject* of the sentence.

Without descending into complex processing of sentences to establish which reference is the subject and which reference is the object, we'll assume that every reference to "you" that's not at the start of a sentence is an object and should become "me" and that if "you" is at the beginning of a sentence, you should assume it's the subject and use "I" instead. This new rule makes your method change slightly:

```ruby
def self.switch_pronouns(text)
  text.gsub(/\b(I am|You are|I|You|Me|Your|My)\b/i) do |pronoun|
    case pronoun.downcase
      when "i"
        "you"
      when "you"
        "me"
      when "me"
        "you"
      when "i am"
        "you are"
      when "you are"
        "i am"
      when "your"
        "my"
      when "my"
        "your"
    end
  end.sub(/^me\b/i, 'i')
end
```

What you do in this case seems odd on the surface. You let `switch_pronouns` process the pronouns and then correct it when it changes "you" to "me" at the start of a sentence by changing the "me" to "I." This is done with the chained `sub` at the end.

Let's try it out:

```ruby
WordPlay.switch_pronouns('Your cat is fighting with my cat')
```

```
my cat is fighting with your cat
```

```
WordPlay.switch_pronouns('My cat is fighting with you')
```

```
your cat is fighting with me
```

```
WordPlay.switch_pronouns('You are my robot')
```

```
i am your robot
```

```
WordPlay.switch_pronouns('I gave you hope')
```

```
you gave me hope
```

```
WordPlay.switch_pronouns('You gave me hope')
```

```
i gave you hope
```

Success!

If you were so cruelly inclined, you could create an extremely annoying bot with this method alone. Consider this basic example:

```
while input = gets
  puts '>> ' + WordPlay.switch_pronouns(input).chomp + '?'
end
```

```
I am ready to talk
>> you are ready to talk?
yes
>> yes?
You are a dumb computer
>> i am a dumb computer?
```

We clearly have some work to do!

Testing the Library

When building a larger application or libraries upon which other applications will depend, it's important to make sure everything is fully tested. In Chapter 8, we looked at using Ruby's unit testing features for simple testing. You can use the same methods here to test WordPlay. Make sure the Minitest gem is installed. If you need help, review Chapter 8.

You'll use the same process as in Chapter 8. Create a file called `test_wordplay.rb` in the same directory as `wordplay.rb` and implement the following basic structure:

```ruby
require 'minitest/autorun'
require_relative 'wordplay'

class TestWordPlay < Minitest::Test
end
```

Now let's write some tests.

Testing Sentence Separation

To add groups of test assertions to `test_wordplay.rb`, you can simply create methods with names starting with `test_`. Creating a simple test method for testing sentence separations is easy:

```ruby
def test_sentences
  assert_equal(["a", "b", "c d", "e f g"], "a. b. c d. e f g.".sentences)

  test_text = %q{Hello. This is a test
of sentence separation. This is the end
of the test.}
  assert_equal("This is the end of the test", test_text.sentences[2])
end
```

The first assertion tests that the dummy sentence `"a. b. c d. e f g."` is successfully separated into the constituent "sentences." The second assertion uses a longer predefined text string and makes sure that the third sentence is correctly identified.

Note Ideally, you'd extend this basic set of assertions with several more to test more complex cases, such as sentences ending with multiple periods, commas, and other oddities. As these extra tests wouldn't demonstrate any further Ruby functionality, they're not covered here, but feel free to try some out!

Testing Word Separation

Testing that the words method works properly is even easier than testing sentences:

```ruby
def test_words
  assert_equal(%w{this is a test}, "this is a test".words)
  assert_equal(%w{these are mostly words}, "these are, mostly, words".words)
end
```

These assertions are simple. You split sentences into words and compare them with predefined arrays of those words. The assertions pass.

This highlights one reason why test-first development can be a good idea. It's easy to see how you could develop these tests *first* and then use their passing or failure as an indicator that you've implemented words correctly. This is an advanced programming concept, but one worth keeping in mind if writing tests in this way "clicks" with you.

Testing Best Sentence Choice

You also need to test your WordPlay.best_sentence method, as your bot will use it to choose the sentence with the most interesting keywords from the user's input:

```ruby
def test_sentence_choice
  assert_equal('This is a great test',
            WordPlay.best_sentence(['This is a test',
                                      'This is another test',
                                      'This is a great test'],
                                 %w{test great this}))

  assert_equal('This is a great test',
                WordPlay.best_sentence(['This is a great test'],
                                     %w{still the best}))
end
```

This test method performs a simple assertion that the correct sentence is chosen from three options. Three sentences are provided to `WordPlay.best_sentence`, along with the desired keywords of "test," "great," and "this." Therefore, the third sentence should be the best match. The second assertion makes sure that `WordPlay.best_sentence` returns a sentence even if there are no matches, because in this case, *any* sentence is a "best" match.

Testing Pronoun Switches

When you developed the `switch_pronouns` method, you used some vague grammatical rules, so testing is essential to make sure they stand up for at least basic sentences:

```
def test_basic_pronouns
  assert_equal("i am a robot", WordPlay.switch_pronouns("you are a robot"))
  assert_equal("you are a person", WordPlay.switch_pronouns("i am a
  person"))
  assert_equal("i love you", WordPlay.switch_pronouns("you love me"))
end
```

These basic assertions prove that the "you are," "I am," "you," and "me" phrases are switched correctly.

You can also create a separate test method to perform some more complex assertions:

```
def test_mixed_pronouns
  assert_equal("you gave me life", WordPlay.switch_pronouns("i gave you life"))
  assert_equal("i am not what you are", WordPlay.switch_pronouns("you are
  not what i am"))
  assert_equal("i annoy your dog", WordPlay.switch_pronouns("you annoy my dog"))
end
```

These examples are more complex, but prove that `switch_pronouns` can handle a few more complex situations with multiple pronouns.

You can construct tests that cause `switch_pronouns` to fail:

```
def test_complex_pronouns
  assert_equal("yes, i rule", WordPlay.switch_pronouns("yes, you rule"))
  assert_equal("why do i cry", WordPlay.switch_pronouns("why do you cry"))
end
```

These tests both fail because they circumvent the trick you used to make sure that "you" is translated to "me" and "I" in the right situations. In these situations, they should become "I," but because "I" isn't at the start of the sentence, they become "me" instead. It's important to notice that basic statements tend to work okay, whereas questions or more elaborate statements can fail. However, for your bot's purposes, the basic substitutions suffice and you can remove these tests.

If you were to focus solely on producing an accurate language processor, you could use tests such as these to guide your development, and you'll probably use this technique when developing libraries to deal with *edge cases* such as these in your own projects.

WordPlay's Source Code

Your nascent WordPlay library is complete for now, and in a state that you can use its features to make your bot's source code simpler and easier to read. Next, I'll present the source code for the library as is, as well as its associated unit test file. As an addition, the code also includes comments prior to each class and method definition, so that you can use RDoc to produce HTML documentation files, as covered in Chapter 8.

Note   Remember that source code for this book is available in the Source Code area at `www.apress.com`, so it isn't necessary to type in code directly from the book.

---

wordplay.rb

Here's the code for the WordPlay library:

```
class String
  def sentences
    self.gsub(/\n|\r/, ' ').split(/\.\s*/)
  end

  def words
    self.scan(/\w[\w\'\-]*/)
  end
end
```

```ruby
class WordPlay
  def self.switch_pronouns(text)
    text.gsub(/\b(I am|You are|I|You|Me|Your|My)\b/i) do |pronoun|
      case pronoun.downcase
        when "i"
          "you"
        when "you"
          "me"
        when "me"
          "you"
        when "i am"
          "you are"
        when "you are"
          "i am"
        when "your"
          "my"
        when "my"
          "your"
      end
    end.sub(/^me\b/i, 'i')
  end
  def self.best_sentence(sentences, desired_words)
    ranked_sentences = sentences.sort_by do |s|
      s.words.length - (s.downcase.words - desired_words).length
    end

    ranked_sentences.last
  end
end
```

test_wordplay.rb

Here's the test suite associated with the WordPlay library:

```ruby
require 'minitest/autorun'
require_relative 'wordplay'
```

```ruby
# Unit testing class for the WordPlay library
class TestWordPlay < Minitest::Test

  # Test that multiple sentence blocks are split up into individual
  # words correctly
  def test_sentences
    assert_equal(["a", "b", "c d", "e f g"], "a. b. c d. e f g.".sentences)

    test_text = %q{Hello. This is a test
of sentence separation. This is the end
of the test.}
    assert_equal("This is the end of the test", test_text.sentences[2])
  end
  # Test that sentences of words are split up into distinct words correctly
  def test_words
    assert_equal(%w{this is a test}, "this is a test".words)
    assert_equal(%w{these are mostly words}, "these are, mostly, words".words)
  end
  # Test that the correct sentence is chosen, given the input
  def test_sentence_choice
    assert_equal('This is a great test',
                 WordPlay.best_sentence(['This is a test',
                                         'This is another test',
                                         'This is a great test'],
                                        %w{test great this}))
    assert_equal('This is a great test',
                 WordPlay.best_sentence(['This is a great test'],
                                        %w{still the best}))
  end

  # Test that basic pronouns are switched by switch_pronouns
  def test_basic_pronouns
    assert_equal("i am a robot", WordPlay.switch_pronouns("you are a robot"))
    assert_equal("you are a person", WordPlay.switch_pronouns("i am a
    person"))
    assert_equal("i love you", WordPlay.switch_pronouns("you love me"))
  end
```

```ruby
# Test more complex sentence switches using switch_pronouns
def test_mixed_pronouns
  assert_equal("you gave me life",
               WordPlay.switch_pronouns("i gave you life"))

  assert_equal("i am not what you are",
               WordPlay.switch_pronouns("you are not what i am"))
end
end
```

Building the Bot's Core

In the previous section, you put together the WordPlay library to provide some features you knew that your bot would need, such as basic sentence and word separation. Now you can get on with the task of fleshing out the logic of the bot itself.

You'll create the bot within a Bot class, allowing you to create multiple bot instances and assign them different names and datasets, and work with them separately. This is the cleanest structure, as it allows you to keep the bot's logic separated from the logic of interacting with the bot. For example, if your finished Bot class exists in bot.rb, writing a Ruby program to allow a user to converse with the bot using the keyboard could be as simple as this:

```ruby
require_relative 'bot'

bot = Bot.new(name: "Botty", data_file: "botty.bot")

puts bot.greeting
while input = gets and input.chomp != 'goodbye'
  puts ">> " + bot.response_to(input)
end
puts bot.farewell
```

You'll use this barebones client program as a yardstick while creating the Bot class. In the previous example, you created a bot object and passed in some parameters, which enables you to use the bot's methods, along with keyboard input, to make the bot converse with the user.

In certain situations, it's useful to write an example of the higher-level, more abstracted code that you expect ultimately to write, and then write the lower-level code to satisfy it. This isn't the same as test-first development, although the principle is similar. You write the easiest, most abstract code first and then work your way down to the details.

Next, let's look at how you expect the bot to operate throughout a normal session and then begin to develop the required features one by one.

The Program's Lifecycle and Parts

So far we have focused on verbal descriptions of what we want to do. In Figure 12-2, however, we take a more visual look at the more overall lifecycle of a bot, and the client accessing it, that we'll develop.

Your entire application will be composed of four parts:

1. The Bot class, within `bot.rb`, containing all the bot's logic and any subclasses.

2. The WordPlay library, within `wordplay.rb`, containing the `WordPlay class` and extensions to `String`.

3. Basic "client" applications that create bots and allows users to interact with them. You'll first create a basic keyboard-entry client, but we'll look at some alternatives later in the chapter.

4. A helper program to generate the bot's data files easily.

Figure 12-2 demonstrates the basic lifecycle of a sample client application and its associated bot object. The client program creates a bot instance and then keeps requesting user input passing it to the bot. Responses are printed to the screen, and the loop continues until the user decides to quit.

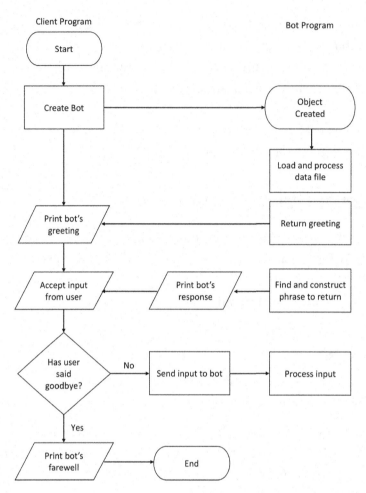

Figure 12-2. *A basic flowchart showing a sample lifecycle of the bot client and bot object*

You'll begin putting together the Bot class and then look at how the bot will find and process its data.

Bot Data

One of your first concerns is where the bot will get its data. The bot's data includes information about word substitutions to perform during preprocessing, as well as myriad keywords and phrases that the bot can use in its responses.

The Data Structure

You'll keep the bot's data in a hash, somewhat like this:

```ruby
bot_data = {
  :presubs => [
    ["dont", "don't"],
    ["youre", "you're"],
    ["love", "like"]
  ],

  :responses => {
    :default   => [
                    "I don't understand.",
                    "What?",
                    "Huh?"
                  ],
    :greeting  => ["Hi. I'm [name]. Want to chat?"],
    :farewell  => ["Good bye!"],
    'hello'    => [
                    "How's it going?",
                    "How do you do?"
                  ],
    'i like *' => [
                    "Why do you like *?",
                    "Wow! I like * too!"
                  ]
  }
}
```

The main hash has two parent elements, `:presubs` and `:responses`. The `:presubs` element references an array of arrays that contain substitutions to be made to the user's input before the bot forms a response. In this instance, the bot will expand some contractions and also change any reference of "love" to "like." The reason for this becomes clear when you look at `:responses`.

Note   The preceding data structure is intentionally lightly populated to save space for discussion of the practicalities. By the end of this chapter, you'll have a more complete set of data to use with your bot. This style of data structure was also covered in Chapter 3.

`:responses` references another hash: one that has elements with the names `:default`, `:greeting`, `:farewell`, `'hello'`, and `'i like *'`. This hash contains all the different phrases the bot will use as responses, or templates used to create full phrases. The array assigned to `:default` contains some phrases to use at random when the bot cannot figure out what to say based on the input. Those associated with `:greeting` and `:farewell` contain generic greeting and farewell phrases.

More interesting are the arrays associated with `'hello'` and `'i like *'`. These phrases are used when the input matches the hash key for each array. For example, if a user says "hello computer," then a match with `'hello'` is made, and a response is chosen from the array at random. If a user says "i like computers," then `'i like *'` is matched and the asterisk is used to substitute the remainder of the user's input (after "i like") into the bot's output phrase. This could result in output such as "Wow! I like computers too," if the second phrase were to be used.

Storing the Data Externally

Using a hash makes data access easy (rather than relying on, say, a database) and fast when it comes to choosing sentences and performing matches. However, because your bot class needs to be able to deal with multiple datasets, it's necessary to store the hash of data for each bot within a file that can be chosen when a bot is started.

In Chapter 9, you learned about the concept of object persistence, where Ruby data structures can be "frozen" and stored. One library you used was called PStore, which stores Ruby data structures in a non-human-readable binary format; and the other was YAML, which is human-readable and represented as a specially formatted text file. For this project, you'll use YAML, as you want to be able to make changes to the data files on the fly, to change things your bot will say, and to test out new phrases without constructing a whole new file each time.

It's possible to create your data files by hand and then let the Bot class load them, but to make life easier, you'll create a small program that can create the initial data file for you, as you did in Chapter 9. An ideal name for it would be bot_data_to_yaml.rb:

```ruby
require 'yaml'

bot_data = {
  :presubs => [
    ["dont", "don't"],
    ["youre", "you're"],
    ["love", "like"]
  ],
  :responses => {
    :default     => [
      "I don't understand.",
      "What?",
      "Huh?"
    ],
    :greeting    => ["Hi. I'm [name]. Want to chat?"],
    :farewell    => ["Good bye!"],
    'hello'      => [
      "How's it going?",
      "How do you do?"
    ],
    'i like *'   => [
      "Why do you like *?",
      "Wow! I like * too!"
    ]
  }
}

# Show the user the YAML data for the bot structure
puts bot_data.to_yaml

# Write the YAML data to file
f = File.open(ARGV.first || 'bot_data', "w")
f.puts bot_data.to_yaml
f.close
```

This short program lets you define the bot data in the bot_data hash and then shows the YAML representation on the screen before writing it to file. The filename is specified on the command line, or defaults to bot_data if none is supplied:

```
ruby bot_data_to_yaml.rb
```

```
---
:presubs:
- - dont
  - don't
- - youre
  - you're
- - love
  - like
:responses:
  i like *:
  - Why do you like *?
  - Wow! I like * too!
  :default:
  - I don't understand.
  - What?
  - Huh?
  hello:
  - How's it going?
  - How do you do?
  :greeting:
  - Hi. I'm [name]. Want to chat?
  :farewell:
  - Good bye!
```

Note that as the YAML data is plain text, you can edit it directly in the file or just tweak the bot_data structure and re-run bot_data_to_yaml.rb. From here on out, let's assume you've run this and generated the preceding YAML file as bot_data in the current directory.

Now that you have a basic data file, you need to construct the Bot class and get its initialize method to use it.

Constructing the Bot Class and Data Loader

Let's create bot.rb and the start of the Bot class:

```
require 'yaml'
require_relative 'wordplay'

class Bot
  attr_reader :name

  def initialize(options)
    @name = options[:name] || "Unnamed Bot"
    begin
      @data = YAML.load(File.read(options[:data_file]))
    rescue
      raise "Can't load bot data"
    end
  end
end
```

The initialize method sets up each newly created object and uses the options hash to populate two class variables, @name and @data. External access to @name is provided courtesy of attr_reader. File.open, along with the read method, opens the data file and reads in the full contents to be processed by the YAML library. YAML.load converts the YAML data into the original hash data structure and assigns it to the @data class variable. If the data file opening or YAML processing fails, an exception is raised, as the bot cannot function without data.

Now you can create the greeting and farewell methods that display a random greeting and farewell message from the bot's dataset. These methods are used when people first start to use the bot or just before the bot client exits:

```
def greeting
  @data[:responses][:greeting][rand(@data[:responses][:greeting].length)]
end

def farewell
  @data[:responses][:farewell][rand(@data[:responses][:farewell].length)]
end
```

Ouch! This isn't nice at all. You have access to the greetings (and farewells) via @data[:responses], but selecting a single random phrase gets ugly fast. This looks like an excellent opportunity to create a private method that retrieves a random phrase from a selected response group:

private

```ruby
def random_response(key)
  random_index = rand(@data[:responses][key].length)
  @data[:responses][key][random_index].gsub(/\[name\]/, @name)
end
```

This method simplifies the routine of taking a random phrase from a particular phrase set in @data. The second line of random_response performs a substitution so that any responses that contain [name] have [name] substituted for the bot's name. For example, one of the demo greeting phrases is "Hi. I'm [name]. Want to chat?" However, if you created the bot object and specified a name of "Fred," the output would appear as "Hi. I'm Fred. Want to chat?"

Note   Remember that a private method is a method that cannot be called from outside the class itself. As random_response is only needed internally to the class, it's a perfect candidate to be a private method.

Let's update greeting and farewell to use random_response:

```ruby
def greeting
  random_response :greeting
end

def farewell
  random_response :farewell
end
```

Isn't separating common functionality into distinct methods great? These methods now look a lot simpler and make immediate sense compared to the jumble they contained previously.

Note   This technique is also useful in situations where you have "ugly" or complex-looking code and you simply want to hide it inside a single method you can call from anywhere. Keep complex code in the background and make the rest of the code look as simple as possible.

The response_to Method

The core of the Bot class is the `response_to` method. It's used to pass user input to the bot and get the bot's response in return. However, the method itself should be simple and have one line per required operation to call private methods that perform each step.

`response_to` must perform several actions:

1. Accept the user's input.

2. Perform preprocessing substitutions, as described in the bot's data file.

3. Split the input into sentences and choose the most keyword-rich sentence.

4. Search for matches against the response phrase set keys.

5. Perform pronoun switching against the user input.

6. Pick a random phrase that matches (or a default phrase if there are no matches) and perform any substitutions of the user input into the result.

7. Return the completed output phrase.

Let's look at each action in turn.

Accepting Input and Performing Substitutions

First, you accept the input as a basic argument to the `response_to` method:

```
def response_to(input)
end
```

Then you move on to performing the preprocessing word and phrase substitutions as dictated by the `:presubs` array in the bot data file. You'll recall the `:presubs` array is an array of arrays that specifies words and phrases that should be changed to another word or phrase. The reason for this is so that you can deal with multiple terms with a single phrase. For example, if you substitute all instances of "yeah" for "yes," a relevant phrase will be shown whether the user says "yeah" or "yes," even though the phrase is only matching on "yes."

As you're focusing on keeping `response_to` simple, you'll use a single method call:

```
def response_to(input)
  prepared_input = preprocess(input).downcase
end
```

Now you can implement `preprocess` as a private method:

private

```
def preprocess(input)
  perform_substitutions input
end
```

Then you can implement the substitution method itself:

```
def perform_substitutions(input)
  @data[:presubs].each { |s| input.gsub!(s[0], s[1]) }
  input
end
```

This code loops through each substitution defined in the `:presubs` array and uses `gsub!` on the input.

At this point, it's worth wondering why you have a string of methods just to get to the `perform_substitutions` method. Why not just call it directly from `response_to`?

The rationale in this case is that you're trying to keep logic separated from other logic within this program as much as possible. This is how larger applications work, as it allows you to extend them more easily. For example, if you wanted to perform more preprocessing tasks in the future, you could simply create methods for them and call them from `preprocess` without having to make any changes to `response_to`. Although this looks inefficient, it actually results in code that's easy to extend and read in the long run. A little verbosity is the price for a lot of flexibility. You'll see a lot of similar techniques used in other Ruby programs, which is why it's demonstrated so forcefully here.

Choosing the Best Sentence

After you have the preprocessed input at your disposal, it's time to split it up into sentences and choose the best one. You can add another line to response_to:

```ruby
def response_to(input)
  prepared_input = preprocess(input.downcase)
  sentence = best_sentence(prepared_input)
end
```

Then you can implement best_sentence as a private method:

```ruby
def best_sentence(input)
  hot_words = @data[:responses].keys.select do |k|
    k.class == String && k =~ /^\w+$/
  end

  WordPlay.best_sentence(input.sentences, hot_words)
end
```

First, best_sentence collects an array of single words from the keys in the :responses hash. It looks for all keys that are strings (you don't want the :default, :greeting, or :farewell symbols getting mixed in) and only a single word. You then use this list with the WordPlay.best_sentence method you developed earlier in this chapter to choose the sentence from the user input that matches the most "hot" words (if any).

You could rewrite this method in any style you wish. If you only ever wanted to choose the *first* sentence in the user input, that's easy to do:

```ruby
def best_sentence(input)
  input.sentences.first
end
```

Or how about the longest sentence?

```ruby
def best_sentence(input)
  input.sentences.sort_by { |s| s.length }.last
end
```

Again, by having the tiny piece of logic of choosing the best sentence in a separate method, you can change the way the program works without meddling with larger methods.

Looking for Matching Phrases

Now you have the sentence you want to parse and the substitutions have been performed. The next step is to find the phrases that are suitable as responses to the chosen sentence and to pick one at random.

Let's extend response_to again:

```
def response_to(input)
  prepared_input = preprocess(input.downcase)
  sentence = best_sentence(prepared_input)
  responses = possible_responses(sentence)
end
```

and implement possible_responses:

```
def possible_responses(sentence)
  responses = []

  # Find all patterns to try to match against
  @data[:responses].keys.each do |pattern|
    next unless pattern.is_a?(String)

    # For each pattern, see if the supplied sentence contains
    # a match. Remove substitution symbols (*) before checking.
    # Push all responses to the responses array.
    if sentence.match('\b' + pattern.gsub(/\*/, '') + '\b')
      responses << @data[:responses][pattern]
    end
  end

  # If there were no matches, add the default ones
  responses << @data[:responses][:default] if responses.empty?

  # Flatten the blocks of responses to a flat array
  responses.flatten
end
```

possible_responses accepts a single sentence and then uses the string keys within the :responses hash to check for matches. Whenever the sentence has a match with a key from :responses, the various suitable responses are pushed onto the responses array. This array is flattened so that a single array is returned.

If no specifically matched responses are found, the default ones (found in :responses with the :default key) are used.

Putting Together the Final Phrase

You now have all the pieces available in response_to to put together the final response. Let's choose a random phrase from responses to use:

```
def response_to(input)
  prepared_input = preprocess(input.downcase)
  sentence = best_sentence(prepared_input)
  responses = possible_responses(sentence)
  responses[rand(responses.length)]
end
```

If you weren't doing any substitutions against the pronoun-switched sentence, this version of response_to would be the final one. However, your bot has the capability to use some of the user's input in its responses. A section of your dummy bot data looked like this:

```
'i like *' => [
  "Why do you like *?",
  "Wow! I like * too!"
]
```

This rule matches when the user says "I like." The first possible response—"Why do you like *?"—contains an asterisk symbol that you'll use to substitute in part of the user's sentence in conjunction with the pronoun-switching method you developed in WordPlay earlier.

For example, a user might say, "I like to talk to you." If the pronouns were switched, you'd get "You like to talk to me." If the segment following "You like" were substituted into the first possible response, you'd end up with "Why do you like to talk to me?" This is a great response that compels the user to continue typing and demonstrates the power of the pronoun-switching technique.

Therefore, if the chosen response contains an asterisk (the character you're using as a placeholder in response phrases), you'll need to substitute the relevant part of the original sentence into the phrase and perform pronoun switching on that part.

Here's the new version of possible_responses with the changes in bold:

```ruby
def possible_responses(sentence)
  responses = []

# Find all patterns to try to match against
  @data[:responses].keys.each do |pattern|
    next unless pattern.is_a?(String)

    # For each pattern, see if the supplied sentence contains
    # a match. Remove substitution symbols (*) before checking.
    # Push all responses to the responses array.
    if sentence.match('\b' + pattern.gsub(/\*/, '') + '\b')
      # If the pattern contains substitution placeholders,
      # perform the substitutions
      if pattern.include?('*')
        responses << @data[:responses][pattern].collect do |phrase|
          # First, erase everything before the placeholder
          # leaving everything after it
          matching_section = sentence.sub(/^.*#{pattern}\s+/, '')

          # Then substitute the text after the placeholder, with
          # the pronouns switched
          phrase.sub('*', WordPlay.switch_pronouns(matching_section))
        end
      else
        # No placeholders? Just add the phrases to the array
        responses << @data[:responses][pattern]
      end
    end
  end

  # If there were no matches, add the default ones
  responses << @data[:responses][:default] if responses.empty?

  # Flatten the blocks of responses to a flat array
  responses.flatten
end
```

This new version of `possible_responses` checks to see if the pattern contains an asterisk, and if so, extracts the correct part of the source sentence to use into `matching_section`, switches the pronouns on that section, and then substitutes that into each relevant phrase.

Playing with the Bot

You have the basic methods implemented in the `Bot` class, so let's play with it asis before looking at extending it any further. The first step is to prepare a better set of data for the bot to use so that your conversations can be more engaging than those with the dummy test data shown earlier in this chapter.

Fred: Your Bot's Personality

In this section, you're going to tweak the `bot_data_to_yaml.rb` script you created earlier to generate a YAML file for your first bot to use. Its name will be Fred, and you'll generate a bot data file called `fred.bot`. Here's `bot_data_to_yaml.rb` extended with a better set of phrases and substitutions:

```ruby
require 'yaml'

bot_data = {
  :presubs => [
    ["dont", "do not"],
    ["don't", "do not"],
    ["youre", "you're"],
    ["love", "like"],
    ["apologize", "are sorry"],
    ["dislike", "hate"],
    ["despise", "hate"],
    ["yeah", "yes"],
    ["mom", "family"]
  ],
  :responses => {
    :default    => [
      "I don't understand.",
      "What?",
```

```ruby
    "Huh?",
    "Tell me about something else.",
    "I'm tired of this. Change the subject."
  ],
  :greeting    => [
    "Hi. I'm [name]. Want to chat?",
    "What's on your mind today?",
    "Hi. What would you like to talk about?"
  ],
  :farewell    => ["Good bye!", "Au revoir!"],
  'hello'      => [
    "How's it going?",
    "How do you do?",
    "Enough of the pleasantries!"
  ],
  'sorry'      => ["There's no need to apologize."],
  'different'  => [
    "How is it different?",
    "What has changed?"
  ],
  'everyone *' => ["You think everyone *?"],
  'do not know'=> ["Are you always so indecisive?"],
  'yes' => [
    "At least you're positive about something!",
    "Great."
  ],
  'family'     => ["Tell me about your family"],
  'you are *'  => [
    "What makes you think I am *?",
    "Are you so sure I am *?"
  ],
  'i am *'     => [
    "Is it normal for you to be *?",
    "Do you like being *?"
  ],
```

```
      'i do not *' => ["Why don't you *?"],
      'what'       => ["Why do you ask?", "Why?", "I don't know. Do you?"],
      'no'         => [
        "Really?",
        "Fair enough."
      ],
      'why does *' => [
        "I don't know why *",
        "Do you already know the answer?"
      ],
      'why can\'t i *' => ["Do you want to *?"],
      'why can\'t you *' => ["Do you want me to *?"],
      'hates *'    => [
        "Why do you think they hate *?"
      ],
      'hate *'     => [
        "Why don't you like *?",
        "Why the dislike of *?"
      ],
      'i like *'   => [
        "Why do you like *?",
        "Wow! I like * too!"
      ]
    }
  }
}
# Show the user the YAML data for the bot structure
puts bot_data.to_yaml

# Write the YAML data to file
f = File.open(ARGV.first || 'bot_data', "w")
f.puts bot_data.to_yaml
f.close
```

If you run this with ruby bot_data_to_yaml.rb fred.bot, you'll end up with a bot data file called fred.bot that contains the necessary data to converse with a basic bot.

The First Real Conversation

Here's a basic program—we'll refer to it as `basic_client.rb`—that can use the Bot class, which reads input from the keyboard and prints the bot's responses to the screen:

```ruby
require_relative 'bot'

bot = Bot.new(name: 'Fred', data_file: 'fred.bot')

puts bot.greeting

while input = gets and input.chomp != 'end'
  puts '>> ' + bot.response_to(input)
end

puts bot.farewell
```

Note   The full code for `bot.rb` is provided a little later in the chapter, so if you run into problems, check it out in case the code you have implemented is missing anything.

It's almost the same as the script we thought of before implementing the Bot class. You used the method names dictated by that program and made it fit. (The completed source for the Bot class is provided in the next section if you want to refer to it.)

Without further ado, give it a try and see if you can have a conversation. Here's a demonstration run:

```
Hi. What would you like to talk about?
I don't know
>> Are you always so indecisive?
Yes, usually
>> Great.
I'm sorry!
>> There's no need to apologize.
So why can't you talk to me properly?
>> Do you want me to talk to you properly?
Yes
```

```
>> At least you're positive about something!
I don't know about that
>> Are you always so indecisive?
Woe is me, why can't I make decisions?
>> Do you want to make decisions?
Everyone does
>> You think everyone does?
```

The bot works! The conversation might be a little stilted and manipulated to use some of the phrases and words covered by your dataset, but with this basic mechanism, and a dataset extended even further, significantly more complex conversations would be possible. Unfortunately, it's outside the scope of this book to provide a large dataset.

In the next section, the final code for the basic bot is presented, and then you'll see how you can extend the bot's functionality further.

Main Bot Code Listing

This section makes available the full source code to the Bot class, bot.rb, including extra documentation that RDoc can use. Also included is the source to a basic bot client that you can use to converse with a bot on a one-on-one basis using the keyboard from the command line.

Note   You will also need the WordPlay class we wrote earlier.

As this code is commented, as opposed to the examples so far in this chapter, I recommend you at least browse through the following code to get a feel for how the entire program operates as a set of parts.

Note   You can also find these listings available to download in the Source Code/ Download area of www.apress.com/.

---

bot.rb

Here's the source code for the main Bot class:

```ruby
require 'yaml'
require_relative 'wordplay'

# A basic implementation of a chatterbot
class Bot
  attr_reader :name

  # Initializes the bot object, loads in the external YAML data
  # file and sets the bot's name. Raises an exception if
  # the data loading process fails.
  def initialize(options)
    @name = options[:name] || "Unnamed Bot"
    begin
      @data = YAML.load(File.open(options[:data_file]).read)
    rescue
      raise "Can't load bot data"
    end
  end

  # Returns a random greeting as specified in the bot's data file
  def greeting
    random_response(:greeting)
  end

  # Returns a random farewell message as specified in the bot's
  # data file
  def farewell
    random_response(:farewell)
  end

  # Responds to input text as given by a user
  def response_to(input)
    prepared_input = preprocess(input.downcase)
    sentence = best_sentence(prepared_input)
    reversed_sentence = WordPlay.switch_pronouns(sentence)
    responses = possible_responses(sentence)
    responses[rand(responses.length)]
  end
```

```ruby
  private

  # Chooses a random response phrase from the :responses hash
  # and substitutes metadata into the phrase
  def random_response(key)
    random_index = rand(@data[:responses][key].length)
    @data[:responses][key][random_index].gsub(/\[name\]/, @name)
  end

  # Performs preprocessing tasks upon all input to the bot
  def preprocess(input)
    perform_substitutions(input)
  end

  # Substitutes words and phrases on supplied input as dictated by
  # the bot's :presubs data
  def perform_substitutions(input)
    @data[:presubs].each { |s| input.gsub!(s[0], s[1]) }
    input
end

  # Using the single word keys from :responses, we search for the
  # sentence that uses the most of them, as it's likely to be the
  # 'best' sentence to parse
  def best_sentence(input)
    hot_words = @data[:responses].keys.select do |k|
      k.class == String && k =~ /^\w+$/
    end

    WordPlay.best_sentence(input.sentences, hot_words)
  end

  # Using a supplied sentence, go through the bot's :responses
  # data set and collect together all phrases that could be
  # used as responses
  def possible_responses(sentence)
    responses = []
```

```ruby
  # Find all patterns to try to match against
  @data[:responses].keys.each do |pattern|
    next unless pattern.is_a?(String)

    # For each pattern, see if the supplied sentence contains
    # a match. Remove substitution symbols (*) before checking.
    # Push all responses to the responses array.
      if sentence.match('\b' + pattern.gsub(/\*/, '') + '\b')
        # If the pattern contains substitution placeholders,
        # perform the substitutions
        if pattern.include?('*')
          responses << @data[:responses][pattern].collect do |phrase|
            # First, erase everything before the placeholder
            # leaving everything after it
            matching_section = sentence.sub(/^.*#{pattern}\s+/, '')

            # Then substitute the text after the placeholder, with
            # the pronouns switched
            phrase.sub('*', WordPlay.switch_pronouns(matching_section))
          end
        else
          # No placeholders? Just add the phrases to the array
          responses << @data[:responses][pattern]
        end
      end
    end

    # If there were no matches, add the default ones
    responses << @data[:responses][:default] if responses.empty?

    # Flatten the blocks of responses to a flat array
    responses.flatten
  end

end
```

basic_client.rb

This basic client accepts input from the user via the keyboard and prints the bot's responses back to the screen. This is the simplest form of client possible:

```ruby
require_relative 'bot'

bot = Bot.new(name: ARGV[0], data_file: ARGV[1])

puts bot.greeting

while input = $stdin.gets and input.chomp != 'end'
  puts '>> ' + bot.response_to(input)
end

puts bot.farewell
```

Use the client like so:

```
ruby basic_client.rb <bot name><data file>
```

Note   You can find listings for basic web, bot-to-bot, and text file clients in the next section of this chapter, "Extending the Bot."

Extending the Bot

One significant benefit of keeping all your bot's functionality well separated within its own class and with multiple interoperating methods is that you can tweak and add functionality easily. In this section, we're going to look at some ways we can easily extend the basic bot's functionality to handle other input sources than just the keyboard.

When you began to create the core Bot class, you looked at a sample client application that accepted input from the keyboard, passed it on to the bot, and printed the response. This simple structure demonstrated how abstracting separate sections of an application into loosely coupled classes makes applications easier to amend and extend. You can use this loose coupling to create clients that work with other forms of input.

Note   When designing larger applications, it's useful to keep in mind the usefulness of loosely coupling the different sections so that if the specifications or requirements change over time, it doesn't require a major rewrite of any code to achieve the desired result.

Using Text Files As a Source of Conversation

You could create an entire one-sided conversation in a text file and pass it in to a bot to test how different bots respond to the same conversation. Consider the following example:

```ruby
require_relative 'bot'

bot = Bot.new(name: ARGV[0], data_file: ARGV[1])
user_lines = File.readlines(ARGV[2])

puts "#{bot.name} says: " + bot.greeting

user_lines.each do |line|
  puts "You say: " + line
  puts "#{bot.name} says:" + bot.response_to(line)
end
```

This program accepts the bot's name, data filename, and conversation filename as command-line arguments, reads in the user-side conversation into an array, and loops through the array, passing each line to the bot in turn.

Connecting the Bot to the Web

One common thing to do with many applications is tie them up to the Web so that anyone can use them. This is a reasonably trivial process using the WEBrick library covered in Chapter 10:

```ruby
require 'webrick'
require_relative 'bot'
```

```ruby
# Class that responds to HTTP/Web requests and interacts with the bot
class BotServlet < WEBrick::HTTPServlet::AbstractServlet

  # A basic HTML template consisting of a basic page with a form
  # and text entry box for the user to converse with our bot. It uses
  # some placeholder text (%RESPONSE%) so the bot's responses can be
  # substituted in easily later.
  @@html = %q{
<html><body>
<form method="get">
<h1>Talk To A Bot</h1>
      %RESPONSE%
<p>
<b>You say:</b><input type="text" name="line" size="40" />
<input type="submit" />
</p>
</form>
</body></html>
  }

  def do_GET(request, response)
    # Mark the request as successful and set MIME type to support HTML
    response.status = 200
    response.content_type = "text/html"

    # If the user supplies some text, respond to it
    if request.query['line'] && request.query['line'].length > 1
      bot_text = $bot.response_to(request.query['line'].chomp)
    else
      bot_text = $bot.greeting
    end

    # Format the text and substitute into the HTML template
    bot_text = %Q{<p><b>I say:</b> #{bot_text}</p>}
    response.body = @@html.sub(/\%RESPONSE\%/, bot_text)
  end
```

```
end
```

```
# Create an HTTP server on port 1234 of the local machine
# accessible via http://localhost:1234/ or http://127.0.0.1:1234/
server = WEBrick::HTTPServer.new( :Port => 1234 )
$bot = Bot.new(name: "Fred", data_file: "fred.bot")
server.mount "/", BotServlet
trap("INT"){ server.shutdown }
server.start
```

Upon running this script, you can talk to the bot using your web browser by visiting http://127.0.0.1:1234/ or http://localhost:1234/. An example of what this should look like is shown in Figure 12-3.

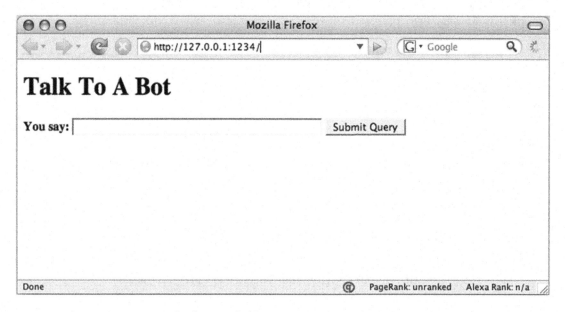

Figure 12-3. *Accessing the bot web client with a web browse*

Alternatively, you could create a CGI script (called bot.cgi, or similar) that could be used with any web hosting provider that provides Ruby as a supported language:

```
#!/usr/bin/env ruby

require_relative 'bot'
require 'cgi'
```

```ruby
# A basic HTML template creating a basic page with a forum and text
# entry box for the user to converse with our bot. It uses some
# placeholder text (%RESPONSE%) so the bot's responses can be
# substituted in easily later
html = %q{
<html><body>
<form method="get">
<h1>Talk To A Bot</h1>
      %RESPONSE%
<p>
<b>You say:</b><input type="text" name="line" size="40" />
<input type="submit" />
</p>
</form>
</body></html>
}
# Set up the CGI environment and make the parameters easy to access
cgi = CGI.new
params = cgi.params
line = params['line'] && params['line'].first

bot = Bot.new(name: "Fred", data_file: "fred.bot")

# If the user supplies some text, respond to it
if line && line.length > 1
  bot_text = bot.response_to(line.chomp)
else
  bot_text = bot.greeting
end

# Format the text and substitute into the HTML template
# as well as sending the MIME header for HTML support
bot_text = %Q{<p><b>I say:</b> #{bot_text}</p>}
puts "Content-type: text/html\n\n"
puts html.sub(/\%RESPONSE\%/, bot_text)
```

Note   You also need to make sure you upload the `bot.rb`, `wordplay.rb`, and bot data file(s).

Bot-to-Bot Conversations

As well as letting users interact with the bot, you can let bots interact with *each other*! Because it only takes a single method on the bot instance to elicit a response, you can pipe responses back and forth between two bots with just a few lines of code:

```ruby
require_relative 'bot'

fred = Bot.new(name: 'Fred', data_file: 'fred.bot')
chris = Bot.new(name: 'Chris', data_file: 'fred.bot')

r = fred.greeting
10.times do
  puts "#{fred.name} said: " + r
  r = chris.response_to(r)
  puts "#{chris.name} said: " + r
  r = fred.response_to(r)
end
```

This could result in the following conversation (it will vary due to the randomness of some of the multiple responses available in the data files):

```
Fred said: Hi. What would you like to talk about?
Chris said: Why?
Fred said: What?
Chris said: I don't know. Do you?
Fred said: What?
Chris said: Why do you ask?
Fred said: I don't understand.
Chris said: Tell me about something else.
Fred said: Tell me about something else.
Chris said: Tell me about something else.
Fred said: I'm tired of this. Change the subject.
```

```
Chris said: What?
Fred said: Why?
Chris said: Tell me about something else.
Fred said: I don't understand.
Chris said: What?
Fred said: Why do you ask?
Chris said: What?
Fred said: Why?
Chris said: Huh?
```

It's not the greatest conversation ever seen, but it's certainly entertaining to see two ersatz therapists getting along with each other. Of course, if you manage to develop two bots that actually have an engrossing conversation, you'll be on the path to artificial intelligence stardom!

The key problem with your bot's data is that none of the default data contains any keywords that can be picked up by other phrases, so both bots are locked in a loop of throwing default phrases at each other. That's why it's important to extend the basic set of data if you want to use the bot for anything that looks impressive!

Summary

In this chapter, we looked at developing a simple chatterbot, developed a library along the way, produced tests for the library, worked with storing our bot's vocabulary in an external file, and looked at a number of ways to extend our project with databases or by hooking it up to a website.

This chapter marks the end of the second part of this book, and you should now have enough Ruby knowledge to pass as a solid, yet still learning, Ruby developer. You should be able to understand the majority of Ruby documentation available online and be able to use Ruby productively either professionally or for fun.

Part 3 of this book digs a little deeper into Ruby's libraries and frameworks, from Ruby on Rails and the Web to general networking and library use. Chapter 16, which looks at a plethora of different Ruby libraries and how to use them, will be particularly useful to refer to as you develop your own programs, so that you don't reinvent the wheel too often!

PART III

Ruby Online

This part of the book looks primarily at Ruby's Internet and networking abilities. The knowledge covered in this part of the book is not essential for developing general Ruby applications, but because the Internet and the Web are important in the scope of modern software development, you're sure to find these chapters useful. This part of the book concludes with a reference-style chapter that covers a choice selection of Ruby libraries and the features they offer.

CHAPTER 13

Two Web Application Approaches: Rails and Sinatra

In this chapter, we're going to look at web application (or web app, for short) frameworks—libraries of code that provide an easily reusable structure and design patterns for developing web applications. If you want to develop something useful for the Web, you'll probably find a web application framework very useful, and Ruby has a wonderful selection of them, of which we'll look at two: Rails and Sinatra.

Background

Ruby's most famous web application framework is the *Ruby on Rails*, and the majority of this chapter will be dedicated to it. We'll walk through developing a (very) basic Rails application and getting it running with a database. After I've covered Rails, we'll take a more cursory look at Sinatra, another library that provides a lightweight approach that is quick and easy to learn.

393

© Carleton DiLeo, Peter Cooper 2021
C. DiLeo and P. Cooper, *Beginning Ruby 3*, https://doi.org/10.1007/978-1-4842-6324-2_13

The Limitations and Benefits of Our Approach

It is very important to note at this stage that web application development is a significant branch of development in general. This book is an introductory Ruby book, rather than a web application development book, so this chapter is focused on giving you a brief walk-through of the concepts involved with Rails and Sinatra, and information on where to go to learn more, rather than exhaustively showing you how to develop complete applications from scratch. Apress has a selection of books specifically about Ruby on Rails and web development available if you wish to learn more and progress further down this line of development. Also, links to further resources and tutorials are provided throughout this chapter.

As well as limitations of space, a key reason for not focusing too much on the details in this chapter is that web application frameworks in particular have a history of changing rapidly. Indeed, this chapter has had to be rewritten twice almost entirely since the first edition of this book in 2006 because the techniques have become obsolete. To prevent you running into too much obsolete code if you come to this book a year or two after publication, we'll focus on the higher-level concepts and look at quick examples of how they relate to code. Then, when you decide to investigate web application frameworks on your own, you'll be informed as to their basic operation, even if the specific techniques have changed.

Pros and Cons of the Frameworks Covered

Rails and Sinatra are easily the two popular web application frameworks used by Rubyists, and they each have distinct pros and cons:

> Rails is a large, robust web application framework that has lots of features baked in. Rails can be used to build applications that are both large and small, but it tends to use more memory and resources than the other frameworks. A typical Rails application will be composed of many tens of files and have a tight structure built of models, views, and controllers (these are explained later). Rails is popular because it's powerful, reasonably standardized, and, admittedly, has the critical mass of community support to keep its popularity growing.

Sinatra is almost the direct opposite of Rails in terms of its qualities. It's fast, lightweight, and pragmatic, and an application can be built within a single Ruby file. There's a lack of any enforced structure (though you could build your own), and fewer features are available out of the box; you will often need to call on other Ruby libraries to fill in the basics, like database support. Despite this, Sinatra is popular due to its extreme simplicity and its suitability for small, agile web applications and services.

Rails: Ruby's Killer App

Due to Rails' significance in making Ruby more popular and its popularity with Rubyists generally, Rails is often called "Ruby's killer app." It's the biggest attractor of new developers to Ruby, and many popular Ruby-related projects online (including Twitter and GitHub) tend to use Rails in some form or another.

Before you can begin to use Rails, it's essential first to know what it is and why it's used, as well as how to get it running, as its installation process is more involved than that of other Ruby libraries.

What Is Rails and Why Use It?

Ruby on Rails is an open source web application development framework. It makes the development of web applications simple. For some of the nontechnical history behind Rails, including the motivation for its development, refer to Chapter 5.

The goal of Rails (as with other web application frameworks) is to make it possible to develop web applications in an easy, straightforward manner and with as few lines of code as necessary. By default, Rails makes a lot of assumptions and has a default configuration that works for most web applications. It's easy to override most of Rails' default assumptions, but these defaults are in place to keep initial application development simple. In Rails parlance, this is commonly called "convention over configuration." That is, there's no need to work on lots of complex configuration files to get going, since sensible defaults will be assumed.

Rails applications operate upon a *model-view-controller* (MVC) architectural pattern. This means that they're primarily split into three sections: *models*, *views*, and *controllers*. These components have the following roles:

- *Models*: These are used to represent forms of data used by the application and contain the logic to manipulate and retrieve that data. In Rails, a model is represented as a class. You can think of models as abstracted, idealized interfaces between controller code and data. These forms of data are not low-level things like strings or arrays, but domain-specific things like users, websites, videos, animals, or classrooms (which could be represented by classes named `User`, `Website`, `Video`, `Animal`, and `Classroom`, respectively).

- *Views*: These are the templates (typically formed of a mixture of HTML and Ruby code) that are used to build up the data that users of the web application see in their browsers or through other clients. Views can be rendered as HTML for web browsers, XML, RSS, or other formats. While views can contain any combination of HTML and Ruby code, typically only the minimal Ruby code necessary to produce the view should be used, as the controller should be handling most of the logic.

- *Controllers*: Controllers provide the logic that binds together models (and their associated data) and views. They process input, call methods made available by models, and deliver data to the views. In Rails, controllers contain methods known as actions that, generally, represent each action relevant to that controller, such as "show," "hide," "view," "delete," and so forth.

The basic relationship between these components is shown in Figure 13-1.

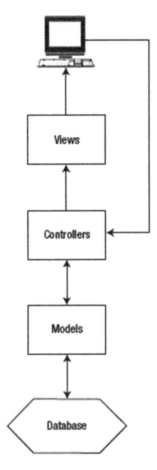

Figure 13-1. *The interactions between an application's users, views, controllers, and models*

Note   You can learn more about the MVC paradigm at `https://en.wikipedia.org/wiki/Model-view-controller`.

The most common motivation to use Rails is that it removes a lot of the groundwork necessary to develop web applications using other technologies. Features such as database access, dynamic page elements (using *Ajax*—Asynchronous JavaScript and XML), templating, and data validation are either preconfigured or take only a few lines of code to configure.

Rails also encourages good development practices. All Rails applications come with support for unit testing (among other forms of testing), and Rails' guiding principles are "don't repeat yourself" (known as DRY) and "convention over configuration."

Installing Rails

The Rails framework is made up of several different libraries, but it's simple to install because all the parts are distributed as gems. The following is a list of Rails' main constituent libraries as of version 6:

- *Rails*: The core library of the Ruby on Rails framework that ties the other libraries together.

- *Action Mailer*: A library that makes it easy to send email from Rails applications. A basic overview of ActionMailer, including how to use it to send mail separately from Rails, is given in Chapter 14.

- *Action Pack*: A framework for handling and responding to requests. The framework includes components to perform routing, define controllers, and render views.

- *Active Record*: An *object-relational mapper* that ties database tables to classes. If you have an ActiveRecord object that references a row in a database table, you can work with that object as you would any other Ruby object (by using attributes and other methods), and changes will be stored in the relevant database table. A basic overview of ActiveRecord was given in Chapter 9.

- *Active Support*: A library that collects a number of support and utility classes used by various Rails features. For example, ActiveSupport implements many useful methods for manipulating times, numbers, arrays, and hashes.

- *Active Job*: A framework for defining tasks that can take place independently of the usual request and response cycle of the web app.

- *ActiveStorage*: Makes uploaded and referencing files in the cloud easy.

- *ActiveModel*: A building block for ActiveRecord. This library allows you to create models using a common template.

- *ActionView*: A framework for handling view template lookup and rendering.

- *ActionText*: Provides rich text editing for Rails. It includes the Trix editor (`https://trix-editor.org/`) to use as a rich text editor in your app.

Generally, you won't need to know or care about each of these elements as a discrete library because you can install them all at once using RubyGems. Before you can install Rails, you must first install Node.js. Visit `https://nodejs.org/en/download/` to find and download the latest Node.js for your OS. Once you've installed node, verify it's installed by running

```
node –version
```

You should get the version of node installed. Make sure it's greater than 8.16.0. Next, you will need to install Yarn. Visit `https://classic.yarnpkg.com/en/docs/install` to find and download the latest Yarn for your OS. Once you've installed Yarn, verify it's installed by running

```
yarn -v
```

Finally, install the Rails gem like so:

```
gem install rails
```

Verify Rails is installed by running the following in a terminal:

```
rails -v
```

Note   Using sudo or run as a superuser on UNIX-like operating systems may fix permissions issues but is not recommended. If you are having issues installing gems, try using either rbenv (`https://github.com/rbenv/rbenv`) or rvm (`https://rvm.io/`) to manage your Ruby environment.

Database Considerations

As Rails is used primarily to develop data-driven web applications, it's necessary to have a database system available to use on your computer.

Database engines are covered in Chapter 9, and you can use all those covered (MySQL, SQLite, and PostgreSQL) with Ruby on Rails. In production, most developers use MySQL or PostgreSQL, as Rails supports these database engines best, but SQLite is the "default" with Rails as it's so easy to set up and is more than fast enough for development purposes (some sites even use it in production with no troubles).

For this chapter's purposes, ensure you have SQLite3 installed and install the SQLite3 gem like so:

```
gem install sqlite3
```

Verify sqlite3 is installed by running the following command in a terminal:

```
sqlite3 -version
```

On Linux, installing the `sqlite3-ruby` gem might raise errors if the SQLite3 libraries are not installed. On Ubuntu and Debian, this is easy to resolve:

```
apt-get install sqlite3 libsqlite3-dev
```

On Red Hat, CentOS, or other Red Hat–derived distributions, you can use the following:

```
yum install sqlite sqlite-devel
```

If you're using a different distribution or have standing issues with getting SQLite3 installed, the best source of help is the many random blog posts you can find on Google by searching for "install sqlite3 [your operating system's name]."

Building a Basic Rails Application

As explained in the previous section, Rails is popular because it makes developing web applications easy. In this section, I'll demonstrate that by showing you how to generate a very basic web application, and we'll take a look through how certain parts of it work.

Creating a Blank Rails Application

As you can use Rails to develop both small and large applications, different types of files are organized into different directories to keep elements separated for tidiness on large projects. A lot of pre-created files are also placed within a new, blank Rails project. The quickest way to look at these files and the overall directory structure is to leap right in and create a new Rails project.

Your project in this chapter will be to create a simple diary app, similar to a blog (or weblog). The resulting application will let you view your diary and add, delete, or edit specific entries.

The basic feature set of being able to create, read, update, and delete items is known as *CRUD* which is a common structure used in web application. For example, a photo gallery site allows you to add, view, edit, and delete photos, which are all CRUD actions. Therefore, the mechanics of developing a basic diary tool are easily transferable to developing most other types of web applications.

Note   CRUD is an acronym to refer to the concept of a system that allows the creation, reading, updating, and deletion of discrete items.

The Rails Command-Line Tool

When you installed Rails, a script called `rails` was also installed. You use the `rails` script to create new Rails projects, their default files, and their directory structure. To use it, navigate to a place in your filesystem where you would like to store Rails projects (possibly creating a `rails` directory in the process) and run `rails new`, specifying an application name as the sole argument:

```
rails new mydiary
```

Tip   By default, SQLite will be specified as the database type in the `database.yml` file generated in the preceding code. If you're going to be using MySQL, however, use `rails mydiary -d mysql` instead. Try `rails -h` if you want to see more of the available command-line options.

A lot of files and directories are produced, but don't feel overwhelmed! You won't even use many of them in this chapter, as they are for more advanced cases that aren't relevant to the very basic web application development we're looking at. In most cases, Rails provides sane defaults anyway, so you don't need to change a lot of files unless you're doing something special. Nonetheless, we'll take a look at what these directories are for in the following section.

Files and Directories Within a Rails Application

In this section, we're going to go through the directories and files created by `rails` and look at what they're for. Don't become overwhelmed by this section. If there's something you don't understand, keep going, as most of the new terms and concepts mentioned here are explained as we use them throughout this chapter.

`rails` generates the following main folders:

- app: Contains most of the Ruby source code and output templates directly associated with the application. It contains several other folders that I'll cover next.

- app/assets: A place to store image and CSS files that can be compiled down to more efficient "packaged" versions later.

- app/javascript: A place to store JavaScript files. JavaScript is in a separate folder from other assets due to Rails 6 adding Webpacker support. Webpacker provides a lot of powerful feature needed for modern JavaScript development. Read more about Webpacker here: `https://github.com/rails/webpacker`.

- app/channel: Contains files for ActionCable. ActionCable is framework that allows Rails to work with websockets.

- app/mailers: Contains code to handle emails. For example, the code for the welcome email would be stored here.

- app/controllers: Contains the controller files. In an empty project, only `application_controller.rb` exists. `application_controller.rb` is an application-wide controller where you can define methods that other controllers will inherit.

- app/helpers: Contains helper files—Ruby source code files that provide methods that you can use from views.

- app/models: Contains a file for each model in the application. In an empty project, no models are yet defined, so this directory is empty.

- app/views: Contains the output templates (views) for the application. Typically, each controller has its own folder under `app/views`, with templates located in those folders. There's also a `layouts` folder that Rails uses to store generic application-wide templates.

- bin: Contains app-tailored scripts that you run from the terminal, for example, `rails` and `bundle`.

- config: An important folder that contains configuration files for the application. For example, `database.yml` is a YAML file with information about the database(s) that the application will use.

- db: A folder to be used for database dumps, backups, and migrations.

- lib: Contains third-party libraries and Rake tasks. Plugins have largely superseded the features offered by libraries that were once placed into `lib`.

- log: Contains log files relating to the operation of the application.

- node_modules: Contains JavaScript libraries and dependencies managed by Webpacker. Webpacker will use npm or Yarn to download libraries and store them here.

- public: Contains non-dynamic files that are accessible under your application's URL scheme, for example, JavaScript libraries (in `public/javascripts`), images (in `public/ images`), and CSS style sheets (in `public/stylesheets`). This folder also includes several "dispatch" scripts and an `.htaccess` file that can be used in certain situations to run your application (such as when/if you choose to use CGI or FastCGI execution methods—neither of which are recommended).

- test: Contains the test subsystems for a Rails application. This folder is covered in more detail later in this chapter in the "Testing" section.

- tmp: Temporary storage area for data created and used by your Rails application (including cache and session files).

I'll briefly mention some of these folders again throughout the rest of the chapter as you create files within them to get your basic application working.

Database Configuration

Earlier I said that Rails applications are generally database dependent. With this in mind, at this stage it's necessary to create a database for your application on your database server.

Note   You *could* develop an app that has no need to permanently store data or operates without a database, but this would be atypical.

By default, your Rails application will use an SQLite database, and it will generate this for itself when you first run your database's migrations (covered later). If you are using any other database engine, however, the technique you'll use to create a database for your application will vary with database type and how you have your database server installed.

Database configuration settings are stored in `database.yml`. Since we are using SQLite, it's not necessary to change these settings at all, but it's worth looking at them nonetheless.

Ignoring the comments, you'll notice three main sections in `database.yml`, called "development," "test," and "production." These sections represent the three different *environments* your application can run under. For example, while developing, you want your application to return verbose error messages and automatically detect changes you make to the code. In production (better thought of as being a "deployment" environment), you want speed, caching, and non-verbose error messages. The test environment is provided so that testing can occur on a different database away from your regular data. The "development" section is used to configure your local development environment.

`database.yml` tells Rails how to access the database associated with the application, so it's essential that the details are correct. If not, you'll get error messages when you try to run your eventual application (though, thankfully, these errors will often tend to give you some great clues as to how to fix the problem).

Using Scaffolding

A Rails application without any models is not a working application at all. Any application you build will need at least one model. In our case, we're first going to focus on the concept of "entries" in our virtual diary.

Rails comes with a concept called *scaffolding* that will generate default (but fully working) code that will do the database and code work necessary to create a model, a controller for that model, and some default views to interact with that model's data. It's possible to do this in gradual steps, or even entirely by hand, but scaffolding enables you to get up and running a lot more quickly.

Think of the Rails generator we used earlier to generate all of the files essential for a Rails project. Scaffolding is the next logical step up from that. Instead of creating the files necessary for a Rails project, scaffolding creates some of the code (including a database *migration* to create the database table for the model) and views necessary to represent a single model within your application.

You can then build your own extra views and controller methods off of this basic scaffolding. It's designed to give you a jump-start without making you code everything from scratch (although you can code from scratch if you want to, particularly if your ambitions differ wildly from what the scaffolding provides).

Note   In Rails, models and database tables typically have a direct relationship. If you have a model called `Entry`, this will by default be related to the database table called `entries`. Rails takes care of the pluralization between model class names and database table names.

For our diary application, entries will initially solely consist of a title and some content. There are other attributes (or "columns" in the database sense) that Rails will add by default to the table, such as `id` (a unique numeric identifier). A directive is also added into the default migration code to create timestamp columns: `created_at` (a timestamp of when the row/associated object was created) and `updated_at` (a timestamp of when the row/associated object was amended last). Because of this automation, it is only necessary to specify the two custom, additional attributes to the scaffold generator to get things going.

To generate scaffolding for your entries table, use the generate script again:

```
rails generate scaffold Entry title:string content:text
```

```
invoke   active_record
create     db/migrate/20200807024733_create_entries.rb
create     app/models/entry.rb
invoke     test_unit
create       test/models/entry_test.rb
create       test/fixtures/entries.yml
invoke   resource_route
route      resources :entries
invoke   scaffold_controller
create     app/controllers/entries_controller.rb
invoke     erb
create       app/views/entries
create       app/views/entries/index.html.erb
create       app/views/entries/edit.html.erb
create       app/views/entries/show.html.erb
create       app/views/entries/new.html.erb
create       app/views/entries/_form.html.erb
invoke     test_unit
create       test/controllers/entries_controller_test.rb
create       test/system/entries_test.rb
invoke     helper
```

```
create      app/helpers/entries_helper.rb

invoke      test_unit

invoke    jbuilder

create      app/views/entries/index.json.jbuilder

create      app/views/entries/show.json.jbuilder

create      app/views/entries/_entry.json.jbuilder

invoke   assets

invoke      scss

create      app/assets/stylesheets/entries.scss

invoke   scss

create      app/assets/stylesheets/scaffolds.scss
```

The scaffolding generator has done a lot of work for us! The generator has created some view files (in app/views/entries) to enable us to see our entries, create new entries, and edit them. It has also produced an "entries" controller (in app/controllers), some dummy tests (in test/*), and a database migration (in db/migrate; note that the migration's filename starts with a timestamp, so it will vary).

But what is a database migration, and why does it matter?

Database Migrations

I've mentioned before that in Rails, models and database tables are directly related. It is necessary, therefore, for the table relating to a Rails model to exist within the database.

Migrations provide a Ruby-based way to define database tables. Instead of doing the SQL yourself, you specify what tables, columns, and indexes you want to exist and run the migration, and Rails' ActiveRecord library does the hard work for you. Even better, you can have multiple migrations for the same table, so that if you decide to add a column to a table later, you create a new migration and specify that you'd like to add a new column.

Migrations are considered desirable because they provide a programmatic way to both upgrade *and* downgrade databases. Since migrations are normal source code, it's also possible to put them into your source code management system and share them between multiple developers, if you wish. Migrations provide abstraction and mechanization to make organizing database changes associated with a Rails application easy.

The scaffolding generator you ran in the previous section produced a database migration. Let's take a look at it to see how it works. You'll find it in the db/migrate directory—it will have a filename ending in "create_entries.rb" because the first part of the filename is timestamped. It should contain the following:

```
class CreateEntries < ActiveRecord::Migration[6.0]
  def change
    create_table :entries do |t|
      t.string :title
      t.text :content

      t.timestamps
    end
  end
end
```

A single migration is defined in a single file as a class that inherits from ActiveRecord::Migration and it creates the entries table using the create_table method, which is supplied with a symbol representing the table name (:entries) and a code block within where the attributes/columns can be defined.

In this case, a string column called title and a text column called content are created. "Timestamp" columns are also created. At the time of writing, these are created_at and updated_at; they store the date and time of when a row was created and when it was last amended, respectively.

Note   The difference between a string column and a text column is that, classically, string columns are for storing short (often fixed-length) textual strings, whereas text columns can store both short strings and very long blocks of text.

Your application has a migration ready to go to create the entries table. To get it to run, you need to invoke a *rake task* (see the following "Rake Tasks" sidebar for more information about these) called db:migrate that will then run all migrations that have not yet been processed:

rake db:migrate

```
== 20200807024733 CreateEntries: migrating
======================================

-- create_table(:entries)

   -> 0.0010s

== 20200807024733 CreateEntries: migrated (0.0011s)
============================
```

The output verifies that the CreateEntries migration was run, and now the entries table exists (with the specified columns) within the database associated with your application. In essence, you now have a Rails application that's ready to be used!

Note   There's a lot more to migrations than this section has scope to cover. Luckily, the Rails documentation team has a great guide specifically about migrations, how they work, and how you can create and customize your own. You can find the migrations guide at https://guides.rubyonrails.org/migrations.html.

RAKE TASKS

Rake tasks are administrative tasks associated with your application that are managed by the Rake tool. Rake, meaning "Ruby Make," is a tool that you can use to process and trigger actions to perform upon Ruby projects and code, and it's used commonly within Rails projects to do things such as start unit tests and perform migrations.

To perform a Rake task, you simply run rake followed by the name of a task:

```
rake <task name>
```

You can also get a list of all the Rake tasks available, like so:

```
rake --tasks
```

With Rails 6, there are 67 tasks by default. To save space, they aren't listed here, but it's worth looking through the list to get a feel for what tasks are available.

Running the Basic, Scaffolded App

You've run the scaffold generator, you've looked at the database migration for your entries table, and you've used the db:migrate rake task to bring your database up to speed. That's all you have to do to get a working application! To try it out, you need to run the server script that provides a basic web server through which to access the application:

```
rails server
```

```
=> Booting Puma

=> Rails 6.0.3.2 application starting in development

=> Run `rails server --help` for more startup options

Puma starting in single mode...

* Version 4.3.5, codename: Mysterious Traveller

* Min threads: 5, max threads: 5

* Environment: development

* Listening on tcp://127.0.0.1:3000

* Listening on tcp://[::1]:3000

Use Ctrl-C to stop
```

At this point, the application sits there doing nothing. This is because it's waiting to serve HTTP requests (such as from your web browser).

Go to your web browser of choice and access the application using the URL given by the output (`http://localhost:3000/` in this case, but it might be `http://127.0.0.1:3000/` on your machine depending on your OS and network setup). You should see a page like the one in Figure 13-2.

Yay! You're on Rails!

Figure 13-2. *The default Rails application index.html page*

The page you're seeing is the `index.html` file from the `public` folder. This is because if no action is found within a Rails application that associates with the URL you're loading from your web browser, a Rails application should return a file from the `public` folder—if any file matches—or an error message. Because the default page to load on a web server is usually `index.html`, `public/index.html` is returned.

When you generated the scaffolding for the `Entry` model, a controller called `entries` was created, as `app/controllers/entries_controller.rb`. By default, you access controller methods in a Rails application using a URL in the format of `http://`*[hostname]*`/`*[controller]*`/`*[action]*.

411

Note Don't worry about this too much, but for completeness, even though `http://[hostname]/` `[controller]/[action]` is a default, it can be superseded. As `entries` has been created as a scaffolded *resource*, you can also use `http://[hostname]/entries/[id]` as an alternative to `http://` `[hostname]/` `entries/show/[id]`, since routes have been automatically created to route requests to certain methods based on the HTTP verb (GET, PUT, POST, or DELETE) used—for example, a DELETE HTTP request can automatically route to the `destroy` action where applicable.

So, with this application, load `http://localhost:3000/entries` (replace `localhost` with whatever hostname is used on your local machine). No action name is specified, but by default an action name of `index` is assumed, and the scaffolding has implemented this. If you're successful, you'll see a basic list of entries, as shown in Figure 13-3.

Entries
Title Content

New Entry

Figure 13-3. The basic list or index view of the entries scaffolding

The list of entries in Figure 13-3 is noticeably bare. This is because your `entries` table has no data in it. The column headings for your table are obvious, though (`Title` and `Content`), and a New Entry link is available.

Clicking New Entry takes you to `http://localhost:3000/entries/new`—the new method within the `entries` controller—and presents you with a page containing a form that allows you to fill out the data for a single entry. This view is demonstrated in Figure 13-4.

New Entry

Title

Content

Create entry

Back

Figure 13-4. The new method of the entries controller, used to create new entries

From this point, you can create new entries, return to the list, edit those entries (the form looks similar to that in Figure 13-4), and delete entries. That covers all the CRUD functions!

With scaffolding, you get a basic but complete data-driven web application with a few lines at the command prompt. However, next you need to look at what the scaffolding generator actually generated and learn how to customize the models, controllers, and views to create the specific application that you want. This experience will be particularly valuable if you choose to pursue Rails development further.

Controllers and Views

In the last section, you put together a basic web application that allowed you to create, edit, list, and delete diary entries. You used scaffolding, which let you put a whole working application together with no direct coding effort required. In this section, you're going to look at what the scaffolding generated, how it works, and how you can extend the application a little.

Controller Actions

The first URL you accessed in your application was `http://localhost:3000/entries`. This URL takes you to the `entries` controller's `index` method. Let's look in `app/controllers/entries_controller.rb` to find it:

```
class EntriesController < ApplicationController
  before_action :set_entry, only: [:show, :edit, :update, :destroy]

  # GET /entries
  # GET /entries.json
  def index
    @entries = Entry.all
  end

  # GET /entries/1
  # GET /entries/1.json
  def show
  end
```

```ruby
# GET /entries/new
def new
  @entry = Entry.new
end

# GET /entries/1/edit
def edit
end

# POST /entries
# POST /entries.json
def create
  @entry = Entry.new(entry_params)

  respond_to do |format|
    if @entry.save
      format.html { redirect_to @entry, notice: 'Entry was successfully
      created.' }
      format.json { render :show, status: :created, location: @entry }
    else
      format.html { render :new }
      format.json { render json: @entry.errors, status: :unprocessable_
      entity }
    end
  end
end

# PATCH/PUT /entries/1
# PATCH/PUT /entries/1.json
def update
  respond_to do |format|
    if @entry.update(entry_params)
      format.html { redirect_to @entry, notice: 'Entry was successfully
      updated.' }
      format.json { render :show, status: :ok, location: @entry }
    else
      format.html { render :edit }
```

```ruby
      format.json { render json: @entry.errors, status: :unprocessable_
      entity }
    end
  end
end

# DELETE /entries/1
# DELETE /entries/1.json
def destroy
  @entry.destroy
  respond_to do |format|
    format.html { redirect_to entries_url, notice: 'Entry was
    successfully destroyed.' }
    format.json { head :no_content }
  end
end

private
  # Use callbacks to share common setup or constraints between actions.
  def set_entry
    @entry = Entry.find(params[:id])
  end

  # Only allow a list of trusted parameters through.
  def entry_params
    params.require(:entry).permit(:title, :content)
  end
end
```

This code shows that Ruby controllers are implemented as classes that inherit from ApplicationController (found in app/controllers/application_controller.rb), which in turn inherits from a core Rails class, ActionController::Base.

When a user tries to access the index method of the entries controller, control is delegated to the index method (or action) in the EntriesController class, shown on its own here:

```
# GET /entries
# GET /entries.json
def index
  @entries = Entry.all
end
```

This code is simple for what it does. It collects all of the Entry objects (represented by rows in the entries table) within the database using @entries = Entry.all.

Entry is the model class and models inherit from ApplicationRecord which inherits from ActiveRecord::Base, which provides methods suitable to navigate and find data in the associated table for that model. Therefore, Entry.all returns all rows (as objects) from the entries table and places them as an array into @entries.

Following on from that, Rails automatically knows to render the correct template for displaying the entries. Let's take a look at how that works now.

Views and Embedded Ruby (ERB)

Now let's look at the equivalent view for the index controller action examined in the previous section. The view template is located in app/views/entries/index.html.erb:

```
<p id="notice"><%= notice %></p>

<h1>Entries</h1>

<table>
  <thead>
    <tr>
      <th>Title</th>
      <th>Content</th>
      <th colspan="3"></th>
    </tr>
  </thead>

  <tbody>
    <% @entries.each do |entry| %>
      <tr>
        <td><%= entry.title %></td>
```

```
      <td><%= entry.content %></td>
      <td><%= link_to 'Show', entry %></td>
      <td><%= link_to 'Edit', edit_entry_path(entry) %></td>
      <td><%= link_to 'Destroy', entry, method: :delete, data: { confirm:
      'Are you sure?' } %></td>
    </tr>
  <% end %>
  </tbody>
</table>

<br>


<%= link_to 'New Entry', new_entry_path %>
```

If you're familiar with both Ruby and HTML, you'll note that this view is basically HTML with Ruby embedded in it (with the Ruby located between <% and %> tags). In Ruby and Rails parlance, this is called an *ERB template*.

Note   The file extension of ERB templates is .erb. Those that are HTML-based typically use the dual extension of .html.erb in Rails. This naming convention allows you to have many erb files with the same root name but for different response types.

The core part of the list view contains this code:

```
<% @entries.each do |entry| %>
  <tr>
    <td><%= entry.title %></td>
    <td><%= entry.content %></td>
    <td><%= link_to 'Show', entry %></td>
    <td><%= link_to 'Edit', edit_entry_path(entry) %></td>
    <td><%= link_to 'Destroy', entry, method: :delete, data: { confirm:
            'Are you sure?' } %></td>
  </tr>
<% end %>
```

This view code results in the main, dynamic part of the page being rendered: the actual list of entries. There are a few key things to note. This whole section is a loop over each element of @entries (using @entries' each method with a code block). You should recall that your controller code placed Entry objects from the database into the @entries array, so the view code iterates over each element (or each entry). Next, two table columns (using the <td> HTML tag) show the current entry's title and content, respectively. This is achieved using the <%= entry.title %> and <%= entry.content %> blocks. Expressions within <%= and %> tags are interpreted and then substituted into the final HTML output.

After the data for the entry has been shown, you reach this:

```
<td><%= link_to 'Show', entry %></td>
<td><%= link_to 'Edit', edit_entry_path(entry) %></td>
<td><%= link_to 'Destroy', entry, method: :delete, data: { confirm: 'Are
you sure?' } %>
</td>
```

The important parts to look at are the calls to the link_to method. link_to is a special method provided by Rails that generates an HTML link to another controller and/or action within the application. Let's look at the first line:

```
<td><%= link_to 'Show', entry %></td>
```

Whereas the general Ruby code in the view is located within <% and %> tags, Ruby code that results in something to be rendered in the document (i.e., shown on the web page) is included within <%= and %> tags (as in the earlier <%= entry.title %> column).

The link_to method accepts the text to use for the link, and then it accepts parameters that specify where the link should go.

In the <%= link_to 'Show', entry %> case, link_to assumes that since it has been passed an entry object, you want to link to the page that will show only that entry—specifically /entries/[id of entry].

In the second example, <%= link_to 'Edit', edit_entry_path(entry) %>, the edit_entry_path shortcut method is used (with the entry object as a parameter) to provide the hash of parameters to link to /entries/[id of entry]/edit.

The last example, <%= link_to 'Destroy', entry, method: :delete, data: { confirm: 'Are you sure?' } %>, provides the entry object, as with the "show" version, but the HTTP DELETE method is specified using the method argument, so link_to is smart enough to realize you want to direct the link to the destroy method of the entries controller in this case.

Separate from these shortcuts, however, let's look at how the parameters of link_to can be manipulated directly to get the results you want.

Let's review the generated output of various link_to examples (assuming a basic Entry object is present in the entry variable):

```
<%= entry.id %>)
```

```
3
```

```
<%= entry.content %>
```

```
This is an example entry.
```

```
<%= link_to 'Show', :action => 'show' %>
```

```
<a href="/entries/show">Show</a>
```

```
<%= link_to entry.title, :action => 'show', :id => entry.id %>
```

```
<a href="/entries/show/3">Example Entry</a>
```

```
<%= link_to 'Show', :action => 'show', :id => entry.id %>
```

```
<a href="/entries/show/3">Show</a>
```

It's important to understand how these examples work, as many elements of views rendered by Rails will contain patterns such as these, whether for generating links, including images, or creating forms to post data back to your application.

At this stage, you might be wondering why you can't write the HTML you want directly into views and then build up the links manually, for example:

```
<a href="/entries/show/<%= entry.id %>"><%= entry.title %></a>
```

instead of

```
<%= link_to entry.title, :action => 'show', :id => entry.id %>
```

The simple answer is *you can*! Stylistically, however, Rails developers prefer to let Rails' *helper methods* (such as `link_to`) do the work of putting together fragments of HTML that might need to change in the future. For example, in the future you might choose to change the "entries" part of the URLs to "entry" for some reason or another, and with Rails you could make changes to the application's routing to do this. The links generated by helpers such as `link_to` would then automatically reflect the new conventions, whereas if you coded them with HTML, as previously, you'd have a lot of searching and replacing to do in your views!

Models and Relationships

So far, your application only has a single model, `Entry`, that relates to diary entries. However, one major benefit the ActiveRecord library provides is the ability to relate models easily to one another. For example, you could create another model called `User` that relates to different people who can post diary entries in your system.

The full depth of ActiveRecord and model relationships (also known as *associations*) can and does take up entire books, so is beyond the scope of this introduction, but in this section, we'll look at a basic example of how ActiveRecord models can relate to one another.

In earlier sections of this chapter, you saw how ActiveRecord objects work at a basic level, for example:

```
entry = Entry.find(1)
entry.title = 'Title of the first entry'
entry.save
```

Columns in the database become attributes that you can get and set on the objects, and you can then save those objects back to the database with the object's `save` method.

If you want to see the previous example in action, try using the Rails console. Similar to irb, the Rails console allows developers to run commands. Unlike irb, Rails console loads the entire Rails environment so that you can access all of the code in your project. Running the console is simple. Using a terminal, go to the root directory of your Rails project and type the following:

```
rails console
```

```
Running via Spring preloader in process 85677

Loading development environment (Rails 6.0.2.2)

irb(main):001:0>
```

Let's imagine that you have a User model that contains columns including a user's name, email address, and other user-related information. Now let's imagine that you directly relate users and entries in your application. You might expect to be able to do things like this:

```
entry = Entry.find(1)
entry.user.name = 'Name of whoever posted the entry'
entry.user.email = 'Their email address'
```

This is, indeed, what one-to-many relationships with ActiveRecord enable. Setting up such a relationship between models is easy. Consider the two models, located in app/models/entry.rb and app/models/user.rb, respectively:

```
class Entry < ApplicationRecord
  belongs_to :user
end
```

You would use this code for the User model:

```
class User < ApplicationRecord
  has_many :entries
end
```

ActiveRecord was designed to allow an almost natural language mechanism of defining model relationships. In our Entry model, we say that Entry objects "belong_to" User objects. In the User model, we say that a User object "has_many" associated Entry objects.

The only thing you need to set up, other than the relationship itself, is a column in the entries table that enables the relationship to work. You need to store the id of the associated user with each Entry object, so you need to add an integer column to entries called user_id. You could do this by creating a new migration and using a directive such as add_column :entries, :user_id, or :integer or by adding the column manually with SQL (through another client).

421

Once the model relationship has been defined and relationships between data have been made—which is as easy as, say, `entry.user = User.find(1)`—you can then access data across the relationship. For example, in a view showing an entry, you might have some view code such as this:

```
<p>Posted by <%= entry.user.name %> at <%= entry.created_at %></p>
```

ActiveRecord also supports *many-to-many* relationships. For example, consider the relationship between fictional `Student` and `Class` models. Students can be associated with more than one class at a time, and each class can contain many students. With ActiveRecord, you can define these relationships using a join table and a `has_and_belongs_to_many` relationship, or through an intermediary model such as `Enrollment`, which defines the links between `Students` and `Classes` using `has_many` with a `:through` parameter.

Note   It's worth pointing out that a model called `Class` wouldn't be allowed in Rails, because there's already a class called `Class` built into Ruby. Beware of reserved words and using names that are already used elsewhere!

The variety of relationships possible are documented in the official Ruby on Rails documentation at `https://guides.rubyonrails.org/association_basics.html`.

Sessions and Filters

A useful feature provided by Rails applications is support for sessions. When a web browser makes a request to your application, Rails silently sends back a cookie containing a unique identifier for that browser. Whenever that browser makes further requests, it sends back the cookie with the unique identifier, so the application always knows when a certain previous visitor is making another request. You can use the session's ability to store information that's specific to a particular visitor for use on future requests.

Sessions are commonly used on websites for features such as shopping carts or keeping track of what pages you've visited. For example, if you add an item to your cart at an ecommerce site, the item chosen is stored in a data store associated with your session's ID. When you come to check out, your session ID is used to look up data specific to your session in the session system's data store and find out what you have in your cart.

To demonstrate basic session storage in your Rails application, you'll count and show a user how many times he or she has accessed actions within your application. To do this, you need to have some way of performing this logic on each request made to the application. You could add logic to every controller action, but an easier way is to use a filter method called before_action.

before_action is a method you can use at the controller class level to define that a method (or, indeed, many methods) should be executed before the method for the controller action of the current request. Filters make it possible to perform generic activities before every request (or before requests to certain groups of methods or certain controllers).

Note   A common use for filters within Rails is to make sure visitors are authenticated and authorized to visit certain controllers and perform certain actions. If you have a controller class called AdminController, you might want to add a before_action that ensures a visitor is logged in to the site as an admin user before you let him or her use the potentially dangerous actions within!

In this example, you'll use before_action to perform some logic before every request to the application. To do this, you'll add some code to app/controllers/application_controller.rb so that every controller in your application (although there is only one in this case, entries) will be subjected to the filter.

Here's app/controllers/application_controller.rb before the new code:

```
class ApplicationController < ActionController::Base
end
```

Here's the same file after implementing your request-counting code (and removing the comments):

```
class ApplicationController < ActionController::Base
  before_action :count_requests_in_session

  def count_requests_in_session
    session[:requests] ||= 0
    session[:requests] += 1
  end
end
```

You use `before_action` with a symbol as a parameter, where the symbol represents the `count_requests_in_session` method.

Tip   Learn more about filters at `https://guides.rubyonrails.org/ action_controller_overview.html#filters`.

Within the `count_requests_in_session` method, a hash provided by Rails called `session` is used. Automatically, `session` is always a data store associated with the current session, so anything you write to it or read from it is always associated with the current session.

In this case, you initialize `session[:requests]` with 0 if it is not already defined, and then you increase the count on the next line. You can access this information from your views now quite easily. Go to `app/views/entries/index.html.erb` and add this line to the top of the file:

```
<%= session[:requests] %>
```

If you now load `http://localhost:3000/entries`, you'll see 1 at the top of the page. Reload the page, and the number increases for each reload. Sessions in action!

Other Features

Although you've managed to create a basic working Rails application so far, I've only covered the bare essentials. In this section, I'll quickly cover a few key areas that you'll want to know about before exploring Rails further independently.

Layouts

In the Rails application developed earlier in this chapter, you let scaffolding do the work of creating views for you. You then looked through the views created to see how they work. The scaffolding generator also created a *layout*, a sort of super-template that can be used to render the generic code around the code specific for a certain action. For example, most HTML documents would start off something like this:

```
<!doctype html>
<html lang="en">
<head>
```

```
<meta charset="utf-8">
<title>Page Title Here</title>
<link rel="stylesheet" href="styles.css">
</head>
<body>
```

And, at the very least, a typical HTML document would end somewhat like this:

```
</body>
</html>
```

In Rails, layouts are special, generic wrapper templates that multiple views can use. Instead of repeating the HTML header and footer code within every view, you can simply embed each view's output into a layout instead. By default, if there's a file with the same base name as the current controller in `app/views/layouts`, it's used as a layout.

In the scaffolded application's case, the layout used was `app/views/layouts/application.html.erb`. Let's take a look at it:

```
<!DOCTYPE html>
<html>
  <head>
    <title>Mydiary</title>
    <%= csrf_meta_tags %>
    <%= csp_meta_tag %>

    <%= stylesheet_link_tag 'application', media: 'all', 'data-turbolinks-
        track': 'reload' %>
    <%= javascript_pack_tag 'application', 'data-turbolinks-track':
        'reload' %>
  </head>

  <body>
    <%= yield %>
  </body>
</html>
```

This layout includes the basic HTML header and footer items, but also uses some special Rails code to include style sheets (with the `stylesheet_link_tag` method), JavaScript, and more that the page relies on.

425

The `<%= yield %>` code yields the rendering process to the view for the current action, so the contents of the current view are rendered at that location.

If you so choose, you can force a view to be displayed without a layout by adding a line at the point of render (i.e., in the relevant method or action) in the `entries` controller, like so:

```
render layout: false
```

You can also specify a different layout to use in this way by supplying a layout name to render instead:

```
render layout: 'some_other_layout'
```

This would then use `app/views/layouts/some_other_layout.html.erb` for the layout of that action's view.

Note   You can learn more about layouts at `https://guides.rubyonrails.org/layouts_and_rendering.html`.

Where to Go Next: References, Books, and Example Apps

Rails has been in popular use since the end of 2004, and it has attracted the interest of thousands of developers, many of whom blog about the framework or release the source of their own Rails applications for free. You can also look to some large-scale Rails applications for inspiration.

The best way to learn Rails, beyond the basics, is to keep up with the new features being added to the framework as it is being developed, to read the source code of other people's applications, and to experiment. Rails isn't something that you can *master* quickly.

This section provides links to several useful references, books, and example applications you can investigate.

Reference Sites and Tutorials

Following are some useful reference sites and tutorials to help you get started using Rails:

- *Official Ruby on Rails API (*`https://api.rubyonrails.org/`*)*: The official documentation for the Ruby on Rails framework. Almost every class and method provided by Rails is documented.

- *Ruby on Rails guides (*`https://guides.rubyonrails.org/`*)*: A useful set of guides for Ruby on Rails written by prominent community members. They're very well written and kept up to date with the latest version of Rails.

- *Getting Started with Rails (*`https://guides.rubyonrails.org/getting_started.html`*)*: A beautifully written introduction to Rails that covers much of the same ground as this chapter. The benefit of this guide, however, is that it will be kept up to date with the latest version of Rails, which may be useful to you in case there are major changes.

Rails Books

There are several books that will walk you through Rails from start to finish, from setting up and looking at scaffolded apps (as in this chapter) to building complete apps with multiple models and customized views that are deployed on the Web.

I recommend investigating the following:

- *Agile Web Development with Rails 4*, by Sam Ruby, Dave Thomas, and David Heinemeier Hansson (Pragmatic Bookshelf, 2013): Many Rails developers consider *Agile Web Development with Rails* to be the canonical Rails tutorial book, particularly as Rails' creator David Heinemeier Hansson has always been involved in its development. Its latest edition came out in September 2013, and it covers Rails 4.0 specifically, although much of it will continue to be relevant now.

- *The Rails Tutorial*, by Michael Hartl: In the past few years, this has essentially become the Rails tutorial. It's a paid-for ebook and set of screencasts, but you can also read the material on the Web for free. It's superb and walks you through the entire process of building a complete Rails app. I strongly recommend you move onto it after reading this book. It's available at `http://railstutorial.org/`.

Sinatra: Lightweight, Simple Web Applications

Sinatra calls itself a "DSL for quickly creating web applications." It's not a framework in the typical sense. It's a library that offers HTTP deployment functionality. In essence, however, it's a very lightweight web application framework that lets you either add HTTP functionality to existing apps or build new ones from scratch as simply as possible.

Sinatra was initially developed solely by Blake Mizerany and first appeared in 2007, but it was not until early 2009 that its popularity exploded, and now there are many developers responsible for it.

To install Sinatra, you can run

```
gem install Sinatra
```

You can visit the project's homepage at `http://sinatrarb.com/` for further instructions.

The Extreme Simplicity of Sinatra

Unlike Rails, there's no enforcement of concepts like MVC or REST in Sinatra. Sinatra is very "at the bare metal" in terms of its functionality. You can write an entire app in a single Ruby file if you wish, or, alternatively, you can develop lots of classes, sprawl your app out over hundreds of files, and really go to town. Sinatra is permissive of almost any development style and offers no Rails-like formula or constraints.

A great way to see how simple a Sinatra app can be is, as always, by trying an example application:

```
require 'sinatra'

get '/' do
  "Hello, world!"
end
```

Place the code in a file named hello_world.rb. Start the Sinatra server by running

```
ruby hello_world.rb
```

A HTTP server will start on your local machine on port 4567. You can try to access it at `http://localhost:4567/`, where upon you should see "Hello, world!" returned.

Other than the necessities of loading Sinatra, the only command is get, which has a single parameter referring to the path ("/") on which to serve the result of the attached code block (which merely returns the string "Hello, world!" in this case).

Note   You can make a Sinatra app run on a different port by specifying a -p [PORT] option on the command line (e.g., ruby `sinatra1.rb -p 1234`). You can see other command-line functions by using the -h option.

When comparing Sinatra with Rails, it's notable that this app is a single file with only a few lines of code. There's no large framework of ancillary code and there's no database. This has its pros and cons, depending on what you're trying to develop. Loading a database library works the same way in a Sinatra app as in a regular Ruby app, if you choose to do so. You might also choose to use PStore or CSV, as we did in Chapter 9. The key point is that it's entirely up to you. Sinatra is completely flexible!

General URL Routing and Parameter Matching

In the previous section, we looked at an app that returned a string on an HTTP GET request for the root path of a URL. It's possible, of course, to take it further:

```
require 'sinatra'
get '/' do
  "Hello, world!"
end

get '/bye' do
  "Leaving already?"
end

get '/time' do
  Time.now.to_s
end
```

In this example, we're serving up different content for different specified URLs—nothing too complex about that. But what if we want to dynamically work with content or parameters provided in the URL? That's possible too:

```
get '/add/:a/:b' do
  (params[:a].to_i + params[:b].to_i).to_s
end
```

Note   For brevity, I'm omitting the `requires` in the examples from here on.

This time we've used a special format to denote a *named parameter* in the URL. These parameters are then made available to the code block in the `params` hash (parameters work in a similar way in Rails).

If we ran the last example and made a request for /add/5/6, then 5 would end up in `params[:a]` and 6 would end up in `params[:b]`, which enables us to add them together and return the result to the HTTP client.

It's also possible to access named parameters with block parameters. This example is functionally equivalent to the last:

```
get '/add/:a/:b' do |a, b|
  (a.to_i + b.to_i).to_s
end
```

Tip   Sinatra also has support for wildcard and regular expression parameters. These are beyond the scope of this introduction, but basic examples can be found in Sinatra's README document at `www.sinatrarb.com/intro.html`.

It's also possible to support other HTTP verbs, such as POST, PUT, and DELETE. You can do this by using the `post`, `put`, and `delete` methods to define blocks instead of using `get`. Here's an example of using `get` and `post` together on the same URL to implement a form:

```
get '/' do
  %q{<form method="post">
      Enter your name: <input type="text" name="name" />
      <input type="submit" value="Go!" />
    </form>}
end
```

```
post '/' do
  "Hello #{params[:name]}!"
end
```

If you visit `http://localhost:4567/`, fill in the text field, and click the Go! button, your web browser will issue a POST HTTP request back to the same URL, and the second method in the example will be executed.

Views, Templates, and Static Files

As with Rails, views make up the part of web applications that users see and interact with in their browsers. In the basic examples in the previous section, we simply returned strings containing HTML from the Sinatra routing methods (get, post, put, and delete). Luckily, you're not consigned to this style, and Sinatra provides some handy shortcuts for making views a lot easier to work with.

Inline and In-File Templates

Sinatra provides easy access to template renderers for ERB, Haml, Builder (used for XML), and Sass (used for CSS) out of the box, assuming that you have their respective gems installed, for example:

```
before do
  @people = [
            { name: "Beatrice", age: 20 },
            { name: "Eugenie", age: 18 },
            { name: "Louise", age: 6 }
            ]
end

get '/' do
  erb %{
    <% @people.each do |person| %>
      <p><%= person[:name] %> is <%= person[:age] %> years old</p>
    <% end %>
  }
end
```

In this case, we're using an ERB template (much as Rails views typically use) supplied as a string to the erb method, which then renders the ERB template into a final string that is returned to the client. This is commonly referred to as an *inline* template. In this case, the output would be as follows:

```
Beatrice is 20 years old

Eugenie is 18 years old

Louise is 6 years old
```

Note   You can learn more about ERB in Chapter 16.

BEFORE FILTERS

Notice that in the first example in this section, the @people variable is defined within a before code block. before blocks are designed to be used for code that is to be executed before every request. Anything that occurs within a before block will be in the same object scope as the processing of the request (as in the get block). Therefore, the before block was used, in this case, to provide a simple data structure for the ERB template to use.

If you were familiar with the Haml, Builder, or Sass templating systems, you could use those in a similar way to render HTML, XML, and CSS, respectively.

It is also possible to store templates at the *end* of the source code file and reference them from the calls to erb, haml, builder, or sass, for example:

```
get '/' do
  erb :index
end

__END__
```

```
@@ index
  <% @people.each do |person| %>
    <p><%= person[:name] %> is <%= person[:age] %> years old</p>
  <% end %>
```

Note   For brevity, the `before` block is not shown in this example.

This example works in exactly the same way as the one prior, except that the template has been moved into a special data area after the main Ruby source code.

In Ruby, if the _END_ delimiter is used, then any text coming after it is not processed as Ruby code but as *input* to the application if the application so chooses to read it. Sinatra can use this functionality to support placing named templates into the source code file itself.

Templates used in this way are prefixed with @@ [name] so that the template can then be referenced by the template rendering commands (erb in this case) by using the symbol representing the name of the template (e.g., erb :index).

Layouts

Similarly to Rails, Sinatra supports layouts for generic templating. For example, complete HTML files tend to have full <html> and <head> definitions, titles, references to style sheets, JavaScript, and so forth. You don't want to code this into every individual template, so instead you can concoct a layout that wraps around your views.

In Sinatra, a layout is defined in the same way as any other template. If you define a template with the name of layout, then it will be used by the template rendering methods (such as erb) by default, for example:

```
before do
  @people = [
              { name: "Beatrice", age: 20 },
              { name: "Eugenie", age: 18 },
              { name: "Louise", age: 6 }
            ]
end
```

```
get '/' do
  erb :index
end

__END__
@@ layout
  <html>
    <head><title>My App</title></head>
  <body>
    <h1>My App</h1>
    <%= yield %>
  </body>
  </html>

@@ index
  <% @people.each do |person| %>
    <p><%= person[:name] %> is <%= person[:age] %> years old</p>
  <% end %>
```

This application has two templates: `layout` and `index`. When the `index` template is rendered, `erb` will notice that there's a template called `layout` and render that first, only yielding to the `index` template when it encounters the `yield` method. This results in a page that contains all of `layout`'s HTML, but with `index`'s specific HTML embedded within.

You can, of course, have more than one layout. For example, if you defined a second layout called `anotherlayout`, you could tell `erb` to render it specifically:

```
erb :index, layout: :anotherlayout
```

You could also choose to render no layout at all:

```
erb :index, layout: false
```

External Templates and Layouts

Having templates and layouts within your source code file can result in a very small, easy-to-understand application, but once your application reaches a certain size, it can become cumbersome—not only to read, but to maintain!

Luckily, you can place templates (including layouts) into external files that Sinatra will load when it comes to render time.

By default, external template files are expected to be in a directory called views located within that of your source code file, although you can override this if you wish using a set directive at the start of your app:

```
set :views, File.dirname( FILE ) + '/templates'
```

Once you have your folder ready, you can place views into it using filenames along the lines of [template name].[format]. For example, assume this is how we're rendering our view:

```
erb :index, :layout => 'mylayout'
```

If no in-file template called index is defined, Sinatra will look for the file index.erb in the views directory (or whatever directory you set). Similarly, if you were using the sass, haml, or builder methods, they would be looking for their own extensions.

The layout situation is very much the same. With the previous line of code, Sinatra would be looking for the mylayout.erb file.

Static Files

Most web applications will rely on static files, often in rendering views. Static files include things like JavaScript files, images, or style sheets. Rather than define templates for these things or serve them programmatically, Sinatra can serve them directly for you.

By default, static files are expected to be in the public subdirectory. As with the external templates directory, however, you can define where you want static files to be if you wish:

```
set :public, File.dirname( FILE ) + '/myfiles'
```

When a request comes in to the Sinatra app for, say, /images/box.gif, Sinatra will first look to see if public/images/box.gif exists before dispatching the request to your application. If the file exists, it will be served up directly. If not, the request will make its way into your app, where it will either be caught with a route or generate an error.

Request Flow Control

So far we've looked at how to make a Sinatra app return content for requests made to specific URLs, but we haven't looked at any flow control.

What if you wanted to only show a page in a certain situation or wanted to redirect someone somewhere else if other conditions are present? What if you needed to raise an error? We'll look at these situations in this section.

Redirection

Let's say that you want to build a simple, scrappy web application that only gives out data if someone uses the right password. You could write it like this:

```
require 'sinatra'

get '/' do
  erb :index, :layout => :layout
end

post '/secretdata' do
  erb :secretdata
end

__END__
@@ layout
  <html><head><title>My App</title></head>
  <body><%= yield %></body></html>

@@ index
  <form method="POST" action="/secretdata">
  Password: <input type="text" name="password" />
  <input type="submit" value="Log in" />
  </form>

@@ secretdata
  Here's our secret data: <code>30'N 12'W</code>
```

Your app is a regular Sinatra app with all of the templates within the source file. The index template features a form that asks for a password that is then sent to the /secretdata action through an HTTP POST request. The "secret data" is then rendered.

In this example, whatever password you type in (or even no password at all) will result in you seeing the secret data. So what if you want to redirect someone back to the form if they get the password wrong? All you have to do is change the /secretdata action:

```
post '/secretdata' do
  redirect '/' if params[:password] != 'xyzzy'
  erb :secretdata
end
```

Now you're using Ruby's regular if construct to see if the password parameter is not equal to 'xyzzy', and if not, you redirect back to the index URL (/).

redirect in Sinatra is a lot simpler than redirect_to in Rails. Its parameter is simply the URL you want to redirect to, whether an absolute URL or a relative one (as used in the prior example). Using an absolute URL, you could redirect the user anywhere:

```
redirect 'http://www.google.com/'
```

Halting

In the last section, we looked at a basic "secret data" app that prevents access to a certain page unless the correct password is supplied. We'll use the context of that example again to explore halting and passing in this section.

Assume that your app is for another computer program to use, rather than web browser–equipped humans. Redirecting to the front page when the password is wrong is not particularly illustrative to an automated client, and typically you'd return an HTTP error code and message instead. In the case of a wrong password, you'd typically return a 403-status code and a "Forbidden" message.

Tip   Learn more about HTTP status codes and messages at https://en.wikipedia.org/wiki/List_of_HTTP_status_codes.

When you want a request to cease and return a particular message (rather than a rendered page), you use Sinatra's `halt` method to *halt* the request. Let's rewrite the /secretdata method from the app in the last section to do this:

```
post '/secretdata' do
  halt 403 if params[:password] != 'xyzzy'
  erb :secretdata
end
```

In this case, you've replaced the redirect with a call to the `halt` method. If you want to set an HTTP status code and return a message, you pass it an array with those items respectively. Alternatively, you could pass an HTTP status code, although it's better to return a message too in case a human *is* accessing your app and doesn't know what 403 really means!

Error Handling

If you try to access a URL on a Sinatra application that isn't handled by one of the route methods, an error page will show up. You can control what this error page looks like by defining a `not_found` block:

```
require 'sinatra'
not_found do
  "<html><body>Sorry, you're lost!</body></html>"
end
```

If you ran this application, every request you made to it would result in the HTML in the `not_found` block being returned because no routes are defined to handle requests to any URL. Note that you could define an external (on internal) view and render it in the typical way with the `erb` method instead, if you wished.

As well as `not_found`, Sinatra offers a way to define a response that should be used when a fatal error occurs in the application. For example, let's build a small application that divides two numbers:

```
require 'rubygems'
require 'sinatra'

set :show_exceptions, false
```

```
error do
  redirect 'http://en.wikipedia.org/wiki/Division_by_zero'
end

get '/divide/:a/:b' do |a, b|
  "#{a.to_i / b.to_i}"
end
```

Note   The set :show_exceptions, false directive is included because, when you're in development mode, Sinatra shows you a helpful "exception" page by default which overrides what you do in error blocks.

If you ran this application and accessed http://127.0.0.1:4567/divide/40/10, you'd be given "4" as a response. Try http://127.0.0.1:4567/divide/10/0, however, and you'll be cheekily redirected to a Wikipedia page all about the perils of dividing a number by zero! This is probably not how you'd want to treat your real-life users, but the point is made.

In a way, the error block has worked in a similar way to the rescue block when handling Ruby exceptions.

Tip   Head back to the "Exceptions and Error Handling" section of Chapter 8 if you need a rescue refresher!

Like rescue, Sinatra's error blocks can also be defined to only respond to certain types of exceptions, whether regular Ruby exceptions or ones of your own creation. A single exception's class or an array of exception classes can be provided as a parameter before the associated code block.

Summary

In this chapter, we looked at how to develop some very basic web applications using Rails and Sinatra. Rails in particular gives you a lot of power out of the box and enables you to develop a fully working, database-driven web application in a short period of time. Sinatra, on the other hand, shows you how *simple* it can be to put smaller web apps together.

We've merely scratched the surface in this chapter, as Rails is a large and complex framework (though simple to use, it has many details that are complex for advanced usage). Entire books larger than this one have been written about Rails, so this chapter merely provides a taste. You can use the references in the previous section to learn more about the framework, and you can investigate the selection of Apress books available about Rails (see www.apress.com). Sinatra also goes a lot deeper than we've been able to scratch here.

Larger frameworks like Rails can seem complex initially, but the complexity of the directory structure and default files created by the rails tool are only there to make your job as a developer easier by providing a familiar structure and separation of concerns. Once you're familiar with the layout and the tools Rails makes available, developing web applications is a simple, organized process.

Let's reflect on the main concepts introduced in this chapter:

- *Ruby on Rails*: A Ruby-based web application development framework developed by David Heinemeier Hansson. See Chapter 5 for the history behind Ruby on Rails.

- *Framework*: A set of libraries and tools that can be used as a foundation for developing applications.

- *Models*: Classes that represent forms of data used by the application and that contain the logic to manipulate and retrieve that data.

- *Views*: Templates and HTML code (more accurately, code that includes both HTML and embedded Ruby code) that produce the pages that users of the web application will see. Views can output data as HTML for web browsers, XML, RSS, and other formats.

- *Controllers*: Classes that process user input and control what data is sent to the views to output. Controllers contain the logic that binds together models, data, and views.

- *Actions*: Methods contained within controllers that are accessed when requests for specific URLs are made on the parent web application.

- *CRUD (create, read, update, delete)*: The four basic actions you can perform upon discrete items and that are common to most web applications. In Rails, these operations can correspond to the PUT, GET, POST, and DELETE HTTP verbs.

- *ActiveRecord*: A library that abstracts databases, rows, columns, and SQL into standard Ruby syntax using classes and objects. It's a major part of the Ruby on Rails framework.

- *Routing*: The process of translating a URL into the desired controller and action by using routing patterns.

- *Session*: A process by which a unique ID is given to a new user of an application, and this unique ID is given back and forth on each further request, thereby making it possible to track that user.

- *Plugins*: Libraries for the Ruby on Rails framework that "plug in" to your applications. Plugins can override Rails' default behaviors or extend the framework with new features you can easily use from your application, such as authentication systems. Plugins are installed on a per-application basis rather than for the Rails framework as a whole.

- *Sinatra*: A lightweight framework (or library) for developing web-facing applications in Ruby without significant amounts of ancillary code. A Sinatra app can be represented in a few lines of code. Its official website is at http://sinatrarb.com/.

In this chapter, we looked at developing web applications under an organized framework, and in the next chapter, we'll look at using Internet protocols more directly. You can combine the techniques covered in Chapter 14 with your Rails applications so that they can communicate with other services available online, such as email, FTP, and data from other websites.

## CHAPTER 14

Ruby and the Internet

In this chapter, we're going to look at how to use Ruby with the Internet and with the various services available on the Internet, from the Web to email and file transfers.

The Internet has recently become an inescapable part of software development, and Ruby has a significant number of libraries available to deal with the plethora of Internet services available. In this chapter, we'll focus on a few of the more popular services: the Web, email (POP3 and SMTP), and FTP, along with how to process the data we retrieve.

In Chapter 15, we'll look at how to develop actual server or daemon code using Ruby along with lower-level networking features, such as *pinging*, *TCP/IP*, and *sockets*. However, this chapter focuses on accessing and using data from the Internet, rather than on the details of Ruby's networking features.

HTTP and the Web

HyperText Transfer Protocol (HTTP) is an Internet protocol that defines how web servers and web clients (such as web browsers) communicate with each other. The basic principle of HTTP, and the Web in general, is that every resource (such as a web page) available on the Web has a distinct Uniform Resource Locator (URL) and that web clients can use HTTP verbs such as GET, POST, PUT, and DELETE to retrieve or otherwise manipulate those resources. For example, when a web browser retrieves a web page, a GET request is made to the correct web server for that page, which then returns the contents of the web page.

In Chapter 10, we looked briefly at HTTP and developed some simple web server applications to demonstrate how Ruby applications can make their features available on the Internet. In this section, we're going to look at how to retrieve data from the Web, parse it, and generate web-compatible content.

© Carleton DiLeo, Peter Cooper 2021
C. DiLeo and P. Cooper, *Beginning Ruby 3*, https://doi.org/10.1007/978-1-4842-6324-2_14

Downloading Web Pages

One of the most basic actions you can perform on the Web is downloading a single web page or document. First, we'll look at how to use the most commonly used Ruby HTTP library, *net/http*, before moving on to a few notable alternatives.

The net/http Library

The net/http library comes standard with Ruby and is the most commonly used library to access websites. Here's a basic example:

```ruby
require 'net/http'

Net::HTTP.start("www.apress.com", use_ssl: true) do |http|
  req = Net::HTTP::Get.new('/sitemap.xml')
  body = http.request(req).body
  puts body.force_encoding("UTF-8")
end
```

This example loads the net/http library, connects to the web server `www.apress.com` (the publisher page of this book), and performs an HTTP GET request for `/sitemap.xml`. The HTML for the page is returned and displayed. The equivalent URL for this request is `www.apress.com/sitemap.xml`, and if you load that URL in your web browser, you'll get the same response as Ruby.

Note   In the example, there was something we haven't learned about: force_ encoding("UTF-8"). This method forces Ruby to output the body of the response using UTF-8 encoding. Depending on what operating system you use, this may or not be needed. Encoding is an important topic in computing, but we will not be covering it in this book. Check out the Ruby docs page for more information: `https://ruby-doc.org/core/Encoding.html`.

As the example demonstrates, the net/http library is barebones. Rather than simply passing it a URL, you have to pass it the URL of the web server and then the resource path. You also have to specify the GET HTTP request type and trigger the request using the `request` method. You can simplify your code by using the URI library that comes with Ruby, which provides a number of methods to turn a URL into the various pieces needed by net/http. Here's an example:

```ruby
require 'net/http'

url = URI.parse('https://www.apress.com/sitemap.xml')

Net::HTTP.start(url.host, url.port, use_ssl: true) do |http|
  req = Net::HTTP::Get.new(url.path)
  body = http.request(req).body
  puts body.force_encoding("UTF-8")
end
```

In this example, you use the URI class (automatically loaded by net/http) to parse the supplied URL. An object is returned whose methods host, port, and path supply different parts of the URL for Net::HTTP to use. Note that in this example you provide three parameters to the main Net::HTTP.start method: the URL's hostname, the URL's port number, and an options hash that configures Net:HTTP to use SSL. The port number is optional, but URI.parse is clever enough to return the HTTP port number of 443.

It's possible to produce an even simpler example:

```ruby
require 'net/http'

url = URI.parse('https://www.apress.com/sitemap.xml')
response = Net::HTTP.get_response(url)
puts response.body.force_encoding("UTF-8")
```

Instead of creating the HTTP connection and issuing the GET explicitly, Net::HTTP. get_response allows you to perform the request in one stroke. We removed use_ssl since get_response determines if SSL is needed from the URL. There are situations where this can prove less flexible, but if you simply want to retrieve documents from the Web, it's an ideal method to use.

Checking for Errors and Redirects

Our examples so far have assumed that you're using valid URLs and are accessing documents that actually exist. However, Net::HTTP will return different responses based on whether the request is a success or not or if the client is being redirected to a different URL, and you can check for these. In the following example, a method called get_web_document is created that accepts a single URL as a parameter. It parses the URL, attempts to get the required document, and then subjects the response to a case/when block:

```ruby
require 'net/http'

def get_web_document(url)
  uri = URI.parse(url)
  response = Net::HTTP.get_response(uri)

  case response
    when Net::HTTPSuccess
      return response.body.force_encoding("UTF-8")
    when Net::HTTPRedirection
      return get_web_document(response['Location'])
    else
      return nil
  end
end

puts get_web_document('https://www.apress.com/sitemap.xml')
puts get_web_document('https://www.apress.com/doesnotexist.xml')
puts get_web_document('https://ruby-doc.org/core')
```

Note `https://ruby-doc.org/core` redirects to the latest version of the Ruby core library. This helps to demonstrate that the redirect is handled correctly.

If the response is of the Net::HTTPSuccess class, the content of the response will be returned; if the response is a redirection (represented by a Net::HTTPRedirection object being returned), then get_web_document will be called again, with the URL specified as the target of the redirection by the remote server. If the response is neither a success nor a redirection request, an error of some sort has occurred, and `nil` will be returned (hence the empty line in the preceding results).

If you wish, you can check for errors in a more granular way. For example, the error 404 means "File Not Found" and is specifically used when trying to request a file that does not exist on the remote web server. When this error occurs, Net::HTTP returns a response of class `Net::HTTPNotFound`. However, when dealing with error 403, "Forbidden," Net::HTTP returns a response of class `Net::HTTPForbidden`.

Note   A list of HTTP errors and their associated Net::HTTP response classes is available at `www.ruby-doc.org/stdlib/libdoc/net/http/rdoc/classes/Net/HTTP.html`.

Basic Authentication

As well as basic document retrieval, net/http supports the *Basic Authentication* scheme used by many web servers to protect their documents in a password-protected area. This demonstration shows how the flexibility of performing the entire request with `Net::HTTP.start` can come in useful:

```ruby
require 'net/http'

url = URI.parse('http://browserspy.dk/password-ok.php')

Net::HTTP.start(url.host, url.port) do |http|
  req = Net::HTTP::Get.new(url.path)
  req.basic_auth('test', 'test')
  puts http.request(req).body
end
```

Note   Authentication is ignored on requests for unprotected URLs, but if you were trying to access a URL protected by Basic Authentication, `basic_auth` allows you to specify your credentials.

Posting Form Data

In our examples so far, we have only been retrieving data from the Web. Another form of interaction is to send data *to* a web server. The most common example of this is when you fill out a *form* on a web page. You can perform the same action from Ruby, for example:

```ruby
require 'net/http'

url = URI.parse('fakeserver.apress.com/form.cgi')

response = Net::HTTP.post_form(url,{'name' => 'David', 'age' => '24'})
puts response.body
```

```
You say David is 24 years old.
```

In this example, you use `Net::HTTP.post_form` to perform a POST HTTP request to the specified URL with the data in the hash parameter to be used as the form data.

Note   `fakeserver.apress.com/form.cgi` is not a working URL. For this code to work, you will need to provide a URL that accepts a HTTP POST.

As with the basic document retrieval examples, there's a more complex, lower-level way to achieve the same thing by taking control of each step of the form submission process:

```ruby
require 'net/http'

url = URI.parse('fakeserver.apress.com/form.cgi')

Net::HTTP.start(url.host, url.port) do |http|
  req = Net::HTTP::Post.new(url.path)
  req.set_form_data({ 'name' => 'David', 'age' => '24' })
  puts http.request(req).body
end
```

This technique also allows you to use the `basic_auth` method if needed.

Using HTTP Proxies

Proxying is when HTTP requests do not go directly between the client and the HTTP server, but through a third party en route. In some situations, it might be necessary to use an HTTP proxy for your HTTP requests. This is a common scenario in schools and offices where web access is regulated or filtered.

net/http supports proxying by creating an HTTP proxy class upon which you can then use and perform the regular HTTP methods. To create the proxy class, use Net::HTTP::Proxy, for example:

```
web_proxy = Net::HTTP::Proxy('your.proxy.hostname.or.ip', 8080)
```

This call to Net::HTTP::Proxy generates an HTTP proxy class that uses a proxy with a particular hostname on port 8080. You would use such a proxy in this fashion:

```
require 'net/http'

web_proxy = Net::HTTP::Proxy('your.proxy.hostname.or.ip', 8080)

url = URI.parse('https://www.apress.com/sitemap.xml')

web_proxy.start(url.host, url.port, use_ssl: true) do |http|
  req = Net::HTTP::Get.new(url.path)
  puts http.request(req).body.force_encoding("UTF-8")
end
```

In this example, web_proxy replaces the reference to Net::HTTP when using the start method. You can use it with the simple get_response technique you used earlier too:

```
require 'net/http'

web_proxy = Net::HTTP::Proxy('your.proxy.hostname.or.ip', 8080)
url = URI.parse('https://www.apress.com/sitemap.xml')

response = web_proxy.get_response(url)
puts response.body.force_encoding("UTF-8")
```

These examples demonstrate that if your programs are likely to need proxy support for HTTP requests, it might be worth generating a proxy-like system even if a proxy isn't required in every case, for example:

```ruby
require 'net/http'

http_class = ARGV.first ? Net::HTTP::Proxy(ARGV[0], ARGV[1]) : Net::HTTP
url = URI.parse('https://www.apress.com/sitemap.xml')

response = http_class.get_response(url)
puts response.body.force_encoding("UTF-8")
```

If this program is run and an HTTP proxy hostname and port are supplied on the command line as arguments for the program, an HTTP proxy class will be assigned to `http_class`. If no proxy is specified, `http_class` will simply reference Net::HTTP. This allows `http_class` to be used in place of Net::HTTP when requests are made, so that both proxy and nonproxy situations work and are coded in exactly the same way.

Secure HTTP with HTTPS

HTTP is a plain text, unencrypted protocol, and this makes it unsuitable for transferring sensitive data such as credit card information. HTTPS is the solution, as it's the same as HTTP but routed over Secure Socket Layer (SSL), which makes it unreadable to any third parties.

Ruby's net/https library makes it possible to access HTTPS URLs, and you can make net/http use it semi-transparently by setting the `use_ssl` attribute on a Net::HTTP instance to `true`, like so:

```ruby
require 'net/http'

url = URI.parse('https://www.apress.com/sitemap.xml')

http = Net::HTTP.new(url.host, url.port)
http.use_ssl = true if url.scheme == 'https'

request = Net::HTTP::Get.new(url.path)
puts http.request(request).body.force_encoding("UTF-8")
```

Note that you use the `scheme` method of `url` to detect if the remote URL is in fact one that requires SSL to be activated.

It's trivial to mix in the form-posting code to get a secure way of sending sensitive information to the remote server:

```ruby
require 'net/http'

# This isn't a working URL, replace with a URL that accepts POST request
url = URI.parse('https://your.serversomewhere.com/form1')

http = Net::HTTP.new(url.host, url.port)
http.use_ssl = true if url.scheme == 'https'

request = Net::HTTP::Post.new(url.path)
request.set_form_data({ 'credit_card_number' => '1234123412341234' })
puts http.request(request).body.force_encoding("UTF-8")
```

net/https also supports associating your own client certificate and certification directory with your requests, as well as retrieving the server's peer certificate. However, these are advanced features only required in a small number of cases and are beyond the scope of this section. Refer to Appendix B for links to further information.

The Open-Uri Library

open-uri is a library that wraps up the functionality of net/http, net/https, and net/ftp into a single package. Although it lacks some of the raw power of using the constituent libraries directly, open-uri makes it a lot easier to perform all the main functions.

A key part of open-uri is the way it abstracts common Internet actions and allows file I/O techniques to be used on them. Retrieving a document from the Web becomes much like opening a text file on the local machine:

```ruby
require 'open-uri'

f = open('https://www.apress.com/sitemap.xml')
puts f.readlines.join
```

As with `File::open`, open returns an I/O object (technically a `StringIO` object), and you can use methods such as `each_line`, `readlines`, and `read`, as you did in Chapter 9:

```
require 'open-uri'

f = open('https://www.apress.com/sitemap.xml')

puts "The document is #{f.size} bytes in length"

f.each_line do |line|
  puts line
end
```

```
The document is 706 bytes in length
```

Also, in a similar fashion to the File class, you can use open in a block style:

```
require 'open-uri'

open('https://www.apress.com/sitemap.xml') do |f|
  puts f.readlines.join
end
```

Note   HTTPS and FTP URLs are treated transparently. You can use any HTTP, HTTPS, or FTP URL with open.

As well as providing the open method as a base method that can be used anywhere, you can use it directly on URI objects:

```
require 'open-uri'

url = URI.parse('https://www.apress.com/sitemap.xml')
url.open { |f| puts f.read }
```

or perhaps:

```
require 'open-uri'
puts URI.parse('https://www.apress.com/sitemap.xml').open.read
```

In addition to acting like an I/O object, open-uri enables you to use methods associated with the object it returns to find out particulars about the HTTP (or FTP) response itself, for example:

```ruby
require 'open-uri'

f = URI.open('https://www.apress.com/sitemap.xml')

puts f.content_type
puts f.last_modified
```

```
application/xml

2020-08-11 00:47:07 UTC
```

Last, it's possible to send extra header fields with an HTTP request by supplying an optional hash parameter to open:

```ruby
require 'open-uri'

f = URI.open('https://www.apress.com/sitemap.xml',
        {'User-Agent' => 'Mozilla/5.0 (platform; rv:geckoversion) Gecko/
          geckotrail Firefox/firefoxversion'})

puts f.read
```

In this example, a "user agent" header is sent with the HTTP request that makes it appear as if you're using Firefox to request the remote file. Sending a user agent header can be a useful technique if you're dealing with a website that returns different information to different types of browsers. Ideally, however, you should use a user agent header that reflects the name of your program.

Tip   The HTTParty gem offers yet another way to fetch data via HTTP and is particularly well suited to interacting with APIs.

Processing Web Content

As you saw earlier, retrieving data from the Web is easy with Ruby. Once you've retrieved the data, it's likely you'll want to do something with it. Parsing data from the Web using regular expressions and the usual Ruby string methods is an option, but several libraries exist that make it easier to deal with different forms of web content specifically. In this section, we'll look at some of the best ways to process HTML and XML.

Parsing HTML with Nokogiri

Nokogiri is a Ruby library designed to make HTML parsing fast, easy, and fun. It's available as a Rubygem via `gem install nokogiri`.

Once installed, Nokogiri is easy to use. The following example loads the library, places some basic HTML in a string, creates a document object, and then searches for H1 tags (using a CSS selector in the `css` method call). It then retrieves the first H1 tag (using `first`, as `css` returns an array) and looks at the HTML within it (using `inner_html`):

```
require 'nokogiri'

html = <<END_OF_HTML
<html>
<head>
<title>This is the page title</title>
</head>

<body>
<h1>Big heading!</h1>
<p>A paragraph of text.</p>
<ul><li>Item 1 in a list</li><li>Item 2</li><li class="highlighted">Item
3</li></ul>
</body>
</html>
END_OF_HTML
```

```
doc = Nokogiri::HTML(html)
puts doc.css("h1").first.inner_html
```

```
Big heading!
```

Nokogiri can work directly with open-uri to load HTML from remote files, as in the following example:

```
require 'nokogiri'
require 'open-uri'
```

```
doc = Nokogiri::HTML(URI.open('https://www.apress.com/us/about'))
puts doc.css("h1").first.inner_html
```

Using a combination of search methods, you can search for the list within the HTML (defined by the <ul> tags, where the <li> tags denote each item in the list) and then extract each item from the list:

```
list = doc.css("ul").first
list.css("li").each do |item|
  puts item.inner_html
end
```

```
<a href="#search" class="search icon">Search</a>

<a href="#menu" class="menu icon">Menu</a>
```

As well as searching for elements and returning an array, Nokogiri can also search for the first instance of an element only, using at:

```
list = doc.at("ul")
```

However, Nokogiri can search for more than element or tag names. It also supports XPath and CSS expressions. These querying styles are beyond the scope of this chapter, but here's a demonstration of using CSS classes to find certain elements:

```
list = doc.at("ul")
highlighted_item = list.at(".search")
puts highlighted_item.inner_html
```

Search

This example finds the first list in the HTML file and then looks for a child element that has a class name of search. The rule .search looks for a class name of search, whereas a rule of #search would search for an element with the ID of search.

Parsing JSON

JavaScript Object Notation (JSON) is a simple, lightweight data format that can represent many different structures of data. Here is an example of a JSON document:

```
[
  {
    "name": "Peter Cooper",
    "gender": "Male"
  },
  {
    "name": "Carleton DiLeo"
    "gender": "Male"
  }
]
```

This JSON document defines a set of people containing two individual persons, each of whom has a name and gender.

JSON is prevalent when it comes to sharing data on the Internet in a form that's easy for machines to parse and is especially popular when using APIs and machine-accessible services provided online, such as Google APIs and other programming interfaces to online services. Due to JSON's popularity, it's worthwhile to see how to parse it with Ruby.

Ruby provides a JSON as part of the standard library. It's very easy to use.

Here's a basic demonstration of parsing a JSON file looking for certain elements:

```ruby
require 'json'

json = <<END_JSON
[
  {
    "name": "Peter Cooper",
    "gender": "Male"
  },
  {
    "name": "Carleton DiLeo",
    "gender": "Male"
  }
]
END_JSON

people = JSON.parse(json, symbolize_names: true)

people.each do |person|
  puts "#{person[:name]} is a #{person[:gender]}"
end
```

```
Peter Cooper is a Male

Carleton DiLeo is a Male
```

In this example, we store JSON in the variable json. Next, we use `JSON.parse` method call to parse the JSON into a Ruby hash. Notice we include the option `symbolize_names`. This option allows us to use a symbol instead of a string to access the hash returned by `JSON.parse`. Using `symbolize_names` isn't necessary, but without it, our code looks like this:

```ruby
people = JSON.parse(json)
people.each do |person|
  puts "#{person['name']} is a #{person['gender']}"
end
```

While functional, it's a little harder to read. The Ruby JSON library has a lot more functionality. Check out the ruby docs page, `https://ruby-doc.com/stdlib/libdoc/json/rdoc/JSON.html`, for more information.

Email

Email predates the invention of the Internet and is still one of the most important and popular technologies used online. In this section, you'll look at how to retrieve and manage email located on POP3 servers, as well as how to send email using an SMTP server.

Receiving Mail with POP3

Post Office Protocol 3 (POP3) is the most popular protocol used to retrieve email from a mail server. If you're using an email program that's installed on your computer (as opposed to webmail, such as Gmail or Microsoft Outlook), it probably uses the POP3 protocol to communicate with the mail server that receives your mail from the outside world.

With Ruby, it's possible to use the net/pop library to do the same things that your email client can, such as preview, retrieve, or delete mail. If you were feeling creative, you could even use net/pop to develop your own anti-spam tools.

Note   In this section, our examples won't run without adjustments, as they need to operate on a real mail account. If you wish to run them, you would need to replace the server name, username, and passwords with those of a POP3/mail account that you have access to. Ideally, you'll be able to create a test email account if you want to play with the examples here, or have a backup of your mail first, in case of unforeseen errors. That's because although you cannot delete mail directly from your local email program, you might delete any new mail waiting on your mail server. Once you're confident of your code and what you want to achieve, you can then change your settings to work on a live account.

The basic operations you can perform with a POP3 server are to connect to it, receive information about the mail an account contains, view that mail, delete the mail, and disconnect. First, you'll connect to a POP3 server to see if there are any messages available for download, and if so, how many:

```
require 'net/pop'
```

```
mail_server = Net::POP3.new('mail.mailservernamehere.com')

begin
  mail_server.start('username','password')
  if mail_server.mails.empty?
    puts "No mails"
  else
    puts "#{mail_server.mails.length} mails waiting"
  end
rescue
  puts "Mail error"
end
```

This code first creates an object referring to the server and then uses the start method to connect. The entire section of the program that connects to and works with the mail server is wrapped within a begin/ensure/end block so that connection errors are picked up without the program crashing out with an obscure error.

Once start has connected to the POP3 server, mail_server.mails contains an array of Net::POPMail objects that refer to each message waiting on the server. You use Array's empty? method to see if any mail is available; if so, the size of the array is used to tell how many mails are waiting.

You can use the Net::POPMail objects' methods to manipulate and collect the server-based mails. Downloading all the mails is as simple as using the pop method for each Net::POPMail object:

```
mail_server.mails.each do |m|
  mail = m.pop
  puts mail
end
```

As each mail is retrieved (or popped, if you will) from the server, the entire content of the mail, with headers and body text, is placed into the mail variable before being displayed on the screen.

To delete a mail, you can use the delete method, although mails are only *marked* for deletion later, once the session has ended:

```
mail_server.mails.each do |m|
  m.delete if m.pop =~ /\bthis is a spam email\b/i
end
```

This code goes through every message in the account and marks it for deletion if it contains the string `this is a spam email`.

You can also retrieve *just* the headers. This is useful if you're looking for a mail with a particular subject or a mail from a particular email address. Whereas `pop` returns the entire mail (which could be up to many megabytes in size), `header` only returns the mail's header from the server. The following example deletes messages if their subject contains the word *medicines*:

```
mail_server.mails.each do |m|
  m.delete if m.header =~ /Subject:.+?medicines\b/i
end
```

To build a rudimentary anti-spam filter, you could use a combination of the mail retrieval and deletion techniques to connect to your mail account and delete unwanted mails before your usual mail client ever sees them. Consider what you could achieve by downloading mail, passing it through several regular expressions, and then choosing to delete depending on what you match.

Sending Mail with SMTP

Whereas POP3 handles the client-side operations of retrieving, deleting, and previewing email, Simple Mail Transfer Protocol (SMTP) handles sending email and routing email between mail servers. In this section, you won't be looking at this latter use, but will use SMTP simply to send mails to an email address.

The net/smtp library allows you to communicate with SMTP servers directly. On many UNIX machines, especially servers on the Internet, you can send mail to the SMTP server running on the local machine and it will be delivered across the Internet. In these situations, sending email is as easy as this:

```
require 'net/smtp'

message = <<MESSAGE_END
From: Private Person <me@privacy.net>
```

```
To: Authors of Beginning Ruby <test@rubyinside.com>
Subject: SMTP email test

This is a test email message.
MESSAGE_END

Net::SMTP.start('localhost', 25) do |smtp|
  smtp.send_message message, 'me@privacy.net', 'test@rubyinside.com'
end
```

You place a basic email in message, using a *here document*, taking care to format the headers correctly (emails require From, To, and Subject headers, separated from the body of the email with a blank line, as in the preceding code). To send the mail, you use Net::SMTP to connect to the SMTP server on the local machine and then use the send_message method along with the message, the from address, and the destination address as parameters (even though the from and to addresses are within the email itself, these aren't always used to route mail).

If you're not running an SMTP server on your machine, you can use Net::SMTP to communicate with a remote SMTP server. Unless you're using a webmail service (such as Hotmail or Yahoo! Mail), your email provider will have provided you with outgoing mail server details that you can supply to Net::SMTP, as follows:

```
Net::SMTP.start('mail.your-domain.com')
```

This line of code connects to the SMTP server on port 25 of mail.your-domain.com without using any username or password. If you need to, though, you can specify port number and other details, for example:

```
Net::SMTP.start('mail.your-domain.com', 25, 'localhost', 'username', ↵
'password', :plain)
```

This example connects to the SMTP server at mail.your-domain.com using a username and password in plain text format. It identifies the client's hostname as localhost.

Note   Net::SMTP also supports LOGIN and CRAM-MD5 authentication schemes. To use these, use :login or :cram_md5 as the sixth parameter passed into start.

File Transfers with FTP

File Transfer Protocol (FTP) is a basic networking protocol for transferring files on any TCP/IP network. Although files can be sent back and forth on the Web, FTP is still commonly used for large files or for access to large file repositories that have no particular relevance to the Web. One of the benefits of FTP is that authentication and access control is built in.

The core part of the FTP system is an *FTP server*, a program that runs on a file server that allows FTP clients to download and/or upload files to that machine.

In a previous section of this chapter, called "The open-uri Library," we looked at using the open-uri library to retrieve files easily from the Internet. The open-uri supports HTTP, HTTPS, and FTP URLs and is an ideal library to use if you want to download files from FTP servers with as little code as possible. Here's an example:

```ruby
require 'open-uri'

output = File.new('MD5SUM.txt', 'wb')
URI.open('ftp://cdimage.debian.org/debian-cd/current/amd64/iso-cd/MD5SUMS')
do |f|
  output.print f.read
end
output.close
```

This example downloads a file from an FTP server and saves its contents into a local file.

Note   The example might fail for you, as your network connection might not support active FTP and might require a passive FTP connection. This is covered later in this section.

However, for more complex operations, the net/ftp library is ideal, as it gives you lower-level access to FTP connections, as net/http does to HTTP requests.

Connection and Basic FTP Actions

Connecting to an FTP server with net/ftp using an FTP URL is a simple operation:

```
require 'net/ftp'
require 'uri'

uri = URI.parse('ftp://cdimage.debian.org/debian-cd/current')

Net::FTP.open(uri.host) do |ftp|
  ftp.login 'anonymous', 'me@privacy.net'
  ftp.passive = true
  ftp.list(uri.path) { |path| puts path }
end
```

drwxr-sr-x	19 ftp	ftp	19 Aug 02 04:00	amd64
drwxr-sr-x	11 ftp	ftp	11 Aug 02 04:00	arm64
drwxr-sr-x	11 ftp	ftp	11 Aug 02 04:00	armel
drwxr-sr-x	11 ftp	ftp	11 Aug 02 04:00	armhf
drwxr-sr-x	19 ftp	ftp	19 Aug 02 04:00	i386
drwxr-sr-x	11 ftp	ftp	11 Aug 02 04:00	mips
drwxr-sr-x	11 ftp	ftp	11 Aug 02 04:00	mips64el
drwxr-sr-x	11 ftp	ftp	11 Aug 02 04:00	mipsel
drwxr-sr-x	7 ftp	ftp	7 Aug 02 04:00	multi-arch
drwxr-sr-x	11 ftp	ftp	11 Aug 02 04:00	ppc64el
drwxr-sr-x	11 ftp	ftp	11 Aug 02 04:00	s390x
drwxr-sr-x	11 ftp	ftp	11 Aug 02 04:00	source
drwxr-sr-x	2 ftp	ftp	4 Jul 06 2019	trace

You use URI.parse to parse a basic FTP URL and connect to the FTP server with Net::FTP. open. Once the connection is open, you have to specify login credentials (much like the authentication credentials when using Net::HTTP) with the ftp object's login method. Then you set the connection type to be passive (this is an FTP option that

makes an FTP connection more likely to succeed when made from behind a firewall—
the technical details are beyond the scope of this book) and then ask the FTP server to
return a list of the files in the directory referenced in your URL (the root directory of the
FTP server in this case).

Net::FTP provides a `login` method that you can use against a `Net::FTP` object, like
so:

```
require 'net/ftp'

ftp = Net::FTP.new('cdimage.debian.org')
ftp.passive = true
ftp.login
ftp.list('*') { |file| puts file }
ftp.close
```

Note   If you know you're going to be connecting to an anonymous FTP server
(one that is public and requires only generic credentials to log in), you don't need
to specify any credentials with the `login` method. This is what happens in the
preceding example.

This example demonstrates a totally different way of using Net::FTP to connect to
an FTP server. As with `Net::HTTP` and `File` classes, it's possible to use Net::FTP within
a structural block or by manually opening and closing the connection by using the
reference object (`ftp` in this case).

As no username and password are supplied, the login method performs an
anonymous login to cdimage.debian.org. Note that in this example you connect to
an FTP server by its hostname rather than with a URL. However, if a username and
password are required, use this code:

```
ftp.login(username, password)
```

Once connected, you use the `list` method on the `ftp` object to get a list of all files in
the current directory. Because you haven't specified a directory to change to, the current
directory is the one that the FTP server puts you in by default. However, to change
directories, you can use the `chdir` method:

```
ftp.chdir('debian-cd')
```

It's also possible to change to any directory in the remote filesystem:

```
ftp.chdir('/debian-cd/current')
```

If you have permission to do so (this depends on your account with the FTP server), you might also be able to create directories. This is done with `mkdir`:

```
ftp.mkdir('test')
```

Performing this operation on an FTP server where you don't have the correct permissions causes an exception, so it's worth wrapping such volatile actions within blocks to trap any exceptions that arise.

Likewise, you can delete and rename files:

```
ftp.rename(filename, new_name)
ftp.delete(filename)
```

These operations will work only if you have the correct permissions.

Downloading Files

Downloading files from an FTP server is easy if you know the filename and what type of file you're trying to download. Net::FTP provides two useful methods to download files: `getbinaryfile` and `gettextfile`. Plain text files and binary files (such as images, sounds, or applications) are sent in a different way, so it's essential you use the correct method. In most situations, you'll be aware ahead of time which technique is required. Here's an example showing how to download a binary file from the official Ruby FTP server:

```
require 'net/ftp'

ftp = Net::FTP.new('cdimage.debian.org')
ftp.passive = true
ftp.login
ftp.chdir('/debian-cd/current/amd64/iso-cd/')
ftp.getbinaryfile('MD5SUMS')
ftp.close
```

`getbinaryfile` accepts several parameters, only one of which is mandatory. The first parameter is the name of the remote file (`MD5SUMS` in this case), an optional second parameter is the name of the local file to write to, and the third optional parameter is a block size that specifies in what size chunks (in bytes) the file is downloaded. If you omit the second parameter, the downloaded file will be written to the same filename in the local directory, but if you want to write the remote file to a particular local location, you can specify this.

One problem with using `getbinaryfile` in this way is that it locks up your program until the download is complete. However, if you supply `getbinaryfile` with a code block, the downloaded data will be supplied into the code block as well as saved to the file:

```
ftp.getbinaryfile('MD5SUMS', 'local-filename', 1024) do |blk|
  puts "A 100KB block of the file has been downloaded"
end
```

This code prints a string to the screen whenever another 1KB of the file has been downloaded. You can use this technique to provide updates to the user, rather than make him or her wonder whether the file is being downloaded.

You could also download the file in blocks such as this and process them on the fly in the code block, like so:

```
ftp.getbinaryfile('MD5SUMS', 'local-filename', 1024) do |blk|
  .. do something with blk here ..
end
```

Each 1KB chunk of the file that's downloaded is passed into the code block. Unfortunately, the file is still saved to a local file, but if this isn't desired, you could use tempfile (as covered in Chapter 9), which is then immediately deleted.

Downloading text or ASCII-based files uses the same technique as in the preceding code, but demands using `gettextfile` instead. The only difference is that `gettextfile` doesn't accept the third block size parameter and instead returns data to the code block line by line.

Uploading Files

Uploading files to an FTP server is possible only if you have write permissions on the server in the directory to which you want to upload. Therefore, none of the examples in this section will work unedited, as you can't provide an FTP server with write access (for obvious reasons!).

Uploading is the exact opposite of downloading, and net/ftp provides `putbinaryfile` and `puttextfile` methods that accept the same parameters as `getbinaryfile` and `gettextfile`. The first parameter is the name of the local file you want to upload, the optional second parameter is the name to give the file on the remote server (defaults to the same as the uploaded file's name if omitted), and the optional third parameter for `putbinaryfile` is the block size to use for the upload. Here's an upload example:

```
require 'net/ftp'

ftp = Net::FTP.new('ftp.domain.com')
ftp.passive = true
ftp.login
ftp.chdir('/your/folder/name/here')
ftp.putbinaryfile('local_file')
ftp.close
```

As with `getbinaryfile` and `gettextfile`, if you supply a code block, the uploaded chunks of the file are passed into it, allowing you to keep the user informed of the progress of the upload:

```
require 'net/ftp'

ftp = Net::FTP.new('ftp.domain.com')
ftp.passive = true
ftp.login
ftp.chdir('/your/folder/name/here')

count = 0

ftp.putbinaryfile('local_file', 'local_file', 100000) do |block|
  count += 100000
```

```
  puts "#{count} bytes uploaded"
end
```

```
ftp.close
```

If you need to upload data that's just been generated by your Ruby script and isn't within a file, you need to create a temporary file with `tempfile` and upload from that, for example:

```
require 'net/ftp'
require 'tempfile'

tempfile = Tempfile.new('test')

my_data = "This is some text data I want to upload via FTP."
tempfile.puts my_data

ftp = Net::FTP.new('ftp.domain.com')
ftp.passive = true
ftp.login
ftp.chdir('/your/folder/name/here')

ftp.puttextfile(tempfile.path, 'my_data')
ftp.close
tempfile.close
```

Summary

In this chapter, we looked at Ruby's support for using various Internet systems and protocols, how Ruby can work with the Web, and how to process and manipulate data retrieved from the Internet.

Let's reflect on the main concepts covered in this chapter:

- *HTTP (HyperText Transfer Protocol)*: A protocol that defines the way web browsers (clients) and web servers talk to each other across a network such as the Internet.

- *HTTPS*: A secure version of HTTP that ensures data being transferred in either direction is only readable at each end. Anyone intercepting an HTTPS stream cannot decipher it. It's commonly used for ecommerce and for transmitting financial data on the Web.

- *HTML (HyperText Markup Language)*: A text formatting and layout language used to represent web pages.

- *Nokogiri*: An HTML and XML parser developed to make it easy to process and parse HTML and XML directly with Ruby. It is noted for its speed, with portions that demand extra performance written in C.

- *POP3 (Post Office Protocol 3)*: A mail server protocol commonly used when retrieving email. You can learn more about the protocol specifically at `www.ietf.org/rfc/rfc1939.txt`.

- *SMTP (Simple Mail Transfer Protocol)*: A mail server protocol commonly used to transfer mail to a mail server or between mail servers. From a typical user's perspective, SMTP is used for sending mail, rather than receiving it. You can learn more about the protocol specifically at `www.faqs.org/rfcs/rfc821.html`.

- *FTP (File Transfer Protocol)*: An Internet protocol for providing access to files located on a server and allowing users to download from it and upload to it.

This chapter covered a variety of Internet-related functions, but in Chapter 15, we're going to look more deeply at networking, servers, and network services. Most of what is covered in Chapter 15 is also applicable to the Internet, but is at a much lower level than FTP or using the Web.

CHAPTER 15

Networking and Sockets

In this chapter, we're going to look at how to use Ruby to perform network-related operations, how to create servers and network services, and how to create persistent processes (*daemons*) that can respond to queries over a network.

Chapter 14 looked at Ruby's Internet capabilities from a high level, like making requests to websites, processing HTML, working with JSON, retrieving email, and managing files over FTP. In contrast, this chapter looks at networking and network services at a lower level.

Let's start with a look at the basic networking concepts we'll be using in this chapter.

Networking Concepts

A *network* is a group of computers connected in some fashion. If you have several computers at home all sharing a wired or wireless router, this is called your *local area network* (LAN). Your computers are probably also connected to the Internet, another form of network. *Networking* is the overall concept of communications between two or more computers or devices, and this chapter looks at how you can use Ruby to perform operations relating to a network, whether a local or global one.

Note If you are experienced with networks and TCP, UDP, and IP protocols, you might wish to skip ahead a little to the "Basic Network Operations" section.

TCP and UDP

There are many types of networks, but the type of network we're most interested in is one that uses *TCP/IP*. TCP/IP is the collective name for two protocols: Transmission Control Protocol (TCP) and Internet Protocol (IP). TCP defines the concept of computers

© Carleton DiLeo, Peter Cooper 2021
C. DiLeo and P. Cooper, *Beginning Ruby 3*, https://doi.org/10.1007/978-1-4842-6324-2_15

connecting to one another, and it makes sure *packets* of data are transmitted and successfully received by machines, in the correct order. IP, on the other hand, is the protocol that's concerned with actually routing the data from one machine to another. IP is the base of most local networks and the Internet, but TCP is a protocol that sits on top and makes the connections reliable.

User Datagram Protocol (UDP) is another protocol like TCP, but unlike TCP, it isn't considered reliable and it doesn't ensure that a remote machine receives the data you sent. When you send data using UDP, you simply have to hope it reached its destination, as you'll receive no acknowledgment of failure. Despite this, UDP is still used for various non-mission-critical tasks, as it's fast and has a low overhead.

Commonly, operations that require a permanent connection (whether over a long period of time or not) between two machines use TCP and TCP-based protocols. For example, almost all services that require authentication to work, such as email access, use TCP-based protocols so that the authentication information can be sent only once—at the start of the connection—and then both ends of the connection are satisfied that connection has been authenticated.

Quick operations where a connection is unimportant or easily repeatable, such as converting domain names and hostnames into IP addresses and vice versa, can run on UDP. If an answer to a query isn't received in sufficient time, another query can simply be issued. UDP is sometimes also used for streaming video and audio due to its low overhead and latency.

IP Addresses and DNS

A machine on an IP-based network has one or many *IP addresses*. Each IP number used on a network must be unique, although each computer has local IP addresses that refer to the current machine (e.g., 127.0.0.1, also known as localhost). When data is sent across the network to a particular IP address, the machine with that address will receive the data.

When you use the Web and access a website such as `www.apress.com`, your computer first asks a Domain Name Service (DNS) server for the IP address associated with the hostname `www.apress.com`. Once it gets the raw address in response (in this case, `207.97.243.208`), your web browser makes a connection to that machine on *port* 80. Machines can make and receive connections on different TCP (or UDP) ports (from a range of 0 through 65,535), and different ports are assigned to different types of services.

For example, port 80 is the default port used for web servers operating over the insecure default HTTP port. (HTTPS/SSL, as used for encrypted web traffic, uses port 443 by default.)

Next in this chapter, we're going to look at how to perform operations over an IP-based network, such as checking the availability of machines on the network, and we'll create basic TCP and UDP clients and servers.

Basic Network Operations

Network programming is usually a difficult process. At the lowest levels, it involves a lot of arcane terminology and interfacing with antique libraries. However, Ruby is not usual, and Ruby's libraries take away most of the complexities usually associated with network programming.

In this section, we're going to look at how to achieve a few basic networking operations, such as checking whether a server is present on a network, looking at how data is routed across the network between two points, and how to connect directly to a service offered on a remote machine.

Checking Machine and Service Availability

One of the most basic network operations you can perform is a *ping*, a simple check that another machine is available on the network or that a service it offers is available.

One ping library that's available is *net-ping*, which is available as a gem with `gem install net-ping`. net-ping can interface with your operating system's `ping` command to get a reliable response. It can also connect directly to services offered by a remote machine to gauge whether it's responding to requests or not:

```
require 'net/ping'

if Net::Ping::External.new('www.google.com').ping
  puts "Pong!"
else
  puts "No response"
end
```

```
Pong!
```

However, if you want to check whether a particular service is available, rather than a machine in general, you can use net-ping to connect to a specific port using TCP or UDP:

```
require 'net/ping'

if Net::Ping::TCP.new('www.google.com', 80).ping
  puts "Pong!"
else
  puts "No response"
end
```

In this instance, you connect directly to `www.google.com`'s HTTP port as if you were a web browser, but once you get a connection, you immediately disconnect again. This allows you to verify that `www.google.com` is accepting HTTP connections.

Performing DNS Queries

Most Ruby networking libraries allow you to specify domain names and hostnames when you want to interact with a remote server and automatically *resolve* these names into IP addresses. However, this adds a small overhead, so in some situations you might prefer to resolve IP addresses ahead of time yourself.

You might also use DNS queries to check for the existence of different hostnames and to check whether a domain is active or not, even if it's not pointing to a web server.

resolv is a library in the Ruby standard library, and it offers several methods that are useful for converting between hostnames and IP addresses:

```
require 'resolv'

puts Resolv.getaddress("www.google.com")
```

```
209.85.229.99
```

This code returns an IP address of `209.85.229.99` for the main Google website. However, if you run the same code several times, you *might* get several different responses. The reason for this is that large websites such as Google spread their requests over multiple web servers to increase speed.

You can also turn IP addresses into hostnames using the getname method, which performs a *reverse* DNS lookup:

```
require 'resolv'

ip = "192.0.34.166"

begin
  puts Resolv.getname(ip)
rescue
  puts "No hostname associated with #{ip}"
end
```

```
34-166.lax.icann.org
```

It's important to note that not *all* IP addresses resolve back into hostnames, as this is an optional requirement of the DNS system.

As well as converting between IP addresses and hostnames, resolv can also retrieve other information from DNS servers, such as the mail server(s) associated with a particular host or domain name. Whereas the records of which IP addresses are associated with which hostnames are called *A records*, the records of which mail servers are associated with a hostname are called *MX records*.

In the previous examples, you've used special helper methods directly made available by the Resolv class, but to search for MX records, you have to use the Resolv::DNS class directly so you can pass in the extra options needed to search for different types of records:

```
require 'resolv'

Resolv::DNS.open do |dns|
  mail_servers = dns.getresources("google.com",
Resolv::DNS::Resource::IN::MX)
  mail_servers.each do |server|
    puts "#{server.exchange.to_s} - #{server.preference}"
  end
end
```

```
alt3.aspmx.l.google.com - 40
alt1.aspmx.l.google.com - 20
alt2.aspmx.l.google.com - 30
aspmx.l.google.com - 10
alt4.aspmx.l.google.com - 50
```

In this example, you've performed a DNS request in a more detailed way using Resolv::DNS directly, rather than the convenient Resolv.getname and Resolv.getaddress helpers, so that you could specify the MX request using the Resolv::DNS::Resource::IN::MX option.

Note   Readers who are savvy with DNS terminology might like to try using CNAME, A, SOA, PTR, NS, and TXT variations of the preceding option, as these are all supported.

MX records are useful if you want to send email to people, but you have no SMTP server you can send mail through, as you can use Net::SMTP (as shown in Chapter 14) directly against the mail servers for the domain name of the email address you want to send to. For example, if you wanted to email someone whose email address ended with @ google.com, you could use Net::SMTP to connect directly to smtp2.google.com (or any of the other choices) and send the mail directly to that user:

```
require 'resolv'
require 'net/smtp'

from = "your-email@example.com"
to = "another-email@example.com"

message = <<MESSAGE_END
From: #{from}
To: #{to}
Subject: Direct email test

This is a test email message.
MESSAGE_END

to_domain = to.match(/\@(.+)/)[1]
```

```
Resolv::DNS.open do |dns|
  mail_servers = dns.getresources(to_domain, Resolv::DNS::Resource::IN::MX)
  mail_server = mail_servers[rand(mail_servers.size)].exchange.to_s

  Net::SMTP.start(mail_server) do |smtp|
    smtp.send_message message, from, to
  end
end
```

> **Note**   You can learn more about DNS at `https://en.wikipedia.org/wiki/Domain_Name_System`.

Servers and Clients

Clients and *servers* are the two major types of software that use networks. Clients connect to servers, and servers process information and manage connections and data being received from and sent to the clients. In this section, you're going to create some servers that you can connect to using net/telnet and other client libraries covered in both this chapter and Chapter 14.

UDP Client and Server

To demonstrate a basic client/server system, UDP is an ideal place to start. Unlike with TCP, UDP has no concept of connections, so it works on a simple system where messages are passed from one place to another with no guarantee of them arriving. Whereas TCP is like making a phone call, UDP is like sending a postcard in the mail.

Creating a UDP server is easy. Let's create a script named udpserver.rb:

```
require 'socket'

s = UDPSocket.new
s.bind(nil, 1234)
5.times do
  text, sender = s.recvfrom(16)
  puts text
end
```

This code uses Ruby's *socket* library, a library that provides the lowest-level access to your operating system's networking capabilities. socket is well suited for UDP, and in this example, you create a new UDP socket and *bind* it to port 1234 on the local machine. You loop five times, accepting data in 16-byte chunks from the socket and printing it to the screen.

Note   The reason for looping just five times is so that the script can end gracefully after it receives five short messages. Later, however, we'll look at ways to keep servers running permanently.

Now that you have a server, you need a client to send data to it. Let's create udpclient.rb:

```
require 'socket'

s = UDPSocket.new
s.send("hello", 0, 'localhost', 1234)
```

This code creates a UDP socket, but instead of listening for data, it sends the string "hello" to the UDP server on localhost at port 1234. If you run udpserver.rb at the same time as udpclient.rb, "hello" should appear on the screen where udpserver.rb is running. You have successfully sent data across a network (albeit on the same machine) from a client to a server using UDP.

It's possible, of course, to run the client and server on different machines, and if you have multiple machines at your disposal, all you need to do is change 'localhost' on the send method to the hostname or IP address of the machine where udpserver.rb is running and ensure the receiver is using an IP address that the sender can reach (e.g., you could bind to 0.0.0.0 to accept connections from any externally facing IP address on your machine).

Note   localhost refers to your local loopback network interface, but this can also sometimes be referred to using the IP address 127.0.0.1 (which will also be picked up through 0.0.0.0), as you will see in the next example.

As you've seen, UDP is simple, but it's possible to layer more advanced features on top of it. For example, because there is no connection involved, you can alternate between client and server modes with a single program, accomplishing a two-way effect. You can demonstrate this easily by making a single program send and receive UDP data to and from itself:

```ruby
require 'socket'

host = 'localhost'
port = 1234
s = UDPSocket.new
s.bind(nil, port)
s.send("1", 0, host, port)

5.times do
  text, sender = s.recvfrom(16)
  remote_host = sender[3]

  puts "#{remote_host} sent #{text}"

  response = (text.to_i * 2).to_s
  puts "We will respond with #{response}"
  s.send(response, 0, host, port)
end
```

```
127.0.0.1 sent 1
We will respond with 2
127.0.0.1 sent 2
We will respond with 4
127.0.0.1 sent 4
We will respond with 8
127.0.0.1 sent 8
We will respond with 16
127.0.0.1 sent 16
We will respond with 32
```

Note   In a real-world situation, you would typically have two scripts, each on a different machine and communicating between each other, but this example demonstrates the logic necessary to achieve that result on a single machine for ease of testing.

UDP has some benefits in speed and the amount of resources needed, but because it lacks a state of connection and reliability in data transfer, TCP is more commonly used. Next, we'll look at how to create some simple TCP servers to which you can connect with net/telnet and other applications.

Building a Simple TCP Server

TCP servers are the foundation of most Internet services. Although lightweight time servers and DNS servers can survive with UDP, when sending web pages and emails around, it's necessary to build a connection with a remote server to make the requests and send and receive data. In this section, you're going to build a basic TCP server that can respond to requests via telnet before moving on to creating something more complex.

Let's look at a basic server that operates on port 1234, accepts connections, prints any text sent to it from a client, and sends back an acknowledgment:

```
require 'socket'

server = TCPServer.new(1234)

while connection = server.accept
  while line = connection.gets
    break if line =~ /quit/
    puts line
    connection.puts "Received!"
  end

  connection.puts "Closing the connection. Bye!"
  connection.close
end
```

Note   This server will go around the main loop permanently. To exit it, press Ctrl+C.

As well as being used to create UDP servers and clients, socket can also create TCP servers and clients. In this example, you create a TCPServer object on port 1234 of the local machine and then enter a loop that processes whenever a new connection is accepted using the accept method on the TCPServer object. Once a connection has been made, the server accepts line after line of input, only closing the connection if any line contains the word quit.

To test this client, you can use your operating system's telnet client (built into Linux and Windows. OS X removed telnet so you will need to install it to use it. Once installed, it is accessible from the command line as telnet.) as follows:

```
telnet 127.0.0.1 1234
Trying 127.0.0.1...
Connected to localhost.
Escape character is '^]'.
Hello!
Received!
quit
Connection closed by foreign host.
```

Alternatively, you can create your own basic client using net/telnet:

```
require 'net/telnet'

server = Net::Telnet::new('Host' => '127.0.0.1',
                          'Port' => 1234,
                          'Telnetmode' => false)
lines_to_send = ['Hello!', 'This is a test', 'quit']

lines_to_send.each do |line|
  server.puts(line)

  server.waitfor(/./) do |data|
    puts data
  end
end
```

481

As with the UDP client and server example, the client and server applications can (and usually would) be placed on different machines. These test applications would work in exactly the same way if the server were located on the other side of the world and the client were running from your local machine, as long as both machines were connected to the Internet.

However, one downside to your TCP server is that it can only accept one connection at a time. If you telnet to it once and begin typing, but then another connection is attempted, it might begin to connect, but no responses will be forthcoming for anything sent. The reason for this is that your TCP server can work with only one connection at a time in its current state. In the next section, we're going to look at how to create a more advanced server that can deal with multiple clients at the same time.

Multi-client TCP Servers

Most servers on the Internet are designed to deal with large numbers of clients at any one time. A web server that can only serve one file at once would quickly result in the world's slowest website as users began to stack up waiting to be served! The TCP server in the previous section operated in this way and would be commonly known as a "single-threaded" or "sequential" server.

Ruby's Thread class makes it easy to create a multithreaded server—one that accepts requests and immediately creates a new thread of execution to process the connection while allowing the main program to await more connections:

```ruby
require 'socket'

server = TCPServer.new(1234)

loop do
  Thread.start(server.accept) do |connection|
    while line = connection.gets
      break if line =~ /quit/
      puts line
      connection.puts "Received!"
    end
```

```
      connection.puts "Closing the connection. Bye!"
      connection.close
  end
end
```

In this example, you have a permanent loop, and when `server.accept` responds, a new thread is created and started immediately to handle the connection that has just been accepted, using the `connection` object passed into the thread. However, the main program immediately loops back and awaits new connections.

GServer

GServer is a Ruby library that used to be part of the standard library but that can now be installed as a Ruby gem using `gem install gserver`, which implements a "generic server" system. It features thread pool management, logging, and tools to manage multiple servers at the same time. GServer is offered as a class, and you produce server classes that inherit from it.

Other than simple management, GServer also allows you to run multiple servers at once on different ports, allowing you to put together an entire suite of services in just a few lines of code. Threading is entirely handled by GServer, although you can get involved with the process if you like. GServer also implements logging features, although, again, you can provide your own code for these functions if you wish.

Let's look at the simplest TCP server possible with GServer:

```
require 'gserver'

class HelloServer < GServer
  def serve(io)
    io.puts("Hello!")
  end
end

server = HelloServer.new(1234)
server.start
server.join
```

This code implements a basic server that simply outputs the word "Hello!" to any client connecting to port 1234. If you telnet to connect to port 1234 (or even a web browser, using http://127.0.0.1:1234/), you'll see the string "Hello!" returned to you before the connection is closed.

In this example, you create a server class called HelloServer that descends from GServer. GServer implements all the thread and connection management, leaving you with only a handful of technicalities to worry about. In this simple example, you only create a single server process, tell it to use port 1234, and start it immediately.

However, even this simple example will work with multiple clients, and if you telnet to it multiple times in parallel, you'll find that all requests are processed successfully. However, it's possible to set a maximum number of allowed connections by supplying more parameters to new:

```
require 'gserver'

class HelloServer < GServer
  def serve(io)
    io.puts("Say something to me:")
    line = io.gets
    io.puts("You said '#{line.chomp}'")
  end
end

server = HelloServer.new(1234, '127.0.0.1', 4)
server.start
server.join
```

The new method for GServer accepts several parameters. In order, they are the port number to run the server(s) on, the name of the host or interface to run the server(s) on, the maximum number of connections to allow at once (set to 4 in this example), a file handle of where to send logging messages, and a true or false flag to turn logging on or off.

As mentioned earlier, you can create multiple servers at once:

```
require 'gserver'

class HelloServer < GServer
  def serve(io)
    io.puts("Say something to me:")
```

```ruby
    line = io.gets
    io.puts("You said '#{line.chomp}'")
  end
end

server = HelloServer.new(1234, '127.0.0.1', 4)
server.start

server2 = HelloServer.new(1235, '127.0.0.1', 4)
server2.start
sleep 10
```

Creating multiple servers is as easy as creating a new instance of HelloServer (or any GServer descendent class), assigning it to a variable, and calling its start method.

Another difference between this example and the last is that at the end you don't call server.join. With GServer objects, join works in the same way as with Thread objects, where calling join waits for that thread to complete before continuing execution. In the first GServer examples, your programs would wait forever until you exited them manually (e.g., using Ctrl+C). However, in the preceding example, you didn't call any join methods and only slept for 10 seconds using sleep 10. This means the servers you created are only available on ports 1234 and 1235 for 10 seconds after running the program, at which point the program and its child threads all exit at once.

Because GServer allows multiple servers to run at the same time without impeding the execution of the main program, you can manage the currently running servers by using several methods GServer makes available to start, stop, and check servers:

```ruby
require 'gserver'

class HelloServer < GServer
  def serve(io)
    io.puts("To stop this server, type 'shutdown'")
    self.stop if io.gets =~ /shutdown/
  end
end

server = HelloServer.new(1234)
server.start
```

```
loop do
  break if server.stopped?
end

puts "Server has been terminated"
```

This time you put the main program into a loop waiting for the server to be stopped. The server is stopped if someone connects and types shutdown, which triggers that server's stop method, leading to the whole server program ending.

You can also check from the process running a GServer whether a GServer is running on a port without having the object reference available by using the in_service? class method:

```
if GServer.in_service?(1234)
  puts "Can't create new server. Already running!"
else
  server = HelloServer.new(1234)
end
```

A GServer-Based Chat Server

With the knowledge picked up in the previous section, only a small jump in complexity is required to build a practical application using GServer. You'll build a simple chat server that allows a number of clients to connect and chat among each other.

The first step is to subclass GServer into a new class, ChatServer, and override the new method with your own so that you can set up variables to store client IDs and the chat log for all the clients to share:

```
require 'gserver'

class ChatServer < GServer
  def initialize(*args)
    super(*args)
    # Keep an overall record of the client IDs allocated
    # and the lines of chat
    @client_id = 0
    @chat = []
  end
end
```

The main part of your program can be like your other GServer-based apps, with a basic initialization and a loop until the chat server shuts itself down:

```
server = ChatServer.new(1234)
server.start

loop do
  break if server.stopped?
end
```

Note   Remember that you can specify the hostname to serve from as the second parameter to `ChatServer.new`. If you want to use this chat server over the Internet, you will need to specify your remotely accessible IP address (or 0.0.0.0) as this second parameter; otherwise, your server might only be available to machines on your local network.

Now that you have the basics in order, you need to create a serve method that assigns the connection the next available client ID (by using the variable @client_id), welcomes the user, accepts lines of text from the user, and shows him or her the latest lines of text entered by other users from time to time.

As the serve method is particularly long in this case, the complete source code of the chat server is shown here, including comments:

```
require 'gserver'

class ChatServer < GServer
  def initialize(*args)
    super(*args)

    # Keep an overall record of the client IDs allocated
    # and the lines of chat
    @client_id = 0
    @chat = []
  end

  def serve(io)
    # Increment the client ID so each client gets a unique ID
    @client_id +- 1
```

```ruby
    my_client_id = @client_id
    my_position = @chat.size

    io.puts("Welcome to the chat, client #{@client_id}!")

    # Leave a message on the chat queue to signify this client
    # has joined the chat
    @chat << [my_client_id, "<joins the chat>"]

    loop do
      # Every 2 seconds check to see if we are receiving any data
      if IO.select([io], nil, nil, 2)
        # If so, retrieve the data and process it...
        line = io.gets

        # If the user says 'quit', disconnect them
        if line =~ /quit/
          @chat << [my_client_id, "<leaves the chat>"]
          break
        end

        # Shut down the server if we hear 'shutdown'
        self.stop if line =~ /shutdown/

        # Add the client's text to the chat array along with the
        # client's ID
        @chat << [my_client_id, line]
      else
        # No data, so print any new lines from the chat stream
        @chat[my_position..(@chat.size - 1)].each_with_index do |line, index|
          io.puts("#{line[0]} says: #{line[1]}")
        end

        # Move the position to one past the end of the array
        my_position = @chat.size
      end
    end

end
end
```

```
server = ChatServer.new(1234)
server.start

loop do
  break if server.stopped?
end
```

The chat server operates primarily within a simple loop that constantly checks whether any data is waiting to be received with the following line:

```
if IO.select([io], nil, nil, 2)
```

IO.select is a special function that can check to see if an I/O stream has any data in its various buffers (receive, send, and exceptions/errors, in that order). IO.select([io], nil, nil, 2) returns a value if the connection with the client has any data received that you haven't processed, but you ignore whether there is any data to send or any errors. The final parameter, 2, specifies that you have a timeout of two seconds, so you wait for two seconds before either succeeding or failing. This means that every two seconds, the else block is executed, and any new messages in the chat log are sent to the client.

If you use telnet to connect to this chat server, a session would look somewhat like this:

```
$ telnet 127.0.0.1 1234

Trying 127.0.0.1...
Connected to localhost.
Escape character is '^]'.
Welcome to the chat, client 1!
1 says: <joins the chat>
2 says: <joins the chat>
Hello 2!
1 says: Hello 2!
2 says: Hello 1!
2 says: I'm going now.. bye!
2 says: <leaves the chat>
quit
Connection closed by foreign host.
```

With the basic GServer principles covered in this and the previous sections, you can create servers that operate to protocols of your own design or even create server programs that can respond to preexisting protocols. All it requires is being able to receive data, process it, and send back the data required by the client. Using these techniques, it's possible to create a mail server, web server, or any other type of server necessary online.

Web/HTTP Servers

As hinted at in the previous section, web servers are also TCP servers and use many of the same techniques covered in the last few sections, such as forking and threading. A web server is a normal TCP server that *talks* HTTP.

However, we're not going to look at HTTP servers directly here, as I covered them previously in Chapter 10, so if you want to recap how to construct a basic web server in, refer to the latter sections of that chapter.

Summary

In this chapter, we've looked at Ruby's support for building lower-level networking tools and servers, as well as using Ruby to develop daemons and other persistently running processes.

Let's reflect on the main concepts covered in this chapter:

- *Network*: A collection of computers connected in such a way that they can send and receive data between one another.

- *TCP (Transmission Control Protocol)*: A protocol that handles connections between two machines over an IP-based network and ensures packets are transmitted and received successfully and in the correct order.

- *UDP (User Datagram Protocol)*: A protocol that allows two computers to send and receive messages between each other where no "connection" is made, and no assurances are made whether the data is received by the remote party.

- *IP (Internet Protocol)*: A packet-based protocol for delivering data across networks. IP also makes provisions for each machine connected to the network to have one or many IP addresses.

- *DNS (Domain Name Service)*: A system of referencing host or machine names against different IP addresses and converting between the two.

- *Ping*: The process of verifying whether a machine with a particular IP is valid and accepting requests by sending it a small packet of data and waiting for a response.

- *Server*: A process that runs on a machine and responds to clients connecting to it from other machines, such as a web server.

- *Client*: A process that connects to a server, transmits and receives data, and then disconnects once a task is completed. A web browser is a basic example of a client.

- *GServer*: A Ruby library that makes developing network servers and services easy. It handles the thread and connection management and allows servers to be created by simply subclassing the GServer class.

This marks the last chapter of narrated, instructional content, with Chapter 16 being a reference-style guide to a wide collection of Ruby libraries (both in the standard library and those available as gems). With this in mind, all of us involved in the production of this book would like to thank you for reading so far and hope you find the following reference chapter and appendixes useful.

I wish you the best on your continuing journey into the world of Ruby. You have only scratched the surface so far! Be sure to look at the remaining chapter of this book to flesh out your Ruby knowledge further.

CHAPTER 16

Useful Ruby Libraries

This chapter is a basic reference to a collection of useful Ruby libraries that you might want to use in your programs. We're going to look at libraries covering a vast array of functionality, from networking and Internet access to file parsing and compression. The libraries in this chapter are in alphabetical order, and each library starts on a new page with the name as the page header for easy browsing. Below each library's title, several subsections follow:

- *Overview*: A brief description of what the library does, its basic functionality, and why you would want to use it.

- *Installation*: Information on where the library is found, how to install it, and how to get it running on most systems.

- *Examples*: One or more examples of how to use the library that demonstrate its various elements of functionality. Example results are included too. This section can be split into multiple subsections, each containing a single example of how to use a particular branch of functionality.

- *Further Information*: Links and pointers to further information about the library, including online references and tutorials.

Unlike the other main chapters in this book, this is a reference chapter, one that you might not necessarily need right away, but that will become useful over time when you want to find out how to perform a certain function. In any case, make sure at least to scan through the list of libraries to get a feel for the variety of Ruby libraries available so that you don't unnecessarily reinvent the wheel when you want to do something a library already does!

© Carleton DiLeo, Peter Cooper 2021
C. DiLeo and P. Cooper, *Beginning Ruby 3*, https://doi.org/10.1007/978-1-4842-6324-2_16

> **Note**   Ruby is in the process of gemifying its standard library. The goal is to
> move all of the Ruby standard library to gems rather than as part of the main Ruby
> codebase. These gems fall into two categories: default and bundled. Default gems
> are part of the Ruby installation and can be required directly. Default gems cannot
> be uninstalled. Bundled gems are installed along with Ruby but can be uninstalled.
> More information at `https://stdgems.org`.

abbrev

The *abbrev* library offers a single method that calculates a set of unique abbreviations for each of a supplied group of strings.

Installation

abbrev is in the standard library, so it comes with Ruby by default. To use it, you only need to place this line near the start of your program:

```
require 'abbrev'
```

Examples

abbrev provides a single method that's accessible in two ways: either directly through `Abbrev::abbrev` or as an added method to the `Array` class. Let's look at the most basic example first:

```
require 'abbrev'
require 'pp'
pp Abbrev::abbrev(%w{Peter Patricia Petal Petunia})
```

```
{"Peter"=>"Peter",
 "Pete"=>"Peter",
 "Patricia"=>"Patricia",
 "Patrici"=>"Patricia",
 "Patric"=>"Patricia",
 "Patri"=>"Patricia",
```

```
"Patr"=>"Patricia",
"Pat"=>"Patricia",
"Pa"=>"Patricia",
"Petal"=>"Petal",
"Peta"=>"Petal",
"Petunia"=>"Petunia",
"Petuni"=>"Petunia",
"Petun"=>"Petunia",
"Petu"=>"Petunia"}
```

abbrev can be useful if you have an input requirement with a number of guessable answers, as you can detect partially entered or erroneous entries more easily, for example:

```
require 'abbrev'

abbrevs = %w{Peter Paul Patricia Petal Pauline}.abbrev
puts "Please enter your name:"
name = gets.chomp

if a = abbrevs.find { |a, n| a.downcase == name.downcase }
  puts "Did you mean #{a.join(' or ')}?"
  name = gets.chomp
end
```

```
Please enter your name:
paulin
Did you mean Paulin or Pauline?
pauline
```

Because the results given by abbrev are the longest unique abbreviations possible, it's viable to rely on them more if the entry dataset is smaller.

Further Information

- *Official documentation for abbrev*: https://ruby-doc.org/stdlib/libdoc/abbrev/rdoc/Abbrev.html

Base64

Base64 is a way to encode 8-bit binary data into a format that can be represented in seven bits. It does this by using only the characters A–Z, a–z, 0–9, +, and / to represent data (= is also used to pad data). Typically, three 8-bit bytes are converted into four 7-bit bytes using this encoding, resulting in data that's 33 percent longer in length. The main benefit of the Base64 technique is that it allows binary data to be represented in a way that looks and acts like plain text, so it can more reliably be sent in emails, stored in databases, or used in text-based formats such as YAML, JSON, and XML.

Note   The Base64 standard is technically specified in RFC 2045 at `www.ietf.`
`org/rfc/rfc2045.txt`.

Installation

The *base64* library is a part of the standard library, so it comes with Ruby by default. To use it, you only need to place this line near the start of your program:

```
require 'base64'
```

Examples

The following two examples show how to convert binary data to Base64 notation and back again. Then we'll look at a third example showing how to make your use of Base64 notation more efficient through compression.

Converting Binary Data to Base64

The base64 library makes a single module, Base64, available, which provides encode64 and decode64 methods. To convert data into Base64 format, use encode64:

```
require 'base64'
puts Base64.encode64('testing')
```

```
dGVzdGluZw==
```

In this example, you only encode data that's already printable (though it's still technically 8-bit data internally), but this is acceptable. However, generally you'd encode binary data from files or other sources:

```
require 'base64'
puts Base64.encode64(File.read('/bin/bash'))
```

```
yv66vgAAAAIAAAAHAAAAwAAEAAAB4xQAAAADAAAABIAAAAAAegAAAIrywA
AAAMAAAAAAAAAAAAAAAAAAAAAAAAAAAAAAAAAAAAAAAAAAAAAAAAAAAAAAAA
AAAAAAAAAAAAAAAAAAAAAAAAAAAAAAAAAAAAAAAAAAAAAAAAAAAAAAAAAAAA
[output continues onwards.. trimmed for brevity..]
```

> **Note**   This example works on OS X and Linux operating systems. On a Windows machine, you could try replacing /bin/bash with c:\windows\system\cmd. exe to get a similar result.

Converting Base64 Data to Binary Data

To convert Base64-encoded data back to the original data, use decode64:

```
require 'base64'
puts Base64.decode64(Base64.encode64('testing'))
```

```
testing
```

Note that if you attempt to decode data that isn't in Base64 format, you'll receive no error in response. Instead, you'll end up with no legitimate data coming back from decode64.

Using Compression to Make Base64 Efficient

Even though Base64 adds 33 percent to the length of a piece of data, it's possible to overcome this by compressing the data before converting it to Base64 and then uncompressing it when you want to convert it back to binary data.

Note   Not all binary data compresses well, although in most cases you'll achieve a reduction of at least 5 percent, usually more.

To compress and uncompress, you can use the zlib library, which is covered later in this chapter, like so:

```
require 'base64'
require 'zlib'

module Base64
  def Base64.new_encode64(data)
    encode64(Zlib::Deflate.deflate(data))
  end
  def Base64.new_decode64(data)
    Zlib::Inflate.inflate(decode64(data))
  end
end

test_data = 'this is a test' * 100

data = Base64.encode64(test_data)
puts "The uncompressed data is #{data.length} bytes long in Base64"

data = Base64.new_encode64(test_data)
puts "The compressed data is #{data.length} bytes long in Base64"
```

```
The uncompressed data is 1900 bytes long in Base64
The compressed data is 45 bytes long in Base64
```

In this example, two new methods have been added to the Base64 module that use zlib to compress the data before converting it to Base64 and then to uncompress the data after converting it back from Base64. In this way, you've received significant space savings.

Read the "zlib" section in this chapter for more information about zlib's operation.

Further Information

The following are some links to good information on the base64 library and on Base64 in general:

- *Standard library documentation for base64*: `https://ruby-doc.org/stdlib/libdoc/base64/rdoc/Base64.html`

- *General information about the Base64 standard*: `https://en.wikipedia.org/wiki/Base64`

- *A practical look at how Base64 works*: `https://email.about.com/cs/standards/a/base64_encoding.htm`

Benchmark

The Benchmark module can be used to measure the time it takes to execute blocks of Ruby code. This can be useful to find which techniques are more efficient than others or to find slow points in your code.

Installation

Benchmark is part of the Ruby standard library, so you're all set to go after loading it in with

```
require 'benchmark'
```

Examples

The simplest example of benchmarking some code is to simply use Benchmark's measure method, like so:

```
require 'benchmark'
puts Benchmark.measure { 10000000.times { rand } }
```

```
0.660000   0.000000   0.660000 (  0.655942)
```

The output shows user CPU time, system CPU time, the sum of both times, and the real time that has elapsed, respectively.

The bm method can be used for a more complicated benchmarking situation where you want to compare the results of multiple approaches. For example, let's try three ways to loop 10 million times:

```ruby
require 'benchmark'

TIMES = 10000000
Benchmark.bm do |b|
  b.report("times") { TIMES.times { rand } }
  b.report("upto") { 1.upto(TIMES) { rand } }
  b.report("loop") {
    i = 0
    loop do
      rand
      i += 1
      break if i == TIMES
    end
  }
end
```

	user	system	total	real
times	0.640000	0.000000	0.640000	(0.648547)
upto	0.650000	0.000000	0.650000	(0.649027)
loop	0.830000	0.000000	0.830000	(0.841448)

This report includes labels for each row and column and demonstrates that manually creating a loop and using a variable to track its progress is slightly slower than using the times method.

Further Information

- *Official documentation for Benchmark*: https://ruby-doc.org/
  stdlib/libdoc/benchmark/rdoc/Benchmark.html

chronic

The chronic library makes it easy to convert dates and times written in almost any format into dates and times that Ruby recognizes correctly internally. It accepts strings such as 'tomorrow' and 'last tuesday 5pm' and turns them into valid Time objects.

Installation

The chronic library isn't part of the Ruby standard library, but it is available as a Rubygem. To install it, use the typical gem installation process (as covered in Chapter 7), like so:

```
gem install chronic
```

Examples

chronic is designed to accept dates and times written in a natural language format and to return valid Time objects. Here are some basic examples:

```
require 'chronic'
puts Chronic.parse('last tuesday 5am')
```

```
2020-03-29 05:00:00 +0100
```

```
puts Chronic.parse('last tuesday 5:33')
```

```
2020-03-29 17:33:00 +0100
```

```
puts Chronic.parse('last tuesday lunchtime')
```

```
2020-03-29 12:00:00 +0100
```

```
puts Chronic.parse('june 29th at 1am')
```

```
2020-06-29 01:00:00 +0100
```

```
puts Chronic.parse('in 3 years')
```

```
2023-04-04 11:30:57 +0100
```

```
puts Chronic.parse('sep 23 2033')
```

```
2033-09-23 12:00:00 +0100
```

```
puts Chronic.parse('2003-11-10 01:02')
```

```
2003-11-10 01:02:00 +0000
```

Chronic.parse will return nil if a date or time isn't recognized.

Note   An extension to the Time class provided by the standard library can also parse times, although at a more preformatted level. See https://ruby-doc.org/stdlib/libdoc/time/rdoc/Time.html for information.

Further Information

- *Documentation for chronic*: https://github.com/mojombo/chronic

Digest

A *digest* (more commonly known as a *hash*—though not the same type of hash as you've used to store data structures in Ruby) is a number or string of data that's generated from another collection of data. Digests are significantly shorter than the original data and act as a form of checksum against the data. Digests are generated in such a way that it's unlikely some other valid data would produce the same value and that it's difficult, if not impossible, to create valid data that would result in the same hash value.

A common use for hashes or digests is to store passwords in a database securely. Rather than store passwords in plain text where they could potentially be seen, you can create a digest of the password that you then compare against when you need to validate that the password is correct. You'll look at an example of this in the "Examples" section.

Installation

The libraries to produce digests in Ruby are called *digest/sha2* and *digest/md5*. Other algorithms like SHA1 and HMAC are available, however. All aforementioned digest libraries are a part of the standard library, so they come with Ruby by default. To use them, you only need to place this line near the start of your program:

```ruby
require 'digest/sha2'
```

or

```ruby
require 'digest/md5'
```

or to require both

```ruby
require 'digest'
```

Examples

Let's look at what a digest of some data can look like:

```ruby
require 'digest/sha2'
puts Digest::SHA2.hexdigest('password')
```

```
5e884898da28047151d0e56f8dc6292773603d0d6aabbdd62a11ef721d1542d8
```

You can use hexdigest (on both Digest::SHA2 and Digest::MD5—more about this later in this section) to produce a digest of any data. The digest is a string of 32 hexadecimal numbers (resulting in 64 characters, as each hexadecimal number is formed using two digits). In this case, the digest is significantly longer than the input data. No matter the input length, a digest generated via Digest::SHA2 is always the same length. For example, here's a digest of a 4000-character input string:

```ruby
require 'digest/sha2'
puts Digest::SHA2.hexdigest('test' * 1000)
```

```
f23eb679397f33bd94ce44d22909189c8f07f3464a4c0e8e36267cf275fd1d38
```

Digest::SHA2 operates using the SHA-2 hashing algorithm. It results in a 256-bit output (this is the default), meaning there are 2^{256} possible hash values. This *almost* guarantees there will be no clashing hash values for legitimate data within a single domain.

Another hashing mechanism provided by Ruby is based on the MD5 hashing algorithm. MD5 produces a 128-bit hash value, giving 340,282,366,920,938,463,463,374,607,431,768,211,456 combinations. MD5 is considered to be less secure than SHA-2, as it's possible to generate "hash collisions," where two sets of valid data can be engineered to get the same hash value. Hash collisions can be used to break into authentication systems that rely on MD5 hashing. However, MD5 is still a popular hashing mechanism, so the Ruby support is useful. You can use Digest::MD5 in exactly the same way as SHA-2:

```ruby
require 'digest/md5'
puts Digest::MD5.hexdigest('test' * 1000)
```

```
b38968b763b8b56c4b703f93f510be5a
```

> **Tip**   There is also a Digest::SHA1 class available in digest/sha1 that provides for the creation of digests of a smaller, less secure length.

Using digests in place of passwords is easy:

```ruby
require 'digest/sha2'

puts "Enter the password to use this program:"
password = gets
if Digest::SHA2.hexdigest(password) ==
                    '5e884898da28047151d0e56f8dc6292773603d0d6aabbdd62
                    a11ef721d1542d8'
  puts "You've passed!"
else
  puts "Wrong!"
  exit
end
```

In this case, the password is stored as a SHA-2 hex digest, and you hash any incoming passwords to establish if they're equal. Yet without knowing what the password is, there's no way you could succeed with the preceding program even by looking at the source code!

You can also generate the raw digest without it being rendered into a string of hexadecimal characters by using the digest method, like so:

```
Digest::SHA2.digest('test' * 1000)
```

As the result is 32 bytes data, it's unlikely you would be satisfied with the output if you printed it to the screen as characters, but you can prove the values are there:

```
Digest::SHA2.digest('test' * 1000).each_byte do |byte|
  print byte, "-"
end
```

```
242-62-182-121-57-127-51-189-148-206-68-210-41-9-24-156-143-7-243-70-74-
76-14-142-54-38-124-242-117-253-29-56-
```

It's worth noting that if you want to store digests in text format, but want something that takes up less space than the 64 hexadecimal characters, the base64 library can help:

```
require 'base64'
require 'digest'

puts Digest::SHA2.hexdigest('test')
puts Base64.encode64(Digest::SHA1.digest('test'))
```

```
9f86d081884c7d659a2feaa0c55ad015a3bf4f1b2b0b822cd15d6c15b0f00a08
qUqP5cyxm6YcTAhz05Hph5gvu9M=
```

Further Information

- *Further information about SHA-2*: https://en.wikipedia.org/wiki/SHA-2

- *Further information about MD5*: https://en.wikipedia.org/wiki/MD5

English

Throughout this book, you've often used special variables provided by Ruby for various purposes. For example, $! contains a string of the last error message raised in the program, $$ returns the process ID of the current program, and $/ lets you add the default line or record separator as used by the gets method. The *English* library allows you to access Ruby's special variables using names expressed in English, rather than symbols. This makes the variables easier to remember.

Installation

The English library is a part of the standard library, so it comes with Ruby by default. To use it, you only need to place this line near the start of your program:

```
require 'English'
```

Examples

Using require 'English' (note the capitalization of the first letter, as opposed to the standard, all-lowercase names adopted by the filenames of other libraries) creates English language aliases to Ruby's special variables, some of which are covered in the following list:

- $DEFAULT_OUTPUT (alias for $>) is an alias for the destination of output sent by commands such as print and puts. By default, it points to $stdout, the standard output, typically the screen or current terminal (see the sidebar "Standard Input and Output" in Chapter 9 for more information).

- $DEFAULT_INPUT (alias for $<) is an object that acts somewhat like a File object for data being sent to the script at the command line, or if the data is missing, the standard input (usually the keyboard or current terminal). It is read-only.

- $ERROR_INFO (alias for $!) refers to the exception object passed to raise, or, more pragmatically, can contain the most recent error message. In the initial form, it can be useful when used within a rescue block.

- $ERROR_POSITION (alias for $@) returns a stack trace as generated by the previous exception. This is in the same format as the trace provided by Kernel.caller.

- $OFS and $OUTPUT_FIELD_SEPARATOR (aliases for $,) can be set or read and contain the default separator as used in output from the print method and Array's join method. The default value is nil, as can be confirmed with %w{a b c}.join, which results in abc.

- $ORS and $OUTPUT_RECORD_SEPARATOR (aliases for $\) can be set or read, and contain the default separator as used when sending output with methods such as print and IO.write. The default value is nil, as typically you use puts instead when you want to append a newline to data being sent.

- $FS and $FIELD_SEPARATOR (aliases for $;) can be set or read, and contain the default separator as used by String's split method. Changing this and then calling split on a string without a split regex or character can give different results than expected.

- $RS and $INPUT_RECORD_SEPARATOR (aliases for $/) can be set or read, and contain the default separator as used for input, such as from gets. The default value is a newline (\n) and results in gets receiving one line at a time. If this value is set to nil, then gets would read an entire file or data stream in one go.

- $PID and $PROCESS_ID (alias for $$) return the process ID of the current program. This ID is unique for every program or instance of a program running on a computer, which is why tempfile uses it when constructing names for temporary files. It is read-only.

- $LAST_MATCH_INFO (alias for $~) returns a MatchData object that contains the results of the last successful pattern match.

- $IGNORECASE (alias for $=) is a flag that you can set or read from that determines whether regular expressions and pattern matches performed in the program will be case-insensitive by default. This special variable is deprecated and only effective in Ruby 1.8 (not Ruby 1.9 or later). Typically, if you required this feature, you'd use the /i flag on the end of a regular expression instead.

- $MATCH (alias for $&) contains the entire string matched by the last successful regular expression match in the current scope. If there has been no match, its value is nil.

- $PREMATCH (alias for $`) contains the string preceding the match discovered by the last successful regular expression match in the current scope. If there has been no match, its value is nil.

- $POSTMATCH (alias for $') contains the string succeeding the match discovered by the last successful regular expression match in the current scope. If there has been no match, its value is nil.

Further Information

- *Standard library documentation for English*: `https://ruby-doc.org/stdlib/libdoc/English/rdoc/English.html`

ERB

ERB is a templating library for Ruby that allows you to mix content and Ruby code. ERB is used as the main template system in Ruby on Rails when rendering RHTML views (see Chapter 13 for more information). Mixing Ruby code with other content results in a powerful templating system.

Installation

The ERB library is a part of the standard library, so it comes with Ruby by default. To use it, you only need to place this line near the start of your program:

```
require 'erb'
```

Examples

ERB works by accepting data written in ERB's template language, converting it to Ruby code that can produce the desired output, and then executing that code.

Basic Templates and Rendering

A basic ERB script might look like this:

```
<% 1.upto(5) do |i| %>
<p>This is iteration <%= i %></p>
<% end %>
```

In this template, Ruby and HTML code are mixed. Ruby code that's meant to be executed is placed within <% and %> tags. Ruby code that's to be evaluated and "printed" is placed within <%= and %> tags, and normal content is left as is.

Running the preceding template through ERB would result in this output:

```
<p>This is iteration 1</p>
<p>This is iteration 2</p>
<p>This is iteration 3</p>
<p>This is iteration 4</p>
<p>This is iteration 5</p>
```

Note   Due to the spacing in the template, the spacing in the output can look odd. Usually added whitespace isn't an issue with HTML or XHTML, but if you're using ERB to output other forms of data, you might need to develop your templates with whitespace in mind.

You use the ERB library to render ERB code from Ruby:

```
require 'erb'
template = <<EOF
<% 1.upto(5) do |i| %>
  <p>This is iteration <%= i %></p>
<% end %>
EOF
puts ERB.new(template).result
```

The `result` method doesn't print the data directly, but returns the rendered template to the caller, so you then print it to the screen with `puts`. If you'd rather have ERB print the output directly to the screen, you can use the `run` method:

```
ERB.new(template).run
```

Accessing Outside Variables

ERB templates can also access variables in the current scope, for example:

```
require 'erb'

array_of_stuff = %w{this is a test}

template = <<EOF
<% array_of_stuff.each_with_index do |item, index| %>
  <p>Item <%= index %>: <%= item %></p>
<% end %>
EOF
puts ERB.new(template).result(binding)
```

```
<p>Item 0: this</p>
<p>Item 1: is</p>
<p>Item 2: a</p>
<p>Item 3: test</p>
```

Note The `result` and `run` methods accept a binding as an optional parameter if you want ERB to have access to variables that are defined in a different (or the current) scope or if you want to "sandbox" the variables to which templates have access. If you allow them access to your main binding, as in the preceding example, remember that code within templates could change the value of the current variables!

Further Information

- *Standard library documentation for ERB*: https://ruby-doc.org/
  stdlib/libdoc/erb/rdoc/ERB.html

json

The json library enables you to parse and create JSON (JavaScript Object Notation) from Ruby objects. JSON is a popular data interchange format that's commonly used in web-based APIs and within JavaScript applications. It's also possible to read JSON easily as it's notated entirely in plain text.

Installation

The json library is part of the standard library, so all we need to do is require it in.

Examples

Here's an example of a very simple JSON document:

```
{"name":"Maggie Robertson","age":37,"interests":["Golf","Bridge","Food"]}
```

This is essentially a hash with numerous keys and values, with the values being a string, number, and an array of strings respectively.

To convert this plain text JSON into a hash we can use within a Ruby program, we can do this:

```
require 'json'

json_data = %{
  {"name":"Maggie Robertson","age":37,"interests":["Golf","Bridge","Food"]}
}

obj = JSON.load(json_data)
puts obj.class
puts obj.keys
```

```
Hash
name
age
interests
```

Likewise, you can go from a Ruby hash to JSON by using a to_json method that the json library introduces to all objects:

```
require 'json'
person = {
  name: 'Maggie Robertson',
  age: 37,
  interests: ['Golf', 'Bridge', 'Food']
}

puts person.to_json
```

```
{"name":"Maggie Robertson","age":37,"interests":["Golf","Bridge","Food"]}
```

Further Information

- *Introducing JSON*: www.json.org/json-en.html

- *JSON tutorial*: www.w3schools.com/js/js_json_intro.asp

- *Ruby JSON documentation*: https://ruby-doc.org/stdlib/libdoc/json/rdoc/JSON.html

logger

logger is a library developed by Hiroshi Nakamura and Gavin Sinclair that provides sophisticated logging features to Ruby applications. It supports automatic log rotation and multiple urgency levels and can output to file, to standard output, or to standard error handles. Ruby on Rails uses logger as its main logging system, but you can use it from any Ruby application.

Installation

The logger library is a part of the standard library, so it comes with Ruby by default. To use it, you only need to place this line near the start of your program:

```
require 'logger'
```

Examples

To use logger, you create `Logger` objects and then use the methods provided by the objects to report events that occur while your program is running. The first step is to get a `Logger` object.

Setting Up a Logger

Loggers can write to standard output, standard error, or to a file. Specify a file handle or filename to `Logger.new`. For example, here's how to write log messages directly to the screen or terminal:

```
require 'logger'
logger = Logger.new(STDERR)
```

Use this code to write log messages to file:

```
logger = Logger.new('mylogfile.log')
logger = Logger.new('/tmp/some_log_file.log')
```

You can also specify that a log file ages daily, weekly, or monthly (old log files are suffixed with date indicators):

```
logger = Logger.new('mylogfile.log', 'daily')
logger = Logger.new('mylogfile.log', 'weekly')
logger = Logger.new('mylogfile.log', 'monthly')
```

Last, it's possible to create a logger that only creates a log file up to a certain size. Once the log file hits that size, logger copies the existing log file to another filename and then starts a new log file. This is known as *log rotation*:

```
logger = Logger.new('mylogfile.log', 10, 100000)
```

This logger logs files to `mylogfile.log` until it reaches 100,000 bytes in length, whereupon the logger renames the log file (by suffixing it with a number) and creates a new `mylogfile.log`. It keeps the ten most recent but unused log files available.

Logging Levels

There are five different logging levels, ranked in order of severity, as follows:

- DEBUG: The lowest severity, used for debugging information for the developer

- INFO: General information about the operation of the program, library, or system

- WARN: A nonfatal warning about the state of the program

- ERROR: An error that can be handled (as with a rescued exception)

- FATAL: An error that is unrecoverable and that forces an immediate end to the program

Whenever you start a logger, you can specify the level of messages it should track. If a message is of that level or above, it will be logged. If it's below that level, it will be ignored. This is useful so that during development you can log every debug message, whereas when your program is being used for real, you only log the important messages.

To set the severity level of a logger, use the logger's `sev_threshold` method. This level ensures *only* FATAL messages are logged:

```
logger.sev_threshold = Logger::FATAL
```

This level ensures every message of all levels is logged:

```
logger.sev_threshold = Logger::DEBUG
```

Logging Messages

Each `Logger` object provides several methods to allow you to send a message to the log. The most commonly used way is to use the `debug`, `info`, `warn`, `error`, and `fatal` methods, which all create log messages of their respective severity:

```
require 'logger'
logger = Logger.new(STDOUT)

logger.debug "test"
logger.info "test"
logger.fatal "test"
```

```
D, [2020-08-11T11:06:06.805072 #9289] DEBUG -- : test
I, [2020-08-11T11:06:06.825144 #9289] INFO -- : test
F, [2020-08-11T11:06:06.825288 #9289] FATAL -- : test
```

Log messages are notated by their severity as a single letter, the date and time of their creation, the process ID of which process created them, and their severity label, followed by the actual message. Optionally, the program name might be present, if it was specified in the logging method, with the normal message coming from a block, like so:

```
logger.info("myprog") { "test" }
```

```
I, [2020-08-11T11:09:32.284956 #9289] INFO -- myprog: test
```

You can also assign a severity to a log message dynamically, like so:

```
logger.add(Logger::FATAL) { "message here" }
```

```
F, [2020-08-11T11:13:06.880818 #9289] FATAL -- : message here
```

To use different severities, pass the severity's class (`Logger::FATAL`, `Logger::DEBUG`, `Logger::INFO`, and so on) as the argument to `add`.

Closing a Logger

You close a logger as you would a file or any other I/O structure:

```
logger.close
```

Further Information

- *Standard library documentation for logger*: `https://ruby-doc.org/stdlib/libdoc/logger/rdoc/Logger.html`

Nokogiri

The *Nokogiri* library is a fast HTML, XML, SAX, and Reader parser with XPath and CSS selector support.

Installation

The Nokogiri library isn't part of the Ruby standard library, but it is available as a Rubygem. To install it, use the typical gem installation process (as covered in Chapter 7), like so:

```
gem install nokogiri
```

Alternatively, you can download the source from Nokogiri's GitHub repository. The link is provided in the following "Further Information" subsection.

Examples

Nokogiri is a fast XML and HTML parser with full CSS3 selector and XPath support.

A great way to start using it is to see how easy it is to parse an HTML page:

```
require 'rubygems'
require 'nokogiri'
require 'open-uri'

doc = Nokogiri::HTML(URI.open('https://www.apress.com/'))

doc.css('p').each do |para|
  puts para.inner_text
end
```

In this example, we've used open-uri to make the retrieval of a website a lot quicker. Nokogiri will, however, also accept strings if you want to process local or user-supplied XML or HTML data.

The document is processed as HTML by Nokogiri, thanks to the use of Nokogiri::HTML (Nokogiri::XML can be used to process XML). We've then used the css method on the document to search for all paragraphs (the <p> tag in HTML). Any CSS selector can be specified as an argument. For example, if you wanted to search for all <li> tags under a <div> with an ID of "story," you'd use the selector #story li.

The each method is then used to iterate over each paragraph, and the inner_text method is used to return the plain text contents of the tag.

Further Information

- *Nokogiri homepage*: www.nokogiri.org/

- *CSS Selector tutorial*: www.w3schools.com/css/css_selectors.asp

- *Nokogiri GitHub repository*: https://github.com/sparklemotion/nokogiri

pp

pp is a "pretty printer" that provides better formatted output than a simple `puts` `something.inspect` or p command. It presents a cleaner look at data structures that are properly tabulated and spaced, unlike `inspect` or p's output.

Installation

The pp library is a part of the standard library, so it comes with Ruby by default. To use it, you only need to place this line near the start of your program:

```
require 'pp'
```

Examples

To use pp, simply use the pp method, followed by the object whose structure you wish to display. Here's a basic comparison of `inspect` and pp:

```
person1 = { :name => "Peter", :gender => :male }
person2 = { :name => "Carleton", :gender => :male }
people = [person1, person2, person1, person1, person1]
puts people.inspect
```

```
[{:name=>"Peter", :gender=>:male}, {:name=>" Carleton", :gender=>:male},
{:name=>"Peter", :gender=>:male}, {:name=>"Peter", :gender=>:male},
{:name=>"Peter", :gender=>:male}]
```

```
pp people
```

517

```
[{:name=>"Peter",  :gender=>:male},
{:name=>"Carleton",  :gender=>:male},
{:name=>"Peter",  :gender=>:male},
{:name=>"Peter",  :gender=>:male},
{:name=>"Peter",  :gender=>:male}]
```

As demonstrated, pp is mostly useful when dealing with complex objects whose data
cannot fit on a single line. Here's a more contrived example:

```
require 'pp'

class TestClass
  def initialize(count)
    @@a = defined?(@@a) ? @@a + 1 : 0
    @c = @@a
    @d = [:a => {:b => count }, :c => :d] * count
  end
end

pp TestClass.new(2), STDOUT, 60
pp TestClass.new(3), $>, 60
pp TestClass.new(4), $>, 60
```

```
#<TestClass:0x357000
  @c=0,
  @d=[{:a=>{:b=>2}, :c=>:d}, {:a=>{:b=>2}, :c=>:d}]>
#<TestClass:0x354364
  @c=1,
  @d=
    [{:a=>{:b=>3}, :c=>:d},
     {:a=>{:b=>3}, :c=>:d},
     {:a=>{:b=>3}, :c=>:d}]>
#<TestClass:0x3503f4
  @c=2,
  @d=
    [{:a=>{:b=>4}, :c=>:d},
```

```
{:a=>{:b=>4}, :c=>:d},
{:a=>{:b=>4}, :c=>:d},
{:a=>{:b=>4}, :c=>:d}]>
```

Where it's practical, pp fits data onto a single line, but when more data is to be shown than could fit on a single line, pp formats and spaces that data accordingly.

Note that in the preceding example, the pp calls are in this format:

```
pp TestClass.new(4), $>, 60
```

With no parameters, pp assumes a display width of 79 characters. However, pp supports two optional parameters, which set the destination for its output and the width of the output field. In this case, you output to the standard output and assume a wrapping width of 60 characters.

Further Information

- *Standard library documentation for pp*: https://ruby-doc.org/stdlib/libdoc/prettyprint/rdoc/PrettyPrint.html

RedCarpet

RedCarpet is a library that converts specially formatted text documents (in a formatting known as *Markdown*) into valid HTML. The reasoning behind languages such as Markdown is that most users prefer to write their documents in a clean format, rather than be forced to use HTML tags everywhere and create documents that don't read well as plain text. Markdown allows you to format text in a way that makes documents look good as plain text, but also allows the text to be converted quickly to HTML for use on the Web. This makes languages such as Markdown popular for use with posting and commenting systems online, and many blog authors even first write their posts in languages such as Markdown before converting them for publication.

Installation

RedCarpet isn't part of the Ruby standard library, but it is available as a Rubygem. To install it, use the typical gem installation process (as covered in Chapter 7), like so:

```
gem install redcarpet
```

519

Examples

An example Markdown document might look like this:

```
This is a title
===============

Here is some _text_ that's formatted according to [Markdown][1]
*specifications*. And how about a quote?

 [1]: http://daringfireball.net/projects/markdown/

> This section is a quote.. a block quote
> more accurately..

Lists are also possible:

* Item 1
* Item 2
* Item 3
```

In the following example, we'll assume this document is already assigned to the variable markdown_text to save space on the page.

Here's how to convert Markdown syntax to HTML:

```
require 'redcarpet'

markdown_text=<<MARKDOWN
This is a title
===============

Here is some _text_ that's formatted according to [Markdown][1]
*specifications*. And how about a quote?

 [1]: http://daringfireball.net/projects/markdown/

> This section is a quote.. a block quote
> more accurately..

Lists are also possible:
```

```
* Item 1
* Item 2
* Item 3
MARKDOWN

markdown = Redcarpet::Markdown.new(Redcarpet::Render::HTML)
puts markdown.render(markdown_text)
```

```
<h1>This is a title</h1>

<p>Here is some <em>text</em> that&#39;s formatted according to <a
href="http://daringfireball.net/projects/markdown/">Markdown</a>
<em>specifications</em>. And how about a quote?</p>

<blockquote>
<p>This section is a quote.. a block quote
more accurately..</p>
</blockquote>

<p>Lists are also possible:</p>

<ul>
<li>Item 1</li>
<li>Item 2</li>
<li>Item 3</li>
</ul>
```

The output HTML correctly resembles the Markdown syntax when viewed with a web browser.

To learn more about the Markdown format and its syntax, visit the official Markdown homepage, as linked in the following section.

Further Information

- *Official RedCarpet homepage*: https://github.com/vmg/redcarpet

- *Official Markdown format homepage*: https://daringfireball. net/projects/markdown/

StringScanner

StringScanner is a library that lets you "walk through" a string, matching patterns one at a time, while only applying them to the remainder of the data that you haven't yet matched. This is in stark contrast to the standard scan method that automatically returns all matching patterns immediately.

Installation

StringScanner is in the standard library, so it comes with Ruby by default. To use it, you only need to place this line near the start of your program:

```
require 'strscan'
```

> **Note**   It's important to recognize that the filename doesn't match the name of the library, or class in this case. Although most library developers tend to keep names consistent, not all do!

Examples

The best way to see StringScanner's feature set is to see it in action:

```
require 'strscan'
string = StringScanner.new "This is a test"
puts string.scan(/\w+/)
puts string.scan(/\s+/)
puts string.scan(/\w+/)
puts string.scan(/\s+/)
puts string.rest
```

```
This
is
a test
```

In this example, you step through the string by first matching a word with scan, then whitespace, then another word, and then more whitespace, before asking StringScanner to give you the rest of the string with the rest method.

However, scan will return content only if the specified pattern matches at the current position in the string. For example, this doesn't retrieve each word:

```
puts string.scan(/\w+/)
puts string.scan(/\w+/)
puts string.scan(/\w+/)
puts string.scan(/\w+/)
```

```
This
nil
nil
nil
```

After the first scan, the pointer for string is waiting at the whitespace after "This," and scan must match the whitespace for it to continue. One way to get around this would be like so:

```
puts string.scan(/\w+\s*/)
puts string.scan(/\w+\s*/)
puts string.scan(/\w+\s*/)
puts string.scan(/\w+\s*/)
```

In the preceding example, you'd retrieve the words and any whitespace located after each word. Of course, this might not be desirable, so StringScanner also provides other useful methods for scanning through strings.

scan_until scans through the string from the current position until the specified pattern matches. All the data from the start of the scan, until and including the match, is then returned. In this example, you perform a normal scan and pick off the first word, but then you use scan_until to scan all text until you reach a number:

```
string = StringScanner.new "I want to live to be 100 years old!"
puts string.scan(/\w+/)
puts string.scan_until(/\d+/)
```

```
I
want to live to be 100
```

You can also use `scan_until` to give a different solution to the previous "scan for each word" problem:

```
string = StringScanner.new("This is a test")
puts string.scan_until(/\w+/)
puts string.scan_until(/\w+/)
puts string.scan_until(/\w+/)
puts string.scan_until(/\w+/)
```

Another useful method is `unscan`, which gives you the opportunity to roll back a single scan:

```
string = StringScanner.new "I want to live to be 100 years old!"
puts string.scan(/\w+/)
string.unscan
puts string.scan_until(/\d+/)
string.unscan
puts string.scan_until(/live/)
```

```
I
I want to live to be 100
I want to live
```

You can also retrieve the current position of the scanner in the string:

```
string = StringScanner.new "I want to live to be 100 years old!"
string.scan(/\w+/)
string.unscan
puts string.pos
string.scan_until(/\d+/)
puts string.pos
string.unscan
string.scan_until(/live/)
puts string.pos
```

524

```
0
24
14
```

You can use pos to set or override the position of the scanner too:

```
string = StringScanner.new "I want to live to be 100 years old!"
string.pos = 12
puts string.scan(/...../)
```

```
ve to
```

Note   StringScanner isn't a subclass of `String`, so typical methods provided by `String` won't necessarily work. However, `StringScanner` does implement some of them, such as `<<`, which concatenates data onto the end of the string.

Further Information

- *Standard library documentation for StringScanner*: https://ruby-doc.org/stdlib/libdoc/strscan/rdoc/StringScanner.html

tempfile

Temporary files are intended for a single, one-time purpose. They're ephemeral files that you use to store information temporarily but that are quickly erased. In Chapter 9, you looked at the creation of temporary files using several techniques, but tempfile provides an easy and standard way to create and manipulate them.

Installation

tempfile is in the standard library, so it comes with Ruby by default. To use it, you only need to place this line near the start of your program:

```
require 'tempfile'
```

Examples

tempfile manages the creation and manipulation of temporary files. It creates temporary files in the correct place for your operating system, and it gives them unique names so that you can concentrate on the main logic of your application.

To create a temporary file, use `Tempfile.new`:

```
require 'tempfile'
f = Tempfile.new('myapp')
f.puts "Hello"
puts f.path
f.close
```

```
/tmp/myapp1842.0
```

Tempfile.new creates a temporary file using the given string as a prefix in the format of `<supplied name>-<program's process ID>.<unique number>`. The returned object is a `Tempfile` object that delegates most of its methods to the usual `File` and `IO` classes, allowing you to use the file methods you're already familiar with, as with `f.puts` earlier.

To use the data in your temporary file, you can close it and reopen it quickly:

```
f.close
f.open
```

If you specify no arguments to `f.open`, it will reopen the temporary file associated with that object. At that point, you can continue to write to the temporary file or read from it:

```
require 'tempfile'
f = Tempfile.new('myapp')
f.puts "Hello"
f.close
f.open
puts f.read
f.close!
```

```
Hello
```

The preceding code creates a temporary file, writes data to it, closes the temporary file (which flushes the written data out to disk from the memory buffers), and then reopens it for reading.

The last line uses close! instead of close, which forces the temporary file to be closed and permanently deleted.

Of course, you can flush the buffers manually, so you can use the same temporary file for reading and writing without having to close it at any point:

```ruby
require 'tempfile'
f = Tempfile.new('myapp')
f.puts "Hello"
f.pos = 0
f.print "Y"
f.pos = f.size - 1
f.print "w"
f.flush
f.pos = 0
puts f.read
f.close!
```

```
Yellow
```

> **Note**   By default, temporary files are opened in the w+ mode.

In some situations, you might want to use temporary files, but not allow tempfile to put them in a place that can be seen by other programs or users. Tempfile.new accepts an optional second argument that specifies where you want temporary files to be created:

```ruby
f = Tempfile.new('myapp', '/my/secret/temporary/directory')
```

As with other file-related classes, you can use Tempfile in block form:

```ruby
require 'tempfile'

Tempfile.open('myapp') do |f|
  f.puts "Hello"
  f.pos = 0
```

```
  f.print "Y"
  f.pos = f.size - 1
  f.print "w"
  f.flush
  f.pos = 0
  puts f.read
end
```

Yellow

Note   You use `Tempfile.open` instead of `Tempfile.new` when using a block.

The benefit of using block form in this case is that the temporary file is removed automatically, and no closing is required. However, if you want to use a temporary file throughout the scope of a whole program, block form might not be suitable.

Further Information

- *Standard library documentation for tempfile*: `https://ruby-doc.org/stdlib/libdoc/tempfile/rdoc/Tempfile.html`

uri

You use the uri library to manage Uniform Resource Identifiers (URIs), which are typically referred to as Uniform Resource Locators (URLs). A URL is an address such as `www.apress.com/`, `ftp://your-ftp-site.com/directory/filename`, or even `mailto:your-email- address@privacy.net`. uri makes it easy to detect, create, parse, and manipulate these addresses.

Installation

uri is in the standard library, so it comes with Ruby by default. To use it, you only need to place this line near the start of your program:

```
require 'uri'
```

Examples

In this section, you'll look at a few examples of how to use the uri library to perform basic URL-related functions.

Extracting URLs from Text

URI.extract is a class method that extracts URLs from a given string into an array:

```
require 'uri'
puts URI.extract('Check out https://www.apress.com/ or email mailto:me@
apress.com').inspect
```

```
["https://www.apress.com/", "mailto:me@apress.com"]
```

You can also limit the types of URLs that extract should find:

```
require 'uri'
puts URI.extract('https://www.apress.com/ and mailto:me@apress.com',
['https']).inspect
```

```
["https://www.apress.com/"]
```

If you immediately want to use the URLs one by one, you can use extract with a block:

```
require 'uri'

email = %q{Some cool Ruby sites are https://www.ruby-lang.org/ and ↵
https://www.apress.com/ and https://www.w3.org/}

URI.extract(email, ['http', 'https']) do |url|
  puts "Fetching URL #{url}"
  # Do some work here...
end
```

Parsing URLs

A URL in a string can be useful, particularly if you want to use that URL with open-uri or net/http, for example. However, it can also be useful to split URLs into their constituent sections. Doing this with a regular expression would give inconsistent results and be prone to failure in uncommon situations, so the URI class provides the tools necessary to split URLs apart easily:

```
URI.parse('https://www.apress.com/')
```

```
=> #< URI::HTTPS https://www.apress.com/>
```

URI.parse parses a URL provided in a string and returns a URI-based object for it. URI has specific subclasses for FTP, HTTP, HTTPS, LDAP, and MailTo URLs, but returns a URI::Generic object for an unrecognized URL that's in a URL-type format.

The URI objects have a number of methods that you can use to access information about the URL:

```
require 'uri'
a = URI.parse('https://www.apress.com/')
puts a.scheme
puts a.host
puts a.port
puts a.path
puts a.query
```

```
https
www.apress.com
443
/
nil
```

Note that URI::HTTP is smart enough to know that if no port is specifically stated in an HTTP URL, the default port 80 must apply. The other URI classes, such as URI::FTP and URI::HTTPS, also make similar assumptions.

With more complex URLs, you can access some extended data:

```
require 'uri'
url = 'https://www.x.com:1234/test/1.html?x=y&y=z#top'
puts URI.parse(url).port
puts URI.parse(url).path
puts URI.parse(url).query
puts URI.parse(url).fragment
```

```
1234
/test/1.html
x=y&y=z
top
```

The uri library also makes a convenience method available to make it even easier to parse URLs:

```
u = URI('https://www.test.com/')
```

In this case, URI(url) is synonymous with URI.parse.

As well as URI.parse, you can use URI.split to split a URL into its constituent parts without involving a URI object:

```
URI.split('https://www.x.com:1234/test/1.html?x=y&y=z#top')
```

```
=> ["http", nil, "www.x.com", "1234", nil, "/test/1.html", nil,
    "x=y&y=z", "top"]
```

URI.split returns, in order, the scheme, user info, hostname, port number, registry, path, opaque attribute, query, and fragment. Any elements that are missing are nil.

Note   The only benefit of URI.split is that no URI object is created, so there can be minimal gains in memory and processor usage. However, generally it's more acceptable to use URI() or URI.parse so that you can address the different elements by name, rather than rely on the order of elements in an array (which could change between versions of the library).

Creating URLs

You can also use uri to create URLs that meet the accepted specifications. At their simplest, you can use the URI subclasses for each protocol to generate URLs by passing in a hash of the elements you want to make up the URL:

```
require 'uri'
u = URI::HTTP.build( host: 'apress.com', path: '/')
puts u.to_s
puts u.request_uri
```

```
http://apress.com/
/
```

Note that to_s returns the entire URL, whereas request_uri returns the portion of the URL that follows the hostname. This is because libraries such as net/http would use the data from request_uri, whereas libraries such as open-uri can use the entire URL.

You could also pass in :port, :query, :fragment, :userinfo, and other elements to the URI subclasses to generate more complex URLs.

Here's an example of creating an FTP URL:

```
ftp_url = URI::FTP.build( userinfo: 'username:password',
host: 'ftp.example.com',
path: '/pub/folder',
typecode: 'a')

puts ftp_url.to_s
```

```
ftp://username:password@ftp.example.com/pub/folder;type=a
```

Also note that uri is good at adjusting URLs in a safe manner, as you can set the various attributes to new values, as well as read them:

```
require 'uri'
my_url = "http://www.test.com/something/test.html"
url = URI.parse(my_url)
url.host = "www.test2.com"
```

```
url.port = 1234
puts url.to_s
```

```
http://www.test2.com:1234/something/test.html
```

Further Information

- *Standard library documentation for uri*: https://ruby-doc.org/
  stdlib/libdoc/uri/rdoc/URI.html

- *Information about URLs and URIs*: https://en.wikipedia.org/
  wiki/URL

zlib

zlib is an open source data-compression library. It's a significant standard in data compression, and you can manipulate zlib archives on almost every platform. Notably, zlib is often used to compress web pages between servers and web browsers, is used in the Linux kernel, and forms a key part of many operating system libraries.

You can use zlib from Ruby as a mechanism to compress and uncompress data.

Installation

zlib is in the standard library, so it comes with Ruby by default. To use it, you only need to place this line near the start of your program:

```
require 'zlib'
```

Examples

Under zlib, compression and uncompression are called *deflating* and *inflating*. The quickest way to compress (*deflate*) data is by using the Zlib::Deflate class directly:

```
require 'zlib'

test_text = 'this is a test string' * 100
```

```
puts "Original string is #{test_text.length} bytes long"
compressed_text = Zlib::Deflate.deflate(test_text)
puts "Compressed data is #{compressed_text.length} bytes long"
```

```
Original string is 2100 bytes long
Compressed data is 46 bytes long
```

This test text compresses extremely well, as it's the same string repeated 100 times over. However, on normal data, it's more practical to see compression rates of around 10 to 50 percent.

Restoring compressed data requires `Zlib::Inflate`:

```
require 'zlib'
test_text = 'this is a test string' * 100
puts "Original string is #{test_text.length} bytes long"
compressed_text = Zlib::Deflate.deflate(test_text)
puts "Compressed data is #{compressed_text.length} bytes long"
uncompressed_text = Zlib::Inflate.inflate(compressed_text)
puts "Uncompressed data is back to #{uncompressed_text.length} bytes in
length"
```

```
Original string is 2100 bytes long
Compressed data is 46 bytes long
Uncompressed data is back to 2100 bytes in length
```

Note   The compressed data returned by zlib is full 8-bit data, so might not be suitable to use in emails or in formats where regular plain text is necessary. To get around this, you can compress your data using zlib as usual and then use the base64 library to turn the compressed results into plain text.

zlib also comes with classes to help you work directly with compressed files. Files compressed with the zlib algorithm are often known as *gzipped* files, and `Zlib::GzipWriter` and `Zlib::GzipReader` make it easy to create and read from these files:

```
require 'zlib'

Zlib::GzipWriter.open('my_compressed_file.gz') do |gz|
  gz.write 'This data will be compressed automatically!'
end

Zlib::GzipReader.open('my_compressed_file.gz') do |my_file|
  puts my_file.read
end
```

```
This data will be compressed automatically!
```

Further Information

- *Standard library documentation for zlib*: https://ruby-doc.org/ stdlib/libdoc/zlib/rdoc/Zlib.html

Ruby Primer and Review for Developers

This appendix is designed to act as both a Ruby primer and review, useful both to developers who want to brush up rapidly on their Ruby knowledge and to those who are new to the language but who have existing programming knowledge and want to get a quick overview.

If you're a new programmer or at least are new to concepts such as object orientation, scripting languages, and dynamic languages, you'll want to read through Chapter 2 and continue with the rest of the book instead of depending on this appendix to teach you about Ruby. This appendix is designed for either those who have finished reading the rest of this book and want to brush up on the basics or those who want to look quickly through some basic elements of Ruby syntax in the flesh.

With that in mind, this appendix isn't instructional, as most of the other chapters in this book are. A lot of concepts will be covered at a quick pace with succinct code examples. References to more explanatory detail found in this book are given where possible.

The Basics

In this section, I'll give a brief overview of the Ruby programming language, its concepts, and how to use the Ruby interpreter.

Definition and Concepts

Ruby is an open source, object-oriented programming language created and maintained by Yukihiro Matsumoto (among others). Languages such as Perl, LISP, Smalltalk, and Python have inspired the syntax and styling of the language. It is cross-platform and runs on several different architectures, although its informal "home" architecture is Linux on x86.

© Carleton DiLeo, Peter Cooper 2021
C. DiLeo and P. Cooper, *Beginning Ruby 3*, https://doi.org/10.1007/978-1-4842-6324-2

Among other things, Ruby has automatic garbage collection, is (mostly) portable, supports multitasking (both native and its own cooperative "green" threads), has a large standard library, and supports most features associated with dynamic languages (such as closures, iterators, exceptions, overloading, and reflection).

Ruby is an interpreted language. This is in opposition to languages that are *compiled*. Code developed in languages such as C and C++ has to be compiled into *object code* that represents instructions supported by a computer's processor. Ruby, however, is compiled down into platform-independent bytecode that is run by a virtual machine. Python, Java, and C# share this characteristic, although they all run on different virtual machine implementations and have different execution characteristics. Table A-1 highlights some key differences between several popular programming languages.

Table A-1. *Feature Comparison Between Several Popular Programming Languages*

Language	Object-Oriented?	Reflective?	Dynamically Typed?	Interpreted?
Ruby	Yes	Yes	Yes	Yes (usually)
C	No	No	No	No
C++	Yes	No	No	No
C#	Yes	Yes	Yes	Yes, through VM
Perl	Partially	Partially	Yes	Yes
Java	Yes, mostly	Not generally	No	Yes, through VM
Python	Yes	Yes	Yes	Yes
Golang	Partially	Yes	No	No

Ruby has been developed with the "principle of least surprise" in mind, so the way you'd expect things to work is usually a valid way of doing something. This means Ruby is very much a "there's more than one way to do it" type of language, in the same vein as Perl but quite different in philosophy from languages such as Python, where having one clear process to achieve something is seen as the best way to do things.

Note   A useful resource is the official Ruby site's "Ruby From Other Languages" section at `www.ruby-lang.org/en/documentation/ruby-from-other-languages/`, where you'll find in-depth comparisons of Ruby against C, C++, Java, Perl, PHP, and Python.

One important concept in Ruby is that almost everything is an object. For example, the following line of code calls a primitive, internal method called `puts` with a single argument of 10. `puts` prints its arguments to the screen:

```
puts 10
```

```
10
```

Note   You could run this as a complete Ruby program or perform it in an interactive manner using Ruby's irb tool.

The following line of code calls the `class` method on the numeric object 10. Even the literal number 10 is an object in this situation. The result demonstrates that 10 is an object of the `Integer` class:

```
puts 10.class
```

```
Integer
```

Ruby's reflection, overriding, object orientation, and other dynamic features make it possible for developers to entirely override the behaviors of even built-in classes such as `Integer`. It's possible to make `Integer` objects work in totally different ways. You can override `Integer` to the point that 2 + 2 could well equal 5. Although some developers already experienced with languages such as Java and C see this as a downside, this level of control over the internals of the language gives Ruby developers a significant amount of power. The key is to use that power carefully.

The Ruby Interpreter and Running Ruby Code

As Ruby is an interpreted language, Ruby code is executed using the Ruby interpreter. On most platforms, that makes running a Ruby script as easy as this:

```
ruby name_of_script.rb
```

Note   Ruby program files usually end with the extension of `.rb`, although this isn't a strict requirement.

The Ruby interpreter has a number of options. You can ask the Ruby interpreter to print out its version details using the `-v` (version) option:

```
ruby -v
```

```
ruby 3.0.0p0 (2020-12-25) [x86_64-darwin17]
```

You can also execute Ruby commands directly from the command line, using `-e`:

```
ruby -e "puts 2 + 2"
```

```
4
```

You can learn more about the Ruby interpreter's command-line options by typing `man ruby` (on UNIX-related platforms) or by visiting a web-based version of the Ruby *man* page at `https://linux.die.net/man/1/ruby`.

Note   On Microsoft Windows, you might choose to associate the Ruby interpreter directly with any `.rb` files so that you can double-click Ruby files to execute them.

On UNIX-related platforms, it's possible to add a "shebang" line as the first line of a Ruby script so that it can be executed without having to invoke the Ruby interpreter explicitly, for example:

```
#!/usr/bin/ruby
puts "Hello, world!"
```

You can take this script, give it a simple filename such as `hello` (no `.rb` extension needed), make the file executable (using `chmod`), and run it directly using its filename rather than having to invoke the Ruby interpreter explicitly. Chapter 10 covers this technique in more depth. More information about the shebang line specifically is available at `https://en.wikipedia.org/wiki/Shebang_(Unix)`.

Interactive Ruby

With the normal Ruby interpreter also comes an interactive Ruby interpreter called *irb*. This allows you to write Ruby code in an immediate, interactive environment where the results of your code are given as soon as you type it. Here's an example irb session:

```
# irb
irb(main):001:0> puts "test"
test
=>nil
irb(main):002:0> 10 + 10
=> 20
irb(main):003:0> 10 == 20
=>false
irb(main):004:0> exit
```

irb gives you the results of methods and expressions immediately. This makes it an ideal tool for debugging or putting together quick snippets of code and for testing concepts.

Expressions and Flow Control

Expressions, logic, and flow control make up a significant part of any developer's tools in any programming language. This section looks at how Ruby implements them.

Basic Expressions

Ruby supports expressions in a style familiar to almost any programmer:

```
"a" + "b" + "c"
```

```
abc
```

```
10 + 20 + 30
```

```
60
```

```
("a" * 5) + ("c" * 6)
```

```
aaaaacccccc
```

```
a = 10
b = 20
a * b
```

```
200
```

You can assign the results of expressions to variables, which you can then use in other expressions.

Method calls, variables, literals, brackets, and operators can all combine so long as sub-expressions always feed values of the correct type into their parent expressions or provide methods that allow them to be *coerced* into the right types. The next section covers this topic in more depth. (Expressions are covered in depth in Chapter 3.)

Class Mismatches

Ruby is a dynamic language, but objects aren't converted between different classes automatically (in this sense Ruby is a *strongly* typed language). For example, this expression is valid in JavaScript:

```
"20" + 10
```

```
30
```

However, in Ruby, you get an error response with the same expression:

```
TypeError (no implicit conversion of Integer into String)
from (irb):1:in `+'
from (irb):1
```

In Ruby, you can only use objects that are of the same class or that support automatic translation between classes (*coercion*) in operations with one another (usually via methods called things like to_s and to_h, for conversions to strings and hashes, respectively).

However, Ruby comes with a set of methods that exist on many types of objects, which make conversion easy, for example:

```
"20" + 10.to_s
```

```
"2010"
```

In this example, the number 10 is converted to a string "10" in situ with the to_s method. Consider this inverse example, where you convert the string "20" into an integer object using the to_i method before adding 10 to it:

```
"20".to_i + 10
```

```
30
```

Note   Methods are covered in depth in Chapters 2, 3, and 6, as well as later in this appendix.

The to_s method provided by all number classes in Ruby results in a number being converted into a String object. Programmers might recognize this concept as similar to *casting*.

Other conversions that can take place are converting integers to floats using to_f, and vice versa with to_i. You can convert strings and numbers using to_s, to_i, and to_f. Many other classes support to_s for converting their structure and other data into a string (the Time class provides a good demonstration of this). This topic is covered in Chapter 3 in the section "Converting Objects to Other Classes."

Comparison Expressions

Comparison expressions in Ruby, as in most other languages, return `true` or `false`, except that in some situations comparisons might return `nil`, Ruby's concept of "null" or nonexistence, for example:

```
2 == 1
```

```
false
```

```
2 == 2
```

```
true
```

```
(2 == 2) && (1 == 1)
```

```
true
```

```
x = 12
x * 2 == x + 1
```

```
false
```

```
x * x == x ** 2
```

```
true
```

In each of the preceding examples, you test whether variables, literals, or other expressions are equal to one another using == (symbolizing "is equal to"). You can check that multiple expressions result in `true` (logical "and"—if x and y are `true`) using && (symbolizing "and").

As in other languages, the concept of a logical "or" is symbolized by ||:

```
(2 == 5) || (1 == 1)
```

```
true
```

This expression is true because even though 2 is not equal to 5, the other sub-expression *is* true, meaning that one *or* another of the expressions is true, so the whole comparison is also true.

Last, it can be useful to negate expressions. You can do this with the ! operator, as in many other programming languages. For example, you might want to see if one thing is true but another thing is false. Here's an example:

```
(2 == 2) && !(1 == 2)
```

```
true
```

The expression is true because both sub-expressions are true. 2 is equal to 2, and 1 is *not* equal to 2.

You can also check that one thing is not equal to another with the inequality operator ! =:

```
(2 == 2) && (1 != 2)
```

```
True
```

Flow

Ruby supports a few different forms of flow control. In this section, you'll see several techniques you can use for branching and looping. (All the topics in this section are covered in more depth in Chapter 3.)

Branching and Conditional Execution

The simplest form of conditional execution is with just a single line using if or unless:

```
puts "The universe is broken!" if 2 == 1
```

This example won't print anything to the screen because 2 is not equal to 1. In this case, if performs the comparison before the rest of the line is executed.

Ruby also supports a multiline construction:

```
if 2 == 1
  puts "The universe is broken!"
end
```

This multiline construction is less space efficient than the previous, single-line construction, but it allows you to put multiple lines between the condition and the end of the block, which isn't possible with the "end of line" technique.

Note   unless is the opposite of if. It executes code if the expression is false (or nil), rather than true. Some Rubyists think of it as "if not," because unless acts like if with the expression negated. Other developers avoid it entirely due to the potential confusion it can cause.

Ruby also supports the else directive:

```ruby
if 2 == 1
  puts "The universe is broken!"
else
  puts "The universe is okay!"
end
```

```
The universe is okay!
```

If the expression (2 == 1 in this example) is true, the main block of code is executed, *else* the other block of code is. There's also a feature called elsif that lets you chain multiple ifs together:

```ruby
x = 12
if x == 1 || x == 3 || x == 5 || x == 7 || x == 9
  puts "x is odd and under 10"
elsif x == 2 || x == 4 || x == 6 || x == 8
  puts "x is even and under 10"
else
  puts "x is over 10 or under 1"
end
```

The preceding rather obtuse example demonstrates how you can use if, elsif, and else in tandem. The only thing to note is that end always finishes an if (or unless) block, whether end is on its own or features elsif and else blocks too. In some languages, there's no need to delimit the end of if blocks if they contain only a single line. This isn't true of Ruby.

Note   JavaScript and C# coders will be used to `else if`. Ruby's uses `elsif` instead.

Ruby also supports another construction familiar to C#, C++, Java, and JavaScript coders, called `case` (known as `switch` in C#, C++, Java, and JavaScript):

```ruby
fruit = "apple"
color = case fruit
when "orange"
    "orange"
when "apple"
    "green"
when "banana"
    "yellow"
else
    "unknown"
end
puts color
```

```
green
```

This code is similar to the `if` block, except that the syntax is a lot cleaner. A `case` block works by processing an expression first (supplied after `case`), and then the `case` block finds and executes a contained when block with an associated value matching the result of that expression. If no matching when block is found, then the `else` block within the `case` block will be executed instead.

The Ternary Operator (Conditional Expressions)

Ruby supports a construction called the *ternary operator*. Its usage is simple:

```ruby
x = 10
puts x > 10 ? "Higher than ten" : "Lower or equal to ten"
```

```
Lower or equal to ten
```

The ternary operator works like so:

```
expression ? true_expression : false_expression
```

It works like an expression, but with built-in flow control. If the initial expression is true, then the first following expression will be evaluated and returned. If the initial expression is false, then the final following expression will be evaluated and returned instead.

Loops

Ruby supports loops in a similar way to other programming languages. For example, while, loop, until, next, and break features will be familiar (although with possibly different names) to most programmers.

Note   Ruby also supports iteration and code blocks, which can prove a lot more powerful than regular loops. These are covered later in this appendix and in Chapters 2, 3, and 6.

Loop techniques are covered in Chapter 3, but some basic demonstrations follow. Here's a permanent loop that you can break out of using break:

```
i = 0
loop do
  i += 1
  puts i
  break if i > 100
end
```

Note   It's worth noting that unlike in C# or JavaScript, you cannot increment variables by 1 with variable++ in Ruby. variable = variable + 1 or variable += 1 is necessary instead.

Here's a while loop, using next to skip even numbers (using the % modulo operator):

```
i = 0
while (i < 15)
  i += 1
```

```
  next if i % 2 == 0
  puts i
end
```

```
1
3
5
7
9
11
13
15
```

> **Note**   until is the opposite of while. until (i >= 15) is equivalent to while (i < 15).

Further looping techniques are covered in Chapter 3 and throughout the book.

Object Orientation

Ruby is considered a *pure* object-oriented language, because everything appears to Ruby as an object. An earlier example in this appendix demonstrated this:

```
puts 10.class
```

```
Integer
```

Even literal data (such as strings or numbers embedded directly in your source code) is considered to be an object, and you can call the methods made available by those objects (and/or their parent classes).

> **Note**   Object orientation, classes, objects, methods, and their respective techniques are covered in full in Chapters 2 and 6. This section presents merely a brief overview.

Ruby implements object orientation in a simple way (syntax-wise), but offers more dynamic features than other major languages (see Chapter 6 for many examples of such features).

Objects

Objects in Ruby have no special qualities beyond objects that exist in any other object-oriented programming language. However, the key difference between Ruby and most other major object-oriented languages is that in Ruby everything is an object. With this in mind, you can call methods on almost everything and even chain methods together:

```
something.function3.function2.function1
```

Periods are used between an object and the method to call, as in C# or JavaScript. In this example, you call the function3 method on the something object, then the function2 method on the result of that, and then the function1 method on the result of that. A real-world demonstration can illustrate

```
"this is a test".reverse
```

```
tset a si siht
```

```
"this is a test".reverse.upcase.split(' ').reverse.join('-')
```

```
SIHT-SI-A-TSET
```

This example is deliberately long to demonstrate the power of method chaining in Ruby. This example takes your string "this is a test", reverses it, converts it to uppercase, splits it into words (splitting on spaces), reverses the position of the words in an array, and then joins the array back into a string with each element separated by dashes. (Objects are covered in depth in Chapters 2, 3, and 6.)

Classes and Methods

Ruby classes are similar in style to those in C# or Java, but keep the benefits of Ruby's dynamic features. Let's look at an example class definition:

```ruby
class Person
  def initialize(name, age)
    @name = name
    @age = age
  end

  def name
    return @name
  end

  def age
    return @age
  end
end
```

This class features an `initialize` method that is called automatically when you create a new instance of that class. Two parameters or arguments are accepted (name and age) and assigned to instance variables. Instance variables are variables associated with a particular instance of a class and begin with an @ sign (as in @name). Java developers should recognize @name as being similar to this.name.

After the initializer come two methods (name and age) that act as basic accessors. They simply return the value of their respective instance variables.

Note   In Ruby, if no value is explicitly returned from a method, the value of the last expression is returned instead. Therefore, `return` @name and just @name as the last line in the name method would be equivalent.

With the preceding class definition, it's trivial to create new objects:

```ruby
person1 = Person.new('Chris', 25)
person2 = Person.new('Laura', 23)
puts person1.name
puts person2.age
```

```
Chris
23
```

One benefit of Ruby is that you can add features to classes even if they've already been defined. Within the same program as before, you can simply "reopen" the class and add more definitions:

```ruby
class Person
  def name=(new_name)
    @name = new_name
  end

  def age=(new_age)
    @age = new_age
  end
end
```

These new methods are added to the `Person` class and are automatically made available to any existing instances of that class. These new methods are *setter* methods, as signified by the equals sign following their names. They allow you to do this:

```ruby
person1.name = "Barney"
person2.age = 101
puts person1.name
puts person2.age
```

```
Barney
101
```

Ruby can simplify most of the preceding work for you though, as it provides the `attr_accessor` helper method that automatically creates accessors and setter methods within a class for you:

```ruby
class Person
attr_accessor :name, :age
end
```

You can also create *class methods*: methods that don't exist within the scope of a single object, but that are bound directly to the class, for example:

```ruby
class Person
  @@count = 0
```

```ruby
def initialize
    @@count += 1
end

def self.count
    @@count
end
end

a = Person.new
b = Person.new
c = Person.new
puts Person.count
```

3

This `Person` class implements a `count` class method (notice that it is defined as `self.count`, rather than just `count`, making it a class method). The `count` class method returns the value of a class variable (`@@count`) that stores the total number of `Person` objects created so far. Class variables begin with two @ signs and exist within the scope of a class and all its objects, but not within the scope of any specific object. Therefore, `@@count` equals 3 and only 3 once you've created three `Person` objects.

This section has given only a brief overview of classes, objects, and their special variables. For a detailed look at classes and objects, refer to Chapter 6.

Reflection

Ruby is often called a *reflective* language, as it supports reflection. Reflection is a process that allows a computer program to observe and modify its own structure and behavior during execution. This functionality can seem like a novelty to developers experienced with C#, C++, and Java, but it's incredibly important in terms of Ruby's operation and Ruby's ability to define domain-specific languages, making other forms of development easier.

A brief demonstration of reflection is the ability to programmatically retrieve a list of all the methods associated with any object or class in Ruby. For example, here's how to display a list of all methods of the `Hash` class:

Hash.methods

[:[], :try_convert, :ruby2_keywords_hash?, :ruby2_keywords_hash, :new,
:allocate, :superclass, :<=>, :<=, :>=, :==, :===, :included_modules,
:include?, :ancestors, :attr, :attr_reader, :attr_writer, :attr_accessor,
:freeze, :inspect, :public_instance_methods, :instance_methods,
:const_missing, :protected_instance_methods, :private_instance_methods,
:const_set, :constants, :remove_class_variable, :class_variable_get,
:class_variable_set, :class_variable_defined?, :const_get, :const_
defined?, :<, :>, :public_constant, :class_variables, :private_constant,
:deprecate_constant, :singleton_class?, :const_source_location, :to_s,
:class_eval, :include, :module_exec, :module_eval, :prepend, :undef_
method, :alias_method, :class_exec, :remove_method, :method_defined?,
:name, :private_class_method, :public_method_defined?, :private_method_
defined?, :protected_method_defined?, :public_class_method, :define_
method, :autoload, :autoload?, :instance_method, :public_instance_method,
:dup, :itself, :yield_self, :then, :taint, :tainted?, :untaint, :untrust,
:untrusted?, :trust, :frozen?, :methods, :singleton_methods, :protected_
methods, :private_methods, :public_methods, :instance_variables,
:instance_variable_get, :instance_variable_set, :instance_variable_
defined?, :remove_instance_variable, :instance_of?, :kind_of?, :is_a?,
:tap, :display, :hash, :class, :singleton_class, :clone, :public_send,
:method, :public_method, :singleton_method, :define_singleton_method,
:extend, :to_enum, :enum_for, :=~, :!~, :nil?, :eql?, :respond_to?,
:object_id, :send, :__send__, :!, :!=, :__id__, :equal?, :instance_eval,
:instance_exec]

Similarly, you can retrieve a list of methods available on a String object directly:
"testing".methods

[:unicode_normalize, :unicode_normalize!, :ascii_only?, :to_r, :unpack,
:encode, :encode!, :unpack1, :%, :include?, :*, :+, :count, :partition,
:+@, :-@, :<=>, :<<, :to_c, :==, :===, :sum, :=~, :next, :[], :casecmp,
:casecmp?, :insert, :[]=, :match, :match?, :bytesize, :empty?, :eql?,
:succ!, :next!, :upto, :index, :rindex, :replace, :clear, :chr, :getbyte,

:setbyte, :scrub!, :scrub, :undump, :byteslice, :freeze, :inspect,
:capitalize, :upcase, :dump, :downcase!, :swapcase, :downcase, :hex,
:capitalize!, :upcase!, :lines, :length, :size, :codepoints, :succ,
:split, :swapcase!, :bytes, :oct, :prepend, :grapheme_clusters, :concat,
:start_with?, :reverse, :reverse!, :to_str, :to_sym, :crypt, :ord, :strip,
:end_with?, :to_s, :to_i, :to_f, :center, :intern, :gsub, :ljust, :chars,
:delete_suffix, :sub, :rstrip, :scan, :chomp, :rjust, :lstrip, :chop!,
:delete_prefix, :chop, :sub!, :gsub!, :delete_prefix!, :chomp!, :strip!,
:lstrip!, :rstrip!, :squeeze, :delete_suffix!, :tr, :tr_s, :delete,
:each_line, :tr!, :tr_s!, :delete!, :squeeze!, :slice, :each_byte, :each_
char, :each_codepoint, :each_grapheme_cluster, :b, :slice!, :rpartition,
:encoding, :force_encoding, :valid_encoding?, :hash, :unicode_normalized?,
:clamp, :between?, :<=, :>=, :>, :<, :dup, :itself, :yield_self, :then,
:taint, :tainted?, :untaint, :untrust, :untrusted?, :trust, :frozen?,
:methods, :singleton_methods, :protected_methods, :private_methods,
:public_methods, :instance_variables, :instance_variable_get, :instance_
variable_set, :instance_variable_defined?, :remove_instance_variable,
:instance_of?, :kind_of?, :is_a?, :tap, :display, :class, :singleton_
class, :clone, :public_send, :method, :public_method, :singleton_method,
:define_singleton_method, :extend, :to_enum, :enum_for, :!~, :nil?,
:respond_to?, :object_id, :send, :__send__, :!, :!=, :__id__, :equal?,
:instance_eval, :instance_exec]

Note   Future versions of Ruby may show different results.

The results given by the `methods` method might seem overwhelming at first, but over time they become incredibly useful. Using the `methods` method on any object allows you to learn about methods that aren't necessarily covered in this book (or other books) or that are new to the language. You can also use `methods` to retrieve a list of class methods, because classes are also objects in Ruby!

This section provides only a taste of reflection, but the topic is covered in more detail in Chapter 6.

Reopening Classes

It's trivial to override already defined methods on classes. Earlier in this appendix, I mentioned that, if you so wish, you can adjust the Integer class so that 2 + 2 would equal 5. Here's how you do that:

```ruby
class Integer
  alias_method :old_plus, :+

  def +(other_number)
    return 5 if self == 2 && other_number == 2
    old_plus other_number
  end
end

puts 2 + 2
```

5

The first thing this code does is to enter the Integer class, so you can define methods and perform actions within it. Next, you make an alias from the addition operator/method (+) to a new method called old_plus. This is so you can still use the normal addition feature, though with a different name.

Next, you redefine (or "override") the + method and return 5 if the current number is 2 and the number you're adding to the current number is also 2. Otherwise, you simply call old_plus (the original addition function) with the supplied argument. This means that 2 + 2 now equals 5, but all other addition is performed correctly.

You can redefine nearly any method within Ruby. This can make testing essential because you (or another developer) might incorporate changes that affect classes and objects being used elsewhere within your program. Testing is covered in Chapters 8 and 12.

Method Visibility

It's possible to change the visibility of methods within Ruby classes in one of three ways. Methods can be public (callable by any scope within the program), private (callable only within the scope of the instance the methods exist upon), and protected (callable by any object of the same class). Full details about method visibility are available in Chapter 6.

To encapsulate methods as public, private, or protected, you can use two different techniques. Using the words public, private, and protected within a class definition causes the methods defined thereafter to be encapsulated in the respective fashion:

```ruby
class MyClass
  def public_method
  end

  private
  def private_method1
  end

  def private_method2
  end

  protected
  def protected_method
  end
end
```

You can also explicitly set methods to be encapsulated in one way or another, but only after you've first defined them, for example:

```ruby
class MyClass
  def public_method
  end

  def private_method1
  end

  def private_method2
  end

  def protected_method
  end

  public :public_method
  private :private_method1, :private_method2
  protected :protected_method
end
```

Declarations such as this should come after you define the methods, as otherwise Ruby won't know what you're referring to.

Data

As everything is an object in Ruby, all forms of data represented within Ruby are also objects, just of varying classes. Therefore, some Ruby developers will try to correct you if you refer to *types* rather than *classes*, although this is merely pedantry.

In this section, we'll take a quick look at some of the basic data classes in Ruby.

Strings

Strings in Ruby are generally unexceptional, except for the object-oriented benefits you gain. Previously in this appendix, we looked at how powerful classes and methods can be when working on strings:

```ruby
"this is a test".reverse.upcase.split(' ').reverse.join('-')
```

```
SIHT-SI-A-TSET
```

The `String` class offers a plethora of useful methods for managing text. I'll cover several of these in the "Regular Expressions" section. However, if you want to see what other methods strings offer, it's easy: just execute `"test".methods`.

Regular Expressions

In Ruby, regular expressions are implemented in a reasonably standard way. If you're familiar with regular expressions, Ruby's techniques shouldn't seem alien:

```ruby
"this is a test".sub(/[aeiou]/, '*')
```

```
th*s is a test
```

```ruby
"this is a test".gsub(/[aeiou]/, '*')
```

```
th*s *s * t*st
```

```
"THIS IS A TEST".gsub(/[aeiou]/, '*')
```

```
THIS IS A TEST
```

```
"THIS IS A TEST".gsub(/[aeiou]/i, '*')
```

```
TH*S *S * T*ST
```

---

sub performs a single substitution based on a regular expression, whereas gsub performs a global substitution. As in other languages, you use the /i option to make the regular expression case-insensitive.

Ruby also makes matching easy, with the match method of String returning a special MatchData array you can query:

```
m = "this is a test".match(/\b..\b/)
m[0]
```

```
is
```

```
m = "this is a test".match(/\b(.)(.)\b/)
m[0]
```

```
is
```

```
m[1]
```

```
i
```

```
m[2]
```

```
s
```

The latter example demonstrates how you can parenthesize elements of the regular expression to separate their contents in the results. m[0] contains the full match, whereas m[1] onward matches each set of parentheses.

You can also scan through a string, returning each match for a regular expression:

```
"this is a test".scan(/[aeiou]/)
```

```
['i', 'i', 'a', 'e']
```

```
"this is a test".scan(/\w+/)
```

```
['this', 'is', 'a', 'test']
```

Methods such as split also accept regular expressions (as well as normal strings):

```
"this is a test".split(/\s/)
```

```
['this', 'is', 'a', 'test']
```

Regular expressions are covered in more depth in Chapter 3, and are used throughout the book.

Numbers

Integers and floating point numbers are available in Ruby and operate mostly as you'd expect. Numbers support all common operators such as modulus (%), addition, subtraction, division, multiplication, and powers (**).

A key consideration with numbers in Ruby is that unless you explicitly define a number as a floating point number, it won't be one unless it contains a decimal point, for example:

```
10 / 3
```

```
3
```

In this situation, 10 and 3 are both considered integers, so integer division is used. If integer division is what you're after—and it might be in some cases—then you're fine. But if you're after floating point division, you need to do something to ensure that at least one of the values involved is recognized as a floating point number. You can generate a floating point value in one of three ways as follows:

- By invoking the `to_f` method to convert an integer to its floating point equivalent

- By writing the number with a decimal point, even if you just add ".0" to the end

- By invoking the `Float()` initializer method to convert an integer to a floating point value

Here are some examples:

```
10.to_f / 3
```

```
3.33333333333335
```

```
10.0 / 3
```

```
3.33333333333335
```

```
10 / Float(3)
```

```
3.33333333333335
```

Which method you choose to make the 10 be recognized as a `Float` object can be largely influenced by the situation, so it's useful to see all your options.

Numbers are covered in depth in Chapter 3.

Note   You can produce roots easily by raising a number to the power of *1 divided by the root desired*. For example, you can find the square (2) root of 25 with `25 ** 0.5`.

Arrays

As in other programming languages, arrays act as ordered collections. However, in Ruby specifically, arrays are ordered collections of *objects*, because everything in Ruby is an object! Arrays can contain any combination of objects of any class.

At first sight, Ruby arrays work much like arrays in any other language, although note that you work on an array using methods, because an array itself is an object. The following example shows the invocation of the Array class's push method:

```
a = []
a.push(10)
a.push('test')
a.push(30)
a << 40
```

```
[10, 'test', 30, 40]
```

Notice the use of a different form of pushing objects to an array with the << operator on the last line of the preceding example.

You can then retrieve elements like so:

```
puts a[0]
puts a[1]
puts a[2]
```

```
10
test
30
```

Note   Although [ ] defines an empty literal array, you can also use Array.new to generate an empty array if you prefer to stick to object orientation all the way.

Arrays are objects of class Array and support a plethora of useful methods, as covered in full in Chapter 3.

Hashes (Associative Arrays)

Hashes (also known as associative arrays) exist as a concept in many programming languages. Hashes are data structures that let you associate keys with values.

Ruby's implementation of hashes is straightforward and should be familiar to Python developers, despite some minor syntax changes, for example:

```
fred = {
  'name' => 'Fred Elliott',
  'age' => 63,
  'gender' => 'male',
  'favorite painters' => ['Monet', 'Constable', 'Da Vinci']
}
```

fred refers to a basic hash that contains four elements that have keys of 'name', 'age', 'gender', and 'favorite painters'. You can refer back to each of these elements easily:

```
puts fred['age']
```

```
63
```

```
puts fred['gender']
```

```
male
```

```
puts fred['favorite painters'].first
```

```
Monet
```

Hashes are objects of class Hash and come with a large number of helpful methods to make hashes easy to navigate and manipulate, much like regular arrays. It's important to note that both hash element keys and values can be objects of any class themselves, as long as each element key is distinct. Otherwise, previously existing values will be overwritten. Hashes and associated methods and techniques are covered in detail in Chapter 3.

In Ruby 1.9 and above, a new style of defining hashes is available and is preferred in modern Ruby. It would allow the previous example to be written like so:

```
fred = {
  name: 'Fred Elliott',
  age: 63,
  gender: 'male',
  favorite_painters: ['Monet', 'Constable', 'Da Vinci']
}
```

Complex Structures

Because hashes and arrays can contain other objects, it's possible to create complex structures of data. Here's a basic example of a hash containing other hashes (and another hash containing an array at one point):

```
people = {
  fred: {
    name: 'Fred Elliott',
    age: 63,
    gender: 'male',
    favorite_painters: ['Monet', 'Constable', 'Da Vinci']
  },
  janet: {
    name: 'Janet S Porter',
    age: 68,
    gender: 'female'
  }
}

puts people[:fred][:age]
puts people[:janet][:gender]
puts people[:janet].inspect
```

```
63
female
{:name=>"Janet S Porter", :age=>68, :gender=>"female"}
```

This example presents a hash called `people` that contains two entries with keys of `:fred` and `:janet`, each of which refers to another hash containing information about each person. These sorts of structures are common in Ruby. They are covered in more depth in Chapter 3 and throughout this book. Typically, compared to other languages, the syntax is simple, and in Ruby, the simplest answer is usually the right one.

Input/Output

Ruby has powerful input/output (I/O) support, from the ability to create, read, and manipulate files through to database support, external devices, and network connectivity. These topics are covered in full in this book (primarily in Chapters 9, 14, and 15), but this section presents a basic overview of the most important forms of I/O.

Files

Ruby's support for file I/O is powerful compared to that of other languages. Although Ruby supports traditional techniques for reading and manipulating files, its object-oriented features and tight syntax offer more exciting possibilities. First, here is the traditional way you'd open and read a file (as when using a more procedural language):

```
lines = []
file_handle = File.open("/file/name/here", "r")

while line = file_handle.gets
 lines<< line
end

file_handle.close
```

Note   You would need to replace `/file/name/here` with a legitimate path for this to work asis.

This example opens a file in read-only mode and then uses the file handle to read the file line by line before pushing it into an array. Let's look at a Ruby-specific technique:

```
lines = File.readlines('/file/name/here')
```

Ruby's file handling and manipulation support is particularly deep and extensive, so it's out of the scope of this chapter. However, the preceding examples should have provided a glimpse into what's possible, and files are covered in full in Chapter 9 of this book.

Databases

There are several ways to connect to database systems such as MySQL, MongoDB, PostgreSQL, Oracle, SQLite, and Microsoft SQL Server from Ruby. Typically, a "driver" library is available for each of the main database systems, although these don't come with Ruby by default. You typically install database driver libraries using the RubyGems Ruby library packaging system, or you might need to download and install them manually. Explaining how to use such libraries is beyond the scope of this appendix, but they are covered in full in Chapter 9.

Ruby also has libraries that can provide more standardized interfaces to various driver libraries. Consider looking at *sequel* for this.

Web Access

Ruby comes with libraries that make accessing data on the Web incredibly easy. At a high level is the open-uri library, which makes it easy to access data from the Web. This example retrieves a web page and returns an array containing all the lines on that page:

```
require 'open-uri'
URI.open('https://www.apress.com/').readlines
```

open-uri is a convenience library that provides an open method that allows you to load data from URLs. open returns a File handle (technically a Tempfile object) that works in the same way as any other File object, allowing you to use methods such as readlines to read all the lines of the data into an array. (This topic is covered in significantly more depth in Chapter 14.)

Ruby also provides lower-level libraries, such as net/http. Here's an example of retrieving a file from a website and displaying it on the screen:

```ruby
require 'net/http'

Net::HTTP.start('www.apress.com', use_ssl: true) do |http|
  req = Net::HTTP::Get.new('/sitemap.xml')
  puts http.request(req).body
end
```

```
<?xml version="1.0" encoding="UTF-8"?><sitemapindex xmlns="http://
www.sitemaps.org/schemas/sitemap/0.9"><sitemap><loc>https://
www.apress.com/sitemap-books-aa.xml</loc><lastmod>2020-08-
12T15:47:18.948Z</lastmod></sitemap><sitemap><loc>https://www.apress.
com/sitemap-books-gp-1.xml</loc><lastmod>2020-08-12T15:47:19.113Z</
lastmod></sitemap><sitemap><loc>https://www.apress.com/sitemap-
books-gp-2.xml</loc><lastmod>2020-08-12T15:47:19.298Z</lastmod></
sitemap><sitemap><loc>https://www.apress.com/sitemap-books-
gp-3.xml</loc><lastmod>2020-08-12T15:47:19.486Z</lastmod></
sitemap><sitemap><loc>https://www.apress.com/sitemap-books-gp-4.xml</
loc><lastmod>2020-08-12T15:47:19.663Z</lastmod></sitemap></sitemapindex>
```

This example connects to the web server at www.apress.com and performs an HTTP GET request for /sitemap.xml. This file's contents are then returned and displayed. The equivalent URL for this request is www.apress.com/sitemap.xml, and if you load that URL in your web browser, you'll get the same response as this Ruby program.

net/http also lets you make requests using other HTTP verbs such as POST and DELETE, and it is the most flexible HTTP library for Ruby. Refer to Chapter 14 for full information.

Libraries

This section looks at how you can organize code into multiple files and manage libraries within Ruby.

File Organization

Ruby libraries don't need to be packaged in any special way (unlike, say, Java's JAR archives). Ruby does have a library packaging system called RubyGems (covered in the next section), but its use is entirely optional. The simplest way to create a library is to create a Ruby file containing classes and methods and use `require` to load it. This technique is similar in C# (using) or JavaScript (import).

Let's assume you have a file called `mylib.rb` containing the following:

```ruby
class MyLib
  def self.hello_world
    puts "Hello, world!"
  end
end
```

And then you have another file like so:

```ruby
require_relative 'mylib'
MyLib.hello_world
```

This program loads in mylib.rb and includes its classes, methods, and other particulars into the current runtime environment, meaning that MyLib.hello_world calls the correct routine.

Ruby searches through its library folders in a specific order (and usually the current directory too, as in the previous example), as dictated by the special variable $:. This variable is an array that can be manipulated like any other array. You can push, pop, and otherwise change the order and directories in which your program searches for libraries.

This topic is covered in depth in Chapter 7, and demonstrations of several Ruby libraries are offered in Chapter 16. A basic Ruby library is also created from scratch in Chapter 12.

Packaging

RubyGems (`https://rubygems.org/`) is a packaging system for Ruby libraries and applications. Each package within the RubyGems universe is called a *gem* or RubyGem (in this book, both terms are used interchangeably). RubyGems makes it easier to distribute, update, install, and remove libraries and applications on your system. A further system called Bundler makes it possible to "bundle" together gems in the context of a single Ruby project that you might be working on.

RubyGems has been included by standard with Ruby since Ruby 1.9, but was previously an optional, third-party technology.

Before the advent of RubyGems, Ruby libraries and applications were distributed in a basic fashion in archive files or even as source code to copy and paste from the Web. RubyGems makes it easier and more centralized and also takes care of any prerequisites and dependencies required when installing a library. For example, here's how to install the Ruby on Rails framework:

```
gem install rails
```

Note   On some platforms, you will have permissions issues installing gems. Avoid using `sudo` as a work around since it will cause issues. Instead, try using `rbenv` (`https://github.com/rbenv/rbenv`) or `rvm` (`https://rvm.io/`) to manage your Ruby install.

This installs the gems that make up Rails along with all their dependencies. Bundler provides an alternative whereby gems are defined within a special file and then the Bundler tool automatically installs the required dependencies for you.

You can uninstall gems in as simple a fashion:

```
gem uninstall rails
```

If you have multiple versions of the same gem(s) installed, gem will ask you which version(s) you want to remove.

By default, gems are searched for in the default repository, hosted at `RubyGems.org`. There is documentation on the official RubyGems site if you want to create your own account to be able to release your own gems via the site.

Optionally you can run your own gems repository on your own website or by using the RubyGems server software. This is less common and requires users of your gems to specify your server name at the same time as installing the gem. I would not advise this.

RubyGems and Bundler are covered in Chapter 7, and several RubyGems are documented in Chapter 16.

Useful Resources

This appendix provides links to useful Ruby resources that are available online, from websites to chatrooms and mailing lists.

As the Internet is ever changing, some resources that were available at the time of writing may no longer be available to you. When you find that to be the case, it's worth using a search engine to search for the keywords involved, as the site you're looking for might have simply changed URLs.

Tutorials and Guides

The Internet is host to a significant number of tutorials and guides on how to use various features of Ruby and its libraries. Often there are multiple tutorials on how to do the same thing in different ways, and tutorials can appear quickly after libraries are released. This is why it's worth subscribing to a few Ruby-related Twitter feeds and other news sources so that you can learn about the latest action as it happens.

However, in this section are links to a number of useful tutorials and guides that are more perennially useful.

General Ruby Tutorials and Information

Try Ruby! (`https://try.ruby-lang.org/`): An online Ruby interpreter with a built-in tutorial.

Ruby in Twenty Minutes (`www.ruby-lang.org/en/documentation/quickstart/`): A basic primer to the bare essentials of Ruby. This guide won't be of any use to readers of this book, but might be useful to forward to others who are interested in Ruby and want to get a quick look at the language from a beginner's point of view.

© Carleton DiLeo, Peter Cooper 2021
C. DiLeo and P. Cooper, *Beginning Ruby 3*, https://doi.org/10.1007/978-1-4842-6324-2

Learn Ruby (`http://rubylearning.com`): A collection of short tutorials and ebooks on various aspects of Ruby, by Satish Talim. It's ideal as a quick recap on various topics. Satish also runs Ruby-related online classes.

Ruby Tapas (`www.rubytapas.com`): Short screencasts covering various Ruby topics.

Ruby on Rails

Getting Started with Rails (`https://guides.rubyonrails.org/getting_started.html`): An excellent walk-through of how to use Rails from a basic point of view. Covers creating a very basic application and provides links to further resources. Well worth reviewing after reading Chapter 13 of this book.

The Rails Tutorial Book (`www.railstutorial.org/book`): A book by Michael Hartl that is available to read in its entirely online. This is what I recommend if you want to learn Rails from scratch.

Other

SQL Tutorial (`www.w3schools.com/sql/`): A comprehensive SQL tutorial, expanding on what is covered in Chapter 9 of this book.

References

The resources covered in this section are general references to Ruby and Ruby on Rails. For specific tutorials and guides to doing certain things, you need to refer instead to the "Tutorials and Guides" section later on in this appendix.

Ruby

Official Ruby Homepage (`www.ruby-lang.org/`*)*: The official Ruby homepage.

Ruby-Doc.org (`www.ruby-doc.org/`*)*: A documentation site built by the Ruby community that features documentation for the core API, standard libraries, and other miscellaneous Ruby bits and pieces. Its primary maintainer is James Britt, who has been involved with Ruby documentation for many years.

Ruby Core Documentation (`https://ruby-doc.org/core/`*)*: Documentation for the core elements of Ruby 2.3 (at the time of writing), such as the included classes (`Array`, `Hash`, etc.), as well as most of the standard library. This URL will redirect to the documentation for the latest production version of Ruby as it changes over time.

Ruby Standard Library Documentation (`https://ruby-doc.org/stdlib/`*)*: Documentation for the Ruby standard libraries. Each library is presented separately, making it easier to read than the core documentation.

Clean Ruby (`www.apress.com/gp/book/9781484255452`*)*: Learn how to make better decisions and write cleaner Ruby code.

Ruby on Rails

Official Rails Homepage (`https://rubyonrails.org/`*)*: The official homepage for the Ruby on Rails framework. It features screencasts, tutorials, and links to many useful Rails references.

Rails API Documentation (`https://api.rubyonrails.org/`*)*: API documentation for the entire Ruby on Rails framework in RDoc format. This is the most useful reference documentation for Ruby on Rails, as almost all Rails techniques and methods are covered.

Ruby on Rails Guides (`https://guides.rubyonrails.org/`*)*:
Well-written walk-through guides for various Rails features,
such as how to get started with Rails and how to use the
internationalization features, routing, and database migrations.

Ruby-Related Content

Aggregators and News

RubyFlow (`www.rubyflow.com/`*)*: A community-driven link blog
for all things related to Ruby and Rails. It's very popular and
a great way to keep up with the day-to-day Ruby news and to
promote your own blog posts.

Ruby News (`www.ruby-lang.org/en/news/`*)*: The official news
site for the main implementation of Ruby. It is only updated
sporadically and when there are key release or security
announcements.

/r/ruby on Reddit (`https://reddit.com/r/ruby`*)*: An area of the
popular Reddit community discussion and bookmarking site
dedicated to Ruby-related items.

Riding Rails (`https://weblog.rubyonrails.org/`*)*: The official
blog for Ruby on Rails, updated by several core Rails developers
and activists. The blog focuses on sporadic announcements of
interesting uses or deployments of Rails, as well as new Rails
features.

Ruby Weekly (`https://rubyweekly.com/`*)*: A weekly Ruby
and Rails email newsletter with almost 40,000 subscribers. It's
produced by your humble author and is highly recommended if
you want to stay up to date with Ruby news on a frequent basis.

Forums

Ruby Forum (`www.ruby-forum.com/`*)*: A popular help and
discussion forum.

Mailing Lists

Mailing lists are like forums, but based on email. People subscribe to a "list," and then all
messages sent to that list are received by all the subscribers. There are also archives of
email lists available on the Web for reference or for those who don't want to sign up for
the list:

Ruby Mailing Lists (`www.ruby-lang.org/en/community/`
`mailing-lists/`*)*: The official page on the Ruby site that provides
information about the official Ruby mailing lists.

Ruby-Talk Mailing List: Ruby-Talk is the most popular Ruby
mailing list, where all aspects of Ruby development are discussed.
You can subscribe via the preceding link.

Ruby-Talk Mailing List Archives (`http://blade.nagaokaut.`
`ac.jp/ruby/ruby-talk/index.shtml`*)*: Offers web access to
more than 400,000 posts made to the Ruby-Talk mailing list and
includes a search feature.

ruby-core (`http://blade.nagaokaut.ac.jp/ruby/ruby-`
`core/index.shtml`*)*: A mailing list dedicated to discussing
implementation details and the development of Ruby. Those who
are developing the Ruby language use this list. However, it isn't a
list on which to ask general Ruby questions.

Note   It's important when using a mailing list that you look at the format and tone
of other posts and don't offend anyone. If your postings sound too demanding or
are of the wrong tone, you might not get any responses.

Chat

On the Internet, there are several ways you can discuss topics with other users in real time. For example, Slack and Discord provide real-time chat via a desktop, mobile, or web app:

> *Ruby on Rails Slack channel (`www.rubyonrails.link/`)*:
> A community of Ruby on Rails developers from all over the world.

> *Ruby Discord Server (`https://discord.gg/bHB8Jkx`)*: A Discord
> server where developers discuss and seek help on various Ruby
> topics.

Index

A

Arrays/lists
  elements, 61, 62
  iteration, 65, 66
  methods
    addition/concatenation, 67
    certain item, 68
    empty array, checking, 67
    first/last elements, accessing, 68
    reversing order, 69
    subtraction/difference, 67
  popping, 63
  splitting strings into arrays, 64
abbrev library
  examples, 494, 495
  installation, 494
access_granted? method, 184
ActiveRecord, 293
add_person method, 288
add_room method, 190
a.rb file, 199
ARGV, 304
attr_accessor method, 188, 326

B

Base64
  definition, 496
  examples, 496, 498, 499
  installation, 496

basic_method, 147
Benchmark module
  definition, 499
  examples, 499, 500
  installation, 499
  profiling, 242–244
  simple, 239–241
Bots, 343
  building core, 360, 361
  code listing
    basic client, 383
    bot.rb, 379, 381, 382
  data loader, 367, 368
  data structure, 363, 364
  extend
    Bot-to-Bot conversation, 388, 389
    connect to Web, 384, 386, 387
    text files, 384
  history, 344
  lifecycle and parts, 361, 362
  playing
    conversation, 378, 379
    Fred, 375, 377
  store data, 364, 366
Branching/conditional execution, 545–547
Building blocks
  converting objects to other
    classes, 90, 91
  dates and times, 83–86
  ranges, 87

© Carleton DiLeo, Peter Cooper 2021
C. DiLeo and P. Cooper, *Beginning Ruby 3*, https://doi.org/10.1007/978-1-4842-6324-2